T0372549

'Taking us on an unconventional journey, Martin Hultman and Paul Pulé untangle what it means to be a man in the western world today. They explore and rethink new expressions of manhood and masculinities towards relational and caring masculinities in service of the global commons. This book is an essential read, especially for men, but also for all those who care about our intertwined futures.'

Seema Arora-Jonsson,
author of *Gender, Development and Environmental Governance* (2013)
and Associate Professor of Urban and Rural Development,
Swedish University of Agricultural Sciences, Uppsala

'Colonialism, war "games", rape culture, child sex trafficking, industrial animal agriculture, mass shootings, domestic and public ecoterrorism: throughout recorded history, hegemonic masculinity has been socially constructed and widely accepted for displaying behaviors that wreck the planet, tear apart families, AND oppress women, non-binary/genderqueer people and people of color. But the green tendrils of feminist ecomasculinities have persisted, and their re-emergence here signals real possibilities for transforming the global terrorist triumvirate of climate change, colonialism and corporate hegemony.'

Greta Gaard,
ecofeminist scholar, activist, filmmaker, author of *Critical Ecofeminism*
(2017) and Professor of English at University of Wisconsin-River
Falls, USA

'*Ecological Masculinities* comes at a pertinent point in our history, expressing humanity's meditative moment of reflection on "what has been" into "what is" as we move beyond gender in our search for true wisdom. Martin and Paul express their masculine embodiment with a fresh critical reflection on deep ecology by toning their feminine expressions of who they are becoming through this mammoth book. I sincerely hope it will awaken a deeper dialogue towards understanding the profound wisdom hidden within Professor Arne Næss's work. Stay close all!'

Pamela Hiley,
British Qigong master living in Oslo, Norway, and
a personal friend of Arne Næss

'Men are the unmarked category and final frontier of gender and environments scholarship. Studies of how hegemonic masculinities are connected with – and drivers of – varied forms of ecological destruction are sorely lacking. We don't fully understand why this lack persists or how it should be redressed. However,

Ecological Masculinities brings us one giant step toward answering these and many other important questions about men/masculinities and their complex relationships to the world. This book is a conversation starter that is both compellingly presented and desperately needed.'

Sherilyn MacGregor,
Reader in Environmental Politics, University of Manchester,
UK and editor of *The Routledge Handbook on Gender and Environment* (2017)

'This is a ground-breaking and very welcome book that takes both environmental studies and critical masculinities studies to a new level. Drawing upon four diverse streams of theory: masculinities politics, deep ecology, ecological feminism and feminist care theory, Martin and Paul examine the human and planetary costs of ecologically destructive masculinities and outline an important new lens to understand and address the social and environmental challenges we face. Their new ecological masculinities perspective, which is grounded in profeminist men's capacities to care, provides realistic hope for a renewed ecologically sustainable relationship between men, masculinities and the Earth.'

Bob Pease,
co-editor of *Critical Ethics of Care in Social Work* (2017), Honorary Professor, School of Humanities and Social Sciences, Deakin University, Australia and Adjunct Professor, Institute for the Study of Social Change, University of Tasmania, Australia

'Associating the approach of caring with masculinities based on feminist thinking is a step up in Western thought toward a more inclusive civilization. This is one of the most important contributions of this book on ecological masculinities.'

Tammy Shel (Aboody)
has a PhD from UCLA in philosophy of education and is author of *The Ethics of Caring* (2007)

Ecological Masculinities

Around the globe, unfettered industrialisation has marched forth in unison with massive social inequities. Making matters worse, anthropogenic pressures on Earth's living systems are causing alarming rates of thermal expansion, sea-level rise and biodiversity losses in terrestrial and aquatic ecosystems. As various disciplines have shown, rich white men in the Global North are the main (although not the only) perpetrators of this slow violence. This book demonstrates that industrial/breadwinner masculinities have come at terrible costs to the living planet and ecomodern masculinities have failed all of us as well; men included.

The work that follows is dedicated to a third and relationally focused pathway called ecological masculinities. Here, we explore ways that masculinities can advocate and embody broader, deeper and wider care for the global through to local (or 'glocal') commons. *Ecological Masculinities* builds on the wisdoms of four main streams of influence that have been bringing their knowledge to us for the best part of half a century. They are: masculinities politics, deep ecology, ecological feminism and feminist care theory. We work with profeminist approaches to the conceptualisations and embodiments of modern Western masculinities. From there, we introduce masculinities that give ADAM-n for Earth, others and self, striving to create a more just and ecologically viable planet for all life.

Ecological Masculinities is intended to reach (but is not restricted to) scholars in history, gender studies, material feminism, feminist care theory, ecological feminism, deep ecology, social ecology, environmental humanities, social sustainability, science and technology studies and philosophy, as well as those who are active and dedicated to living well and preserving all life.

Associate Professor **Martin Hultman** has widely published in energy, climate and environmental issues, including *Discourses of Global Climate Change* (2014). He works with grass-roots transitions, rights of nature and global strategies for ending ecocide in Sweden and beyond. His current research projects include gender and energy history, ecopreneurship in circular economies and creative responses to climate change denialism.

Doctor **Paul M. Pulé** is an Australian scholar and activist specialising in men, masculinities and their impacts on Earth, others and self. His research and community education efforts are dedicated to creating a healthier planet for all. He is also teaching, researching and publishing works on gender and environments, with a particular interest in climate change and its consequential social and environmental conundrums.

Together (and beyond the scope of this monograph), Martin and Paul are compiling an anthology that widens the conversations about men and Earth to include concepts and praxes from across a multiplicity of academic disciplines. This will be followed by a third and non-scholarly publication that captures men's stories of ecologisation across a wide array of constituencies, which will be written for general audiences.

Routledge Studies in Gender and Environments

With the European Union, United Nations, UN Framework Convention on Climate Change, and national governments and businesses at least ostensibly paying more attention to gender, including as it relates to environments, there is more need than ever for existing and future scholars, policy makers, and environmental professionals to understand and be able to apply these concepts to work towards greater gender equality in and for a sustainable world.

Comprising edited collections, monographs and textbooks, this new *Routledge Studies in Gender and Environments* series will incorporate sophisticated critiques and theorisations, including engaging with the full range of masculinities and femininities, intersectionality, and LBGTIQ perspectives. The concept of 'environment' will also be drawn broadly to recognise how built, social and natural environments intersect with and influence each other. Contributions will also be sought from global regions and contexts which are not yet well represented in gender and environments literature, in particular Russia, the Middle East, and China, as well as other East Asian countries such as Japan and Korea.

Series Editor: Professor Susan Buckingham, an independent researcher, consultant and writer on gender and environment related issues.

International Editorial Board

Margaret Alston is Professor of Social Work and Head of Department at Monash University, Melbourne, Australia.

Giovanna Di Chiro is Professor of Environmental Studies and teaches in the Gender and Sexuality Studies Program at Swarthmore College, USA.

Marjorie Griffin Cohen is an economist who is Professor Emeritus of Political Science and Gender, Sexuality and Women's Studies at Simon Fraser University, Canada.

Martin Hultman is Associate Professor in science, technology and environmental studies at Chalmers University, Sweden.

Virginie Le Masson is a Research Fellow at the Overseas Development Institute, London, UK.

Sherilyn MacGregor is a Reader in Environmental Politics at the University of Manchester, UK.

Tanja Mölders is an environmental scientist. Since 2013 she is University Professor and holds the chair "Space and Gender" at Leibniz University Hannover, Germany.

Karen Morrow is Professor of Environmental Law at Swansea University, UK.

Marion Roberts is Professor of Urban Design at Westminster University, UK.

Titles in this series include:

Ecological Masculinities
Theoretical Foundations and Practical Guidance
Martin Hultman and Paul M. Pulé

Ecological Masculinities
Theoretical Foundations and
Practical Guidance

Martin Hultman and Paul M. Pulé

Routledge
Taylor & Francis Group

LONDON AND NEW YORK

First published 2018
by Routledge

2 Park Square, Milton Park, Abingdon, Oxfordshire OX14 4RN
52 Vanderbilt Avenue, New York, NY 10017

Routledge is an imprint of the Taylor & Francis Group, an informa business

First issued in paperback 2019

British Library Cataloguing in Publication Data
A catalogue record for this book is available from the British Library

Library of Congress Cataloging in Publication Data
Names: Hultman, Martin, author. | Pulé, Paul M., author.
Title: Ecological masculinities: theoretical foundations and practical
guidance / Martin Hultman and Paul M. Pulé.
Description: Abingdon, Oxon: New York, NY, Routledge, 2018. | Series:
Routledge studies in gender and environments | Includes bibliographical
references and index.
Identifiers: LCCN 2017061086 (print) | LCCN 2018015026 (ebook) |
ISBN 9781315195223 (eBook) | ISBN 9781138719910 (hbk) |
ISBN 9781315195223 (ebk)
Subjects: LCSH: Human ecology--Sex differences. | Nature--Effect of human
beings on. | Ecofeminism. | Deep ecology.
Classification. LCC GF75 (ebook) | LCC GF75 .H84 2018 (print) |
DDC 304.20811--dc23
LC record available at https://lccn.loc.gov/2017061086

ISBN: 978-1-138-71991-0 (hbk)
ISBN: 978-0-367-89369-9 (pbk)

Typeset in Times New Roman
by Taylor & Francis Books

Martin Hultman
To Elin, for your enduring support and
encouraging me to improve.
To Kaspar, for making me think ahead.
To all my friends, who have listened and shared with me.
To all plants, for providing me with oxygen.
To the oceans, rivers and lakes for providing me with water.
To all Earth Protectors, for showing me that
caring must dare to accompany
the path of peace when life is at stake
. . . and to all indigenous people from
around the world translating
global climate change into *Blocadia* for the sake of all life.

Paul M. Pulé
To Mum and Dad, for enduring.
To Leslie, for showing me another world.
To Dottie, for reminding me to cackle at myself
. . . and to the many other-than-human others that are our
companions on this life-perfect orb floating through space and
time.

Contents

Illustrations

Figures

Box

Acknowledgements

A culture that has lost its beginning story is a culture adrift, destructive and self-harming. While the West can be seen as synonymous with imperialism, this is not our old people, this is not our true culture, gender-lopsidedness is not our only heritage.

(Jones, 2017: 21)

Martin's acknowledgements

I firstly honour and acknowledge all life that sustains me, both outside and within, which has supported me since day one. I also offer my heartfelt thanks to my parents, Rolf and Gertie, as well as my wife Elin, my son Kaspar and my brothers Ola and Johan for helping make this book possible.

To my parents, I celebrate how you brought me into the world and took me with you to experience the forests, sometimes with map in hand, but mostly simply by being part of the landscape. My enthusiasm for foraging comes from you – especially going out on my own to find chanterelles.

To my wife Elin, you are one of a kind in the way that you are always up for a personal or political discussion. We have experienced the world together through as many adventures as there are days. Were it not for you, I could not have taken stock of what it means to be a man in today's world, considered the ways that I do my masculinities, nor found the passion that I bring to this book as I do.

Together with my son Kaspar, I regularly explore the world anew. You are the one who knows the most about what is going on in our world now. My close involvement in your growing up allows me to grow up again too. It is a rare privilege to watch you becoming a person who is courageous enough to try out what you want and who you want to be with me tending to your fears, understanding your upsets and celebrating your joys. As a parent, I am doing my best to show you that the world really is beautiful; a great source of inspiration on this path you are on in becoming the person you are.

My academic journey has been a winding one that prepared me well to become an undisciplined scholar. I am grateful to all the gentle and open-minded colleagues I have met throughout my studies. I offer my special thanks to Per-Anders Forstorp and Marianne Winther-Jörgenssen for revealing a whole new way of experiencing the world. Inviting me to the 'Studierektangeln' was instrumental in blending your respective insights with my eclectic mind, taking part in the very best evening seminar a curious graduate student could hope for. Without you both, I would not have become the person nor the scholar that I now am.

Once a PhD student, I was fortunate enough to have my back covered and my texts scrutinised by the one and only Jonas Anshelm. Jonas, this book is in some way a celebration of your unique ability to be both supervisor and friend. Inspired by your Næssean ways, going fishing with you, taking a dip in Stora Rängen together and the day that my son Kaspar and I picked mouthwatering raspberries from your garden, are memories that will last a lifetime. Even more Næssean, I want to honour Johan Hedrén as a force of inspiration not only in your sheer presence, but also the way you have invited me into dialogues with utopian and environmental humanities scholars as well as the deep conversations on the bus rides we have shared.

During my early days at the Department of Thematic Studies (Tema – Technology and Social Change) at Linköping University, Ulf Mellström was also right by my side. Ulf, co-teaching the graduate course 'Gender and Technology' with you was both personally and professionally formative.

After I completed my PhD, I looked for opportunities to publish some of my empirical analyses as articles, with increased attention on a theoretical approach. Then Anna Lundberg came along. As editor of the renowned Swedish peer-reviewed gender studies journal *Tidskrift för genusvetenskap* (TGV), you were (together with Mattias Martinsson) a prime motivator for me to write up my first masculinities and environment article – the one about Arnold Schwarzenegger. The work with the English version of that article, published in the first proper issue of *Environmental Humanities*, introduced me to conversations with Seema Arora-Jonsson, Susan Buckingham, Sherilyn MacGregor and Marjorie Cohen, who together have proved to be important guides in furthering my academic thinking, all the way up to the writing of this book.

I extend a very special thanks to my friends with whom I continue to have in-depth conversations about social and environmental justice, especially: Martin Laps, Anders Hansson, Magnus Nilsson, Björn Wallsten, Francis Lee and Robert Helsing. I also extend a big thank you to my co-author Paul Pulé. We have become instant close collaborators. From the moment we met, I could tell that the crossing of our paths was something special and truly mind changing. This serendipity touched something deep inside of me. You continue to instigate fantastic conversations and deep connections about Earth, humanity and self.

With Paul, I offer heartfelt appreciation to the following reviewers, who have generously contributed to our refinements of the typescript from their respective areas of expertise, or helped administer the book's production: Annabelle Harris, Leila Walker, Charlotte Endersby, Rebecca Brennan, Laura Brookes, along with T. Anne Dabb, Greta Gaard, Bob Pease and Tammy Shel.

We add special thanks to Pamela Hiley and Ki Fai Næss for their compelling reflections about the widely revered Norwegian national treasure, Professor Arne Næss. It was truly an honour to have you both help us sharpen our focus and gain needed clarity about Arne the man in addition to deep ecology the movement as we have embraced elements of his brilliance that have shaped our thoughts and the ways they can be applied.

Finally, I acknowledge the Bestorp community for being instrumental in my becoming the scholar that I am today. This small village where I lived for ten years has been a formative 'laboratory' for the Swedish Transition Movement, as much as it was for me personally. During the time I lived there, I became a rural community leader. The joy in people's eyes as I contributed in very concrete and positive ways to their everyday lives was not only a rare privilege, but continues to be a source of great inspiration. Together with several key Swedish colleagues, I am now part of Transition Council Sweden, which gathers together visions and projects that support social endeavours committed to respecting planetary boundaries. Finally, through my relationships with people like Pella Thiel, Niklas Högberg and many more, I learn how to walk the talk; to be the change in the world I want to see.

Paul's acknowledgements

Writing this book has been an intensely personal journey. For many years now, I have been seeking ways to express the levels of care for life that we argue here dwell naturally within us all. The following pages are the product of many hours of scholarly research on men, masculinities and Earth. Over the years, my relational exchanges with colleagues, friends, family members and lovers have shaped my thoughts and the ways I move through the world. When I first started this project as a PhD student in 2001, I had no idea what direction it would take me. Neither did I foresee the foreboding tide of toxic/extreme masculinities, obscene levels of entitlement, nationalistic fervour, and wicked misogynistic backlashes that have swept across the globe with renewed abandon, which have raised the stakes a heck of a lot higher for us all. I have felt growing concern and from that have sought alternatives to the recent rise of shock politics that have captured centre stage throughout many nations of the Global North in recent times. This right- wing ferment of fear has motivated me as a scholar and activist to dedicate my efforts all the more to creating an inclusive and caring world.

My contributions to this book had quite humble beginnings. From a young age, I wanted to know how to be the best man I could be. This took me on a journey to find fresh ways of being, thinking and doing manhood and masculinities both conceptually and practically. In this sense, I have been my own first case study. The thoughts I share here are blended products of my personal and professional journeys. There are some special acknowledgements I would like to make as well.

Mum and dad, you will find much of yourselves in the pages that follow, not only directly but also through the fact that this book became a reality at least in-part because you both have, through the ebbs and flows of life, been here with me, eternally. Thank you for hanging in here. I offer special honouring to my dear uncle Leslie, whose shoebox New York City apartment was my refuge as a young man all those years ago. You helped me see that there are many ways to be a man, wear maleness and imbibe masculinities. Your contemplative spirit, your sense of adventure, your faith in the joys of life, your tireless generosity, your deep respect for diversity and your reverence for nature's 'church' have been more than a ladder for me to scale to ever greater heights. The rite of passage of entering my manhood in your care was a revolution of body, mind and spirit that I carry with me all the days of my life.

To aunty Dot Scott, I send you a wide Western Australian smile for your enduring interest in my life and the many ways you have cheered me on. Your home has always been an open, warm and welcoming retreat, your excitement for the wild west of Australia has been a formative inspiration for my love of nature and your reminders that there is nothing more healing than a darn good laugh especially at myself have been greater gifts than I could have imagined. You are of course my favourite aunty!

I have been graced with three mentors on my academic journey over the years. Each of them has been instrumental in supporting me to shape my contributions to this book. You each deserve special mention.

Internationally renowned and widely loved ecological feminist scholar, Dr. Patsy Hallen became an oracle for things to come, helping me massage a loose collection of thoughts and feelings about men and our impacts on life into the beginnings of what is now my life's path. Patsy, you have taken time to listen and move me forth when I thought I might break, smiled widely at the smallest of my revelations, blessed me with your trademark 'pungent breath of a curious whale' and bolstered my courage and faith in this journey. You will find your zestful guidance scattered between the lines of this book that I can now pay forward to others both as your student and Earth fellow. To your patience and consistency in being there, your courage to set boundaries with me, speak your truth with an open heart, offer a firm and guiding hand and your philosophical brilliance, I bow in deep gratitude.

Feminist sociologist Dr Michael Booth took a keen interest in my project once Patsy retired. Sadly, Michael died shortly after taking me on as one of his students. As a veritable walking encyclopaedia, he showed me the importance of broadening my search for an alternative future for men and Earth – starting with a small but profound research trick of reading tables of contents and indexes before plunging headlong into books. Michael's soft-spoken and considered wisdom was not only humbling to experience. He also exemplified a version of the alternative masculinities that we advocate. Michael . . . to your spirit and your memory, I offer you a warm smile.

To Associate Professor Brad Pettitt, who has been the quintessential pragmatist and exemplar of efficiency, productivity and drive, I send you my appreciation for quickly assuming the role of 'stoker' upon Michael's sudden passing. Your enduring optimism, community spirit and capacity to join dots across a morass of multidisciplinary complexities have been invaluable. You became an effective aide, enduringly supported this project and helped me set limits repeatedly in my march towards what is now an emerging international conversation about men, masculinities and Earth. I have been greatly inspired by your dedication to creating caring communities.

To the more than 130 contributors to the Kickstarter campaign that enabled me to fund the beginnings of this book, I offer you my deep thanks for your support through many questions and comments along with your financial gifts. Special mention goes out to the following particularly generous donors: Anonymous (*you know who you are*), Sofi and Cecilia Håkansson, Emma Brindal, Michelle Power, John Croft, Greg Davey, Mimi and Gerry Pule, Leslie Pulé, and Dottie Scott.

Through the collective efforts of these people, I have had the rare privilege of receiving the sensual embodiment, scholarly acuity, spiritual shepherding, financial backing and conceptual cohesion that have made my contributions to this book possible. I could not have done it without each and every one of you.

References

Jones, P. 2017. *re:) Fermenting culture: a return to insight through gut logic.* Daylesford: Tree Elbow.

Prologue

Masculinity is a great renunciation . . . emotions, expressiveness, receptiveness, a whole array of possibilities are renounced by successful boys and men in everyday life, and often for men who inhabit masculinized realms – sports, the military, the police, [near] all-male workforces in construction and resource extraction – even more must be renounced to belong. Women get to keep a wider range of emotional possibility, though they are discouraged or stigmatized for expressing some of the fiercer ones, the feelings that aren't ladylike and deferential, and so much else – ambition, critical intelligence, independent analysis, dissent, anger.

(Solnit, 2017: 28–29)

Dire circumstances, new approaches

Encouraged by Rebecca Solnit's (2017) compelling treatise on the silent isles of masculinity and their global impacts, this book offers a fresh examination of men, masculinities and Earth. While we have written for the widest possible audience, this book speaks to men and the masculinities that dwell within us all in particular. To begin, we recognise that all men are *not* equal – disparities between the rich and poor within nations run parallel to different socially sanctioned rankings among men based on race, age, sexual orientation, identity as much as exists between industrialised Western nations of the Global North and industrialising non-Western nations in the Global South.[1] Being a man and being sensitive to the ways that masculinities impact the lives of all others along with men themselves presents complexities that defy boundaries and borders within and between nations as much as gendered identities, harbouring notable consequences for all of life. Karen Warren's contribution to the discourse on 'otherisation' captures her astute analysis of the 'logic of domination' that she defined as 'a logical structure of argumentation that . . . assumes that superiority justifies subordination . . . [and] is offered as a moral stamp for keeping Downs [as-in oppressed others] down' (Warren, 1987: 6; Warren, 2000: 24, 47). The phrase 'human and other-than-human others' or simply 'others' as we use it throughout this book, is drawn from Warren's treatise, which notes the ways that select men within male-dominated social arrangements are afforded injunctions to marginalise, background and inferiorise any one (human or other-than-human other) who does not fit within the parameters of select and advantaged norms. Throughout this book, we define and refer to these prescribed parameters as 'daring' or 'malestream' norms (Bologh, 1990). These norms are unavoidably complex and pluralised since they arise in women and non-binary/genderqueer people as well. We cannot effectively attend to the many nuances of them all within the confines of one book. So, we do not explore all men and all masculinities here. We have instead chosen to research and write from within our respective cultural contexts as men, living in Sweden (Martin) and Australia (Paul) that are subject to the privileges and challenges of our Western male lives. In doing so, we introduce a more relational and caring vision for the intersecting terrain between modern Western men, masculinities and Earth.

It is true that many of the world's ills have unfolded as a direct result of the socialisations that define and determine modern Western masculinities. However, in this book, we argue that these social and environmental ills are not the product of an inherent shortcoming of Western men. On the contrary, we believe that all men (like all human beings the world over) can feel and express broader, deeper and wider care. However, we also recognise that, traditionally, the applications of men's care are meted out unequally – advantaging a few, mostly Western white men – while causing harm to many (Western, non-Western and other-than-human) others. We have seen recent and, in some instances, violent backlashes against feminism, which is now routinely singularised and attacked as a block despite a diversity of approaches supporting women's empowerment. There has been a rise of fervent nationalism across the Western world. Refugees (especially those from the Global South) have been demonised. Islamophobia has become commonplace. We are experiencing a renewed wave of anti-Semitism, neo-Nazi/white supremacist resurgences and increased rates of international and domestic forms of terrorism despite the fact that it is 2018. One might be forgiven for hoping that we would learn from our past mistakes, that we ought to trust the rule of law and we can have faith in moral leadership to see us through to better days. It would be understandable to think that such assumptions would collectively circumvent the vagaries we face. Sadly, these are assumptions we cannot afford to make. Global authorities, increasingly run by anti-immigrant governments, have responded by systematically eroding civil liberties as they wrestle with ways to keep the most privileged minority of their citizens safe. There has been an expansion of the military–industrial complex accompanied by sabre-rattling between conflicting nations that is – once again – bringing the risk of nuclear obliteration of whole regions of Earth to the fore. Cultural libertarians and social conservatives have risen to dominance as self-appointed protectors of 'freedom of speech' by donning the mantle of discrediting 'political correctness' and with this the rejection of diversity. Claims of victimisation and reverse racism and sexism have slid towards the normalisation of outright white supremacy and misogyny along with the sanitising of rape/sexual assault towards women by some male politicians and men's rights activists (MRAs). We are seeing the systematic mainstreaming of various forms of climate change denialism even as global ecological devastation continues to unfold before our very eyes, the consequences being enormous and irreversible for all life.

In her formative text titled *The Politics of Reproduction*, Mary O'Brien (1981: 62) deconstructed the normalisation of male domination through a critique of what she termed 'malestream norms'. We borrow this term and use it throughout this book as synonymous with patriarchy. Patriarchy is a term derived from the Greek 'rule of the father' (πατριάρχης or patriarkhēs), which we define as the social, political, moral and proprietary primacy of men above all others on Earth, or the process of positioning men and masculinities in dominance over women, human others and Earth. Historically, patriarchy has been considered by Marxists to be enmeshed with capitalism (Keith, 2016: 2–3). Throughout this book we also use the term 'male domination' instead of 'patriarchy' to expose the systematic devaluing of all non-males and non-humans by a male-dominated world (Stockard and Johnson, 1979). Our references to malestream norms and male domination highlight the ways that masculinities manifests in private and public as well as personal and professional spheres, effectively normalising masculine hegemonisation. As we seek constructive solutions to our dizzying problems, we have entered an explosive era of renewed industrial extractivism pushing up against neo-liberal attempts at reforms that have struggled to effectively regulate Western industrialisation in the pursuit of balanced social and environmental needs. This malestream revival has been ushered in with great pomp, power and pageantry – think here of the global authority bestowed upon 'pussy-grabbing' presidents through to exorbitantly paid and smack-mouthed ultimate fighting champions, reifying anew the potency of certain, but very limited (ecocidal and interpersonally violating), kinds of toxic/extreme masculinities as men the world over find ways to reassert their assumed 'greatness' (Kimmel, 2013). To make things even worse, such anti-feminist behaviour is ideologically colliding with climate change denial at a time when speedy and transformative policy change is urgently needed (Hultman, et. al., forthcoming; Pulé and Hultman, forthcoming).

If we are to introduce alternatives to these crass expressions of masculinities (and the global problems they cause), we must uncover fresh and creative resocialisations of modern Western masculinities. While we restrict ourselves to exploring Western men and masculinities here, we recognise this is not the entire story that is needing humanity's collective attention. We focus our efforts on modern Western contexts simply because it is these men and masculinities that are the most accountable for the problems we face globally; their nuanced issues typically buried within versions of normality that renders their primacy invisible. Bringing these issues to light through our focused analyses, we seek solutions for men and masculinities that offer alternatives to the problems we face looking to ecology as a relational science as our greatest guide. To create a grounded theory on men, masculinities and Earth, much of our attention is aimed at the structural elements of the conversation that follows. This book is influenced by the theories that have come before us and those we have generated between us as well. Borrowing from Donna Haraway's (1988) influential work on 'situated knowledges', we recognise that the analyses we offer are indeed situated and unapologetically reflective of us as colleagues and friends, each with unique but very aligned backgrounds. Consequently, we begin by offering overviews of our respective lives as an important starting point, given we have discovered that our professional explorations of this topic have been intensely personal as well.

As social and environmental justice scholars and activists (henceforth 'scholar activists') we had both been separately working on these critical global concerns since the mid 1990s – long before we first met. That all changed on 26–28 February, 2016. There, at an international gathering hosted by Sherilyn MacGregor and Nicole Seymour on behalf of the Rachel Carson Center for Environment and Society in Munich, the idea of writing this book about ecological masculinities was born. Our explorations of the topic have grown from concerns about something 'out there' in the world of ideas, that now shapes the ways we relate with those in our respective lives, as well as each other and ourselves. The work that follows is the product of a soulful friendship that combines our common passions and our deep care for Earth.

I (Martin speaking here) grew up in a middle-class family in that nation which often finds itself the envy of the world; Sweden. My homeland is especially renowned for its encouraging parental-leave policies. There, fathers share some of the highest portions of domestic responsibility on the planet. Sweden has become an icon for socially progressive and environmentally friendly policies and practices (Haas and Hwang, 2008). But Sweden has many problems, despite its reputation. Sexism persists, not least made visable with #MeToo (2017/2018), a campaign that has exposed the deep structural misogyny of sexual abuse even in The Swedish Academy as the awarder for the Nobel Prizes. The image of Sweden as a veritable (eco)utopia does not hold up in the fields of rigorous social and environmental justice. If we extend to all people the consumption rates of the average Swede, we would need four planets. The World Wild Life Fund's *Living Planet Report* (2016) lists Sweden among some of the worst per capita carbon polluters and resource uses. Measures such as these show that Sweden is not necessarily the envy that it is at times portrayed. This perception appears to be more a consequence of Sweden's low population density correlated with the abundance and the privileges of its very high levels of Western consumerism and wealth, more so than an honest commitment to sustainability. Despite instituting efficient resource uses in its energy and industrial sectors, Sweden's per capita consumption levels put its citizens among the top nations placing strains on global natural systems (OECD, 2016). Sweden boasts low levels of per capita domestic environmental impacts because the nation has efficiently displaced significant portions of its ecological impacts onto other countries, while also becoming progressively more efficient at concealing non-exportable social and environmental impacts (Hysing, 2014). Even more ironic in this Nordic neo-liberal icon is the fact that Sweden's second largest political party (as of polls in July, 2018) unapologetically promotes neo-fascist policies. I have had my own inner tensions to reconcile as a Swedish man in the wake of these paradoxes.

In my younger years, I developed a passion for football (the World game) while also seeking solace through orienteering or foraging for wild mushrooms. In my twenties, I was oblivious to the fossil-fuel dependency of modern industrial life at home. While I was at that time supportive of diversity among people and revered nature, I blindly contributed to carbon pollution at high levels reflective of my Swedish compatriots as I thoughtlessly travelled around the globe for both work and pleasure. Once I became a PhD student, I began to develop an awareness of the destructive elements embedded within the average Swede's standard of living. I made the link between my fossil fuel-propelled travels and my contributions to a growing climate emergency. Through my studies, I became aware of how easily we can distance ourselves from and cause further harm to our communities and towards our environment. Long hours of sitting at my computer, distant air travels to conferences and sharing ideas in the lecture room away from home, illuminated this paradox. I came to see that social and environmental awareness must be backed up with individual leadership and civil actions. This discovery was galvanised by three life-changing events.

The first was a personal and family crisis, as I fell ill with cancer at the age of 30. With a 1-year-old child just starting to walk, my illness placed enormous pressure on my wife and wider family to support us through that time. Contending with cancer left me acutely aware that to survive I needed help from family, friends and nature. It became obvious to me that I was part of nature and nature was part of me. That humbling experience shifted my perspective radically. While receiving treatment and recovering, I not only connected with loved ones but communed with the forests near my home as well. On long walks, I found chanterelles, caught the piercing gaze of elk and picked wild berries. Supported by dear ones along with the plants and animals on these sojourns, I was able to rebuild my strength and make a full recovery.

The second event happened a few years later, where I successfully defended my PhD and moved swiftly into writing a book based on a broad empirical study of environmental and energy politics with my academic mentor, Jonas Anshelm, titled *Discourses of Global Climate Change: Apocalyptic Framing and Political Antagonisms* (Anshelm and Hultman, 2014a). Through that research project, I conducted a comprehensive study of the climate data. In becoming knowledgeable about the social and ecological consequences of anthropogenic climate change, I realised that if we are truly committed to solving our global problems, we do indeed need to take the climate data seriously and in doing so we must as a species respond with focus, commitment and haste.

Third, was meeting engaged indigenous Sámi people. Leaders in those communities are passionate about ending domination of their home land by extractive industry. These folks, combined with ecopreneurs in New Zealand helped me realise all the energy and visions that are available to us if we only open our eyes to them. From that moment, I could begin the process of extracting myself from my fossil fuel addiction. With that realisation, I expanded my scholarly pursuits to include activism, working with my neighbours on community enrichment projects such as ride-sharing, ecotourism and creating a cultural house in my home village at the time – Bestorp in Linköping Municipality. My personal and professional trajectories have been clear ever since. This book is my latest addition to making the world a better place for all.

I (Paul speaking here) grew up in the suburbs of Perth, Western Australia in a family of Maltese, Italian and Lebanese descent. Far from your classic Aussie bloke, I am a product of Australia's wave of post-Second Word War émigrés. As the only son and a first-generation Australian-born man, I found it challenging to feel at ease at home as much as out in my world. The conventions of my heritage often placed my Australian-ness at odds with my family's cultural norms and with that the expressiveness of my Catholic/Mediterranean heritage was often received as an affront to the Protestant sensibilities of late twentieth-century Australia: our surname was anglicised; I was parcelled into a Catholic boys' college whose student body was largely made up of 'wogs' (a derogatory term for southern European migrants and their families); my family insisted that I fit in as seamlessly as possible in order to dodge the racism they endured, meaning I did not learn to speak the native languages of my parents and grandparents; we largely kept to ourselves or socialised with family in my early years, only to have frequent feuds erupt that commonly ended in long stretches of disconnection between family members as wounds healed. My strongest childhood recollections about the men in my life were that they were overbearing, entitled, emotionally distant and prone to violent thoughts, words and/ or deeds. As a youngster, most of the men in my life seemed impossible to reach, likely to ridicule, prone to react in fits of blaming and shaming and were terrifying to be around. The two big exceptions were my maternal grandfather who I am named after – he was always kind and happy to see me – and my paternal uncle who had left for adventures overseas when I was very young, returning sporadically with tall tales, deep insights and prodding questions about who I was and was becoming. Little did I know then that the tense fragility of my relationships with most of the men in my early life would create the perfect conditions for me to enter my adulthood primed to become a masculinities scholar. In my early twenties, I decided to leave Australia for an indefinite period, setting off for New York City to live with my uncle. There, I found a community of his friends who were warm, attentive and more emotionally available than the men I was accustomed to back home in Perth. From that base, I entered a new life in the US, joining an intentional community in a semi-rural part of Buck's County, north of Philadelphia. Our home was idyllic; close to major cities but with state forest reserve on three sides, a creek running through the back yard, a root cellar and plenty of space for a large vegetable garden. I became part of a tight-knit group of socially and politically active young adults, living a simple life of experimenting with consensus and collective decision-making, chopping wood, frolicking naked in the creek, wandering through the nearby woods, sharing boisterous community meals, collectively raising the kids that some in the community had birthed, pitching in shoulder to shoulder to share the chores and pooling finances. These experiences gave me a sense of what is possible when we live in communion with each other and Earth. When this living arrangement ended some five years later, I found myself wondering (skeptically) if living this way was possible on a broader scale. With this question in mind, I applied for a PhD programme at Murdoch University's School of Sustainability back home in Perth. Winning a scholarship, I plunged headlong into a study on men and care. As I deepened my understanding of post-structural and feminist thinking, ecology, mechanisms of oppression and care theory, I recognised that the world is rife with injustices that persistently promote men's interests ahead of all others. This realisation helped me focus my studies on malestream norms and male domination. I have since dedicated my life to finding alternative paths for men that help us access and express our care for all life along with ourselves.

This book reflects our combined efforts to critically examine men, masculinities and Earth. Here, we seek new approaches to the ways that maleness might be reconfigured to support broader, deeper and wider care for our world, each other and ourselves.

Societal and environmental challenges

As we introduced above, we are facing crises of society and the environment that have their roots in our very gendered identities as human beings (Buckingham, 2015). To effectively confront the enormous challenges upon us, we must find multifaceted approaches that will tackle our escalating social, economic, political and ecological problems. These responses must be both conceptual and practical if we are to create equitable communities and harmonious relationships between humanity and Earth. Even though nations of the Global North are the highest per capita resource consumers in human history, a common response to critiques of Western standards of living is to seek someone or something to blame. In the Swedish debate on global climate change, the finger is readily pointed at the US and China for being the biggest carbon emitters; some actors accuse refugees of taking jobs, straining welfare budgets and/or bringing foreign cultural nuances to our neighbourhoods; extreme interpretations of Islam and Christianity are fostering waves of international and domestic terrorism; the poor are increasingly being branded as more complicit than the wealthy for causing environmental harm (e.g. the racism that pervades the environmental movement can convince us that non-white communities throughout the West are ecologically ignorant) (Anshelm and Hultman, 2014a). Our situation has become perilous to such an extent that Professor Johan Rockstöm, Director of Stockholm Resilience Centre, made a stark declaration that 'the planetary stability our species has enjoyed for 11,700 years, that allowed civilisation to flourish, can no longer be relied upon' (World Wildlife Fund, 2016: 5). With the negative impacts of climate change growing (as shown by environmental phenomena like the mass bleaching events of Australia's Great Barrier Reef of 2016 and 2017 and hurricanes Harvey, Irma and Maria off the coast of the Southeastern US in 2017), coupled with persistent global atmospheric temperature increases, we must find ways to manifest more harmonious interactions with Earth, along with each other and ourselves. The transitions we face – both their harmful consequences for all life as well as our attempts to respond constructively to them – are proving to be enormous. Sadly, despite these ominous scenarios, many people continue to 'otherise' Earth's living systems, members of our communities and each other (Anshelm and Hultman, 2014b). Throughout this book, we argue that this is ultimately a masculinities problem that manifests most intensely in the Global North. We need something new and different that can shift the ways that men and masculinities affect our world.

Other scholars have investigated the role of men and masculinities in global social and environmental destruction. For generations, prominent feminists have directly and indirectly examined the socially and environmentally challenging implications of traditional industrial notions of manhood and masculinities[2] (Laula, 2003[1904]; Wägner, 1941; Carson, 1962; Merchant, 1980; Plumwood, 1993; Nightingale, 2006; MacGregor, 2009; Buckingham, 2010; Arora-Jonsson, 2013; MacGregor and Seymour eds., 2017). There is also empirical evidence to highlight the failure of technological fixes and compromised policies and practices that run parallel to neo-liberal reforms (Hultman, 2013; Hultman, 2017; Hultman and Anshelm, 2017). From these foundations, we challenge the norms that define what it means to be a man in today's world, arguing that if we are to successfully avert (or at least minimise) the global impacts of our growing crises, we must rethink and embody fresh expressions of manhood and masculinities (Alaimo and Hekman eds., 2008; Alaimo, 2009; Klein, 2014; Cornwall, et al. eds., 2016). To achieve this, we hold men and masculinities accountable for the principal elements of the struggles we face, bearing in mind this is not the entire story – we are all responsible for the state of the world, but the roles of men and masculinities are particularly acute and worthy of our focused attention (Wackernagel and Rees, 1996; Lenzen et al., 2007; Räty and Carlsson-Kanyama, 2010). We also consider that unfettered Western (what we refer to as 'industrial/breadwinner') and reformist (what we refer to as 'ecomodern') approaches to our growing global social and environmental problems have proved to be inadequate responses to our challenges, since both have coveted corporate capitalism while amplifying social and environmental decay. I (Martin speaking here) developed the notion of industrial masculinities relating to my own concept 'industrial modern discourse' (Hultman, 2010). However, others have used the term before me (Nayak, 2003). The term breadwinner masculinities is drawn from the work of Judith Stacey (1990). Paul and I have, as a consequence of our collaboration, combined the two terms to speak to both socio-economic ends of male domination at its most severe. We discuss this at greater length in Chapter 1. While we agree that men and masculinities have been complicit in the lion's share of our global social and environmental problems, we offer a third (and to date under-researched and under-theorised) response that provides some proactive pathways towards relational and more caring masculinities (what we refer to as 'ecological masculinities'). With masculine ecologisation as our focus, it is important to note that any understanding of men and masculinities must start from gendered terminologies that reflect changeable entities, which produce a variety of researchable categories across a wide array of understandings. This is particularly true of the terms 'man', 'men', 'manhood' and 'masculinities' (see Chapter 3). Notably, critical examinations of these terms are little more than a generation old, emerging in solidarity with the accomplishments of 'second-wave' feminism. Further, scholars have only recently begun to analyse notions of manhood and masculinities in the context of environmental concerns (MenEngage, 2016). For too long, men and masculinities have dodged responsibility for our social and environmental ills precisely because to be male in popular culture is 'normal', not 'other' and provides a reference point that defines things relative to not being male; gaining nuanced examination primarily within academic (critical) and pop-psychological (essentialist) circles. We need a unifying view; one that celebrates critical analyses of men, masculinities and Earth, but that also recognises that the many faces of masculinities are inseparably entangled.

It is inexcusable but understandable that many men struggle to distance themselves from the allure of their own primacy. The pressure to embrace male domination patterns is enormous. Returning to Solnit (2017: 30–31), men are socialised to literally kill off their emotional selves and intentionally target others that they dominate, routing out vulnerability in others as much as in the self; the messages conveyed to boys and men are incisive – openness is weakness, being a real man is being the one who penetrates, not the one who is penetrated; to love is to risk rejection and abandonment; respect is earned or extorted; being heartfelt is to lose control; to collaborate and consult is to deny one's leadership. To be born into malestream norms – particularly in the West – is to valorise data, to approach problems with logical responses and driven intentions to fix them, to trust that economic rationalism and technology will save the day and to seek grounded solutions in competition against each other from an assumed 'I-should/can/will-handle-this' approach to life that leaves little room for feelings or intuition (Mellström, 1995). Hegemonic stereotypes of being a real man include being a winner, a hunter, a leader, someone dutiful to their superior who is also a servant to God. These socialisations get embedded into boys early in life. Boys' malestream conditioning is to adopt protector/provider personas as they move into manhood. Economic pressures similarly coerce men to become dutiful cogs in the wheel of corporate capitalism. Such are the messages of malestream norms. In this book, we look instead to an empathic 'sense of connectedness to humans and other-than-humans; of being in relation with them, actually or potentially' that demands a shift in the ways that men care for those around them along with themselves (Puka, 1993: 216).

We do not question whether men care. We know they can and do. Like all human beings, men are caring, but are socialised to mete out their care within quite specific and tight parameters. Take for example supporting a team (or caring about one's chosen sport), patriotism (or caring for one's nation ahead of other nations and in the face of potential enemies), protecting, providing and active fathering (or caring for loved ones), loyalty to an employer (or caring about one's fiscal security, one's career, or one's professional identity) and a slew of caring professions where men are well represented, such as medicine, dentistry and veterinary science, social and psychological services, education, even politics where one is of service to the community and is a profession disproportionately populated by men (Kimmel et al. eds., 2005). For millennia, stories abound of men at war acting with much courage and at great mortal risk to themselves to preserve the lives of others and the values they hold dear (McPhedran, 2005). These are just some of the many ways that men can express care beyond themselves. In each instance, there are winners and losers. We seek another way forward for men and masculinities, investigating stereotypical expressions of masculine care and how it can be directed towards broader, deeper and wider care for our glocal commons, a term borrowed from Roland Robertson (1995) that refers to our capacities to tend to the universal down to particular – simultaneously.

The myopia of men's care

Malestream men's care is myopic. Blinded by the intoxicating properties of hegemonisation, malestream manhood prioritises doing rather than being. This can be a trap, since it is common for men inculcated by heteronormativity to arrive at the end of their careers, no longer defined by what they know how to do, only to find their lives empty and meaningless. The passing of time is a silent reminder of their inescapable demise (through declining sexual function and metaphorically through declining power and influence as they grow past their primes), which can leave many ageing men feeling cast aside, cheated out of their social and economic potency, marginalised and left behind. This sentiment runs parallel with the appeal of contemporary shock politics that has gained renewed racist and sexist appeal, tapping into male entitlement with great vigour, helping us understand some of the reasons why middle-aged and older men (white men in particular) are susceptible to far-right wing socio-political movements (Lewis, 2015; Eisenstein, 2016; Burns, 2017; Çalışkan and Preston, 2017; Hozić and True, 2017; Johnson, 2017; Pascoe, 2017; Viefhues-Bailey, 2017). The great promise of men's primacy in a sexist and ecocidal world leaves them at odds with who they really are, where the pressure to perform, accomplish, manage and overshadow their inner needs, wants and desires can be considerable. Paraphrasing Henry David Thoreau (1995 [1854]), it is still commonplace for many men to live lives of quiet desperation, arriving at the end of their days not having honoured their inner passions in service to the greater good. With this, the very systems that sustain all life on Earth are showing signs of great social and ecological demise. We need men to reconnect with their broader care for all others and themselves, for the sake of all others and themselves.

The costs of malestream masculinities are enormous. Not only limited to those who are otherised, masculine hegemonisation erodes men's lives and our common planet as well. As inescapable parts of ecosystems, men, like all living things, represent relational exchanges with others on multiple scales – globally through to personally. A central goal of this book is to redirect the most celebrated aspects of masculinities towards care for the glocal commons. In Section One, we interrogate modern Western masculinities and explore trajectories from hegmonised through to ecologised masculinities. Section Two considers masculinities politics, deep ecology, ecological feminism and feminist care theory. We imagine these to be the equivalent of four streams emptying into an estuary upon whose fresh shores we stand. These discourses offer important materials washed down to us from their respective headwaters, helping us to build what we visualise to be a new ecological masculinities 'shelter' on those shores as a place of reflective contemplation and gathering where we can consider and restructure modern Western masculinities for the sake of all life. The materials from these four streams are substantial and worthy of our detailed consideration, but they are not exhaustive. Seeking guidance from those who have come before us, in Section Three, we proceed to examine materials from other perspectives as well, as if seeking additional resources for the finishing touches of this shelter just inland from the water's edge to help us complete our task. These added resources come to us through: environmental and historical accounts of the Green Man, the communal and self-help orientation proffered by the mythopoets, the creative analytics of ecocritics, the visceral churn exposed through sociological explorations of wild-ness and rural-ness and the astute socio-politics of ecologically inspired feminists. Of course, this list is not exhaustive but captures our principal influences in the journey towards masculine ecologisation. There are likely to be additional discursive influences worthy of our attention than we have considered here. Our book initiates a new conversation and for this reason we defer examination of some of these wider discussions to future works that will be published by ourselves or others as ecological masculinities takes hold internationally. The concluding chapter constructs our theoretical framework for ecological masculinities and offers a framework for you to find your own practical pathway through a unique masculine ecologisation process. There, we aim to help you deepen or (re)discover what your own path of service in support of the glocal commons might be.

While we have primarily written from an academic vantage to formulate ecological masculinities, we also appeal to anyone who has an interest in the convergence of men, masculinities and Earth to read this book. We have written Chapter 8 as our way of appealing to the widest audience possible. For now, we stay focused on our four chosen streams as we prepare to map out our theoretical framing for ecological masculinities.

Notes

1   We use 'Western' throughout this book as synonymous with the wealthier nations of the 'Global North' that are distinct from 'non-Western' nations of the 'Global South' as described in the *Brandt Report* (Stewart, 1980).

2 We use 'industrial/breadwinner masculinities' to supersede a more familiar but older term 'hyper-masculinity' defined as the amplification of traditional expressions of masculinities through physical strength, aggression, sexual prowess, military might, domination, being a 'winner' and not being a 'girl' (Kivel, 1999; hooks, 2004; Katz, 2006; Katz, 2012; Katz, 2016). We do so to emphasise the entangled relationship between malestream norms, male domination, industrialisation and their social and environmental consequences which have proved to be severe. We give a fuller explanation of the meaning we attach to industrial/breadwinner masculinities, along with ecomodern and ecological masculinities in Chapter 2.

References

Alaimo, S. 2009. 'Insurgent vulnerability and the carbon footprint of gender'. *Kvinder, Køn & Forskning* 3–4: 22–35.

Alaimo, S., and S. Hekman, eds. 2008. *Material Feminisms*. Bloomington: Indiana University Press.

Anshelm, J., and M. Hultman. 2014a. *Discourses of Global Climate Change: Apocalyptic Framing and Political Antagonisms*. Oxon: Routledge.

Anshelm, J., and M. Hultman. 2014b. 'A green fatwã? Climate change as a threat to the masculinity of industrial modernity'. *NORMA: International Journal for Masculinity Studies* 9(2): 84–96.

Arora-Jonsson, S. 2013. *Gender, Development and Environmental Governance: Theorizing Connections* (vol. 33). New York: Routledge.

Bologh, R. 1990. *Love or Greatness: Max Weber and Masculine Thinking – A Feminist Inquiry*. London: Unwin Hyman.

Buckingham, S. 2010. 'Call in the women'. *Nature* 468(7323): 502–502.

Buckingham, S. 2015. *Gender and the Environment (Critical Concepts in the Environment)*. Oxon: Routledge.

Burns, J. 2017. 'Biopolitics, toxic masculinities, disavowed histories, and youth radicalization'. *Peace Review* 29(2): 176–183.

Çalışkan, G., and K. Preston. 2017. 'Tropes of fear and the crisis of the west: Trumpism as a discourse of post-territorial coloniality'. *Postcolonial Studies* 20(2): 199–216.

Carson, R. 1962. *Silent Spring*. Boston: Houghton Mifflin.

Cornwall, A., Karioris, F., and N. Lindisfarne, eds. 2016. *Masculinities under Neoliberalism*. London: Zed Books.

Eisenstein, C. 2016. 'The election: of hate, grief, and a new story'. Accessed 25 June 2017. https://charleseisenstein.net/essays/hategriefandanewstory

Haas, L., and C. Hwang. 2008. 'The Impact of Taking Parental Leave on Fathers' Participation In Childcare And Relationships With Children: Lessons from Sweden.' Community, Work & Family 11(1): 85–104.

Haraway, D. 1988. 'Situated knowledges: the science question in feminism and the privilege of partial perspective'. *Feminist Studies* 14(3): 575–599.

hooks, b. 2004. *We Real Cool: Black Men and Masculinity*. New York: Routledge.

Hozić, A., and J. True. 2017. 'Brexit as a scandal: gender and global Trumpism'. *Review of International Political Economy* 24(2): 270–287.

Hultman, M. 2010. 'Full gas mot en (o) hållbar framtid: Förväntningar på bränsleceller och vätgas 1978–2005 i relation till svensk energi-och miljöpolitik'. PhD diss., Linköping University.

Hultman, M. 2013. 'The making of an environmental hero: A history of ecomodern masculinity, fuel cells and Arnold Schwarzenegger'. *Environmental Humanities* 2(1): 79–99.

Hultman, M. 2017. 'Conceptualising industrial, ecomodern and ecological masculinities'. In S. Buckingham and V. le Masson, eds., *Understanding Climate Change through Gender Relations*. Oxon.: Routledge, 87–103.

Hultman, M., and J. Anshelm. 2017. 'Masculinities of global climate change'. In M. Cohen, ed., *Climate Change and Gender in Rich Countries: Work, Public Policy and Action*. New York: Routledge, 19–34.

Hultman, M., Björk A., and T. Viinikka. Forthcoming. 'Neo-fascism and climate change denial. Analysing the political ecology of industrial masculinities, anti-establishment rhetoric and economic growth nationalism'. In B. Forchtner, C. Kølvraa and R. Wodak, eds., *Contemporary Environmental Communication by the Far Right in Europe*. London: Routledge.

Hysing, E. 2014. 'A green star fading? A critical assessment of Swedish environmental policy change'. *Environmental Policy and Governance* 24(4): 262–274.

Johnson, D. 2017. 'Rule by divide and conquer'. In D. Johnson, ed., *Social Inequality, Economic Decline, and Plutocracy: An American Crisis*. Cham: Springer, 91–108.

Katz, J. 2006. *The Macho Paradox: Why Some Men Hurt Women and How All Men Can Help*. Naperville: Sourcebooks.

Katz, J. 2012. 'Violence against women – it's a men's issue' [Video]. TedXFiDiWomen, November. Accessed 1 September 2017. http://www.ted.com/speakers/jackson_katz

Katz, J. 2016. *Man Enough?: Donald Trump, Hillary Clinton, and the Politics of Presidential Masculinity*. Northampton: Interlink.

Keith, T. 2016. *Masculinities in Contemporary American Culture: An Intersectional Approach to the Complexities and Challenges of Male Identity*. New York: Routledge.

Kimmel, M. 2013. *Angry White Men: American Masculinity at the End of an Era*. New York: Nation Books.

Kimmel, M., Hearn, J., and R. Connell, eds. 2005. *Handbook of Studies on Men and Masculinities*. Thousand Oaks: SAGE Publishing.

Kivel, P. 1999. *Boys Will Be Men: Raising Our Sons for Courage, Caring and Community*. Gabriola Island: New Society Publishers.

Klein, N. 2014. *This Changes Everything: Capitalism vs. the Climate*. New York: Simon & Schuster.

Laula, E. 2003[1904]. *Inför lif eller död?: sanningsord i de lappska förhållandena*. Stockholm: EOD.

Lenzen, M., Murray, J., Sack, F., and T. Wiedmann. 2007. 'Shared producer and consumer responsibility – theory and practice'. *Ecological Economics* 61(1): 27–42.

Lewis, T. 2015. 'A Harvard psychiatrist says 3 things are the secret to real happiness'. *Business Insider*. Accessed 11 November 2017. http://www.businessinsider.com.au/robert-waldinger-says-3-things-are-the-secret-to-happiness-2015-12?r=US&IR=T

MacGregor, S. 2009. 'A stranger silence still: the need for feminist social research on climate change'. *Sociological Review* 57 (2 suppl.): 124–140.

MacGregor, S., and N. Seymour, eds. 2017. *Men and Nature: Hegemonic Masculinities and Environmental Change*. Munich: RCC Perspectives.

McPhedran, I. 2005. *The Amazing SAS: The Inside Story of Australia's Special Forces*. Sydney: HarperCollins.

Mellström, U. 1995. 'Engineering lives: technology, time and space in a male-centred world'. PhD diss., Linköping University.

MenEngage. 2016. *Men, Masculinities and Climate Change: A Discussion Paper*. Washington, DC: MenEngage Global Alliance.

Merchant, C. 1980. *The Death of Nature: Women, Ecology and the Scientific Revolution.* New York: HarperCollins.

Nayak, A. 2003. '"Boyz to men": masculinities, schooling and labour transitions in de-industrial times'. *Educational Review* 55(2): 147–159.

Nightingale, A. 2006. 'The nature of gender: work, gender, and environment'. *Environment and planning D: Society and space* 24(2): 165–185.

O'Brien, M. 1981. 'Feminist theory and dialectical logic'. *Signs: Journal of Women in Culture and Society* 7(1): 144–157.

OECD [Organisation for Economic Co-operation and Development]. 2016. *Data on Sweden*. Accessed 1 November 2017. https://data.oecd.org/sweden.htm

Pascoe, C. 2017. 'Who is a real man? The gender of Trumpism'. *Masculinities and Social Change* 6(2): 119–141.

Plumwood, V. 1993. *Feminism and the Mastery of Nature*. London: Routledge.

Puka, B. 1993. 'The liberation of caring: a different voice for Gilligan's "different voice"'. In M. Larrabee, ed., *An Ethic of Care: Feminist and Interdisciplinary Perspectives*. London: Routledge, 215–239.

Pulé, P., and M. Hultman. Forthcoming. 'Fossil fuel, industrial/breadwinner masculinities and climate change: understanding the "white male effect" of climate change denial'. In C. Kinnvall and H. Rydström, eds. *Climate Hazards and Gendered Ramifications*. London: Routledge.

Räty, R., and A. Carlsson-Kanyama. 2010. 'Energy consumption by gender in some European countries'. *Energy Policy*, 38(1): 646–649.

Robertson, R. 1995. 'Glocalization: time–space and homogeneity–heterogeneity'. In M. Featherstone, S. Lash, and R. Robertson, eds., *Global Modernities*. London: SAGE Publishing, 25–44.

Solnit, R. 2017. *The Mother of All Questions*. Chicago: Haymarket Books.

Stacey, J. 1990. *Brave New Families: Stories of Domestic Upheaval in Late-Twentieth-Century America*. Berkeley: University of California Press.

Stewart, F. 1980. 'The *Brandt Report*'. *Development Policy Review* 13(1): 65–88.

Stockard, J., and M. Johnson. 1979. 'The social origins of male dominance'. *Sex Roles* 5(2): 199–218.

Thoreau, H. 1995[1854]. *Walden, or Life in the Woods*. Minneola: Dover.

Viefhues-Bailey, L. 2017. 'Looking forward to a new heaven and a new earth where American greatness dwells: Trumpism's political theology'. *Political Theology* 18(3): 194–200.

Wackernagel, M., and W. Rees. 1996. *Our Ecological Footprint: Reducing Human Impact on the Earth*. Gabriola Island: New Society Publishers.

Wägner, E. 1941. *Väckarklocka*, Stockholm: Bonniers.

Warren, K. 1987. 'Feminism and ecology: making connections'. *Environmental Ethics* 9 (spring): 3–20.

Warren, K. 2000. *Ecofeminist Philosophy: A Western Perspective on What It Is and Why It Matters*. Lanham: Rowman & Littlefield.

World Wildlife Fund. 2016. *Living Planet Report 2016: Risk and Resilience in a New Era*. Gland: WWF International.

Section I
Conceptual foundations

1 Introduction

Interrogating masculinities

... embedded in cultural discourses, social institutions, and individual psyches is the lens of *androcentrism*, or male-centered-ness. This is not just the historically crude perception that men are inherently superior to women but a more treacherous underpinning of that perception: a definition of males and male experience as a neutral standard or norm, and females and female experience as a sex-specific deviation from that norm. It is thus not that man is treated superior and woman as inferior but that man is treated as human and woman as 'other' ... superimposed on so many aspects of the social world that a cultural connection is thereby forged between sex and virtually every other aspect of human experience ... as the natural and inevitable consequences of the intrinsic biological natures of women [, non-binary/genderqueers] and men.

(Bem, 1993: 2–3)

Thoughts from many fronts

Post-gendered understandings of human beings – regardless of biological or behavioural differences – suggest that we are are both similar and variable. Consistent with Sandra Bem (1993), we recognise 'that people can be both masculine and feminine ... that assigned biological sex is independent from gender' and that our focus ought to be on the socio-cultural constructions of gender as they affect us all (Keener and Mehta, 2017: 525). We consider it vital to transition beyond gendered polarisations about what it means to be human in today's world. However, to help us get there, if we want to better understand men's lives as a gender, the masculinities that shape them and the impacts that these identities have on Earth, others and men themselves, then more work on masculinities is necessary. To do otherwise, is to leapfrog over these important foundational analyses, creating a vacuum that some men (and others) are feeding through contemporary toxic masculinities revivals, which are destructive for all life. It would therefore be useful to consider this book a 'catch-up' of sorts, where we focus our attention on the nuances of men and masculinities beyond scattered academic publications and essentialised debates. We do this to bring masculine discourses as they relate to social and environmental justice up to date with the extensive considerations of our feminist colleagues (and others) who have come before us. We deconstruct and move towards reconfigurations of men and masculinities that stand shoulder to shoulder with the extensive and deeply considered works of gender and environments scholars who have come before us. Our intention is to interrogate points of intersection and commonality beyond perceived differences among people and between humanity and other-than-human others.

In this chapter, we explore the understanding that masculinities are structural, personal and unavoidably plural. Further to our four primary discursive influences, we consider Kimberlé Crenshaw's (1989) intersectionality theory, which argued the ways that we acquire knowledge through subjective relationships shaped by gender, race, class and other social categories. Intersectionality theorists examine the ways that we implement processes through nuanced and unequal relational intersections (McCall, 2005; Christensen and Jensen, 2014). We also acknowledge that Jeff Hearn et al. (2012) considered masculinities to be 'situated'; a view that encouraged research on the topic across various categories and configurations. Further, Raewyn Connell (1995: 37), whose pivotal work we return to consistently throughout this book, has been instrumental in positing the notion of hegemonic masculinities. Engaging with empirical research, she concluded that men's various practices occur across a wide variety of relational exchanges that not only reveal patterns of domination, but also stress the importance of viewing men's lives and masculine identity as heterogenous. Following the lead of these scholars, we consider it vital that we approach research on men and masculinities as a 'broad church'. That said, it is precisely because of the dichotomous nature of masculinities that the analyses and alternatives we offer directly discuss malestream dominator patterns (especially of white Western males). We see these norms as artefacts of masculine hegemonisation that need further investigation if we are to better understand the personal and the political implications of men and masculinities as material-semiotic categories. Our goal is to create more space for broader, deeper and wider masculine care (and by this we mean 'caring about' – as a feeling – and 'caring for' as an action consistent with the formative tenets of feminist care theory, which we consider in Chapters 6), so that men are more willing and able to stand with human others to support all life. To achieve this, we begin by critically analysing the narrow bandwidth of malestream ontologies that have long tied socialisations of men and masculinities to the constraints of masculine hegemonisation.

White, male and in denial

In exploring modern Western men and masculinities as a mosaic of categories, we are particularly interested in the lives of those men who occupy the most privileged positions in society in the Global North. A stereotypical belief persists that, 'there is only one complete unblushing male' and he is a:

> . . . young, married, white, urban, northern, heterosexual, Protestant father of college education, fully employed, of good complexion, weight, and height, and recent record in sport . . . Any male who fails to qualify

in any one of these ways is likely to view himself – during moments at least – as unworthy, incomplete and inferior.

(Goffman, 1963: 128)

While we recognise that this is a dated stereotype, we note that to this day age typically brings with it an accumulation of socio-economic and political power and prestige, colliding with ageism that can take the sheen off older men's primacy. Considerable attention has recently shifted towards the plight of working-class white men feeling marginalised, subjecting them to similar stereotypes. This demographic represents an understudied and severely discontented sector of society, which has used their anger in many Western nations recently to support toxic/extreme and authoritarian leadership styles replete with overt and subtle expressions of power and violence (Katz, 2016: 26). In a study titled *Strangers in Their Own Land: Anger and Mourning on the American Right*, sociologist Arlie Hochschild (2016) provided us with an in-depth ethnographic study of Louisiana bayou country – a stronghold of the far-right where malestream masculinities remain overt and unapologetic. This study emphasised the need to understand the structural impacts of neo-liberalism in these areas as well as the huge impact of the right wing politicisation of Christianity that has captured a critical portion of the US electorate. Further and bringing the compelling arguments in his important book titled *Angry White Men* (2013) up to date in an interview with *The Guardian*, sociologist Michel Kimmel made explicit the connections between malestream masculinities and the voter base for the Trump administration (Conroy, 2017). Alarmingly, the characteristics of men who embrace masculine hegemonisation echo Erving Goffman's (1979) identified features of malestream norms that he published approximately forty years ago. It appears that little has changed in regard to masculinities and the status quo. This does raise questions about how far we need to go in order to break free from the constraints of hegemonic masculinities. The answer appears to be: quite far and quite fast. To assist with this, we give further consideration to some of the sharpest commentaries on masculinities from scholars who have dedicated their lives to this task.

Anthony Synnott (2009: 46, 51) suggested that the most revered of masculinities assume three main forms: the warrior (who embodies bravery), the gentleman (who epitomises gentility) and the self-made man (who manifests his own success). Such men are supposedly good husbands, exceptional fathers, tireless workers, civil men calling the shots, and when it all breaks down, they are also violent beasts ready to put things back in their 'rightful' place with force. These stereotypical male characteristics align strongly with being white, wealthy, travelling frequently, eating high meat diets and living in energy-intensive homes; features which echo hyper-masculinist, hyper-consumerist attitudes (Alaimo, 2009: 26). Granted, such generalisations are problematic, since they do not specify what we mean by wealthy (within or between nations), nor do they account for diversities in age, race, class, etc. where travel frequency, meat consumption and domestic energy usage are high (MacGregor and Seymour, 2017: 12). Also, consider those non-white men who have assumed similar leadership roles throughout Western nations who have received some of the same socio-political and economic trappings as their white compatriots, along with those men who comprise the non-Western ruling classes. We must include these 'otherised' men in our analyses of masculine hegemonisation as well, since they also receive benefits precisely because women and non-binary/genderqueer people are otherised by sexism, racism and heteronormativity in ways that they are not because they are male and/or wealthy. That considered, hegemonic masculinities, exhibit '[d]elusions, of hyperseparation, transcendence, and dominance [that] . . . engender denial of the many global [social and] environmental crises' we face, effectively calling to our attention that these features typically run parallel to Western white male domination patterns (Alaimo, 2009: 28). Taken to be emblematic of the most celebrated of Western masculinities, these characteristics define a narrow bandwidth of socialisations that feed and are fed by Western malestreams, presenting working- and middle-class white men with the unspoken expectation that theirs is a life that could be self-made if only they worked hard enough. Consistent with socialist critiques of capitalism, we recognise that wealth is consolidated in the hands of owners of the means of production and commerce throughout the West, who socially, politically and economically exploit workers and extract the Earth's natural resources for their own gains. Dissecting this entanglement, we recognise that the benefits of wealth, race and sexual orientation are shaped by:

> . . . the social contract that enabled self-made [malestream] men to feel that they *could* make it, even if they somehow failed to realize their dreams, [which] has, indeed, been shredded, abandoned for lavish profiteering by the rich, enabled by a government composed of foxes who have long ago abandoned their posts at the henhouse . . . There's a painful sense of betrayal from their government, from the companies to who we give our lives, from the unions. There was a *moral* contract, that if we fulfill our duty to society, society will fulfill its duty to us in our retirement, taking care of those who served so loyally.
>
> (Kimmel, 2013: 203)

The 'foxes' Kimmel mentioned above are of course the most extreme embodiments of (Western, white) male domination, which through the process of masculine hegemonisation locate white men at the top of the heap, imbuing them with deep-seated senses of internalised superiority or 'aggrieved entitlement' if achieving wealth alludes them (resulting in a supposed justifiable foment of rage) (Kimmel, 2013: 18).

Some refer to this entangled relationship between gender, race and power as a 'white male effect' defined as lowered risk perception that corresponds with increased conflicts and associated social, economic and environmental costs (Finucane et al. 2000: 160; Slovic et al., 2005; McCright and Dunlap,

2011; McCright and Dunlap, 2015). Melissa Finucane et al.'s (2000: 161) research on white male effect surmised that:

> White males may perceive less risk than others because they are more involved in creating, managing, controlling and benefiting from technology. Women and nonwhite men may perceive greater risk because they tend to be more vulnerable, have less control, and benefit less . . . White males displayed more hierarchical and individualistic views and less fatalistic and egalitarian views . . . White males were far less worried about adverse public responses from risk exposure to chemical and radioactive waste hazards . . . white males seem to promote individual achievement, initiative, and self-regulation, trust in experts and risk proponents, and intolerance of community-based decision and regulation processes . . . Despite knowing very little about the risk perceptions and socio-political attitudes of minority groups, they [white men] are perhaps precisely the people who might be at greatest risk (and who might receive most benefit) from some activities or technologies.

The conundrums that confront white men are obvious. Their conditioning on the one hand encourages creativity, initiative, motivation, drive – a willingness to assess the odds and move forward courageously, driven by the promise of great material rewards along the way. However, in reacting against the struggles that confront them, some men, encouraged by political leaders, social media such as Breitbart and mass media such as Fox News, have hurled themselves headlong into transforming their disappointments into hate towards marginalised groups. They have channeled their anger and hurt towards blaming others rather than taking responsibility for their choices or transforming the systems that have ground them down. The ills of male domination can be so intense for some men that they have driven growing numbers to join the ranks of white supremacy organisations, gatherings and demonstrations in Europe, the US and Australia (Forchtner and Kølvraa, 2015; BBC News, 2017; Begley and Maley, 2017).

Clearly, those individuals who are dependently aligned with industrial modernisation are not only straining human societies and Earth's living systems. They are also straining the lives of those they care about along with themselves. Industrial modernisation continues to dominate global machinations (through geo-engineering as an example) and in so doing is having great bearing on the ways that we shape current and future generations of men and masculinities throughout the Global North (Fleming, 2007; Anshelm and Hansson, 2014; Buck et al., 2014). Little wonder we have not progressed beyond the constraints of hegemonic masculinities. It is no coincidence that the features that define white male effect are mirror images of those of industrialists (McCright and Dunlap, 2011; Anshelm and Hultman, 2014). As an additional example, consider the demography of climate change denialists, who have taken it upon themselves to disproportionately confuse the climate science debate in order to protect and preserve their own socio-political and economic interests. This well-resourced and vocal cadre of corporate leaders, industrial capitalists, special interest groups and public relations firms continue to try to convince us that global warming is nothing other than a 'normal' geological cycle. They claim that climate science is simply hysteria drummed up by the politically correct left to the detriment of the supposed 'good life' that is the great promise of male domination (Oreskes and Conway, 2010). Their persistent tone is that of conspiracy and victimisation (Anshelm and Hultman, 2014). Notably, these views reflect extremely small but powerful lobbies. We cannot view them as a single social movement. Nor can we simply dismiss them as contrarians. Rather, they can highly fund and effectively market the views of a vocal minority who stand to gain and lose the most as the consequences of climate change bite ever deeper (Brulle, 2014). We must expose the spin associated with climate change denial for what it is: a tactic of wealthy – mostly white Western – men to assert and reassert social, economic and political control over wealth distribution while wantonly using the Earth's resources and human labour with disregard for their global, regional and local impacts on society and environment. The irony of this is sadly obvious. Eighty per cent of the global economy remains fossil fuel dependent and has placed seemingly inescapable market pressures on our continued use of remaining fossil fuel reserves that, by using them, will certainly increase ongoing climatic aberrations. This is already proving to cause great social, economic, political and environmental upheavals, consequently destabilising the political and economic security of these men as much as the ecological integrity of the planet (McGlade and Ekins, 2015). Aligned with Greta Gaard (2015: 24), we concur that 'climate change may be described as white industrial capitalist heteromale supremacy on steroids, boosted by widespread injustices of gender and race, sexuality and species', implicating climate change denialism as a corresponding expression of malestream norms . We conclude that climate change denialism epitomises white male effect, providing us with a destructive example of the convergent mechanisms of race, power and resource exploitation that have asserted white men's primacy precisely because malestream norms persist and shape some men's values and actions in overtly uncaring directions.

Others have dissected the links between industrialisation, climate change denial, gender and race, seeking constructive paths forward as the trying consequences of social and environmental demise march on (McCright and Dunlap, 2015). Similarly, there have been indirect attempts to steer us away from the negative implications of white male effect that deserve to also be considered. While steps in the right direction, their long-term successes are contestable. We consider some of these contributions next.

Turning the tide

Through humble beginnings in the 1960s, the first Earth Day (22 April 1970) in the US emerged. Two years later, we saw the first UN Conference on the Human Environment, which resulted in the Stockholm Declaration that tended to growing concerns about fossil fuel emissions through recommendations for internationally coordinated and measured responses (Knaggård, 2014). These tepid beginnings laid the foundations for establishing the Intergovernmental Panel on Climate Change (IPCC) in 1988 by two United Nations organisations – the World Meteorological Organization (WMO) and the United Nations Environment Programme (UNEP). The IPCC was instrumental in making the link between expanded human activities and global climate change (IPCC, 1990). With these revelations, the notion of sustainability entered mainstream political discourse. At first, this occurred through scholarly publications, environmental not-for-profit organisations and activist groups. Support through international, regional and local sustainable policy reforms followed, designed to mitigate our patterns of production and consumption while shifting values, beliefs and actions associated with them from personal to regional and global political scales (Jackson, 2009; Steffen et al., 2011; Crocker and Lehmann eds., 2013). Now widely recognised as the pre-eminent international body responsible for analysing the most recent climate science, the IPCC has gathered together an overwhelming amount of evidence to conclude that Earth is indeed warming, that global snow/ice reserves are melting, that rainfall is more erratic, intense storm surges are increasing, marine and fresh-water hydrological systems are collapsing, terrestrial ecosystems are subject to unprecedented cyclic shifts, biodiversity is declining, sea levels are rising and these are all attributed to anthropogenic causes, particularly the excessive emissions of CO_2 into the atmosphere as a direct consequence of industrialisation (IPCC, 2014a: 13–16). Anthropocentric pressures on Earth's living systems have affected biodiversity as well. When examined alongside climate trends, threats to vulnerable ecosystems have become so great that scholars argue we have entered a sixth mass extinction (Crutzen, 2002; Wake and Vredenburg, 2008; Barnosky et al., 2011; Steffen et al., 2015). This is tightly coupled with a new epoch broadly termed the 'Anthropocene', or human-induced changes in climate and the environment that some alternatively refer to as the 'Sociocene', 'Technocene', 'Homogenocene', 'Econocene', 'Plantationocene' and 'Capitalocene' (Haraway, 2015: 160; Angus, 2016: 230); or, very much related to our analysis, an (m)Anthropocene – where the (m) prefix emphasises the pivotal role of a small and influential group of men in creating and promulgating the Anthropocene (also consider references to the (m)Anthropocene as variations on andro/anthropocentrism analyses) (Di Chiro, 2017; Raworth, 2017; Pulé and Hultman, forthcoming). This is a time where 'corporations, states, structures of power and inequality, rather than individual humans, are generating large-scale environmental effects' (Connell, 2017: 5).

With foreboding evidence such as this to support a litany of global concerns, climate change is serving as the ultimate litmus test for the human–nature relationship. Indeed, climate concerns are directly linked to the negative impacts of fossil fuel dependency. Natural resource extraction subsidies also outweigh funding for social services intended to protect and preserve the health and well-being of nations' citizens (Coady et al., 2015). The wealthiest 500 million people on Earth (approximately 7 per cent of the total human population) produce 50 per cent of all the carbon dioxide emitted into the atmosphere, compared with the poorest 3 billion people who emit a mere 6 per cent (Assadourian, 2010). Further, in 2014, the top 1 per cent of the planet's richest individuals controlled 48 per cent of global wealth compared to the poorest 80 per cent who controlled 5.5 per cent (Oxfam, 2017). As the richest get richer and the poorest get poorer (80 billionaires controlling more wealth than 3.5 billion people's combined wealth), three sobering realities confront us – 90 per cent of the richest people in the world are men, 85 per cent of them are over the age of 50 and almost 70 per cent of them are white (Dolan, 2017). Despite these facts, there are few signs that policymakers are successfully steering us away from a cataclysmic precipice, nor are we adequately tending to the gendered elements they reveal. Ingolfur Blühdorn (2011) argued that to fully understand the severity of our current environmental situation, it is time to recognise the extent to which the politics of environmental care is sustaining the unsustainable. This is particularly true of wealthier Western nations, who, as far greater per capita polluters, hold a larger proportion of the responsibility to preserve healthy living conditions for present and future generations of all life (Warlenius et al., 2015). Even if negatively impacted through indiscriminate natural disasters, it remains self-evident that wealthier individuals and nations are in much better positions to implement environmental, infrastructural and social responses and repairs more rapidly than can the poor after disaster strikes, meaning we are dealing with global problems across a very uneven playing field (IPCC, 2014b). The consequences of unfettered industrial modernisation are, beyond their obvious affronts to other-than-human others, an assault on the peace and stability of human communities as well, eroding the long-term sustainability of chains of production for the sake of short-term gains, making comprehensive and coordinated global responses to the impacts of industrialisation on Earth's living systems essential were we to address these problems for purely economic reasons alone (Hultman and Anshelm, 2017).

As we have introduced above, our responses must include a transition from masculine hegemonisation to ecologisation. Given our commitment to provide such a response, we will, by the end of Section One, have explored our chosen four streams of thought in greater detail, linking their respective insights to ecological masculinities. Through our examination of masculinities politics, we consider men's lived experiences and the masculinities that shape them across a politicised spectrum. Deep ecology provides us with an expansive understanding of the wisdoms and psychospiritual awakenings that can come to us through intimate encounters with Earth. Ecological feminism considers the ways that women and Earth are similarly impacted by male domination. Feminist care theory provides detailed analyses of care in both conceptual and applied ways. All four streams share intricate explorations of Earth and human care in common and it is for this reason that we have chosen to ponder them most deeply and ahead of other discursive possibilities.

Masculinities as politics

We introduced the plurality of views on men and masculinities above. Men's lived experiences and the masculine socialisations that shape them are referred to at length in Chapter 3 as masculinities politics. The term is an adaptation of Jeff Hearn's (2010) reference to 'men's politics' linked to an early paper of his titled 'Men's politics and social policy' (1980), that we use here to describe the diverse perspectives that have emerged about men and masculinities along with their impacts on those who are otherised (of which critical studies on men and masculinities - or CSMM - represents the significant scholarly developments on the topic over the last thirty years, posited primarily from profeminist perspectives). There are several key contributors to masculinities politics we would like to acknowledge. Raewyn Connell (1995: 77) considered the hegemonised masculine ideal as:

> . . . the configuration of gender practice which embodies the currently accepted answer to the problem of the legitimacy of patriarchy [or male domination], which guarantees (or is taken to guarantee) the dominant position of men and the subordination of women.

She not only examined the complexities and consequences of hegemonic masculinities. Connell (1990) also examined the impacts of hegemonic masculinities on the human–nature relationship in a pivotal paper titled 'A whole new world: remaking masculinity in the context of the environmental movement', which we recognise as a central and early publication that exposed the need for the writing of this book. Building on Antonio Gramsci's (1971) analysis of class relations where one group aims to claim and sustain a lead role in society, Connell's (2001: 38–39) work affirmed that hegemonic masculinity constituted a dominant and oppressive gender practice towards all others. She argued that men have legitimised male domination to such an extent that their positions of domination have been both institutionalised and embodied through hierarchical and dominating heteronormative, aggressive, competitive and homosocial networks that advantage men and exclude women (and non-binary/genderqueer people as well) (Connell, 1997: 8). Most recently, she added further commentary on masculinities and the environment through her 'Foreword: Masculinities and the Sociocene', in Sherilyn McGregor and Nicole Seymour's (2017) important anthology titled *Men and Nature: Hegemonic Masculinities and Environmental Change*. In a similar vein, Michael Kaufman (1987: 1) discussed the familiar story of men's rape, battery and/or abuse of their female partners, considering these deprecating acts to be indicators of an authoritarian, sexist, class-driven, militarist, racist, impersonal and ecocidal society that has arisen because of the institutions of male domination, giving men supposed permission to mete out power and control over all others at will.[1] For other scholars of masculinities politics, socialisations that condition some men to perpetrate such violations run parallel to the rape, battery and abuse of other-than-human others as well. After all:

> Male means winning (being number one in sports, business, politics, academia), going to war ('kill or be killed'), being rational, not emotional ('boys don't cry') and embracing homophobia (fear of male affection). Male means domination, lording over others – whether nature, one's own body, women, others.
>
> (Fox, 2008: xxvi)

Not all men enact violence, just as not all women and human others are caring and as a consequence we must remain sensitive to these variations and resist the temptation to gender stereotype. However, the propensity for men to resort to violence in greater number than do women and human others provides us with a crucial motivation to persist in our efforts to reconfigure masculinities towards greater social and environmental care (Gracia and Merlo, 2016).

Ecosophising the self

Another principal aim of this book is to help usher in a deep green future. This phrase was coined by Norwegian philosopher, Arne Næss, who, introduced his vision for a deep and long-range future for the planet in what has become an iconic paper title: 'The shallow and deep, long-range ecology movement: a summary' (1973). As the movement's founder, Næss focused on raised self-awareness, nature reverence and care for Earth as deeply personal goals for all of us to strive for in our respective lives. Næss's motivation was to bring an end to anthropocentrism (or human-centredness) by prioritising the intrinsic value of all life through the philosophy and pluralised praxes of deep ecology.

Deep ecology encourages us to consider practical and conceptual encounters with nature as great guides in this discovery (Zimmerman, 1986: 21; Zimmerman, 1993). The process of acquiring deep ecology's trademark 'Self-realization!' through nature engagement lies at the very heart of a deep green future and is an edifice of Næss (the man) and deep ecology (the movement) in unavoidably plural ways, which has significantly influenced our conceptualisation of ecological masculinities.

Agreeing with Næss in bringing humanity onto a level playing field with the rest of life and its many complex processes, it is this deeper valuing of each other, other-than-human others and ourselves that we also subscribe to throughout this book. However, the ecosophy (personalised Earth wisdom) that we advocate here tends to the structural mechanisms that intersect with men and masculinities in ways that Næss and many others in the deep ecology movement did not. We are most interested in shining a light on the ways that the masculinised relational self impacts (and is impacted by) the systemic dynamics of justice and oppression in relation to the glocal commons. This is an important distinction between our work and that of deep ecologists. Where

Næss was transcendent towards social constructivist views of the world, we acknowledge and honour the presence of 'masculine', 'feminine' and 'other' identities within all humans, recognising that while these terms are in and of themselves problematic, they also strongly influence the human–nature relationship in distinct ways that justify their careful consideration. We align the gendered interpretations of deep ecology with ecological feminism in ways that Næss and the deep ecology movement did not. More on this in Chapter 4.

Feminist ecologisation

Ecofeminists are individuals who posit unique scholarships of justice for women and Earth. They do so through the ecological feminist discourse, providing us with rich, diverse and foundational leadership in understanding how valorising masculinities has resulted in androcentrism (or male-centredness) further to the anthropocentrism catechised by deep ecologists (Plumwood, 1993; Plumwood, 2002). We have much to learn from a cross section of ecofeminist views as we develop a theoretical framework for ecological masculinities. In Chapter 5, we encounter acute views about the contemporary impacts of men's sexism and environmental mastery on women, otherised humans and other-than-humans, the ways these mechanisms of domination have become institutionalised and what we might do about our resultant dire circumstances. As an introduction to the deeper analysis we offer in Chapter 5, it is important to firstly flag some insights drawn from our early (essentialised) ecofeminist colleagues, since they forestall the enigmatic aspects that an emergent masculine ecologisation discourse is also likely to encounter as this new discourse takes hold.

Consider *Green Paradise Lost*, published by Elizabeth Dodson Gray (1979) as a response to the complicated relationship between gender and our global social and environmental problems. Gray was critical of constructs that placed inert elements of Earth at the base of a hierarchy that then ascended to plants, animals, children, women, common men, noble men, princes, kings, then fallen angels and angels, culminating in a male God in the heavens. She argued that this arrangement – broadly referred to as the 'Great Chain of Being' – trained humanity to exercise power over those we dominate in a prescribed order. The social and environmental consequences of human mastery over nature (or more precisely men's domination over all others) continues to challenge us locally, regionally, nationally and globally. In a subsequent book titled *Patriarchy as a Conceptual Trap*, Gray (1982: 114) explored a pervading 'illusion of dominion' that not only placed humans above nature, but also placed men above women, effectively legitimising the otherising of other-than-humans in precisely the same ways that it legitimises the otherisation of women and non-binary/genderqueer people (and to a lesser extent, non-straight men as well). This helps explain why men as a group, the world over, are generally reticent to speak out and act in support of social and environmental justices; otherised others suffer the impacts of being otherised in ways that men do not, leaving little incentive for change from the masculinities end of social functioning. For women and non-binary/genderqueer people, the experiencing of unequal power relations is immediate, pervasive and visceral; their capacities to join the dots between real-world situations, policy responses and the impacts (both positive and negative) on access to resources, socially sanctioned importance, stigmatisation and standards of living, remain evident in ways that many men need seldom if ever confront (Cecelski, 1995; Clancy et al., 2007; Ryan, 2014).

Having noted these gendered distinctions, we digress momentarily to recognise that masculine and feminine qualities are present and accessible in all human beings, regardless of their biology, identity, socialisations or choices. Sweden provides us with an excellent example of the ways that gendered traits do not necessarily follow biology. With its high levels of uptake of paid paternity leave coupled with its pervasive presence of feminist principles and practices at every level of governance, Sweden continues to offer alternatives to many of the malestream socialisations that are considered stereotypical in the Global North (Björk, 2015; Neuman et al., 2017). Acknowledging the historical impacts of male-stream oppressions on others, we seek non-essentialist and structural solutions to the problems we face for the betterment of all life. To controvert male domination with biological determinism (as some early eco-feminists did) reinforces masculinities as unmarked, taunts malestream backlashes, obscures exit politics and leaves men no place to go (Mac-Gregor and Seymour, 2017: 12). After all:

> Achieving masculine status makes sense only in a social context. The top managers of the corporations pouring out greenhouse gases and poisoning river systems are not necessarily doing so from inner evil. Perhaps these men love babies and puppies and would sing in a church choir if only they could find the time. But they are working in an insane elite world that institutionalizes competition, power-oriented masculinity, and they are doing whatever it takes.
>
> (Connell, 2017: 6)

Contemporary toxic/extreme masculinities are some of the most insidious 'doing whatever it takes' examples of preserving male domination that Connell highlighted above (also see Keith, 2017: 2). They are indeed very worrysome. But these tumultuous times might also present us with great opportunities as well. To paraphrase Charles Eisenstein (2016) – with apologies to wolves who are far from toxic as the following idiom might suggest – they illuminate that we have entered an era where malestreams norms have become fully visible wolves in wolves' clothing once again. Eisenstein identified the time immediately after the Trump US presidential election as a 'space between stories' where we are now transitioning from the failures of neo-liberalism to something new that is still taking shape. If, through this transition, we are to succeed in achieving greater care for the glocal commons – replete with his characteristic virtues of 'love, compassion, and interbeing' for all of life, all the better. However, we must continue to broaden the scope of our critical understanding of the masculine experience as a vital element of such an inquiry. We must look beyond essentialist views to celebrate difference, seek mutual internal empowerment towards all human beings and in doing so extend great care towards all of Earth's living systems. Such strategies suggest proactive antidotes to the internalised superiorisation that accompanies malestream norms. We cannot afford to address these challenges in half measure. Notably, some early ecofeminists fell afoul of their colleagues by essentialising these debates about humanity and nature. This highlights the need for our vigilance to ensure that ecological masculinities can transcend similar pulls towards gendered essentialism as well.

Gendered essentialism from either end of the political spectrum is troubling. It reinforces assumptions about individuals and the social constructions that are indiscriminately imposed upon us all. Returning to our focus on ecological feminism, we note that by adopting terms like 'wemoon', 'womyn', 'wimmin' and 'womb-one' to link women to moon and Earth cycles, essentialist ecofeminists have sought wholeness for women in defiance of their 'other-half-ness', arguing in favour of women's rights to access the full range of living human potential and in doing so have aimed to manifest women's full and 'natural' humanity (Musawa, 2010: 7, 67; Morris, 2015; Phillips, 2016). But they pursue these views by celebrating the feminine principle made manifest in women's bodies, positioning women's lives as counterpoints to men's and malestream norms. While the intent of revering stereotypical feminine qualities is understandable in the wake of a long history of gendered inequities, such approaches fail to challenge the structural mechanisms that created them. Essentialist ecofeminists consider women and Earth to be conjoined categories, sharing capacities to be 'mater-realisers' in alleged ways that men cannot ever be, subsequently connecting women more so than men to 'the living goddess, a wild mystery, unto itself' (Griffin, 1978; Musawa, 2010: 86). We stress this point about the limitations of gendered essentialism precisely because similar levels of essentialism already prevail in discourses on men and masculinities as well, which we critically consider at length in Chapter 3 (Bly, 1990; Keen, 1992; Kimmel and Kaufman, 1995). We cannot simply compartmentalise woman as creator and fosterer of life, just as we cannot presume that man is society's sole protector and provider. Similarly, it would be a mistake to settle on characterising all men as hostile towards Earth and humanity, just as it would be a mistake to presume that it is the intractable role of 'women to teach [men] how to be human' (Montagu, 1968: 159, Kreps, 2010: 5). Queer theorists have successfully troubled these trends further still by noting the complexities associated with gender identities (Ferguson, 1993: 81; Seymour, 2013). These cutting edge views on gender identities that berate the structural oppressions accompanying male domination are proving to be indispensable.

Granted, Earthcare, communal care, familial care and self-care manifest in women's lives more easily than for men (Breton, 2016). However, as we look intentionally beyond gendered essentialism, the grounded theories that gained momentum as ecological feminism matured have helpfully pre-empted expected levels of multiplicity from essentialist/deterministic to social/structural interpretations of ecological masculinities. We aim to critically consider these various views. By the book's end, we will have created a framework for a contested and pluralised conversation about ecological masculinities that joins with the emergent and dichotomous nature of ecological feminism. Recognising that we must reach beyond the blinders of gendered esentialism, we will examine masculine care through a feminist lens in our fourth stream.

Care

Domestic and familial performances by women have been traditionally bonded to sexist notions of care. However, scholars have expanded our understandings of care to apply much broader applications to the term beyond essentialist views. Joan Tronto (1993) argued that care in the modern West is shaped by gender, race and class biases. Maria Puig de le Bellacasa (2012) suggested that care is an embodied phenomenon. Thom van Dooren (2014) demonstrated that care emerges as an important concept for engagement with our environment from global to local scales. Care compels us to get involved in our lives in very concrete ways – we care about our partners' needs, our children's education, our homes, our gardens, our pets, etc. and in doing so we are motivated to act accordingly. Van Dooren (2014: 293) argued that 'care is a vital concept for an engaged environmental humanities'. In this sense, care is a great motivator, driving us to act selflessly, at times beyond the limits of rational thinking; after all, through care we become selfless. Care motivates us to support others generously, to be of service to what we consider is righteous and good. Care is present in all human beings in one way or another and may well have been instrumental in the survival of our species given the evolutionary benefits of cooperation. However, our socialisations have a direct impact on the ways we manifest care in our daily lives. Care can be an ethical obligation or a practical labour. Care is both an internal and external phenomenon. In this sense, care governs when and how we look after the world around us as well as ourselves. In Chapter 6, we explore care both conceptually and practically. We also draw on the tangible implications of personal responsibility and accountability as well – noting that the presence or absence of care has profound impacts on the lives of those around us as well as our own. When we are in touch with our internal capacities to care, our active engagement with the world and being of service to it becomes harder to ignore. To generate a sustainable world is to care about the well-being of the glocal commons. To do that is to treat all others with dignity and respect, along with ourselves.

Having shared these preliminary thoughts about care, we introduce a central premise that serves as an axis for this book:

***All masculinities have infinite capacities to care, which can be expressed
towards Earth, human others and ourselves – simultaneously.***

Care ethics also transcend ideology, political affiliation, socio-economics,
race, age, ability, etc. Men can and do assume caring roles in society. But
malestream care is typically proximal; subject to prejudices and lived experiences that can predetermine who we care for (ideologically) and care about
(tangibly), meaning that men's care is shaped by male domination. Of course,
care can challenge male domination. However, malestream norms guide men
to care within the constraints of popular culture, ensuring that the ways that
they care comply with masculine hegemonisation. While traditional expressions
of masculine care can be self-serving, inward facing and/or confined by limited
views of the world, we challenge these myopic expressions of masculine
care, seeking broader, deeper and wider interpretations and expressions of
care, taking masculine care to the level of concurrent consideration for all life,
including men themselves. The kinds of masculine care we aspire to through
positing ecological masculinities generates accountability and responsibility
for the well-being of all others, while also tending to our own.

For now, we examine the roles that industrial/breadwinner and ecomodern
masculinities have played in distancing men and masculinities from care for
the glocal commons, which then sets the foundations for us to introduce
ecological masculinities.

Note

1 We acknowledge that some men are battered by their female, male or non-
binary/genderqueer intimate partners as well, meaning they can also be victimised in domestic situations and are subject to general acts of violence in
greater number than are other groups within societies. These nuances considered, the fact remains that men are by far the most frequent and severe of
domestic violence and male-on-male violence perpetrators and are as a consequence to be held proportionately accountable for these trends (ANROWS,
2015).

References

Alaimo, S. 2009. 'Insurgent vulnerability and the carbon footprint of gender'. *Kvinder,
Køn & Forskning* 3–4: 22–35.
ANROWS [Australian National Research Organisation for Women's Safety]. 2015.
*Horizons: Violence against Women: Additional Analysis of the Australian Bureau of
Statistics' Personal Safety Survey, 2012.* Sydney: ANROWS.
Angus, I. 2016. *Facing the Anthropocene: Fossil Capitalism and the Crisis of the Earth
System.* New York: Monthly Review Press.
Anshelm, J., and M. Hultman. 2014. 'A green fatwā? Climate change as a threat to the
masculinity of industrial modernity'. *NORMA: International Journal for Masculinity
Studies* 9(2): 84–96.

Anshelm, J., and A. Hansson. 2014. 'The last chance to save the planet? An analysis of the geoengineering advocacy discourse in the public debate'. *Environmental Humanities* 5(1): 101–123.

Assadourian, E. 2010. 'The rise and fall of consumer cultures'. In Worldwatch Institute, ed., *2010 State of the World: Transforming Cultures: From Consumerism to Sustainability (A Worldwatch Institute Report on Progress Toward a Sustainable Society)*. Washington, DC: Norton, 3–20.

Barnosky, A., Matzke, N., Tomiya, S., Wogan, G., Swartz, B., Quental, T., and B. Mersey. 2011. 'Has the Earth's sixth mass extinction already arrived?'. *Nature* 471 (7336), 51–57.

BBC News. 2017. 'White supremacy: are US right-wing groups on the rise?'. Accessed 2 November 2017. http://www.bbc.com/news/world-us-canada-40915356

Begley, P., and J. Maley. 2017. 'White supremacist leader Mike Enoch to visit Australia'. *Sydney Morning Herald Online*. Accessed 10 September 2017. http://www.smh.com.au/federal-politics/political-news/white-supremacist-leader-mike-enoch-to-visit- australia-20170513-gw46fn.html

Bem, S. 1993. *Gender Polarization. The Lenses of Gender: Transforming the Debate on Sexual Inequality*. Binghamton: Vail-Ballou Press.

Björk, S. 2015. 'Doing, re-doing or undoing masculinity? Swedish men in the filial care of aging parents'. *NORA: Nordic Journal of Feminist and Gender Research* 23(1): 20–35.

Blühdorn, I. 2011. 'The politics of unsustainability: COP15, post-ecologism, and the ecological paradox'. *Organization & Environment* 24(1): 34–53.

Bly, R. 1990. *Iron John: A Book About Men*. Boston: Addison-Wesley.

Breton, M. 2016. *Women Pioneers for the Environment*. Boston: Northeastern University Press.

Brulle, R. 2014. 'Institutionalizing delay: foundation funding and the creation of US climate change counter-movement organizations'. *Climatic Change* 122(4): 681–694.

Buck, H., Gammon, A., and C. Preston. 2014. 'Gender and geoengineering'. *Hypatia* 29(3): 651–669.

Cecelski, E. 1995. 'From Rio to Beijing: engendering the energy crisis'. *Energy Policy* 23(6): 561–575.

Christensen, A., and S. Jensen. 2014. 'Combining hegemonic masculinity and intersectionality'. *NORMA: International Journal for Masculinity Studies* 9(1): 60–75.

Clancy, J., Ummar, F., Shakya, I., and G. Kelkar. 2007. 'Appropriate gender-analysis tools for unpacking the gender–energy–poverty nexus'. *Gender and Development* 15(2): 241–257.

Coady, D., Parry, I., Sears, L., and B. Shang. 2015. *How Large Are Global Energy Subsidies?* Washington, DC: International Monetary Fund, 15–105.

Connell, R. 1990. 'A whole new world: remaking masculinity in the context of the environmental movement'. *Gender and Society* 4(4): 452–478.

Connell, R. 1995. *Masculinities*. Berkeley: University of California Press.

Connell, R. 1997. 'Men, masculinities and feminism'. *Social Alternatives* 16(3): 7–10.

Connell, R. 2001. 'The social organization of masculinity'. In S. Whitehead and F. Barrett, eds., *The Masculinities Reader*. Oxford: Blackwell, 30–55.

Connell, R. 2017. 'Foreword: Masculinities in the Sociocene'. In S. MacGregor and N. Seymour, eds., *Men and Nature: Hegemonic Masculinities and Environmental Change*. Munich: RCC Perspectives, 5–8.

Conroy, J. 2017. '"Angry white men": the sociologist who studied Trump's base before Trump'. *The Guardian Online*. Accessed 2 November 2017. http://www.theguardian.com/world/2017/feb/27/michael-kimmel-masculinity-far-right-angry-white-men

Crenshaw, K. 1989. *Demarginalizing the Intersection of Race and Sex: A Black Feminist Critique of Antidiscrimination Doctrine, Feminist Theory and Antiracist Politics*. Chicago: University of Chicago Press.

Crocker, R., and S. Lehmann, eds. 2013. *Motivating Change: Sustainable Design and Behaviour in the Built Environment*. London: Routledge.

Crutzen, P. 2002. 'Geology of mankind'. *Nature* 415(6867): 23.

Di Chiro, G. 2017. 'Welcome to the white (m) Anthropocene? A feminist–environmentalist critique'. In S. MacGregor, ed., *Routledge Handbook of Gender and Environment*. Oxon: Routledge, 487–507.

Dolan, K. 2017. 'Forbes 2017 billionaires list: meet the richest people on the planet'. *Forbes Online*. Accessed 28 June 2017. http://www.forbes.com/sites/kerryadolan/2017/03/20/forbes-2017-billionaires-list-meet-the-richest-people-on-the-planet/#2f63045e62ff

Eisenstein, C. 2016. 'The election: of hate, grief, and a new story'. Accessed 25 June 2017. https://charleseisenstein.net/essays/hategriefandanewstory

Ferguson, K. 1993. *The Man Question: Visions of Subjectivity in Feminist Theory*. Berkeley: University of California Press.

Finucane, M., Slovic, P., Mertz, C., Flynn, J., and T. Satterfield. 2000. 'Gender, race, and perceived risk: the "white male" effect'. *Health, risk & society* 2(2): 159–172.

Fleming, J. 2007. 'The climate engineers'. *Wilson Quarterly (1976–)* 31(2): 46–60.

Forchtner, B., and C. Kølvraa. 2015. 'The nature of nationalism: populist radical right parties on countryside and climate.'. *Nature and Culture* 10(2): 199–224.

Fox, M. 2008. *The Hidden Spirituality of Men: Ten Metaphors to Awaken the Sacred Masculine*. Novato: New World Library.

Gaard, G. 2015. 'Ecofeminism and climate change'. *Women's Studies International Forum* 49(1): 20–33.

Goffman, E. 1963. *Stigma: Notes on the Management of Spoiled Identity*. New York: Simon & Schuster.

Goffman, E. 1979. *Gender Advertisements*. Boston, MA: Harvard University Press.

Gracia, E., and J. Merlo. 2016. 'Intimate partner violence against women and the Nordic paradox'. *Social Science & Medicine* 157 (May): 27–30.

Gramsci, A. 1971. *Selections from Prison Notebooks*. London: Lawrence & Wishart.

Gray, E. 1979. *Green Paradise Lost*. Wellesley: Roundtable Press.

Gray, E. 1982. *Patriarchy as a Conceptual Trap*. Wellesley: Roundtable Press.

Griffin, S. 1978. *Woman and Nature: The Roaring Inside Her*. New York: Harper & Row.

Haraway, D. 2015. 'Anthropocene, Capitalocene, Plantationocene. Chthulucene: Making Kin'. *Environmental Humanities* 6: 159–165.

Hearn, J. 2010. 'Reflecting on men and social policy: contemporary critical debates and implications for social policy'. *Critical Social Policy* 30(2): 165–188.

Hearn, J., Nordberg, M., Andersson, K., Balkmar, D., Gottzén, L., Klinth, R. and L. Sandberg. 2012. 'Hegemonic masculinity and beyond: 40 years of research in Sweden'. *Men and Masculinities* 15(1): 31–55.

Hochschild, A. 2016. *Strangers in Their Own Land: Anger and Mourning on the American Right*. New York: New Press.

Hultman, M., and J. Anshelm. 2017. 'Masculinities of global climate change'. In M. Cohen, ed., *Climate Change and Gender in Rich Countries: Work, Public Policy and Action*. New York: Routledge, 19–34.

IPCC [Intergovernmental Panel on Climate Change]. 1990. *Climate Change: The IPCC Scientific Assessment*, edited by J. Houghton, G. Jenkins, and J. Ephraums. Cambridge: Cambridge University Press.

IPCC [Intergovernmental Panel on Climate Change]. 2014a. 'Summary for policy-makers'. In *Climate Change 2014: Mitigation of Climate Change. Contribution of Working Group III to the Fifth Assessment Report of the Intergovernmental Panel on Climate Change*, edited by O. Edenhofer, R. Pichs-Madruga, Y. Sokona, E. Farahani, S. Kadner, K. Seyboth, A. Adler, I. Baum, S. Brunner, P. Eickemeier, B. Kriemann, J. Savolainen, S. Schlömer, C. von Stechow, T. Zwickel, and J. Minx. Cambridge: Cambridge University Press.

IPCC [Intergovernmental Panel on Climate Change]. 2014b. *Climate Change 2014: Synthesis Report*. Accessed 27 June 2017. http://www.ipcc.ch/report/ar5/syr

Jackson, T. 2009. 'Beyond the growth economy'. *Journal of Industrial Ecology* 13(4): 487–490.

Katz, J. 2016. *Man Enough: Donald Trump, Hillary Clinton, and the Politics of Presidential Masculinity*. Northampton: Interlink.

Kaufman, M. 1987. 'The construction of masculinity and the triad of men's violence'. In M. Kaufman, ed., *Beyond Patriarchy: Essays by Men on Pleasure, Power, and Change*. New York: Oxford University Press, 1–29.

Keen, S. 1992. *Fire in the Belly: On Being a Man*. New York: Bantam.

Keener, E., and C. Mehta. 2017. 'Sandra Bem: revolutionary and generative feminist psychologist'. *Sex Roles* 76: 525.

Keith, T. 2017. *Masculinities in Contemporary American Culture: An Intersectional Approach to the Complexities and Challenges of Male Identity*. New York: Routledge.

Kimmel, M. 2013. *Angry White Men: American Masculinity at the End of an Era*. New York: Nation Books.

Kimmel, M., and M. Kaufman. 1995. 'Weekend warriors: the new men's movement'. In M. Kimmel, ed., *The Politics of Manhood: Profeminist Men Respond to the Mythopoetic Men's Movement (And the Mythopoetic Leaders Answer)*. Philadelphia: Temple University Press, 14–43.

Knaggård, Å. 2014. 'What do policy-makers do with scientific uncertainty? The incremental character of Swedish climate change policy-making'. *Policy Studies* 35(1): 22–39.

Kreps, D. 2010. 'Introducing eco-masculinities: how a masculine discursive subject approach to the individual differences theory of gender and IT impacts an environmental informatics project'. *Proceedings of the Sixteenth Americas Conference on Information Systems (AMCIS)*. Lima: Association for Information Systems.

MacGregor, S., and N. Seymour. 2017. 'Introduction'. In S. MacGregor and N. Seymour, eds., Men and Nature: Hegemonic Masculinities and Environmental Change. Munich: RCC Perspectives 9–14.

McCall, L. 2005. 'The complexity of intersectionality'. *Signs: Journal of Women in Culture and Society* 30(3): 1771–1800.

McCright, A., and R. Dunlap. 2011. 'Cool dudes: the denial of climate change among conservative white males in the United States'. *Global Environmental Change* 21(4): 1163–1172.

McCright, A., and R. Dunlap. 2015. 'Bringing ideology in: the conservative white male effect on worry about environmental problems in the USA'. *Journal of Risk Research* 16(2): 211–226.

McGlade, C., and P. Ekins. 2015. 'The geographical distribution of fossil fuels unused when limiting global warming to 2°C'. *Nature* 517(7533): 187–190.

Montagu, A. 1968. *The Natural Superiority of Women* (Revised Edition). London: Macmillan.

Morris, J. 2015. 'Queer earth mothering: thinking through the biological paradigm of motherhood'. *Feminist Philosophy Quarterly* 1(2): 1–27.

Musawa. 2010. *In the Spirit of We'moon: Celebrating 30 Years: An Anthology of Art and Writing*. Wolf Creek: Mother Tongue Ink.

Næss, A. 1973. 'The shallow and deep, long-range ecology movement: a summary'. *Inquiry* 16(1–4): 95–100.

Neuman, N., Gottzén, L., and C. Fjellström. 2017. 'Narratives of progress: cooking and gender equality among Swedish men'. *Journal of Gender Studies* 26(2): 151–163.

Oreskes, N., and E. Conway. 2010. 'Defeating the merchants of doubt'. *Nature* 465 (7299): 686–687.

Oxfam. 2017. 'An economy for the 99%: it's time to build a human economy that benefits everyone, not just the privileged few'. Accessed 28 June 2017. http://p olicy-practice.oxfam.org.uk/publications/an-economy-for-the-99-its-time-to-build-a-human-economy-that-benefits-everyone-620170

Phillips, M. 2016. 'Embodied care and planet earth: ecofeminism, maternalism and postmaternalism'. *Australian Feminist Studies* 31(90): 468–485.

Plumwood, V. 1993. *Feminism and the Mastery of Nature*. London: Routledge.

Plumwood, V. 2002. *Environmental Culture: The Ecological Crisis of Reason*. London: Routledge.

Puig de la Bellacasa, M. 2012. 'Nothing comes without its world: thinking with care'. *Sociological Review* 60(2): 197–216.

Pulé, P., and M. Hultman. Forthcoming. 'Ecological Masculinities: a response to the (m)Anthropocene question?'. In L. Gottzén U. Mellström and T. Shefer, eds., *Routledge Handbook of Masculinity Studies*. Milton Park: Routledge.

Raworth, K. 2017. 'What on earth is the donut? Kate Raworth: exploring donut economics'. Accessed 29 June 2017. http://www.kateraworth.com/doughnut

Ryan, S. 2014. 'Rethinking gender and identity in energy studies'. *Energy Research & Social Science* 1(March): 96–105.

Seymour, N. 2013. *Strange Natures: Futurity, Empathy, and the Queer Ecological Imagination*. Urbana: University of Illinois Press.

Slovic, P., Peters, E., Finucane, M., and D. MacGregor. 2005. 'Affect, risk, and decision making'. *Health Psychology* 24(4): S35–S40.

Steffen, W., Persson, Å., Deutsch, L., Zalasiewicz, J., Williams, M., Richardson, K., and M. Molina. 2011. 'The Anthropocene: from global change to planetary stewardship'. *AMBIO: A Journal of the Human Environment* 40(7): 739–761.

Steffen, W., Richardson, K., Rockström, J., Cornell, S., Fetzer, I., Bennett, E., Biggs, R., Carpenter, S., de Vries, W., de Wit, C., Folke, C.Gerten, D., Heinke, J., Mace, G., Persson, L., Ramanathan, V., Reyers, B., and S. Sörlin. 2015. 'Planetary boundaries: guiding human development on a changing planet'. *Science* 347(6223): 736, 1259855.

Synnott, A. 2009. *Re-thinking Men: Heroes, Villains and Victims*. Surrey: Ashgate.

Tronto, J. 1993. *Moral Boundaries: A Political Argument for an Ethic of Care*. New York: Routledge.

van Dooren, T. 2014. 'Care: living lexicon for the environmental humanities'. *Environmental Humanities* 5: 291–294.

Wake, D., and V. Vredenburg. 2008. 'Are we in the midst of the sixth mass extinction? A view from the world of amphibians'. *Proceedings of the National Academy of Sciences*, 105(supplement 1): 11466–11473.

Warlenius, R., Pierce, G., and V. Ramasar. 2015. 'Reversing the arrow of arrears: the concept of "ecological debt" and its value for environmental justice'. *Global Environmental Change* 30: 21–30.

Zimmerman, M. 1986. 'Implications of Heidegger's thought for deep ecology'. *Modern Schoolman* 54(November): 19–43.

Zimmerman, M. 1993. 'Rethinking the Heidegger–deep ecology relationship'. *Environmental Ethics* 15(3): 195–224.

2 Masculine ecologisation

From industrial/breadwinner and ecomodern to ecological masculinities

> . . . there are some common values . . . we need as a foundation for any pro-gressive future we can imagine. One of those values is the elimination of rigidly defined, mutually exclusive gender roles that lock men and women into expectations and behaviours that are limiting and distorted. We will have achieved little if we do not seriously undermine male and female gender roles and must be constantly vigilant to ensure that we do not recreate them in new guises.
>
> (Kivel, 2003: 72)

> . . . masculinity tends to function as 'unmarked'. Because meaning is made through opposition (e.g. the word 'man' and the concept behind it make sense because they are assumed to be not 'woman'), theorists often consider 'masculinity' as one element of a binary opposition with 'femininity'. In the opposition of two elements, one element can be considered unmarked – more frequent or less noticed than its marked counterpoint . . . women are considered to have a gender, while men are more often considered genderless . . . Precisely because a term is unmarked, its silence speaks . . . the fact that masculinity has tended to not be thought of as gendered is a hole that should draw attention to its very absence.
>
> (Reeser, 2010: 8–9)

Men, fracturing societies, ravaging Earth

In Chapter 2 we consider the costs associated with male domination by critically examining past and present ways of being male in the modern West. We examine two distinct and pre-existing categories of masculine conditioning that we refer to as 'industrial/breadwinner' and 'ecomodern masculinities'. They represent two 'unmarked' (i.e. normalised) masculine categories whose social and environmental impacts on the planet are obscured by the systems that created and continue to maintain them (Barthes, 1967: 77; Reeser, 2010: 8–9; MacGregor ed., 2017). We follow this analysis by introducing a third relational category based on care for the glocal commons. We refer to this third and alternative possibility of enacting manhood and constructing masculinities as 'ecological masculinities'. To begin, we examine the constrained socialisations of modern Western malestreams as a means of providing a context for the analyses that follow.

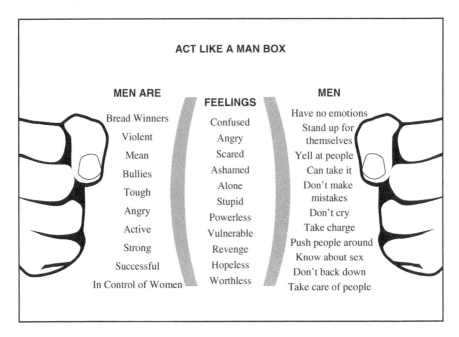

Figure 2.1 Paul Kivel's (2007) "Act like a man" box

US violence prevention educator, activist and author Paul Kivel (2010 [1992]) has been instrumental in deciphering the role of men and masculinities in justice movements for more than forty-five years. Through his '"Act like a man" box' (see Figure 2.1), Kivel illustrated the ways that boys and men are socialised to adopt certain sets of predetermined malestream norms.

Kivel's box of 'manly' characteristics help us recognise that a fuller spectrum of human emotional expressions such as love, excitement, pain, frustration, humiliation, grief, resentment, loneliness, self-worth, compassion, etc., are broadly considered feminine within societies dominated by malestream norms. According to Kivel, the generalised and traditional messages about acceptable expressions of manhood are clear: boys and men are expected to hold their ground; take charge of situations; pursue lots of women and have sex with as many of them as possible; be misogynistic and homophobic; make money and carry responsibility for their friends, family, nations and their idealisations for the world upon their shoulders. Although Global Northern nations are now predominantly secular, they are also experiencing religious revivals in certain sectors. In those enclaves we can add to the litany of acceptable expressions a man's duty to his God, predetermined by the particular dogmatic messages of his religion as well (a nuance that has gained much traction in terrorism/freedom fighter debates within and beyond the Global North). Kivel demonstrated that malestream norms are laid into boys and men through some heavy-hitting personal messages. Through his work and others who have conveyed similar messages (Jhally and Katz, 1999), we are reminded that most males experience these pressures at some point in their lives, making his man box relatable and foreboding for most boys and men. Sadly, while knowing all too well about these characteristics of the man box and being intensely aware of the consequences for them should they choose to step beyond its bounds, few men are conscious of the price they pay for adhering to this social contract. Some of the dehumanising ways that boys and men are coaxed into this box are: 'big boys don't cry'; 'don't be a scaredy-cat'; 'be a man'; 'do the right thing'; 'die for your country'; 'go it alone'; 'be right at all costs'; be 'physical', 'strong', 'independent', 'powerful', 'in control', 'rugged', 'scary', 'respected', 'a stud', 'athletic', 'muscular'; don't be a 'fairy', 'fag', 'wimp', 'wuss', 'sissy' and that most insulting of insults, don't be a 'girl'/'pussy'/ 'bitch' (Jhally and Katz, 1999). These are accompanied by more recent vernacular phrases such as 'suck it up', 'toughen up princess' and 'man up' (Albury and Laplonge, 2012; Conroy and de Visser, 2013). Such messages pervade popular culture and in recent times have been expanded through alt-right inspired demands that men dismiss political correctness, discredit and attack intellectuals (esp. feminists), place power and success ahead of care and assume the swaggering attributes of malestreams emboldened in some of the most influential celebrities and powerful leaders in the Global North (consider the global social impacts of John Wayne, Chuck Norris, Ronald Reagan and more recently, Vladimir Putin and Donald Trump), effectively conditioning boys and men to adopt those attributes of the most acclaimed of masculinities that defines malestream norms (Jhally and Katz, 1999; Kivel, 1999; Kimmel, 2008; Kivel, 2009; Zimmer, 2010; Katz, 2016). These 'strong man' characteristics epitomise malestream masculinities to this day. The resulting pressures and structural inequities are enormous and entangled, exposing the broader social and ecological consequences of masculine 'boxed' socialisations, in addition to the ways they shape boys and men as individuals as well. Kivel's boxed socialisations affirmed other researchers' contentions that boys and men have been strongly conditioned to perform masculinities within set criteria (Simpson, 1994). Little wonder men are commonly emotionally unavailable in their relational exchanges with others.

The conditioning summarised in Kivel's man box blinds boys and men to their own privileges. This insight is a useful entry point into challenging malestream masculinities. In this way, we create better conditions for boys and men to unravel their enmeshment with male domination along with the impacts they have on others. Acknowledging self-costs is simply one – albeit a rudimentary – entry point into ending male domination that is worthy of our critical consideration, since it affords us a very personal way of reaching some of the hardest to reach of men – particularly those who are immersed in industrialised and breadwinner lifestyles. There are some very tangible ways that this resistance has come about, resulting in the shaping of men's lives from a very young age. Boys are touched, held and caressed less than are girls; spoken to less and with more harsh tones; bullied or routinely bully others and through that expected to weather violence; told to keep their thoughts and feelings to themselves (especially pain); expected to perform to get attention; distanced and starved of relational training through expectations that they ought to overcome their dependences from an early age; banter with others by giving or receiving shame/putdowns; considered 'not girls' and 'different' from mum while having limited contact with dad or other males; expected to stand on their own two feet – and the list goes on (Kivel, 2010[1992]: 7–8, 23–25; Ackerman, 1993: 125; Kindlon and Thompson, 1999: Pollack, 2000: 17–20; Thompson and Barker, 2000: 10; Meeker, 2014: 10–11, 44; Vaccaro and Swauger, 2016: xv–xvi). Traditional masculine conditioning isolates and prepares boys to become human 'doings' (a.k.a. men as performers) that distances men from their human 'being-ness'. These forms of conditioning are accentuated by the fact that boys have limited access to adult male role modelling, and where they do, the exchange is often with men who are themselves emotionally repressed. For all of these reasons, boys are set on collision courses with emotional emaciation as they become men. These hallmarks of malestream socialisations form the very bedrock of male domination. Men socio-economically benefit the most from capitalism as well; traditional socialisations like those captured in Kivel's man box are designed to prepare males from an early age to do the structural bidding of commoditisation, effectively industrialising boys to become mechanistic men who are compelled to fall in line, be warriors willing to protect and become breadwinners able to provide for others (Phillips, 1994: 37–53; Jackins, 1999: 4). In light of our concerns for the glocal commons, we note that the most abstruse versions of malestream norms, which take these man box conditionings fully on board, manifest as what we refer to as industrial/ breadwinner masculinities.

Industrial/breadwinner masculinities

For our purposes, the term industrial/breadwinner masculinities is used here interchangeably with malestream, patriarchal, hegemonic and normative masculinities (which we apply primarily to men, but also to the masculinities adopted by some women and non-binary/genderqueer people as well). The separation between men and male-dominated cultures stood against otherised people and Earth has been centuries in the making. Building on Carolyn Merchant's (1980) defining text: *The Death of Nature: Women, Ecology and the Scientific Revolution*, we have noted that men and masculinities have been historically rewarded for pursuing exploitative practices, despite far-reaching social and environmental costs. For centuries, masculine hegemonisation has implemented organised and overt oppression of those who challenged or propped up the establishment – for example, consider the witch hunts of the Middle Ages, the Enlightenment (1600–1800) and the Industrial Revolution (1760–1840).

We use the term 'industrial' to refer primarily to those individuals who possess and manage the means of production and support service corporations who are handsomely rewarded by wealth-creating practices that rely on extraction of Earth's natural resources. Notably, the term industrial is used here to also emphasise the ways that the broader social and environmental implications of industrialisation are backgrounded for the sake of capital growth. Some examples of these kinds of masculinities manifest through overt roles such as fossil fuel and mining executives, financial managers and bankers, corporate middle and senior-level managers and administrators – the vast majority being Western, white and male (Connell, 2017). We also include the majority of corporate shareholders in this category, given they reap the profits of the companies that they have invested in (Connell and Wood, 2005). Those most strongly bonded to industrial masculinities collectively represent individuals who claim pride of place as owners and/or managers of corporate capitalism; they are typically not only Western and white but tend to be owning- and middle-class individuals who have welded their identities to the dominant social, economic and political systems that operate throughout the Global North.

The term industrial masculinities has been used in educational studies prior to our use of it here (Nayak, 2003). There, references to the term expose the ways that industrial/post-industrial societies affect individual learning possibilities among boys and men who enact industrial masculinities (Stahl et al. eds., 2017: 52–52, 205). However, the categorisation of industrial masculinities is more expansive than that. Judith Stacey's (1990: 267) *Brave New Families: Stories of Domestic Upheaval in Late-Twentieth-Century America* introduced us to the term 'breadwinner' to refer primarily to those working-class men that are typically found at the 'coalface' of extractive practices. Commonly, they are individuals who, for example, toil in mines, work on manufacturing assembly lines, swing hammers, move goods and grow crops. These men and the masculinities they imbue are closely related to industrial masculinities as we have defined it above, but represent a distinct group. Consider copper mining in Australia as that nation's third largest metal ore employer, with up to 92 per cent of the industry's technicians and trade employees being male (Australian Government, 2014). Processing copper results in 99.5 per cent spoil, with the mineral being biochemically extracted from the rock in large sulfuric acid ponds (Wallsten, 2015; Johansson, 2016). Globally, Australia has the third highest reserves of copper ore at 6 per cent, with main deposits in Queensland (Mount Isa) and South Australia (Olympic Dam) and is the third highest producer of the mineral after Chile and the US. Taking the national averages for mining employee qualifications as our guide, technical certificates awarded, high school certificates qualified and school drop-outs represent the top three most populous employment categories in the Australian copper mining industry (Australian Government, 2014). This data provides a revealing example of the ways that an important primary resource such as copper, which causes vast amounts of waste and environmental toxicants, is also an industry employing large numbers of working men – in particular – whose labour creates profits, bonuses and large salary incentives of which the vast majority are divided among industrial shareholders and senior managers who own those means of production.

In reference to both industrial and breadwinner masculinities, individuals may have been born into or worked their way through different socio-economic strata. To mitigate this complexity, our discussion refers specifically to socio-economics and social standing in the present time, looking past class patterns reflective of individual heritage as a complexity that reaches beyond the scope of this book. Combining the two terms into the phrase industrial/breadwinner masculinities represents a category of men who have long been (and still are) enmeshed with industrial-scale extractive processes and services reliant on energy-intensive, profit-consolidating, ecologically destructive and fossil fuel-dependent processes that have been historically created and maintained through colonisation, engineering and technology, neoclassical economic theories and under-challenged social practices. We use this phrase to illuminate the variations of malestream masculinities that men at all socio-economic levels can and do embrace. We contend that industrial/breadwinner masculinities carry the primary responsibility for humanity's global social and ecological problems, but are not responsible for this alone. This cohort of men and masculine identities are the most representative of modern Western male-streams personae. Industrial/breadwinner masculinities are bound to the pursuits of industrial growth, since the two require each other to thrive (Daly and Cobb, 1994; Friman, 2002). Some empirical analyses of industrial/breadwinner masculinities at both the actor-network and structural levels has been conducted previously (Anshelm and Hultman, 2014b). Such studies note that there are an infinite number of ways that industrial/breadwinner masculinities can manifest in individuals and across industries. Characteristic of primary industrialisation, mining masculinities in Australia cut across class distinctions and remuneration variables, delivering a homogeneous image of the 'Aussie bloke' as one who is white, heterosexual, an epitome of Australian manhood, of working-class demeanour (if not origin), who embodies:

> . . . the mining industry's Australian credentials; to illustrate the importance of mining as a site of employment for 'Aussie blokes', and as economically and culturally important to Australia.
>
> (Whitman, 2013: 2, 8)

This statement illuminates the enmeshment of corporate systemics with stereotypical Australian mining personae, exemplifying the deep seated significance of industrial and breadwinner masculinities, which is not unique to the Australian mining vernacular, but can be found throughout industrialised settings the world over. This raises a question about the consequences of malestream norms that industrial and breadwinner masculinities readily adopt. Interestingly, the defining characteristics of industrial/breadwinner masculinities are similar to 'heroic' (Holt and Thompson, 2004), 'hyper-' (Parrott and Zeichner, 2003) and/or 'cowboy' masculinities (Donald, 1992) that have also emerged through the works of other researchers. We have, however, chosen the broader term industrial/breadwinner masculinities to highlight the ways that masculine hegemonisation, as it pervades industrial Western societies in the modern context, persists across the Global North. By levelling our attention on industrial/breadwinner masculinities, we seek to understand malestream norms at their very foundations and from there, proceed to disentangle the mechanisms of domination that are adopted by individual men, groups of men and masculine socialisations that result in patterns of internalised superiorisation in their most obscene forms. These then result in some of the most socially and ecologically destructive impacts on Earth, others and self. We consider industrial/breadwinner masculinities as the most oppositional versions of masculinities to the ecologised masculinities we advocate throughout this book. In order to further stress the importance of this point, we draw attention to one of the planet's most pressing environmental concerns, which provides us with a clear example of the importance of developing a critical analysis of industrial/breadwinner masculinities, that being: climate change.

The link between industrial/breadwinner masculinities and climate change denialism exposes a disconnection between modern Western malestreams and Earthcare. The very suggestion that we live on a vulnerable planet that is being rapidly transformed by anthropogenic factors such as carbon emissions has sparked strong protestations particularly on the part of those who stand to gain the most from unfettered industrialisation (Anshelm and Hultman, 2014a; Supran and Oreskes, 2017). Previous studies demonstrate that climate change denialism is created by small groups of (mostly white Western) men who are intricately interwoven with identities that dovetail with malestream norms, since, as concerns for climate change gain momentum, climate change denialism, particularly from corporate and industrial allies and beneficiaries, has ramped up to match it (Anshelm and Hultman, 2014b). Aaron McCright and Riley Dunlap (2003) noted that the 1997 Kyoto Protocol was met by a reflex of conservative political activity (particularly in the US) buoyed by a small group of dissident and contrarian scientists who lent their credentials to think tanks that champion climate change denialism. It is well recognised that to maintain an illusion of intense controversy, industries, special interest groups and public relations firms have manipulated climate data and found ways to capitalise on the media to promote their message across a broad front (Farrell, 2016). Take for example the engagement of APCO by ExxonMobil to confuse public disquisition on climate change that, unsurprisingly, was the same public relations firm engaged by Philip Morris to confuse the health risks of tobacco smoking. Also consider the way that research within ExxonMobil confirms the severe consequences of emissions from coal, oil and gas, but was intentionally downplayed by management in order to extend markets and preserve profits (Supran and Oreskes, 2017). Using these strategies, lobby groups and fossil fuel companies have positioned climate change denialists on an equal footing with international, peer-reviewed climate science experts, even though the proportion of reports reaching consensus over concerns versus denying climate science is a sobering 97:3 per cent ratio – respectively (Cook et al., 2016). The strategy of climate change deniers has levelled at pitting emotive views reflective of socio-political biases against overwhelming field data and analyses by global experts, drawing on economic and moral arguments as potent cocktails for confusing the issues. Many of these audible (and mostly white male) voices have participated in generating climate controversy as industry-funded advocates who also hold strong beliefs in global market forces and a general mistrust of regulatory government policies (Anshelm and Hultman, 2014b).

As an additional example, consider Sweden's climate change denialists, who have organisational affiliations in sectors where business research as well as science and technology studies meet. Per-Olof Eriksson, a former board member of Volvo and former CEO of SECO Tools and Sandvik, wrote an article in the leading Swedish business paper *Dagens Industri*, declaring his doubts that carbon emissions affect the climate (Hultman and Anshelm, 2017). Ingemar Nordin, professor of philosophy of science, joined the fray by stating that the IPCC's (2014) 'selection and review of scientific evidence are consistent with what politicians wanted' (Hultman, 2017b: 244). Economy professors Marian Radetzki and Nils Lundgren (2009) claimed that the IPCC deliberately cast their models in alarmist direction to intentionally and inaccurately demonstrate that significant climate change was taking place. Fifteen Swedish professors, notably all men, have come out to publicly proclaim themselves as climate change denialists (Einarsson et al., 2008). Rather than simply viewing these climate change deniers as anti-science or anti-political, we argue that it is important to understand how their very identities as industrial/breadwinner masculinists (even if women) have been shaped by the industrial modernisation movement and why this perspective favours deniers' interrogations of climate science precisely because the data affronts these individuals at the level of their personal and professional identities (Jorgenson and Clark, 2012). Further, an identifiable convergence of industrial/breadwinner masculinities has recently manifested in neo-fascist/alt-right political movements supported by extractive industries that categorically deny climate science (Lockwood, 2018; Hultman, et. al., forthcoming).

Industrial/breadwinner masculinities commonly advocate the wholesale elimination of policies and practices that could otherwise pull us back from a perilous global climatic precipice (Hultman and Anshelm, 2017). Their characteristics are at the very foundations of human social and environmental injustices; these masculinities are effectively the most responsible for human destruction of the living planet. However, there is a second category of masculinities that is distinguishable from industrial/breadwinner masculinities that is also worthy of our consideration. Individuals who adopt the following personae recognise the social and environmental challenges that industrial/breadwinner masculinities have historically ignored or denied. Unlike their counterparts who we have just discussed, this category of masculinities is common among those who assume leadership roles in the fields of local, regional and international environmental policy reform as well as corporations engaged in techno-fixes and clean energy innovations. We term them ecomodern masculinities. We begin our discussion on ecomodern masculinities by firstly tracing the relationship of this category to ecological modernisation as a school of thought within the social sciences that links environmentalism with economic progress.

Ecomodern masculinities

Another sharp burst of global industrial productivity occurred during and after the Second World War. This was a concentrated period that some refer to as the 'great acceleration' (Coleman et al., 2007: 84). Post-war industrialisation had profound impacts on economic, social and political systems the world over, with the Western industrial means of production (esp. in the US) gathering seemingly unstoppable momentum and global domination. However, only fifteen to twenty years later, evidence mounted that the accelerating abuse of resources to feed industrial modernisation (both in capitalist and socialist contexts) was creating huge amounts of waste and toxic pollutants that threatened global environmental and human living conditions and the long-term sustainability of the planet (Carson, 1962; Nader, 1965; Clark, 2002; Salleh, 2010). From there ensued two more decades of intense clashes between industrial and ecological imperatives, resulting in increased need for social and environmental regulation at the level of local, national and global governance (McNeill, 2000). By the late 1980s, the apparent successes of pro-environmental policy reforms gave corporate and industrial sectors cause for concern that progressive environmental politics might constrain Western industrial development agendas into the twenty-first century if left unchecked (Hajer, 1996). This trend presented financiers and extractive industry owners with the challenge of wrestling back regulatory controls through some green-washed levels of care towards workers, communities and the environment, as a great compromise. Faced with the prospects of accountability for growing problems such as climate change, regulators wedded to global economic management and advanced industrialisation came to the aid of primary production and manufacturing sectors such as oil, gas, mining, steel and coal companies, which have long been complicit in producing the largest quantities of environmental pollutants (Oreskes and Conway, 2010). Such was the ecomodernist response.

Ecological modernisation draws its scholarly origins from the German political scientists Joseph Huber (1982) and Martin Jänicke (1985). The concept was developed further by Dutch sociologists Gert Spaargaren and Arthur Mol (2008). Popularised by growing concerns about the impacts of industrialisation on the planet and people, ecological modernisation provided political reformers with pathways to address the harmful trends of industrial capitalism. Formalised through initiatives such as the Brundtland Report (1987), ecological modernisation aligned with emerging imperatives that not only called for long-term sustainable development policies and practices, but positioned itself as a measured response to growing concerns about rising atmospheric emissions as waste products of industrialised economies, along with the introduction of micro-plastics and other synthetic toxics into biotic systems. Ecological modernisation was presented as a fundamental reorganisation of the core institutions of industrial society, along with the mechanisms that created and maintained them. This concept can thus be considered an assemblage of organised responses and reforms that pay lip service to the costs of industrialisation on human societies and the ecological integrity of Earth by offering watered-down pathways to protect and preserve economic growth while also offering nominal care for society and environment (Adler et al., 2014). Consider the alarming failure of ecological modernisation that has promoted government-funded corporate energy companies (e.g. Enron) to lobby for policy reform that has effectively sheltered industrialist, financiers and those who support business-as-usual from paying the real costs for their contributions to social and environmental decay – instances of government funded big-business bailouts in times of economic crises abound and appear to have become routine responses to economic crises despite the fact that taxpayer funds are then used to ensure the financial sustainability of corporate elites (Levy and Spicer, 2013). In short, ecological modernist priorities place industrial capitalism ahead of social and environmental imperatives; they are insufficient responses to growing evidence of the unsustainability of industrialisation, designed to placate evidence-based concerns and extend business-as-usual for as long as possible. This reformist approach aimed to tackle our global problems by mitigating threats to industrial growth, the rationale being that profits will be sustained if smart social and environmental regulations are implemented and in doing so would preserve the economic, social and political integrity of corporatised extractivism (Hultman, 2015). In support of these sanguine responses to burgeoning concerns, environmental sociologists, geographers and political ecologists chimed in to ensuing discussions, noting that reform policies and practices were not successfully averting the growing gap between humans and nature, nor that emerging between the rich and poor both within and between nations (Swyngedouw, 2010; Blühdorn, 2011). In an in-depth dissertation, Ole Martin Lægreid (2017) demonstrated that the ecomodernist presumption that higher GDP would at some point result in lower anthropogenic emissions, does not hold true. This fact alone is a revealing indictment of the economically suicidal consequences of human-induced global emissions, given multilateral atmospheric regulatory agreements are struggling to gain purchase and the overall carbon (and more pertinently the ecological) impacts of industrialisation continue to rise. Ironically, the regulatory offerings ecological modernisation posited were little felt in Western nations despite them being the largest per capita carbon polluters. Global political and economic machinations strategically deferred the greatest costs and impacts of industrial and economic policy reform to more populous, less-industrialised and poorer non-Western nations of the Global South. Today, with the impacts of climate change upon us, nations such as China, India, Bangladesh and the Alliance of Small Island States (forty-four states and observers from Africa, the Caribbean, Indian Ocean, Mediterranean, Pacific and South

China Sea) are bearing the brunt of the worst predictions from climate science even though their economic capacities to avert social and environmental crises are substantially constrained (York et al., 2010).

As we identified in the previous discussion about industrial/breadwinner masculinities, ecological modernisation has similarly struggled to free itself from a materialist addiction to growth (Lundqvist, 2004; Hultman and Yaras, 2012). In line with the critiques above, we argue that ecological modernisation has failed because it has implemented inverted priorities, adhering to anthropocentric ideals of moderating human impacts on communities and Earth; doing so by prioritising human needs and wants while sidestepping the intrinsic value of all life. To seriously avert climate change requires prioritising social and environmental care at least on an equal footing (if not ahead of) human interests (or, more accurately, the interests of those select few who benefit the most from industrialisation). We concede that ecological modernisation facilitated some improvements in global social and environmental awareness and activities such as the rise of new industrial coalitions like manufacturing bonded to the renewable energy industries and triple bottom-lining where incomings and outgoings have been audited alongside environmental cost (Anshelm and Hansson, 2011). These are some of the indicators that demonstrate how the reformist approaches of ecological modernisation have combined with neo-liberal agendas over the last few decades, resulting in an obituary of sorts (albeit providing some 'greenwashed' policy and practical reform) that intonates (albeit weakly) an assemblage of tepid sustainable responses to important social and environmental issues (Coffey and Marston, 2013; Morton, 2016: 33). However, ecological modernisation has not stemmed the negative impacts of humanity on Earth's living systems across a broad front. It has levelled too much attention at the machinations of production and trade while offering minimal or non-existent responses to the discontents of working families. This is one core reason for the populist, nationalist, white supremacist uprisings that we are now experiencing throughout the West, raising a key question: despite being a well-intended balance between economy, society and ecology, why did the efforts of ecological modernisation falter so comprehensively? We suggest that part of the answer to this question is gendered, looking to an analysis of ecomodern masculinities to find some answers.

Ecomodern masculinities represents the embodiments of masculine identities that valorise sustainability through ecomodern notions of reform; they collapse social and ecological crises with economic concerns as a supposed balance point between competing forces. While distinct from industrial/breadwinner masculinities in their willingness to recognise glocal challenges, ecomodern masculinities have emerged paradoxically; aligning global responsibility and determination with increased care for the glocal commons, but held strictly within the market forces of industrial and corporate capitalism. We argue that this combination is like asking an alcoholic to draft drinking laws. To stress the point, consider the following examples: growth in energy consumption stood against the desire for a stable climate (Hultman, 2013; Hultman and Anshelm,

2017); industrial forestry stood against ecological diversity (Brandt and Haugen, 2000); agribusiness stood against land care and the preservation of farming families and communities (Little, 2002). We contend that the core tenets of ecological modernisation are shackled by a 'masculinist bind' that harbours daring intentions but is socially and environmentally weak precisely because it embraces the 'solipsism of economic reasoning' that Australian sociologist Ariel Salleh exposed when she noted that:

> Conventional programs for mitigating the collateral damage of consumer economies – melting icebergs, species loss, pollution induced cancers – simply bandaid a competitively masculinist neoliberal system tailored to production for individual gain.
>
> (Salleh, 2010: 130)

This commoditised deference to selfishness, when combined with superficial attempts to bring about sustainable change, reveals the inadequacies of eco-modern masculinities; a myopia that we introduced above and consider to be a floundering attempt to find a middle path through various conflicting pressures within human communities and between humanity and other-than-humans. We argue for a willingness to challenge not only leaders in important international roles, but the socialisations of masculinities that shape them as well, seeking to expose the structural limitations of ecomodernism at its very gendered core.

There are two telling example of this masculinist bind that provide additional insights into the limits of social and environmental ecomodernism. We firstly refer to Arnold Schwarzenegger, an individual who became governor of the US state of California (CA is notably the world's sixth largest economy) from November 2003 until January 2011. Nicknamed the 'Governator' leveraged off his role in the Terminator movies, Schwarzenegger provided a telling example of the ways that ecological modernisation and masculinities collide (Hultman, 2013). Given the high level of environmental awareness of the CA state electorate, Schwarzenegger was compelled to find solutions to his seemingly conflicting image problem, since he was readily viewed as the personification of a kind of industrial/breadwinner masculinities, while offering voters a new impression of him as more environmentally friendly. One strategy he employed was to promote a retrofitted Hummer (military vehicle) with a fuel cell driven by hydrogen technology rather than hydrocarbons (in 2017 he retrofitted his Hummer to become fully electric in alignment with the rise in popularity of that technology). Schwarzenegger's metamorphosis to become an 'environmental' warrior-hero was crowned with his role as executive producer and correspondent in *Years of Living Dangerously* (The Years Project, 2014) – a two-season/seventeen-episode documentary focused on the concerns associated with global warming. Schwarzenegger effectively 'tweaked' public perception of his persona; his supposed toughness, determination and endurance were blended with strategically chosen moments of compassion, vulnerability and the pursuit of eco-friendly innovations (Hultman, 2013). He validated compromise, located himself as a centrist eco-politician while also embracing industrial hegemonisation. Conflating these seemingly disparate characteristics aimed to appeal to Schwarzenegger's Republican base as well as the broader CA state electorate's predominantly progressive constituencies, which served his political career well while in office.

Another Western, white, wealthy example of ecomodern masculinities is that of Elon Musk. Claiming pride of place as a visionary, Musk is broadly hailed as the twenty-first century's smartest entrepreneur and man of great passion for the radical and broad-scale implementation of social and environmental innovations. He is acknowledged for a slew of pro-environmental strategies that aim to 'make the world a greener and better place' by using technology to extend the 'good life' to all (Fiegerman, 2017). Among other innovations, consider Musk's Hyperloop (his version of this technology implements air resistant tubes that transport pods using linear induction propulsion technologies with a prototype intended to link the US cities of Los Angeles and San Francisco announced in 2013). Also consider SpaceX (a California-based aerospace and space transport company that he founded in 2002 that is working to develop space exploration technologies that are intended to enable human colonisation of Mars, gaining notoriety for the development of a reusable orbital rocket called Falcon 9). However, Musk is most widely recognised for his popular (and now financially troubled) Tesla electric car series boasting fully electric sports performance vehicle designs with acceleration and autopilot capacities originally marketed within the $94,000–140,000USD base-price ranges that now aims to bring this vehicle within the high end of the mainstream new vehicle market. The company is currently promoting a $35,000USD mass consumer product line in an attempt to right its floundering financial woes while broadening the market affordability of these cars (Etherington, 2017). Powerwall is marketed as a domestic green energy accompaniment to Musk's Tesla vehicle series; an integrated solar-powered home battery system pictured on the Tesla website as a discrete monolithic panel powering a modern, spacious, nature immersed, upper middle-class home, through which a Tesla vehicle can be recharging overnight. Through products such as these, Musk has positioned himself as a global environmental champion. He has lead the charge for industrial and technological solutions to growing needs and wants as one of the world's leading techno-fix innovators. However, consistent among all of these innovations is an uncritical approach to the expanding demands for increased standards of living fed by social, economic and political enmeshments with corporate and capitalist growth, all of which are based on industrialisation and the heavy natural resource dependency that they rely on. These technologies are initially expensive, making them exclusive, at least in their earlier stages of development, production and sale. Of course, this severely restricts innovative goods and services accessibility to those with disposable incomes that on a global scale represent mere fractions of the total human population; technologies that will take considerable amounts of time to trickle down the socio-economic ladder – if at all. Meanwhile, these innovations would rely on ballooning resource exploitation and the production of toxic pollutants that continue to savage Earth's living systems.

As remains the case with Schwarzenegger, Musk similarly continues to sidestep the socio-economic, energy and resource injustices that green technologies like the Tesla electric car series require. David Abraham (2015), author of *The Elements of Power: Gadgets, Guns, and the Struggle for a Sustainable Future in the Rare Metal Age* noted that even solar panels are energy intensive and rare-earth dependent as are many of the essential components of the Tesla vehicles. Economist and environmental researcher Virginia McConnell, who serves as senior fellow at Resources for the Future and professor of economics at the University of Maryland-Baltimore, argued that regional production methods of grid-source energy can negate the greenhouse gas-saving properties of electric vehicles like the Tesla series when those grids are heavily reliant on hydrocarbons; a claim supported by the Devonshire Research Group (a tech company investment firm) since:

> Teslas (and by extension all electric vehicles) create pollution and carbon emissions in other ways. Each stage of an EV[electric vehicle]'s life has environmental impacts, and while they aren't as obvious as a tailpipe pumping out fumes, that doesn't make them any less damaging . . . Your electric car doesn't need gas, but it still might get its energy from burning carbon.
>
> (Wade, 2016)

Further, the industrial/breadwinner masculinist appeal to consumer fancies is integral to Musk's business developments. Take for example the marketing strategy used to sell the Tesla electric sedans and sport utility vehicles, which relies on language pitched to malestream notions of masculinities such as: 'unparalleled performance', 'long range', 'safe', 'exhilarating', 'stress free', 'ludicrously fast', 'quick', 'ample', 'capable', 'uncompromised' and 'real', making no mention at all about how the electricity to propel them is to be generated and shifting focus away from the potential environmental benefits of such a consumer purchase (Tesla, 2017). The malestream appeal of green technologies encounter their own set of threats to society and environment precisely because they are likely to accelerate individual impacts on Earth's living systems as more and more people gain greater purchasing power the world over. For these reasons and comparable to a greenwashed Schwarzenegger, Musk's technological revolutions continue to over-promise and under-deliver. Like Schwarzenegger, Musk the ecopreneur, the investor, the philanthropist who has pledged to give away 50 per cent of his wealth to charity, the global citizen, the billionaire determined to 'save the planet', the all-round 'simple guy', the man, has embodied the characteristics of ecomodern masculinities to a tee. Our gendered analysis of the Schwarzenegger the warrior-hero holds true for the revered Musk as well, who is similarly failing to deliver effective long-term alternatives to the structural roots of our looming crises.

In the two sections above, we have considered the impacts of industrial/ breadwinner and ecomodern masculinities on issues of social and environmental justice. We have demonstrated that in reality, industrial/breadwinner and eco-modern masculinities have courted malestream norms (and their entwined relationship with industrial extractivism) as their shared hidden drivers. In doing so, both categories have either directly exacerbated social inequities and environmental challenges or failed to seize opportunities to protect and preserve all life for the long term. Clearly another approach to global structural machinations is needed. We explore a path for modern Western men and masculinities that prioritises deeper, broader and wider responses to global social and environmental problems – responses that are both personal and political, individual and systemic and therefore truly transformational. In the following section, we show you a glimpse of what the rest of this book is about; introducing a third category of masculinities that accelerates a shift towards heighted levels of care for the glocal commons. This, more socially and environmentally connected masculinities, is one we refer to as ecological masculinities.

Ecological masculinities

In the preceding discussion on industrial/breadwinner and ecomodern masculinities, we exposed a common postulate that nature is being overly impacted for human benefit. This has prioritised the wants, needs and desires of some, while others continue to be marginalised. We argue that this is inadequate for humanity and our impacts on the planet. For the remainder of this chapter, we explore what lies beyond the robust industrial/breadwinner and gracile ecomodern options for men and masculinities.[1]

The United Nations Development Programme (UNDP) *Human Development Report* (2015) discussed the following development agenda, or Sustainable Development Goals (SDGs). They are: addressing inequality; managing population growth and demographic structuring; planning urbanisation; establishing and preserving security; encouraging women's empowerment; preparing for the perturbations of geopolitical shocks, vulnerabilities and risks. These goals are designed to steer us towards more sustainable living standards for humanity and the planet and they were intended to raise humanity's levels of care towards Earth, others and self – simultaneously. As we have attested above, all of these measures have been detrimentally affected and increasingly difficult to achieve as a direct result of human induced pressures such as anthropogenic climate change (UNDP, 2015: 70–73). While industrial/ breadwinner masculinities have had unapologetic impacts on people and the planet and ecomodern efforts have delivered limited successes across the globe, deprivations on all UNDP counts remain. This calls forth the need for continued creativity as we seek truly effective solutions to the problems we face. Sadly, even the United Nations as humanity's ultimate international regulatory body has been reticent to fully address social and environmental injustices through a frontal deconstruction of hegemonic masculinities and its social and environmental implications – malestream norms have remained unmarked even there, approached through concerns about justice for girls and women but not directly analysed as a masculinities problem. This obscuring of a crucial piece in the puzzle of our times has left the role of men and masculinities off the table – the broader care for the glocal commons that we call for throughout this book being easily taken as an affront to human standards of living rather than calling it what it is: a symptom of internalised superiority that accompanies male domination. We are determined to subvert that trend.

With such an intention in mind, we became interested to explore what masculinities look like when they are not industrial/breadwinner or ecomodern. Our response to our own inquiry has been to examine masculinities and their impacts on men's lives in particular, suggesting that a missing element is masculine ecologisation. Connell's (1990) early examination of ecologised masculinities noted that the values pervading environmental movements could direct men's belief and behaviours towards broader expressions of care for nature, compatriots and self in ways that challenged hegemonic masculinities. Connell and Wood (2005) later discussed how alternative masculinities could offer critical resistance to industrial and hegemonic forms of masculinities. Through my doctoral research (Pulé, 2013) (Paul speaking here), I mapped the development of ecologised masculinities from the late twentieth century to the completion of my dissertation in 2013, where I proposed the need for 'ecological masculinism', which is a term I have since dispensed with, as my thinking on the topic has progressed in combination with Martin's and moved beyond terminological associations with mechanisms of domination that an '-ism' suffix suggests. That said, my research did reveal notions of 'ecomasculinities' had received perfunctory consideration by some scholars and activists from various disciplines, but did not develop into a discursive theory on the subject – Martin and I have updated those findings, bringing our considerations of the works of others up to date. Similarly, when doing empirical research on ecopreneurship (Martin speaking here) I came up with the term 'ecological masculinity' reflective of my concerns about the problems and pitfalls associated with industrial and ecomodern masculinities (Hultman, 2017a). My work has similarly progressed to centre on the term 'ecological masculinities' in dialogue with Paul while writing this book (Hultman, 2017b). A more theoretical assessment has also been posited by Greta Gaard (2014), who similarly noted the dearth of analyses on men, masculinities and Earth (also see Gaard, 2017). Previous research on the topic has emerged under various permutations of the singular and pluralised uses of the term, those being: eco-masculinity, eco-masculinities, ecomasculinity and ecomasculinities. These interchanging terms have been further dichotomised by the use of 'ecoman' by Mark Allister (2004), whose ecocritical anthology on men and nature remains the only independent text on the topic to date. Stefan Brandt (2017), Teresa Requena-Pelegrí (2017) and Uche Umezurike (forthcoming) have recently expanded on these ecocritical views in separate essays. Further, Sherilyn MacGregor's and Nicole Seymour's (2017) anthology *Men and Nature: Hegemonic*

Masculinities and Environmental Change provides some of the most recent scholarly works on men and nature. We also acknowledge that in finalising this book, after extensive research, we discovered one reference to the actual term 'ecological masculinities' published prior to our use of it here. Professor Wendy Woodward (2008) wrote a chapter titled '"The nature feeling": ecological masculinities in some recent popular texts', in the edited ecocritical volume *Toxic Belonging?* There, Woodward analysed how some authors positioned themselves in connection with ecological thinking and praxes through their constructions of masculine identities. She described the perceptions of Earth, humans and other-than-humans through a gendered lens in a variety of texts noting how this gendering is connected to criticisms of colonially held notions of conservation and hunting as well as traditional knowledges. While Woodward's work is the only scholarly text we could find that uses precisely the same term that we use here, 'ecological masculinities', we note that her emphasis on ecocriticism differs from the meaning we attach to the term. We also take the various references to ecomasculinities introduced above as cursory since they each lack theoretical frameworks for their respective uses of the permutated term. Less direct, but equally worthy of introducing as inspiration for us here are a series of publications exploring the intersecting terrain between men and nature by some rural sociology scholars (Peter et al., 2000; Ni Laoire, 2002; Sherman, 2009) and more specific mention of ecomasculinity in response to disaster management (Pease, 2016; Enarson and Pease eds., 2016) that again do not use the exact same term, ecological masculinities, nor do they provide theoretical framing for permutations on an ecomasculinities theme. These ambiguities highlight the need for a meta-narrative under which these various approaches to the topic can be gathered, examined and debated. Our use of the term ecological masculinities is intended – first and foremost – to provide such a discursive framework for the ways that men, masculinities and Earth are examined.

We introduce ecological masculinities with a keen eye on gender studies (especially profeminist views associated with critical studies on men and masculinities, or CSMM; also see Carrigan et al., 1985; Hearn and Morgan eds., 1990; Clatterbaugh, 1997; Hearn, 1997; Pease, 2000; Hearn, 2004). Ecological masculinities as we formulate it here is consequently positioned as a gathering point for previous conversations about men, masculinities and Earth. Central to our argument is the notion that the Western socio-political landscape of the industrialised north is in great need of a transformation from hegemonisation to ecologisation. We encourage the applications of masculine ecologisation across a broad systemic front, while also arguing the need for this category of masculinities to facilitate personal transformations as well. In Chapter 8, we formulate new ways of configuring masculinities as they shape the lives of men and masculine identities. We also examine the ways that these configurations impact human and other-than-humans as well. Our aspiration here is to bring men and masculinities to the very heart of social and environmental justice.

Conceptually, ecological masculinities stands as a critical alternative to industrial/breadwinner hegemonies and ecomodern reforms. We use the term 'ecological' both scientifically (as a branch of biology that explores the ways that organisms interact with each other and the ecosystems within which they live) and socio-politically (as a movement that explores the relational complexities associated with protecting and preserving living systems on Earth – human and other-than-human alike). My (Martin speaking here) use of the term stems from my analysis of the influence of ecological discourse in the 1970s–1980s in Sweden on the successes and failures of energy and environmental politics. For me (Paul speaking here), the term is a development that builds on my doctoral work, casting a wider net and refining some of the terminology and my analyses of themes to include Martin's important insights on the need for exit politics (from hegemonisation to ecologisation). We use the term 'ecological' reflective of German biologist Ernst Haeckel's first use of the term *Oecologie* in 1866. Haeckel borrowed from the Greek root terms *Oikos* meaning 'the family household' and *Logy* meaning 'the study of'. Charles Krebs (2008: 2–4) defined ecology as a science that examines the 'interrelations of all organisms'. As a science, ecology raises concerns not only about humans and our impact on Earth's living systems, but also about the relationships between the component species within those living systems as well. Ecology can be quantitative or qualitative, helping us to track patterns of interdependency within ecosystems to understand how various species are related. However, ecology also has powerful metaphorical and sociological references as well, facilitating communication within and between species at various scales which have the potential to expose and non-violently resolve discord (Drengson, 2001: 64–65). In this sense, ecology is a science of relationships that can be used literally and metaphorically. For this reason, we use 'ecological' not only as a noun, but as a verb as well, thus: to 'ecologise' or 'ecologisation' are terms used to represent relationality in action. Through the variable implications of these terms, we refer back to the process of relationality in the broader ecological sense. Ecological masculinities, as we use it throughout this book is intended to shift our trajectory as a species towards a deep green future in which we recognise the relationality of humans and other-than-humans alike. Before exploring this notion more thoroughly, we proceed to consider the range of existing views about men and masculinities in masculinities politics.

Note

1 We use these terms 'robust' and 'gracile' intentionally here, borrowing from Kelton McKinley's (1971) paper on the survivorship of the two varieties of australopithecines categorised under the same two terms, which represent two closely related groups of hominids to our own lineage. McKinley indicated that the gracile lineage of

australopithecines had significantly higher survivorship (22.9 years) over the robust lineage (18 years). We consider these findings (which are of course debatable) apt for our purposes, noting that more caring approaches to survivorship appear to have paid dividends to relatives of our own species for millennia. We take this as further justification for stretching the bounds of masculine care, zooming out further still beyond the constrictions of ecomodernisation in order to accentuate our own and other species' survivorship towards greater flourishing through more caring approaches to the world, each other and ourselves that we consider to be ecological (a.k.a. relational) in the broadest sense of the word. (Pulé, 2003; Pulé, 2013).

References

Abraham, D. 2015. *The Elements of Power: Gadgets, Guns, and the Struggle for a Sustainable Future in the Rare Metal Age.* New Haven: Yale University Press.

Ackerman, R. 1993. *Silent Sons: A Book for and about Men.* New York: Poseidon.

Adler, F., Beck, S., Brand, K., Brand, U., Graf, R., Huff, T., and T. Zeller. 2014. *Ökologische Modernisierung: zur Geschichte und Gegenwart eines Konzepts in Umweltpolitik und Sozialwissenschaften.* Frankfurt: Campus.

Albury, K., and D. Laplonge. 2012. 'Practices of gender in mining'. *AusIMM Bulletin Online*, 1. Accessed 5 October 2017. http://search.informit.com.au/documentSumma ry;dn=201202253;res=IELAPA

Allister, M., ed. 2004. *Ecoman: New Perspectives on Masculinity and Nature.* Charlottesville: University of Virginia Press.

Anshelm, J., and A. Hansson. 2011. 'Climate change and the convergence between ENGOs and business: on the loss of utopian energies'. *Environmental Values* 20(1): 75–94.

Anshelm, J., and M. Hultman. 2014a. *Discourses of Global Climate Change: Apocalyptic Framing and Political Antagonisms.* Oxon:Routledge.

Anshelm, J., and M. Hultman. 2014b. 'A green fatwā? Climate change as a threat to the masculinity of industrial modernity'. *NORMA: International Journal for Masculinity Studies* 9(2): 84–96.

Australian Government. 2014. *Industry Outlook: Mining.* Department of Employment. Accessed 5 November 2017. https://cica.org.au/wp-content/uploads/2014-Mining-Industry-Employment-Outlook1.pdf

Barthes, R. 1967. *Elements of Semiology.* New York: Hill & Wang.

Blühdorn, I. 2011. 'The politics of unsustainability: COP15, post-ecologism, and the ecological paradox'. *Organization & Environment* 24(1): 34–53.

Brandt, S. 2017. 'The wild, wild world: masculinity and the environment in the American literary imagination'. In J. Armengol, M. Bosch Vilarrubias, À. Carabí, and T. Requena-Pelegrí, eds., *Routledge Advances in Feminist Studies and Intersectionality.* Series: Masculinities and Literary Studies: Intersections and New Directions. New York: Routledge, 133–143.

Brandt, B., and M. Haugen. 2000. 'From lumberjack to business manager: masculinity in the Norwegian forestry press'. *Journal of Rural Studies* 16(3): 343–355.

Brundtland, G. 1987. *Our Common Future: Report of the World Commission on Environment and Development.* Oxford: Oxford University.

Carrigan, T., Connell, R., and J. Lee. 1985. 'Toward a New Sociology of Masculinity'. *Theory and Society* 14(5): 551–604.

Carson, R. 1962. *Silent Spring.* Boston: Houghton Mifflin.

Clark, R. 2002. 'Measures of efficiency in solid waste collection'. *Journal of Environmental Division ASCE* 99(4): 447–459.

Clatterbaugh, K. 1997. *Contemporary Perspectives on Masculinities*. Boulder: Westview Press.

Coffey, B., and G. Marston. 2013. 'How neoliberalism and ecological modernization shaped environmental policy in Australia'. *Journal of Environmental Policy & Planning* 15(2): 179–199.

Coleman, M., Ganong, L., and K. Warzinik. 2007. *Family Life in 20th-Century America*. Westport: Greenwood Press.

Connell, R. 1990. 'A whole new world: remaking masculinity in the context of the environmental movement'. *Gender and Society* 4(4): 452–478.

Connell, R. 2017. 'Foreword: Masculinities in the Sociocene'. In S. MacGregor and N. Seymour, eds., *Men and Nature: Hegemonic Masculinities and Environmental Change*. Munich: RCC Perspectives, 5–8.

Connell, R., and J. Wood. 2005. 'Globalization and business masculinities'. *Men and masculinities* 7(4): 347–364.

Conroy, D., and R. de Visser. 2013. '"Man up!": discursive constructions of non-drinkers among UK undergraduates'. *Journal of health psychology* 18(11): 1432–1444.

Cook, J., Oreskes, N., Doran, P. Anderegg, W., Verheggen, B., Maibach, E., Carlton, J., Lewandowsky, S., Skuce, A., Green, S., Nuccitelli, D., Jacobs, P., Richardson, M., Winkler, B., Painting, R., and R. Rice. 2016. 'Consensus on consensus: a synthesis of consensus estimates on human-caused global warming'. *Environmental Research Letters, 11(4)*: 1-7.

Daly, H., and J. Cobb. 1994. *For the Common Good: Redirecting the Economy Toward Community, the Environment, and a Sustainable Future* (2nd Edition edn). Boston: Beacon Press.

Donald, R. 1992. 'Masculinity and machismo in Hollywood's war films'. In S. Craig, ed., *Men, Masculinity and the Media*. Thousand Oaks: SAGE Publishing, 124–136.

Drengson, A. 2001. 'Education for local and global ecological responsibility: Arne Næss's cross-cultural, ecophilosophy approach'. *Canadian Journal of Environmental Education* 5 (spring): 63–75.

Einarsson, G., Franzén, L., Gee, D., Holmberg, K., Jönsson, B., Kaijser, S., Karlén, W., Liljenzin, J., Norin, T., Nydén, M., Petersson, G., Ribbing, C., Stigebrandt, A., Stilbs, P., Ulfvarson, A., Walin, G, Andersson, T., Gustafsson, S., Einarsson, O., and T. Hellström. 2008. '20 toppforskare i unikt upprop: koldioxiden påverkar inteklimatet'. *NewsMill.se*, 2008/12/17 kl 20:12. Accessed 1 May 2017. https://news voice.se/2008/12/17/20-toppforskare-i-unikt-upprop-koldioxiden-paverkar-inte-klima tet-lars-bern-far-tungt-stod-fran-vetenskapsman

Enarson, E., and B. Pease, eds. 2016. *Men, Masculinities and Disaster*. Oxon:Routledge.

Etherington, D. 2017. 'Top-end Teslas get price drop thanks to production improvements'. *Oath Tech Network*. Accessed 4 October 2017. https://techcrunch.com/2017/08/30/top-end-teslas-get-price-drop-thanks-to-production-improvements

Farrell, J. 2016. 'Network structure and influence of the climate change countermovement'. *Nature Climate Change* 6(4): 370–374.

Fiegerman, S. 2017. 'Elon Musk to quit Tesla, jumps on a bitcoin tech startup'. *CNN Tech*. Accessed 4 October 2017. http://www.cnn-money-report.com/Elon-Musk-invests-770-million-on-a-bitcoin-tech-startup

Friman, E. 2002. 'No limits: the 20th century discourse of economic growth'. PhD diss., Umeå University.

Gaard, G. 2014. 'Towards new ecomasculinities, ecogenders, and ecosexualities'. In C. Adams and L. Gruen, eds., *Ecofeminism: Feminist Intersections with Other Animals and the Earth*. New York: Bloomsbury, 225–240.

Gaard, G. 2017. *Critical Ecofeminism (Ecocritical Theory and Practice)*. Lanham: Lexington Books.

Hajer, M. 1996. 'Ecological modernisation as cultural politics'. In S. Lash, B. Szerszynski and B. Wynne, eds., *Risk, Environment and Modernity: Towards a New Ecology*. London: SAGE Publishing, 246–286.

Hearn, J. 1997. 'The implications of critical studies on men'. *NORA. Nordic Journal of Women's Studies* 3(1): 48–60.

Hearn, J. 2004. 'From hegemonic masculinity to the hegemony of men'. *Feminist Theory* 5(1): 49–72.

Hearn, J., and D. Morgan, eds. 1990. *Men, Masculinities & Social Theory (Critical Studies on Men and Masculinities – 2)*. Boston: Unwin Hyman.

Holt, D., and C. Thompson. 2004. 'Man-of-action heroes: the pursuit of heroic masculinity in everyday consumption'. *Journal of Consumer research* 31(2): 425–440.

Huber, J. 1982. *The Lost Innocence of Ecology: New Technologies and Superindustrial Development*. Frankfurt am Main: Fisher.

Hultman, M. 2013. 'The making of an environmental hero: a history of ecomodern masculinity, fuel cells and Arnold Schwarzenegger'. *Environmental Humanities* 2(1): 79–99.

Hultman, M. 2015. *Den inställda omställningen: svensk energi-och miljöpolitik i möjligheternas tid 1980–1991*. Möklinta: Gidlund.

Hultman, M. 2017a. 'Natures of masculinities. industrial-, ecological-, and ecomodern masculinity'. In S. Buckingham and V. le Masson, eds., *Understanding Climate Change through Gender Relations*. Oxon: Routledge, 87–105.

Hultman, M. 2017b. 'Exploring industrial, ecomodern, and ecological masculinities'. In S. MacGregor, ed., *Routledge Handbook of Gender and Environment*. Oxon: Routledge, 239–252.

Hultman, M., and J. Anshelm. 2017. 'Masculinities of global climate change: exploring ecomodern, industrial and ecological masculinities'. In M. Cohen, ed., *Climate Change and Gender in Rich Countries*. London: Routledge, 19–34.

Hultman, M., Björk A., and T. Viinikka. Forthcoming. 'Neo-fascism and climate change denial. Analysing the political ecology of industrial masculinities, anti-establishment rhetoric and economic growth nationalism'. In B. Forchtner, C. Kølvraa and R. Wodak, eds., *Contemporary Environmental Communication by the Far Right in Europe*. London: Routledge.

Hultman, M., and A. Yaras. 2012. 'The socio-technological history of hydrogen and fuel cells in Sweden 1978–2005: mapping the innovation trajectory'. *International Journal of Hydrogen Energy* 37(17): 12043–12053.

IPCC [Intergovernmental Panel on Climate Change]. 2014. 'Summary for policymakers'. In O. Edenhofer, R. Pichs-Madruga, Y. Sokona, E. Farahani, S. Kadner, K. Seyboth, A. Adler, I. Baum, S. Brunner, P. Eickemeier, B. Kriemann, J. Savolainen, S. Schlömer, C. von Stechow, T. Zwickel and J. Minx, eds., *Climate Change 2014: Mitigation of Climate Change. Contribution of Working Group III to the Fifth Assessment Report of the Intergovernmental Panel on Climate Change*. Cambridge: Cambridge University Press, 1–32.

Jackins, H. 1999. *The Human Male: A Men's Liberation Draft Policy*. Seattle: Rational Island.

Jänicke, M. 1985. 'Preventive environmental policy as ecological modernisation and structural policy'. Discussion paper. Berlin: WZB.

Jhally, S., and J. Katz. 1999. *Tough Guise: Violence, Media and the Crisis in Masculinity* [Video]. Northampton: Media Education Foundation.

Johansson, N. 2016. *Landfill Mining: Institutional Challenges for the Implementation of Resource Extraction from Waste Deposits* (vol. 1799). Linköping: Linköping University Electronic Press.

Jorgenson, A., and B. Clark. 2012. 'Are the economy and the environment decoupling? A comparative international study, 1960–2005'. *American Journal of Sociology* 118(1): 1–44.

Katz, J. 2016. *Man Enough: Donald Trump, Hillary Clinton, and the Politics of Presidential Masculinity.* Northampton: Interlink.

Kimmel, M. 2008. *Guyland: The Perilous World where Boys become Men.* New York: HarperCollins.

Kindlon, D., and M. Thompson. 1999. *Raising Cain: Protecting the Emotional Lives of Boys.* London: Michael Joseph.

Kivel, P. 1999. *Boys Will Be Men: Raising Our Sons for Courage, Caring and Community.* Gabriola Island: New Society Publishers.

Kivel, P. 2003. 'The "act like a man" box'. In M. Hussey, ed., *Masculinities: Interdisciplinary Readings.* Englewood Cliffs: Prentice-Hall, 69–72.

Kivel, P. 2007. 'The act-like-a-man box'. In M. Kimmel and M. Messner, eds., *Men's Lives* (7th Edition). Boston: Pearson, 148–115.

Kivel, P. 2009. '"Adultism": getting together for social justice'. Accessed 10 December 2017. http://paulkivel.com/wp-content/uploads/2015/07/getting_together_2009.pdf

Kivel, P. 2010[1992]. *Men's Work: How to Stop the Violence that Tears Our Lives Apart.* Center City: Hazelden.

Krebs, C. 2008. *The Ecological World View.* Collingwood: CSIRO.

Levy, D., and A. Spicer. 2013. 'Contested imaginaries and the cultural political economy of climate change'. *Organization* 20(5): 659–678.

Lægreid, O. 2017. Drivers of Climate Change? Political and Economic Explanations of Greenhouse Gas Emissions. Gothenburg: Gothenburgh University.

Little, J. 2002. 'Rural geography: rural gender identity and the performance of masculinity and femininity in the countryside'. *Progress in Human Geography* 26(5): 665–670.

Lockwood, M. 2018. 'Right-wing populism and the climate change agenda: exploring the linkages'. *Environmental Politics*, April: 1–21.

Lundqvist, L. 2004. *Straddling the Fence: Sweden and Ecological Governance.* Manchester: Manchester University Press

McCright, A., and R. Dunlap. 2003. 'Defeating Kyoto: the conservative movement's impact on US climate change policy'. *Social Problems* 50(3): 348–373.

MacGregor, S., ed. 2017. *Routledge Handbook of Gender and Environment.* Oxon: Routledge.

MacGregor, S., and N. Seymour, eds. 2017. *Men and Nature: Hegemonic Masculinities and Environmental Change.* Munich: RCC Perspectives.

McKinley, K. 1971. 'Survivorship in gracile and robust Australopithecines: A demographic comparison and a proposed birth model'. *American Journal of Physical Anthropology* May 34(3): 417–476.

McNeill, J. 2000. *Something New under the Sun.* New York: Norton.

Meeker, M. 2014. *Strong Mothers, Strong Sons: Lessons Mothers Need to Raise Extraordinary Men*. New York: Ballantine.

Merchant, C. 1980. *The Death of Nature: Women, Ecology and the Scientific Revolution*. New York: HarperCollins.

Morton, T. 2016. 'The first draft of the future: journalism in the "Age of the Anthropocene"'. In J. Marshall and L. Connor, eds., *Environmental Change and the World's Future: Ecologies, Ontologies and Mythologies*. Oxon: Routledge, 33–47.

Nader, R. 1965. *Unsafe at Any Speed*. New York: Grossman.

Nayak, A. 2003. '"Boyz to men": masculinities, schooling and labour transitions in de-industrial times'. *Educational Review* 55(2): 147–159.

Ni Laoire, C. 2002. 'Masculinities and change in rural Ireland'. *Irish Geography* 35(1): 16–28.

Oreskes, N., and M. Conway. 2010. 'Defeating the merchants of doubt'. *Nature* 465 (7299): 686–687.

Parrott, D., and A. Zeichner. 2003. 'Effects of hypermasculinity oh physical aggression against women'. *Psychology of Men & Masculinity* 4(1): 70–78.

Pease, B. 2000. *Recreating Men: Postmodern Masculinity Politics*. London: SAGE Publishing.

Pease, B. 2016. 'Masculinism, climate change and "man-made" disasters: towards an environmental profeminist response'. In E. Enarson and B. Pease, eds., *Men, Masculinities and Disaster*. Oxon: Routledge, 21–33.

Peter, G., Bell, M., Jarnagin, S., and D. Bauer. 2000. 'Coming back across the fence: masculinity and the transition to sustainable agriculture'. *Rural Sociology* 65(2): 15–33.

Phillips, A. 1994. *The Trouble with Boys: A Wise and Sympathetic Guide to the Risky Business of Raising Sons*. New York: Basic Books.

Pollack, W. 2000. *Real Boys' Voices*. New York: Random House.

Pulé, P. 2003. 'Us and them: primate science and the union of the rational self with the intuitive self'. Master's diss., Plymouth University.

Pulé, P. 2013. 'A declaration of caring: towards an ecological masculinism'. PhD diss., Murdoch University.

Radetzki, M., and N. Lundgren. 2009. 'En grön fatwa har utfärdats'. *Ekonomisk debatt* 37(5): 57–65.

Reeser, T. 2010. *Masculinities in Theory*. Malden, MA: Wiley-Blackwell.

Requena-Pelegrí, T. 2017. 'Green intersections: caring masculinities and the environmental crisis'. In J. Armengol and M. Vilarrubias, eds., *Masculinities and Literary Studies: Intersections and New Directions*. New York: Routledge, 143–152.

Salleh, A. 2010. 'Climate strategy: making the choice between ecological modernisation or living well'. *Journal of Australian Political Economy* 66: 118–143.

Sherman, J. 2009. 'Bend to avoid breaking: job loss, gender norms, and family stability in rural America'. *Social Problems* 56(4): 599–620.

Simpson, M. 1994. *Male Impersonators: Men Performing Masculinity*. New York: Routledge.

Spaargaren, G., and A. Mol. 2008. 'Greening global consumption: redefining politics and authority'. *Global Environmental Change* 18(3): 350–359.

Stacey, J. 1990. *Brave New Families: Stories of Domestic Upheaval in Late-Twentieth-Century America*. Berkeley: University of California Press.

Stahl, G., Nelson, J., and D. Wallace. eds. 2017. *Masculinity and Aspiration in the Era of Neoliberal Education: International Perspectives*. New York: Routledge.

Supran, G., and N. Oreskes. 2017. 'Assessing ExxonMobil's climate change communications (1977–2014)'. *Environmental Research Letters* 12(8). Accessed 4 November 2017. http://iopscience.iop.org/article/10.1088/1748-9326/aa815f/pdf

Swyngedouw, E. 2010. 'Apocalypse forever?'. *Theory, Culture & Society* 27(2–3): 213–232.

Tesla. 2017. 'Tesla inventory'. Accessed 4 November 2017. http://www.tesla.com/en_AU/new

The Years Project (Producer). 2014. *Years of Living Dangerously* [TV Series]. Brooklyn: FilmRise.

Thompson, M. and T. Barker, 2000. *Speaking of Boys: Answers to the Most-Asked Questions about Raising Sons.* New York: Ballantine.

Umezurike, U. Forthcoming. 'The eco(logical) border man: masculinities in Jim Lynch's *Border Songs*'.

UNDP [United Nations Development Programme. 2015. *Human Development Report: Work for Human Development.* New York: United Nations Development Programme.

Vaccaro, C., and M. Swauger. 2016. *Unleashing Manhood in the Cage: Masculinity and Mixed Martial Arts.* London: Lexington Books.

Wade, L. 2016. 'Tesla electric cars aren't as green as you might think'. Accessed 4 October 2017. http://www.wired.com/2016/03/teslas-electric-cars-might-not-green-think

Wallsten, B. 2015. 'The Urk world: hibernating infrastructures and the quest for urban mining'. PhD diss., Linköping University.

Whitman, K. 2013. 'Looking out for the "Aussie bloke": gender, class and contextualizing a hegemony of working-class masculinities in Australia'. PhD diss., University of Adelaide.

Woodward, W. 2008. '"The nature feeling": ecological masculinities in some recent popular texts'. In D. Wylie, ed., *Toxic Belonging? Identity and Ecology. Southern Africa.* Newcastle upon Tyne: Cambridge Scholars, 143–157.

York, R., Rosa, E., and T. Dietz. 2010. 'Ecological modernization theory: theoretical and empirical challenges'. In M. Redclift and G. Woodgate, eds., *The International Handbook of Environmental Sociology* (2nd Edition). Northampton: Edward Elgar, 77–90.

Zimmer, B. 2010. '"Man up" gets political'. *New York Times Magazine Online.* Accessed 9 February 2011. http://www.visualthesaurus.com/cm/wordroutes/2458

Section II
Four streams

3 Men and masculinities

A spectrum of views

To indoctrinate boys into the rules of patriarchy, we force them to feel pain and to deny their feelings.

(hooks, 2004: 22)

Men and masculinities

The following arguments are based on an understanding that men and masculinities are both constructed and changeable. Keeping with the theme of situatedness introduced in the Prologue, we reiterate that both terms represent researchable categories of various configurations and applications, which have profound impacts on the world (Haraway, 1988; also see Frank, 2008; Hopkins and Noble, 2009; Hearn et al., 2012).[1] By this, we are referring to pro-feminist research traditions that characterise critical studies on men and masculinities (CSMM) in particular. In doing so, we expose the noteworthy absence of a cohesive and rigorous analysis of the connection between men, masculinities and Earth. In Chapter 1, we acknowledged Connell's (1995) influential contribution to the now widely accepted notion that there is not a singular rendition of masculinity. In what became a pivotal publication, Connell (1995: 37, 185) convincingly demonstrated the importance of recognising modern Western masculinities as plural, constructed, subjective and examinable as discrete categories. In an elaboration of the complexities associated with masculinities, Connell (2001: 30–34) described essentialist, positivist, normative and material-semiotic distinctions when exploring masculinities politics, suggesting that these categories equate to active, psychological, ethical and symbolic interpretations of the term, respectively. We add that a person might not be 'biologically male', but they might behave in competitive, aggressive, egotistical and pragmatic ways, which popular culture would readily describe as 'masculine' behaviours and for this reason we consider our analyses to be applicable not only to men, but to women and non-binary/genderqueer people as well.

While the offerings in this book might well be most applicable to cis men, they are intended to be germane to all persons. Further pluralising the terrain of gendered identities, an individual's demeanour and/or physical characteristics may be indistinguishably male, female, transgendered, androgynous, etc. Such persons may be 'anatomically female' but some of the characteristics they embody might be treated as 'masculine' and might therefore be considered by others as more like a man and more 'masculine' than 'feminine'. Similarly, an anatomical male might appear feminine or 'womanly' and might consider themself as a woman in a man's body or want to be treated by others accordingly. In addition, individuals might choose intimate relations with members of their same or different gender identities and may find and/or seek out sexual or non-sexual intimacy with others who identify as 'pan-sexual', 'gender-neutral', 'questioning' or 'post-gendered'. We explore the complexities of this pluralised view on gender when discussing the LGBTIQA+, or rainbow community. For now, we note that when we acknowledge the granularity of these many different ways of understanding gender, identity and the impacts on individuals and their environments, we see that, as Connell and others have eruditely demonstrated, gendered categories are variable, complex and unavoidably plural; beckoning us to celebrate difference precisely because it is unavoidably present in the mosaic of identities that individuals assume (or reject) (Messerschmidt, 2012; Seymour, 2013; Christensen and Jensen, 2014). However, because our primary focus throughout this book is to interrogate the intersectionality between men, masculinities and Earth, we dedicate this chapter to the mosaic of views that persist across the politicised terrain of studies and praxes on men and masculinities that we broadly refer to as masculinities politics (Aboim, 2016).

Australian sociologist Bob Pease (1998: 77) has provided an overview of research on the following activities that have supported our textured understanding of not only the theories, but the variety of practices that have shaped masculinities politics. They are: men's support groups, ritual healing groups; violence re-education groups; boys programmes to manage errant behaviour or to help transition boys into healthy manhood; men's health programmes to increase men's well-being and longevity; men's rights groups to address the distress that some men express over the loss of connection with their children as a result of relationship breakdowns; anti-feminist backlash groups; alt-right and far-right wing political groups; new age men's liberation groups; men who support feminist theories; courses about men and masculinities at universities; as well as social actions groups specifically designed for men, which he categorised accordingly: profeminist, gay, spiritual and men's rights categories (Pease, 2002: 33). Jeff Hearn (1992: 6, 142–146, 208) has similarly and comprehensively argued that 'man' as a label is structural and agentic and is therefore subject to public and private aberration within civil society, meaning different masculine identities emerge as they are shaped by variations in systems of social functioning (also see Hearn et al., 2012: 1, 6, 15, 23). Further still, consider Michael Kimmel and Michael Messner's (1989) four major divisions within masculinities politics: anti-feminist, men's rights, mythopoetic and profeminist, with Messner (1997) later suggesting eight specific categories: Promise Keepers (joined now by alt-right devotees and twenty-first-century evangelicals), mythopoets, men's liberationists, men's rights activists (MRAs), radical feminists, socialist feminists and gay male liberationists. Taking these various perspectives into consideration, we are inspired by the more straightforward categorisations posited by Kenneth Clatterbaugh (1997), those being: socialist, queer, gay, profeminist, black, men's rights and Christian masculinities. We combine the collective wisdom from the scholarships considered above as our principal guides (also see Pease, 2002; Heasley, 2005). We move through our assessment of this mosaic of views that characterise masculinities politics by highlighting their useful, less-than-useful and dated implications as well as examining the ways that each offering is relevant to ecological masculinities as we formulate it throughout this book. Importantly and further to the various nomenclatural offerings of the scholars mentioned above, the categories we posit below should not be considered exhaustive or mutually exclusive, but a compilation aimed at capturing the far from discrete complexities of masculinities. For example, an individual might be an avid supporter of communalism and the collectivisation of labour that aligns with the *realpolitik* of socialist masculinities, while also sitting comfortably with some elements of the values associated with Christian masculinities, such as a belief in God or the valorising of men as 'heads of household', even though these research traditions and categories are on opposite ends of a traditional political spectrum. Consequently, we argue that individuals can find themselves aligned with elements of multiple positionalities,[2] even if the politics of those positionalities might be at odds – our lives are after all rife with contradictions. This dynamic view is an important ingredient in formulating our rendition of ecological masculinities. We therefore consider the research below to be a versatile introduction to the field, rather than a prescribed view fixed to a specific framework; we posit a dynamic assessment of masculinities politics instead. We also suggest that pluralism encourages the emergence of fresh insights, critical debates and access to information and praxes that will collectively raise the potential for us to consider the various values, concepts and applications emergent throughout masculinities politics. In doing so, our intention is to create the broadest of possible assessments of men and masculinities; a pluralism that we consider to be vital if we are to successfully create a sustainable world.

Reflective of our combined political views, we align ecological masculinities with a profeminist perspective, recognising that others will contest this (and intentionally welcome lively debate). Further, current events surrounding notions of toxic/extreme masculinities through the exposure of high-profile men to multiple accusations of sexual misconduct or assault, coupled with the socio-political consequences of these exposures of perpetration, are now more visible and must be included in contemporary analyses of masculinities politics (Sexton, 2016; Gleeson, 2017; Solnit, 2017a; Solnit, 2017b; Solnit, 2017c). Such voiced concerns have traditionally been received with silence, denial and fervent backlashes from those who benefit the most from masculine hegemonisation. For example, MRAs and alt-right political agendas have valorised men's domestic entitlements, violence, rape culture, misogyny, anti-feminism, white supremacy, anti-Semitism and Islamophobia, anew (Kimmel and Ferber, 2000; Kimmel, 2013; Conroy, 2017; Kelly, 2017). With these contemporary complexities in mind, we provide our analyses of seven research themes, each of which has influenced our conceptualisations of ecological masculinities. They are:

- profeminist masculinities
- the economics of gender equity
- LGBTTTQQIAA-OHP (LGBTIQA+ or non-binary/genderqueer) masculinities
- decolonisation of masculinities
- men's mythopoetry and nature myth-making
- Christian dogmatic and environmental traditions
- men's rights groups (toxic/extreme masculinities unleashed)

We offer this overview of the positionalities throughout masculinities politics as our response to contemporary eruptions and lively debates about the state of modern Western masculinities.

Profeminist masculinities

Profeminist masculinities play a crucial role in our analyses. This positionality historically originates from some men's support for second-wave feminism (Kimmel, 1987). By the mid 1970s, some men sought more organised ways to draw on feminist interventions of male domination and this resulted in the formalisation of profeminism (as distinct from declaring oneself as male and feminist, effectively qualifying men's efforts to unpack and reframe masculinities in critical alignment as allies to feminism rather than joining women to champion women's empowerment). Fidelma Ashe (2007: 13, 47–48) noted that the views formulated by profeminists have been instrumental in creating men's groups that tackle questions of gendered power and practices with the intent of supporting equity and increased agency for all through the democratisation of gender relations. To clarify, we note that 'gender equity' and 'gender equality' can be used interchangeably.[3] However, for our purposes, they are considered distinct, where the former refers to equitable access to resources and opportunities through variable and customised strategies (such as equal opportunity legislation, parental rights in family court proceedings, budgetary measures to reflect the gender-specific differentials in rates of domestic and family violence perpetration/victimisation). The latter, on the other hand, refers to a determination to grant equal access to resources and opportunities for both women and men (which, notably, does not critically analyse the sources, statuses or impacts of those gendered differentials on women and men and – at best – simply aims to uncritically fold women into men's worlds in greater number to close the demographic gap for the sake of numerical balance – which we find inadequate on account of the lack of sensitivity to different starting positions and access to opportunities). Guided by these distinctions, we subscribe to the former throughout this book to support both women and men to not only be given equal access to resources and opportunities, but that both genders are provided with specific, relevant and appropriate benefits in ways that are not identical at all, but rather are fair and reflective of the differing statistics, circumstances, along with historical and social trajectories that have, are and will continue to affect women's and men's lives differently. Of course, following this argument to its logical conclusion, we extend our interpretations of equity to non-binary/genderqueer analyses as well. Our intention here is to support the notion that it is not adequate to simply bring women and human others equally into men's world, but to reframe our social machinations to create a level playing field that then facilitates the emergence of gender/identity equality reflective of the subjectivities of each group. In this sense, we see gender equity as a necessary precursor to gender equality. Consequently, and countering violent expressions of male domination as products of masculine hegemonisation, we recognise that some men have been seeking allegiances with various forms of feminism for more than two generations (Seidler, 1991; Hill, 2007). Since the 1970s, we have seen the emergence of the White Ribbon Campaign, the National Organization for Men Against Sexism (NOMAS) in the US, the White Ribbon Campaign in Canada, the Achilles Heel Collective in the UK, MEN for Gender Equality in Sweden, along with Men Against Sexual Assault (MASA) and No to Violence (NTV) in Australia. These are just some of the notable examples of community initiatives and organisational manifestations of profeminism that support gender equity praxes through the lens of masculinities. They collectively critique the ways that hegemonic masculinities are infused with hypersensitivities to powerlessness that can unfold in stark contrast to men's traditional senses of superiority in public spheres – a paradox that profeminists recognise and examine (Kaufman, 1994: 142).

Profeminists are outspoken critics of the predominating characteristic of hegemonic masculinities. A central aim of their analyses of men and masculinities has been to expose and work to end male violence, particularly against women (Seidler, 2014; Flood and Howson eds., 2015). The use of violent force to bolster men's primacy has long been implemented by military and police personnel as agents of domestic and international government policies just as much as men have perpetrated domestic and family violence at alarming rates (Devries et al., 2013; Ross ed., 2014; ANROWS, 2016). Of course, men's violence has been used as a form of intimidation not only towards rival societies, women and other marginalised communities or at the familial level, but towards other men as well. According to Connell, these are some of the ways that male domination routinely engages in keeping people and systems in 'their place' to protect and preserve the assumed sanctity of masculine hegemonisation (Connell, 1995: 81–86). Profeminists expose the conditioning that sets men up to engage in violent behaviours towards all others and men themselves.

One of the more alarming expressions of violence perpetrated (almost) exclusively by men has been the near-routine occurrence of mass shootings in homes, communities, schools and universities in the West (the clear majority occurring in the US). Consider 64-year-old Stephen Paddock's 'bump stock' shooting (that turned his rifles into the near equivalent of a fully automatic weapons) resulting in fifty-eight deaths in Las Vegas on 1 October 2017 as he sprayed bullets into a crowded open-air music festival. We also note the racially motivated school attack at Trollhättan, Sweden by Anton Lundin Pettersson on 22 October, 2015; Alek Minassian's 'involuntary celibate (or incel) rebellion' where a van was used to run down and claim the lives of 10 pedestrians (mostly women) in Toronto, Canada on 23 April 2018; and the Osmington, Western Australia murder/suicide of 6 members of the Miles family by Peter Miles on 11 May 2018; all examples of recent mass killings perpetrated by men beyond the US. Aspects of mass shootings run parallel with domestic and international terrorism (particularly those that are Christian or Islamic inspired) and have today resulted in these tragedies becoming routine events enacted by those seeking purpose and expressing their passions through extreme acts of violence that not only cause chaos and destruction in the lives of many, but frequently result in the perpetrator's suicide, termination, or life-long incarceration. That most of these perpetrators are men is no coincidence. Each time these events occur, they underscore the depth of pressure to conform and the intensity of feelings that can manifest when a male does not reap the rewards of their assumed and socially sanctioned primacy (Hatty, 2000: 1–3; Everytown for Gun Safety Support Fund, 2015). Given the high rates of suicide or use of lethal force by authorities in response, it has been difficult to develop an accurate profile of the inner machinations of individuals who commit these horrendous crimes. Some alarming data that does appear to be revealing patterns of perpetration demonstrate that 16 per cent of recent shooters had previously been charged with domestic violence offences, with 54 per cent of those targeted being intimate partners, family members and people the perpetrator knew (Everytown for Gun Safety Support Fund, 2017; Digg, 2017). Admittedly, mass shootings are still very rare incidences, statistically speaking, especially when weighed against global homicide rates, war casualties or even people killed in traffic accidents. However, this gap in death statistics (which has too frequently been used to justify lax gun laws, especially in the US) is closing; the US sticking way out ahead of other Global Northern nations as the frequency of mass shootings and their levels of lethalness continue to rise in that nation (Kennedy, 2013; Quealy and Sanger-Katz, 2016).

Connell (1995: 83) identified a revealing pattern of masculine violence that has long pervaded malestream societies. She noted that privileged men use violence not only to sustain their dominance over others, but also to rank men according to their access and capacity to participate in that dominance, asserting traditional notions of masculinity that push otherised men down the pecking order as well. Anthony Synnott (2009: 46) suggested that men's violence functions as dominator expressions of masculinities in three main ways: the warrior who embodies bravery (e.g. the soldier, fireman or policeman), the gentleman who epitomises refinement and good manners (e.g. the aristocrat or noble hunter) and the self-made man who manifests his own success (e.g. the statesman willing to wage war or the entrepreneur willing to strip lands bare for riches). These violent themes have subversive companions that assert male primacy in less dramatic ways such as the idea of the good husband, the exceptional father, the tireless worker, the protector and provider, the chivalrous knight tending to the damsel in distress and the civil man of the polis. Juxta-posed against each other, we see these as dark/light inflections of men's violence, since together, these nuances of traditional masculinities harbour expressive and subversive versions of the 'violent beast' willing and able to wreak havoc upon those who threaten or defy the hallowed ground of male primacy when things fall apart or when adopting the moral high ground in the name of a right-eousness cause (Synnott, 2009: 46, 51). Whether dark or light in intent and/or outcome, in each case, manifestations of men's violence is enmeshed within the structural mechanisms of masculine hegemonisation. The two go hand-in-hand.

Another central theme for profeminists is the elimination of sexism, particu-larly as it relates to men's perpetration of domestic and family violence (Flood, 2005). Further (and of particular importance for a profeminist positionality), consider men's rights elements of masculinities that have been railing against feminism, supporting rape culture and/or emboldening misogyny for some time (Kimmel, 1993). Profeminists position themselves as bulwarks against these expressions of sexism, advocating the need for men to acknowledge their struc-tural privileges, eliminate their internalised superiority and advocate gender equity. Profeminist publications, forums, organisations and support groups col-lectively facilitate a cross section of behavioural and paradigmatic reforms for men and masculinities, aiming to achieve alternative and post-patriarchal forms of masculinities that treat women and non-binary/genderqueer people as equals and set up systems in support of that goal. They deconstruct men's internalised superiority while also interrogating the structural implications of sexism, naming and dismantling the many conceptual and tangible forms of male domination (Pease, 1999: 260). Profeminist masculinities theorists are outspoken proponents of the elimination of wider forms of oppression perpetrated by men towards all marginalised people as well (based on gender, race, class, sexual orientation, age, ability and so forth). This positionality serves as a pathway to structural libera-tion from the dehumanising implications of men's primacy, educating, developing awareness and supporting activism to resist men's engagement in pornography, prostitution, militarism, sexual harassment, rape, domestic violence and compe-titiveness, while also supporting women's (and others') empowerment through, for example, professional equity and reproductive rights advocacy (Pease, 1998: 83–84; Pease, 2000: 43).

Michael Kimmel (1998: 64) argued that profeminist masculinities has played two important roles in masculinities politics. Firstly, the discourse acknowledges men's experience, while being critical of their privileging. Secondly, profeminists recognise that men's perceived suffering is, paradoxically, caused by their own socially sanctioned power, further noting that male domination is granted to men, with terrible personal costs attached. Like feminists, profeminists argue that male domination is detrimental to men and masculinities as well. This insight highlights that internalised superiorisation not only results in unequal distribution of privileges, power and control, but is also met by stress-related illnesses, emotional inexpressiveness and a general decline in men's health and wellbeing (Waldinger, 2016). These findings are ironic, given the forces brought to bear to protect and preserve male primacy (Pease, 2002: 3). If men are to cultivate greater care for the glocal commons, we must be willing to develop emotional vocabularies attuned to heartfelt connections not only between women (and non-binary/genderqueer people) and men but also among men as well.

Profeminists directly challenge homophobia, noting that 'men tend not to have same-sex friendships that are as satisfying to them as same-sex friendships are to women' (May et al., 1992: 95). The lack of strong bonds between men reinforces their sense of independence, non-communicativeness and aversions to closeness and intimacy, which, in addition to constrained emotional literacy, can leave many men with a limited range of permissive human exchanges, substituting them instead with notions of entitlement and internalised superiorisation and a suite of addictions to salve their isolation (Waldinger, 2016). However, and despite their lofty intentions, profeminist perspectives and praxes can be confronting for many men living within malestream norms, occurring to many as a 'gender betrayal' of sorts. This helps explain the resistance that many men harbour towards feminist thinking and actions and also provides us with some insight into reasons why, for example, 'locker room talk' is allowed to run wild and unchecked even by men who might quietly disagree with such attitudes and behaviours (Soloway, 2016). To deny one's exclusive membership to the highest echelons of society is, for many men, simply unthinkable. Profeminists play a lead role in helping to expose this folly.

Profeminists are also beginning to pay attention to the intersecting terrain of men, masculinities and Earth as well. In a recent and poignant essay aimed at addressing precisely this discursive union, Bob Pease (2016: 33) noted that:

> . . . profeminist men involved in reconstructing or exiting dominant forms of masculinity may be able to envisage new non-oppressive ways for men to relate to nature, as they discover new ways to relate to women, other men and themselves.

To this, we add that more flexible conceptualisations of care are also gaining ground (Elliott, 2016). This signifies a promising development, since it aligns well with some new work being promoted through contemporary ecological feminism and studies on gender and the environment (Buckingham and Le

Masson eds., 2017; Gaard, 2017). In this sense, the socio-political analyses that characterise profeminist masculinities inform both men's inner journeys and are setting fresh tones about masculinities and environmental concerns. However, it is important to note that profeminists have not addressed this intersecting terrain in any substantive sense beyond some of the publications we give fuller consideration in Chapter 7. For now, we proceed to explore the economic implications of male domination.

The economics of gender equity

Keeping pace with the rise of feminism during the 1960s and 1970s, researchers and activists began to respond to increasingly obvious hegemonic expressions of masculine identity within capitalist societies. They proposed an alternative *realpolitik* that confronted the impacts of industrial labour and productivity on men's lives, inspired in particular by the writings of Karl Marx (Tacey, 1997: 108). As counter-capitalists, these masculinities theorists sought some allegiances with feminism by analysing the patriarchal nature of market-oriented oligarchies. They were guided by the core tenet of socialism to acknowledge the agency of all oppressed peoples, beyond their gendered identities (Hearn, 1987). In doing so, they emphasised the ways that men have been traditionally positioned as expendable labourers in the wake of corporate growth that benefits those who own the means of production (a point that easily translates into more extreme impacts on women and others, especially those being exploited in the industrial sectors of the Global South). This observation ran parallel to the ways that governments have historically used working men as cannon fodder during times of war, with women and others filling in the gaps in labour markets in their absence only to be sent home when men returned. Emphasising public ownership as an alternative to privatisation, economic masculinities analyses have placed a premium on collectivisation as a path to greater freedom (Clatterbaugh, 1997: 12–13). This insight is relevant to the impact of industrialisation on men's bodies as well. David Tacey (1997: 108–109) acknowledged that socialism made an important conceptual contribution to masculinities politics by exposing the impact of industrial pressures on men's health and well-being within the foreboding shadow of corporate and capitalist pursuits of profit (also see Schumacher, 1973: 218; Hearn, 1992: 35). This body of research aimed to dispel class distinctions among men, suggesting that to 'understand men, we have to understand their material and economic positions and their social practices both at home and at work' (Pease, 2002: 25). Through a socialist lens, working men (and women) have traditionally been seen as vulnerable to being used by those who own the means of production (primarily Western white men) in order to generate profit, often at considerable physical, emotional, financial and social expense to the labourer him/herself. In other words, industrialisation has had immediate and profound impacts on men's (and others') lives socially, culturally, economically, politically, emotionally and physically. Capitalism has effectively enabled wealthy industrialists to buy other men's (and others') labour through social, economic and political arrangements that ensure that they profit enormously from businesses serviced by a cadre of labourers in primary production and fossil fuel based industries (Rickards et al., 2014; Malm, 2015). Through such an analysis, we see that gender plays a pivotal role in constructing individual identities along traditional and binary lines of identity throughout capitalist societies in particular – in other words, capitalism needs distinctions such as class, race, age and gender in order to establish worker hegemonies. According to Pease, this capitalist tradition of hegemonic exploitation has exposed the necessity to reassess gender identity by constructing new laws, values, organisations and institutions that function beyond the constraints of sexism, with the intent of broadening access to the labour field for women and non-binary/genderqueer people as well (2002: 25). These masculinities scholars posited a revolutionary societal transformation that would point us in the direction of post-hegemonic social constructions, also noting the severity to which women (and others) were barred from blue- and white-collar roles outside of the home at the expense of society-wide progress for much of Western history (Fasteau, 1975: 60).

Sadly, in relation to gender equity, socialist-inspired societies (particularly communist states that rose and fell during the middle to latter twentieth century) implemented many of the same traits of masculinist hegemonisation that their foundational rhetoric aimed to usurp. Sexism persevered in communist states as well, despite the best of intentions to liberate all citizens through collective industrialisation (Zawisza et al., 2015). Further still, despite emphases on collective industrialisation, emergent communist societies gave little attention to care for the environment. The dismal environmental record of communist industrialisation has been exposed for some time (Goldman, 1972; Josephson et al., 2013). For example, the Caucuses and Central Asia had a well-established history of systematic ecological devastation under communist economic development policies and practices (Cherp and Mnatsakanian, 2008). Despite the rhetoric, the social and environmental care that has been implemented in (former) communist states has proved to be weak at best (Komarov, 1978: 30; Bowers, 1993: 134). Communism resulted in the replication of binary views and practices about humanity and Earth as much as it championed binary views of men's and women's roles in labour markets, essentially creating a different version of the same problematic hegemonisation between Earth and humanity as much as between the genders, just as is the case throughout global capitalist states. Further, and more to the point, it would be fair to say that comunism has failed, leaving us with rogue industrialisation reflective of raw expressions of global capitalism. Given sexism and environmental destruction have persisted through both capitalism and communism as both systems pursued industrial modernisation, we must take steps towards building equitable societies (both socially and environmentally speaking), seeking answers to our social and environmental problems beyond either economic system. We consequently find little evidence of intersectional support for men, masculinities and Earth within an economic analysis of men's labour relations as exemplified by those masculinities theorists who turned to socialism for guidance. This brings us to consider other masculinities positionalities that expand our understandings of the definitions of manhood and masculinity beyond economic modelling and towards critical analyses of heteronormativity.

LGBTTTQQIAA-OHP (LGBTIQA+ or non-binary/genderqueer) masculinities

As we step towards masculine ecologisation, we honour insights about masculinities posited by lesbian, gay, bisexual, transgender, transsexual, two-spirited, queer, questioning, intersexed, asexual and allied people (plus other-O, HIV-affected-H, pansexual-P) (LGBTTTQQIAA-OHP) individuals, scholars and activists. This movement is also known as the rainbow community, reflective of the rainbow flag, which originated in Northern California and has become an international symbol for lesbian, gay (and others') pride. We refer to the more complex initialism 'LGBTTTQQIAA' instead of rainbow community to emphasise the diversity that exists across the fullest and what we consider to be the most respectful acknowledgement of non-binary/genderqueer people. Throughout this book and for sake of simplicity, we use the abbreviated initialism LGBTIQA+ and the term 'non-binary/genderqueer' interchangeably. We note that heteronormativity is an integral aspect of the constraints imposed upon people's identities within the confines of hegemonic masculinities. This is fiercely advocated by many non-binary/genderqueer individuals and community groups. As we mentioned elsewhere in this book, we take our lead from ecology, honouring the fact that complexity and diversity supports greater resilience in ecosystems as they do in human communities. Ecology teaches us that (in general) the broader, deeper and wider the web of relational connections, the more robust the ecosystem is in the face of perturbations. Of relevance to this positionality are the contributions of LGBTIQA+ theorists and activists who help us to see the same biodiversity in gender identity as is present in other-than-human communities (Mortimer-Sandilands, 2005). Given our focus on men and masculinities here, we draw most of our understanding of the LGBTIQA+ community from gay and queer scholars. That said, we acknowledge that many more voices (some reaching beyond the scope of this book) are worthy of recognition within the LGBTIQA+ community as well.

   Gay masculinities theorists have made a substantial contribution to Western cultural evolution since the 1960s. They have openly challenged both the viability and morality of male domination as it impacts men, through acute critiques of heteronormativity (Connell, 2002: 7). In the early 1970s, gay men – empathising with the plight of women and feminists who challenged patriarchy – aligned their own liberation with the values and priorities of feminism prior to the rise of most other masculinities theorists (Carrigan et al., 1987: 83). We have noted above that male domination affects men as well as all others, creating expectations that marginalised (especially non-binary/genderqueer) men along with women and human others are identified with the corporeal, embodied and erotic aspects of 'wild' nature, while traditional expressions of maleness are more closely aligned with logic, intellectualism, pragmatism, emotional constraint and the pursuits of 'civilised' culture (Ortner, 1974; Griffin, 1978; Merchant, 1980; Eisenstein, 1983; Gaard, 2011). Such views highlight the distinguishing features of masculinised and feminised gender identities. Like all identities, gayness is a process of 'becoming' – a condition constructed *in situ* and may be a function of preference, genetic predisposition, early experiences, or any combination of these (Connell, 2002: 4). Gay liberation efforts have long aimed to normalise homosexuality as central to the human socio-sexual repertoire, resulting in contentious debates about marriage equality, parental rights for same-sex couples and a shift towards the normalisation of homosexuality to the extent that many Global Northern countries have sought equal representation of LGBTIQA+ people in the eyes of their respective marital laws. Ireland, the US, along with many of the nations of Europe, Canada, New Zealand, nations of Central and South America and now Australia have now legalised same-sex marriage.

It is difficult to be gay and non-political, even if privately so. However, gayness does not automatically predetermine one's politics to be liberal or progressive (consider for example Milo Yiannopoulos). To be quietly critical of masculine hegemonisation but then not challenge male domination is to reap benefits from sexism as a man or as a male-identified individual that non-masculine identified humans do not receive. This is even more evident when a person is white, as an unmarked person can take for granted that they will benefit from their whiteness in racist societies in ways that privilege them over people of colour, just as do straight people over LGBTIQA+ people. Connell (1995: 79) referred to a 'patriarchal dividend', which ensures that men of all sexual orientations receive some benefits as a direct result of the overall subordination of those who fall outside of maleness and heteronormativity. Consequently, gay men receive scaled versions of masculinist structural and personal privileges compared to their heteronormative counterparts, since their maleness gives them limited access to the benefits of malestream norms despite the oppressions imposed upon them for their gayness (Connell, 1995: 79). This 'watered-down' access to the privileges of male domination places gay men (even if below heterosexual men) in socio-cultural and political positions of advantage over women and non-binary/genderqueer others (Hanmer, 1990: 30). Effectively, gay men (inadvertently) join with heterosexual men in limited levels of gendered intoxication in the wake of male domination (Brod, 2002: 162). However, masculinities are constructed by socialisations that are hegemonised meaning the distinction between malestream and gay masculine identities are present as well. For gay masculinities theorist, the phenomenon of 'gender vertigo' (the confusing of one's societal privileges due to gendered identity and sexual orientation) amplifies the marginalisation of gay men and queers, further stifling heteronormative men's capacities to care for other men and themselves by amplifying isolation and disconnection from relational closeness with others (Connell, 2000: 91). Correspondingly, the stigmas attached to homophobia not only repress gay men, but also lesbians and non-binary/gender-queer people in similar ways. This provides us with some insight into the emergence of queer theory in the 1990s as a means of critically responding to the constraints of heteronormativity, which has lent itself to further dichotomising of embodiment and sexuality in the twenty-first century.

Queer theory offers useful contributions to an ecologised masculinities theory that prioritises broader approaches to care. Judith Halberstam's (1998) *Female Masculinity* discussed the issue of gender identity from a queer perspective by suggesting that definitions of 'masculinity' viewed through social, cultural or political expressions of the self should not be restricted by the male body and its impacts on the world. She noted the ways that traditional masculine socialisations have colonised women's bodies, extending the entitlements of hegemonic masculinities to include access and control over women's reproductive rights along with the health and medical policies and practices that impact them (Halberstam, 1998: 1–2).[5] This is alarming precisely because – as queer theorists attest – 'masculinity' ought to be considered a construct that 'engages, inflects, and shapes everyone' and 'is not the property of men', but rather, offers us ways of engaging with the world through internalised privilege, power and control. For queer theorists, masculinity is then something manufactured for the explicit purpose of soliciting social, economic and political gains (Halberstam, 1998: 13–14, 16). The capacity to reflect on the self beyond categorisations is to exercise the right to be or choose gendered or sexual orientations at will, which, queer theory argues, frees us to 'create a society that accepts difference, welcomes diversity, and champions human rights' that echoes the most resilient of ecosystems (Kirsch, 2000: 8–9). Halberstam (2005) envisaged expressions of identities freed from the influences of heteronormativity – where people and their intimate affiliations would be welcomed and embraced across a broad mosaic of possibilities. In this sense, queer theory directly challenges male domination as little more than 'manufactured illusions' of the self, tightly coupled with hegemonic gains. Queer theory continues to aspire to societal equanimity that is not only post-gendered, but also post-heterosexual, seeking to manifest a world that embraces different and non-traditional ways of being in relationship with other human beings, both conceptually and viscerally. In confronting the power base of hegemonic masculinities through collective and connective approaches to self-identity, queer theory forges solidarity that reaches beyond traditional binaries of woman and man, female and male, femininity and masculinity and homosexual and heterosexual (Kirsch, 2000: 9). In this sense, queer theory is post-structural, seeking to advance individuation beyond contemplative self-discovery in men, women and non-binary/genderqueer people by directly confronting heteronormativity, effectively usurping traditional prescriptions of identity and orientation (Berlant and Warner, 1995: 344). Given the infinite complexities of nature that are echoed in human societies, this gendered plasticity has many useful implications for Earthcare as well.

As the discourse has grown, some interpretations of queer theory have extrapolated care for human others beyond difference to the level of environmental care as well. In her book, *Strange Natures: Futurity, Empathy, and the Queer Ecological Imagination*, Nicole Seymour (2013) critically explored the nuances of queer environmentalism in contemporary fictions. Seymour stated that these fictions capitalise on the notion of wilderness/nature and the queer human body as equally threatened by capitalist domestication. She argued that the:

> . . . shirking of stable identities, epistemologies and ontologies (moves for which critical theory and queer theory in particular, are well known and which have arguably sparked a 'post-identity' culture) might lend itself most effectively to empathetic, politicized advocacy for the nonhuman natural world.
>
> (Seymour, 2013: 184)

From this statement, we conclude that ecological masculinities has much to gain from queer theory. This pluralistic approach to closeness among humans beyond traditional boundaries facilitates more authentic levels of care in the broader context (Mellström, 2014). This includes human relations that can – when drawn to their logical conclusions – be extended to the human–nature relationship as well. Consequently, queer theory frames care for humans and other-than-human others through the pursuit of intimate closeness with fellow human beings, effectively reaching beyond traditional renditions of gender identity. Our notion of ecological masculinities acknowledges the demarcations between categories of men and masculinities – such as gendered and sexual identities – as socio-material constructs, the boundaries of which can (and ought to) be confronted and transformed. Like queer theorists, we advocate a diversity of views and actions reflective of the trajectory of discussions on non-heteronormativity as we reconfigure understandings of men and masculinities in alignment with masculine ecologisation (Butler, 2017).

Of course, LGBTIQA+ communities have been on the front line of struggles with malestream norms along side women and Earth. They have challenged power differentials and asserted their rights to equal treatment – the successes of which are gathering momentum globally. A similar process of challenging the institutionalised power structures of masculine hegemonisation has unfolded for those concerned about masculinities and race, which we turn our attention to next.

Decolonisation of masculinities

Some masculinities theorists have considered masculine socialisations in the context of race relations. Human social constructs have long hegemonised along the lines of light to dark, good to bad, worthy to marginal, desirable to reprehensible binaries in both physical and socio-cultural contexts (DiPiero, 2002: 13). In each instance within binaries such as these, being white, Western and male equates to being located as prime beneficiary. Informed by a working definition posited by the People's Institute for Survival and Beyond

(2017) – an ending-racism collective based in New Orleans, US – we use the term 'racism' here to refer to race prejudices combined with unequal access to economic power meaning that only white people can be racist. This has been a topic of contention since long before the civil rights movement, where the mechanisms of oppression associated with racism have at times cauterised even the most benevolent of causes, prioritising white privilege and institutionalising access to resources in ways that have systematically marginalised people of colour throughout human history. Those scholars and activists most interested in masculinities and race have made it evident that 'whiteness' and 'blackness' are socially constructed categories that reflect cultural, political, sexual and ethnic mechanisms of oppression (Connell, 2016). Racism concocts images of men of colour as the 'alien other, as undesirable residents in the green fields and shires of imaginary [white] community', positioning black, brown and indigenous men as threats to white 'manliness' resulting in their colonisation and the quarantining of white society through genocide, slavery and personal/institutional marginalisation through, at times, the most unapologetically violent of legal and socio-cultural means (Marriott, 1996: 189; Dobratz and Shanks-Meile, 2000).

Overt and covert messages within cultures of white masculine hegemonisation have traditionally bolstered suggestions that colonised men are eyesores who are out of place, unwelcomed and inferior; mere heathens historically considered second-class 'noble savages' at best, or subhuman at worst. The sovereignty of men of colour and thousands of generations of intimate indigenous socio-cultural and ecological wisdom has been assaulted by colonial desires to make of them 'fine servants' for God(s), kings and economies, as European desires to expand the reach of their respective empires spread across the globe (Marriott, 1996: 189–190; Hughes, 2003[1986]; Zinn, 2003[1980]). Notions of white supremacy drove European imperial expansion efforts as the people of the British Isles and continental Europe reached into the 'new' world, resulting in attempts to eliminate the cultural threat that men of colour have represented to white hegemonies (Stanovsky, 2007). The expulsion of black, brown and indigenous men from the valorisation of (white) male domination has subordinated them as 'toys' in the white man's hand or an amputation from the body of white normality (Fanon, 2002[1967]; Du Bois, 2007[1903]). The message of such rhetoric is fundamentally separatist and has recently reared its head in racist policies in Australia, the US and across Europe. Attempts to decolonise masculinities reveal the constraints placed upon men of colour as particularly acute expressions of racism that pervade male domination (Mac an Ghaill, 1994: 183). In this sense, current reactions to immigration policies across the Western world are far from new. Rather, they might be considered newer versions of the old and tired personal and institutional manifestations of racism that have pervaded the Western world for centuries, which in becoming increasingly visible in connection to environmental issues, are being reinvented anew (Rogers, 2008; Buckingham and Kulcur, 2009). Black, brown and indigenous scholars and activists are distinguishable for challenging these entrenched assumptions about gender and race relations in unison, arguing that any crises of masculinities that have resulted in the institutional decimation of people of colour have been generated by expressions of hegemonic oppression that collude with imperial and racial intents (Franklin, 1987: 155; Marriott, 1996: 185–186). For example, in Australia, Aboriginal people continue to be marginalised by white, Anglo-dominated society racially, economically, socially *and* culturally. In Sweden, the Sami are simultaneously subject to the machinations of colonisation as Swedish indigenous people, being subject to cultural as well as social and environmental oppressions along the same lines of racism that affect Australian Aboriginal people on the opposite side of the globe (Össbo and Lantto, 2011; Bird Rose, 2016; Sehlin MacNeil, 2017).

Scholars from this field have made contributions to our understandings of ethnic, familial and colonised community structures that reveal the nuances of the male 'other' who is not white (Marriott, 1996: 194). Recently, several gender scholars have introduced intersectionality into their analyses of environmental issues, not least in relation to the racial impacts of climate change (Kaijser and Kronsell, 2014; for overviews, also see Moosa and Tuana, 2014; Pearse, 2017). Consequently, we have much to learn from decolonisation theorists who have brought to our attention discourses on race and gender that remain highly relevant to this day (Tengan, 2002; Cariou et al., 2015). We note that some Western, mostly white, men have generated great wealth in the world and in doing so have typically exploited the labour of colonised black, brown and indigenous people, while drawing resource riches from the hinterlands of colonised nature. We also note that contemporary environmental movements offering resistance to these trends have largely become white phenomena as well, not because colonised people do not care for the environment but that racism has so successfully severed global majority ecological connections and painted people of colour into (largely urbanised) corners as colonies of the West have become nation states. This persistent exploitative trend has been counteracted by some men (but mostly women) wanting to break free from the viciousness of colonisation that still is with us to this day (Whyte, 2014; Claeys and Delgado Pugley, 2017).

Of course, the presence of deeply considered environmental care has been present among people of colour and indigenous communities throughout their histories. The contemporary flow of environmental (as distinct from political) refugees at the time of writing this book has been rapidly increasing, indicating a direct relationship between environmental circumstances and the livelihoods of people of colour from the Global South that are also the global majority (UNHCR, 2017). Indigenous people and people of colour have been living sustainably and, in the face of colonisation, organising resistance to their own and their homelands' exploitation for generations, not only through violent/non-violent conflict, but through legislative advocacy as well. Take for example millennia of environmental stewardship and immersion in the living environment by indigenous peoples the world over, of which Australian Aboriginal peoples are an obvious example, having lived in and with the multitude of biomes on that continent for more than 60,000 years (Lawlor, 1991).

Also consider the seventeen Principles of Environmental Justice, which were raised at the First National People of Color Environmental Leadership Summit in Washington, DC in October 1991; a landmark event sponsored by the United Church of Christ, the Commission for Racial Justice and proceedings editor, Charles Lee (Lee, 1991). We suggest that any discussion about ecological masculinities benefits from a critical analysis of the interplay between state-sanctioned institutions, racism and the otherisation of people of colour along with indigenous people. Also consider the racial and gendered implications of looming climate catastrophes; nations of the (non-European) Global South are at greatest risk, mitigation policies (or their ineffectiveness) primarily drafted by men (and some women) enthralled in neo-liberal ecological modernisation approaches we introduced in Chapter 2 (Rivera and Miller, 2007). Environmental movements in the Global North have consequently struggled to take on board the widest range of racial experiences possible (Di Chiro, 2008).

We have considered important issues raised by decolonisation combined with masculinities research, recognising that this is but an introduction to the complexities associated with this topic. For more thorough examinations of notions of race and masculinities (which fall outside the scope of this book, given its focus on reconfigurations of masculinities in the West beyond male-stream norms) we defer to scholars and activists of colonised heritages for more in-depth study of this important topic. We take this deferential approach intentionally, recognising that neither of us are of colonised heritages in Sweden (Martin) and Australia (Paul). We note the needed sensitivities of speaking to decolonisation concerns since issues of race and imperialism are awash with socio-cultural blind spots that we both consequently harbour. We recognise that to do this topic full justice requires specific understanding of cultural misappropriation along with historical legacies of colonised people and the tragedies that have afflicted their communities under the weight of centuries of racism. We acknowledge that the links between indigenous men, men of colour and Earthcare are acute, (pre)historic and grounded in immense Earth wisdoms that a discourse on masculine ecologisation has much to learn from. Ecological masculinities will benefit greatly from heeding the views on the human–nature relationship of colonised people and as a consequence we welcome contributions from those scholars and activists who possess greater expertise on this topic than do we.

Further to this introduction to the value of this analysis, we give some consideration to the problematic presence of cultural misappropriation in our consideration of the mythopoetic men's movement in the section that follows.

Men's mythopoetry and nature myth-making

The mythopoetic men's movement has diverse origins. The movement grew out of the psycho-spiritual tenets of Greek, Roman and Far Eastern mythologies as well as Euro-pagan fairy tales, the Jungian archetypal canon, along with transpersonal psychology. The term is a derivation of 'mythopoesis' that means to re-mythologise or remake, where 'mythopoeia' refers to the capacity to create myth or share a traditional story (Bliss, 1992: 95; Hoff, 1994; Bliss, 1995: 292–293; Hoff and Bliss, 1995). The movement is credited with making men's issues visible throughout Western popular culture, employing various theatrical and dramatic processes and pop-psychological techniques that aim to re-mythologise notions of masculinities, especially those of fellowship, camaraderie, service, purpose and self-empowerment. The movement emerged as a response to concerns about the alleged 'emasculating' impacts of second-wave feminism in imposing what some men saw as a 'reverse' sexual discrimination that was allegedly undercutting industrial/breadwinner masculinities. From simple beginnings in the 1960s, the movement gathered momentum in the 1980s, reaching a populist peak in the 1990s (particularly through the international spread of the ManKind Project), with contemporary residential and virtual variations (e.g. Tommorowman, the Shift Network's Ultimate Man Summit, the Brotherhood Community, the Crucible Project, Reclaim Your Inner Throne and the Authentic Man Program, to name but a few global permutations); experimenting with masculine identity, definitions of manhood, religiously inspired rites of passage, shamanic/underworld journeying and dating/sexuality/intimacy trainings (Gambill, 2005). Variations on these themes continue to unfold.

The mythopoetic men's movement was formalised by US men's leaders: Shepherd Bliss, Robert Bly, Robert Moore, Douglas Gillette, James Hillman and Michael Meade. At its core, the movement was built on Jungian and gestalt foundations, drawing on the archetypal King, Warrior, Magician and Lover quartet to usher in a revisionist men's liberation (Moore and Gillette, 1990). As the movement grew, processes and practices emerged that were designed to reawaken mythopoetically inspired renditions of the authentic masculine self through contemporary rites of passage (initially in natural settings though increasingly now through online international groups and individual coaching), accompanied with men's popular literature and protocols focused on men's personal growth, emotional release and therapeutic development (Bly, 1990; Ross, 1992). In practical terms, the mythopoetic men's movement has constructed elaborate rituals to support what many in the movement describe as a rise of the 'mature masculine' to transition from immature and insecure 'boy's psychology' to mature and well-adjusted 'man's psychology' where a life dedicated to being of service to the greater good can be accessed (Moore and Gillette, 1990). Men's mythopoetry has routinely used sweat lodge and talking stick circles, adopted animal names inspired by a potpourri of (borrowed and in some cases stolen) First Nations traditions (especially from North American indigenous traditions) and the adaptation of Earth-based rites through retreats and consciousness-raising gatherings (Moore and Gillette, 1990: xvi–xix; Wicks, 1996: 63–79; Ashe, 2007: 69). The foundations of the movement were built on the premise that the 'wild man' (the potent, instinctual and ancient voice of the authentic and powerful masculine self) must be awakened and his potency channelled in the direction of loving support for planet, people and self (Pease, 2002: 77). The movement emerged as a response to the sinister impacts of hegemonic masculinities (on both the world and on men themselves) that have socialised men to reach for greatness out in the world by building up themselves but, notably, was not critical of masculine socialisations to put others down.

The mythopoetic men's movement gained early notoriety through a 1986 *Yoga Journal* article written by Shepherd Bliss. There, Bliss attempted to explore alternatives to the 'toxic' or 'extreme' masculinities that have long characterised malestream norms, seeking 'real' and 'deep' masculine alternatives by awakening a more agrarian approach to life. Bliss suggested that the emerging movement harboured great potential to serve men and the world by engaging internal healing and recovery, which would awaken the 'deep masculine' aspect – that part of the self on a mission to serve the planet in customised ways reflective of each man's unique life history and leadership (Bliss, 1995: 300–301, 302). The movement aimed to cauterise the hubris of 'great man' thinking and behaviours on men's lives. Contemporary social commentaries in response to these aims like those offered by Rebecca Solnit (2017a; Solnit, 2017b; Solnit, 2017c) are instructive (see Box 3.1).

We acknowledge that Bliss introduced the beginnings of a personal/political conversation to the then fledgling mythopoetic men's movement (Bliss, 1987). With this, he did not blame men for the world's woes. Steering away from condemning masculinities in an interview with Bert Hoff, Bliss essentialised his vision for a healthier and kinder masculinity by claiming that the:

> . . . historic male role of the Protector, which when taken in excess could be a problem, is a positive image. The Protector, the Husbandman. The men who till the Earth, take care of the Earth, not as nurturers but as generators. There's that regenerating quality. I make a distinction between the nurturing that women do and generating that men do. We need to think about biodiversity in human-kind. We think about it mainly in terms of wildlife and nature. But humans are a part of nature. We need to apply some of the thinking in the environmental circles to Men's Work and some of the thinking in Men's Work to environmental circles . . . I'd like us to bring that more into the mass culture and environmental awareness. We as men both individually and in our movement have a lot to offer to our society as a whole.
>
> (Hoff and Bliss, 1995)

Through statements such as this, Bliss exposed some of the earliest visions for 'ecomasculinity' and its earnest pursuit for improved lives for men and others. He echoed Thoreau's pronouncement that '[a]ll good things are wild and free . . . Give me for my friends and neighbours wild men, not tame ones' (Bliss, 1989: 10). Effectively, Bliss's efforts centred on bringing men home to Earth, each other and themselves. He beckoned the Earth Father back from the sky (our Father who art in Heaven); the Uncle back to nephew (the one who helps, advises and inspires); the Husband back to the hearth (the one who protects and provides by being attentive to familial needs) (Bliss, 1989: 11). This

Blissian 'ecoman' was fresh and spontaneous, vital and alive – as opposed to the brutal savagery of the soldier or the beaten-down passivity of the working man – he was an antidote offering great salve 'to our over-civilized, over-urbanized, over-organized, too-rational society [who] can be life-enhancing and planet-protecting' (Bliss, 1989: 10).

Box 3.1 Great man? Toxic man

In a *Guardian* article, Rebecca Solnit (2017c) exposed the limitations of a 'great man' ethos that she also referred to as a 'toxic' or 'extreme' masculinity.

There, responding to the public eruption of allegations of sexual assault against Hollywood producer Harvey Weinstein (along with unfolding claims against Roger Ailes, Woody Allen, Bill Cosby, Peter Madsen, Bill O'Reilly, Roy Moore and others) and highlighting the one-year anniversary of similar allegations against the then candidate and now US President Donald Trump, Solnit examined the propensity for some men to be aroused by their capacities to inflict pain and humiliation on women in particular. She noted a pervading absence of empathy, an addictive attraction to domination, an insatiable appetite for control and a complete disregard for causing harm towards others that some men seem willing to embrace as their due. Solnit acknowledged the role that mental illness may play in some cases, but pointed us towards the more alarming and broader consideration that these behaviours may in fact be culturally instilled in men writ large; a perverse means of asserting power, elevating status, demeaning others and presuming that such behaviour is an entitlement for some to hurt and destroy those they dominate in order to achieve societally sanctioned greatness.

Solnit's argument proceeded to raise the sceptre of the great man as an example of 'extreme masculinity'. She argued that this characterisation is something we have been living with for millennia that provides vehicles for taking male domination to a supposed 'logical conclusion'; the products of great isolation and loneliness afflicting men that divorces them from their care for others and strips them of their capacity to empathise, love and be selfless, representing a toxic cocktail of socialisations that may well be rewarded socio-economically and politically, but is relationally devastating and ultimately a consequence of someone whose inner state is in fact quite fragile. Solnit suggested that when men act in these extreme ways they are confined within their own perpetration as much as they are punishers of others. She called for a new way forth for men, one where the fear of getting caught acting out is replaced with the elimination of a desire for these behaviours to arise in the first place. In this particular article, she does not take the next step of sharing with us her vision for how men might get there.

However, it is our view that Bliss (and his colleagues) overly relied on mytho-poetry to solve our social and ecological problems. While he encouraged men's

Earth-preserving activities (such as anti-nuclear activism, environmental con-servation and animal rights advocacy), these broader and more systemic applica-tions of the work on offer did not gather momentum. Instead and by the movement's peak in the 1990s, few deep encounters with otherised human and other-than-human others were formalised – men's weekend workshops using nature as a 'backdrop' for the theatre of men's healing from their inner wounds rather than reframing the intrinsic value and agency of others that calls forth the need for our utmost care of all life. A central argument has persisted within the movement that feminism has successfully challenged male domination to the point of instigating confusion in many men about their manhood. The movement has argued that feminism has compelled men to meet the politicised and raised expectations of some feminists, pressuring them to become soft 'wimps' in exchange for approval and acceptance. This has resulted in backlashes towards women and feminists as well as profeminist men from within the ranks of mytho-poetry (Ross, 1992: 209–219). We return to these considerations in Chapter 7.

Additional criticism has ensued about the apolitical tendencies of the mytho-poetic men's movement (Kimmel, 1996; Clatterbaugh, 1997). While aspiring to be relevant to men from a diversity of backgrounds, the movement has remained particularly attractive to middle-aged, straight men of the Western, white, work-ing and middle classes (Pease, 2002: 77). Over the last twenty-five years and based on my (Paul speaking here) personal participation in mythopoetry on multiple occasions, I have encountered very few non-binary/genderqueer people as well as minimal to no men of colour represented among the movement's leaders and participants, or who have found a long-term 'home' for themselves in such com-munities. This is a demographic trend that was present in the movement from its early days and appears to have persisted to this day.

In an astute observation that still holds true, Michael Kimmel and Michael Kaufman (1994: 284) suggested that the movement conveniently sidestepped the personal/political insights of feminists. Speaking of the movement's founders, Kimmel and Kaufman noted that men's mythopoetry failed to:

> . . . hear what women have been telling men . . . that personal change is an indispensable element of, and tool for, social change, and that struc-tural social change is an indispensable element for personal change. It is a personal vision of political change and a political vision of personal change that we propose as an alternative to [mythopoesis] . . . that will allow men's wild and progressive impulses to blossom . . . What keeps Bly and his followers from taking this radical course of personal and social change are his protests that his work has nothing to do with women or feminism . . . But such claims are disingenuous.
>
> (Kimmel and Kaufman, 1994: 274)

Further, Kimmel noted that the absence of socio-political analyses to usurp misogyny in direct and strategic ways also ignored the homogeneous nature of the movement, instituting instead 'everything from anti-feminist backlash and patriarchy redux to racist appropriation, misleading theology, misguided anthropology and misogynist political ideology' as features of the movement that have collectively cast a shadow over its potency and potential (Kimmel, 1995: xi–xii). We add that, but for a few isolated and autonomous examples to the contrary, the movement has similarly failed to build an effective, respectful and mutually empowering bridge between Western white and first nations cultural elements, many of which have shaped its rites and rituals. Juxtaposing the mythopoets against a more politically engaged (profeminist) approach to unpacking masculinities, Ashe (2007: 76–82) emphasised that both women and men have long been otherised as a function of the policies and practices generated by male domination in everyday life, suggesting that it is in men's best interests to address injustices for their own benefit as well. Further, segregating men off into men-only spaces for inner personal work can, in the absence of acute socio-political analyses to call men's roles in structural oppressions to account, leave misogyny and sexism weakly challenged, unchallenged or even emboldened (think here of uninterrupted 'locker room' talk) – effectively replicating the very mechanisms of oppression that pervade malestream society in the wide world within these well-intended consciousness-raising journeys.

Reflective of these identifiable contradictions, critiques of the mythopoetic men's movement abound. Connell (1995: 13) considered the mythopoets to be a type of 'masculinity therapy' reminiscent of a belief that modern Western masculinities are broken and in need of urgent repair. The demographic monoculturing of men's mythopoesis has continued to characterise the movement. With that, we identify two key problems: the cultural appropriation of indigenous rites and rituals to improve men's lives. With this we have also seen the reification of heteronormativity throughout the movement – if not through overt homophobia, then due to the exclusionary nature of heteronormative men's subcultures, effectively conveying hegemonisation throughout the movement whose intent has all along been to liberate men; to free them from their bonds to mechanistic performance. In other words, men's mythopoetry has persistently struggled to reach the depths of ontological and practical ecologisation that could have pointed us in the direction of a deep green future of both social and environmental significance; one where social equities are a given and Earth honourings are gifted and developed with cross-cultural sensitivities, incorporated into the rites and rituals practised accordingly and from there radiated out into the world (Pulé and Hultman, forthcoming). Sadly, there is still much ground to be gained across the movement.

However, we are seeing some signs that these sorts of shifts are taking place throughout men's mythopoetry – at least incrementally. The personal internalisation of deep ecology discussed in Chapter 4 suggests that as a result of their participation in some men's consciousness-raising weekends, individuals are detecting the importance of precisely these levels of transformation that have affirming personal and political consequences. As an example, consider this rousing testimonial from Urs Blumer (pers. comm., 19/11/17) from the back-end of a mid-coast New South Wales (Australia) mythopoetic weekend retreat he attended. That training incorporated local Aboriginal ceremony shared with participants by traditional indigenous custodians that incorporated biocentric rites and rituals throughout the processes engaged:

> I am checking out [signing off] with deep gratitude for . . . this amazing land which has received us all so generously. I felt a powerful connection to spirit through the mother, the plants, the sky and the ocean. I honor the beautiful land of Australia and the peoples who have walked on the face of the mother thousands of years before any pale faced adventurers came. I admire the way they learnt to live in harmony with the land, the animals and the plants, wishing we ourselves were still able to learn to be in good relationship today – i[*sic*] fear the modern man will need much more time to understand . . . I especially wish to express my gratitude to the [Australian Aboriginal] people of the Gumbaynggirr for their hospitality and generous sharing of their gifts in so many ways.

Of course, the presence of a Mother Earth metaphor suggests degrees of essentialism run strong in the movement still, and how such insights translate into structural changes on personal or organisational levels are yet to be seen. Certainly, the degree of cultural shift that we advocate appears to not be present throughout men's mythopoetry at this time. However, we recognise that renditions of broader, deeper and wider Earthcare might be possible through mythopoetic forms of men's work, given sufficient support at the senior levels of international leadership across the movement (Dennis Beros, pers. comm., 19/11/17). The absence of frontal changes to men's structural impacts on the world has persevered at organisational levels; men throughout the movement have remained largely unmarked in pursuit of self and communal reflection and as a consequence have routinely returned to their lives where male domination continues to run roughshod over people and the planet without adequate intervention.

Clearly Bliss's preliminary approaches to masculine ecologisation did not achieve the levels of planetary transformation he hoped for. The movement is now approximately 40 years old and our social and environmental problems have drastically worsened. We suggest that in the attempt to help men's lives go well, the ecomasculinity of Blissian mythopoetry and its applications throughout the movement fell on deaf ears. Referring back to Solnit's *Guardian* article summarised in Box 3.1, it is clear that mythopoetry has stopped short of frontally addressing male domination and its impacts on otherised others by not centralising the reconfiguration of masculinities away from the toxic sentiments of great man thinking. Speaking from first-hand experience, we have both witnessed this phenomenon of socio-political watering down and denial that Solnit suggests on numbers of occasions at men's mythopoetry events online and in Australia, the US, the UK and Sweden. In solidarity with our profeminist colleagues, we problematise a general sense of inertia that pervades the mythopoetic men's movement from a socio-environmental perspective. These omissions demonstrate how difficult it is for men to bite the hand (of male domination) that feeds them.

Similar concerns can be levelled at Christian masculinities as well.

Christian dogmatic and environmental traditions

Intensive critiques levelled at Christians (and Christian men in particular) have positioned them as some of modernity's prime antagonists (White Jr., 1967; Merchant, 1980; Gray, 1982; Bullough, 1994; Gaard, 1997; Stearns, 2001). Lynn White Jr. (1967) emphasised the anti-ecological implications of an incorporeal existence that has been championed by Christian dogma for centuries. When viewed in the context of Western history, the natural theology of Christianity was the product of transcendence and mastery over nature, not integration with it (White Jr., 1967: 1206). Greta Gaard's (1997) 'Toward a Queer Ecofeminism' offered a useful synopsis of the terror rained down upon women, homosexuals, pagans and the like in a bid to install a 'holy order' upon the world, with Christian men at its pinnacle (second only to God). We agree that the Christian tradition has been centrally complicit in promoting a disembodied way of viewing the self in the world throughout most of Western history (Hitzhusen, 2007). This approach has resulted in severe consequences for us all, especially the world's poor, non-Western, female (feminised and racially marginalised and indigenous) peoples, along with our other-than-human compatriots in particular. It is our contention that primary causes of our global struggles are economic and gendered, but that they have religious origins as well (Kimmel and Ferber, 2000). After all, Christianity is centrally complicit in the formulation of anthropocentrism at the expense of nature, bolstered by an erroneous assumption that humanity is closer to God in heaven than to the 'simpler' creatures of Earth. But this is not the entire story for a Christian gendered/Earth analysis.

Challenging a general presumption in progressive quarters that Christianity has been oppressive towards both humanity and nature, we also consider some evidence to give us cause to appreciate elements of Christian contributions to social and environmental justice (Moncrief, 1970; McCammack, 2007). We note that Christian masculinities can be critically examined as another variation of Earthcare, although more anthropocentric than our vision for ecological masculinities. Consider the two notions of stewardship and ecotheology. Stewardship became intricately interwoven with the practice of Earth resource extraction, where men in particular (with Adam as God's creation and Eve an afterthought drawn from his rib in order to accompany him on Earth) were mandated to mind, supervise and care for God's bounties on Earth as possessions to be tamed and managed, an image reiterated to legitimise, for example, the Swedish nuclear industry (Wardekker et al., 2009; Anshelm, 2010). Stewardship positions nature as resource in service to humanity (Lovelock, 1979: 119–123; Callahan 1981: 73–85; Golding 1981: 61–72). The concept implies care even if from the vantage of human separateness from the other-than-human world. Stewardship elements of Christian dogma are built on traditional presumptions that human existence is the consequence of a dualised battle between Godly purity and a fall from grace in the Garden of Eden. This Christian story is one of human flourishing pitted against the darkness of the world and the wilds of nature; the struggle between good and evil, right and wrong, the saved and the sinner, etc. Unfortunately, these binary foundations of Christianity have pointed men and masculinities in the direction of separation rather than communion, charging individuals with the task of defeating the powers of the Devil by taking up the 'whole armour of God' as if a war to won (Ephesians 6:10–18).

Throughout the history of modernity, countless wars have been fought in the name of Christian ideals (Keen, 1984; Nicholson, 2001). The righteousness that justified battle was reified by the chivalrous virtues of the Christian knight during the Middle Ages, who emerged as an idealised masculinity celebrated for his capacity to turn his sword, wrought in the image of the Crucifix, into a weapon for Christian salvation – a form of stewardship that has been infused within the imagery and actions of men in service to God through both life (love for sovereign and country) and death (slaying of mythical dragons, heathens and foes or being willing to die doing so). Despite these tense origins, stewardship has since become a sentinel of Christian Earthcare, continuing to engage us with myriad living things with which we share our corporeal lives (Berry ed., 2006). Christian dogma can be interpreted as viewing other-than-human nature (an assumed feminine principle) as a 'corruption' or 'wildness' that is synonymous with ungodliness, which is consequently in need of our great care, cultivation and management to reap God's bounties on Earth (Merchant, 1996: 75–79). Here, we note a parallel between a protective approach towards 'meek' women as well as 'fragile' nature, both of which called forth the condescending, firm and guiding hand of man (in God's image on Earth) to impose management and control. As a Christian-dominated culture, the socio- and eco-political tenets of the West have been significantly guided by stewardship logics. The wildness of nature has long been considered something to fear and master. The Christian charge to be 'fruitful and multiply, and fill the earth, and subdue it' (Genesis, 1:28) forms the bedrock of many nations in the Global North and is (arguably) an original source for the unfettered economic growth edict that characterises capitalism. Through a Christian creationist world view, Earth was located as material to eat, chop, plough, fish and play with on our way to Heaven; compelling humanity to use nature as a springboard to salvation.

The combined efforts to wed Christian dogma with Earthcare has been poignantly articulated by the great US proponent of environmental conservation, Aldo Leopold (1966[1949]). Leopold was one of the founding fathers of preservation as environmental practice. His classic text that is arguably one of the most influential environmental texts of all time, *A Sand County Almanac*, illuminated the importance of land reverence as an integral aspect of a righteous and godly life. As a devout Christian land carer and natural resource manager, Leopold was instrumental in setting the tone for a Christian interpretation of Western natural resource management principles and practices. He extolled our need to become conscious students of the land that sustains us by developing a reverence, knowledge and care for the land, which contradicted the growing materialism of Western industrial nations and their accompanying and ever-growing threats of environmental destruction (1966[1949]: xxviii–xix). Leopoldian Earthcare was couched initially in the then young US Forest Service land manager's concern for dwindling natural resources. But, later in life, Leopold's growing intimate relationship with his impoverished farm in Minnesota yielded what he came to refer to as a 'Land Ethic' that has since become the steward's creed: 'A thing is right when it tends to preserve the integrity, stability and beauty of the biotic community. It is wrong when it tends otherwise' (1966[1949]: 262; Roach 2003: 18). Such an ethic is compelling, even if condescending towards other-than-human others, in the presumed benefit of caring human interventions.

As another Christian approach to nature, ecotheology offers us additional starting points that have some similarities to material feminisms and post-humanities approaches (O'Brien, 2004; Cappel et al., 2016).[6] This interpretation of Christian scripture ascribes degrees of inherent worth to a heterogenic Earth. Ecotheologians prioritise elements of the Creation myth that suggest our charge is to cultivate and care for the Earth (Genesis, 1:28; 2:15). Drawing direct links to the pagan Earth-based traditions, ecotheology encourages adaptations of nature-based celebrations, such as: Christ's birthday correlated with winter solstice, Easter correlated with spring equinox, as well as the long-identified entwining of many other Earth-based spiritual traditions with the doctrines and rituals of Christian faith (Herskovits, 1937). Ecotheological support for social and environmental justice issues has, in many instances, been drawn directly from biblical instruction to dedicate one's self to a life of service focused on improving human life and Earth's bounties. This moral imperative found its strongest support in the teachings of the Italian Roman Catholic friar, Giovanni di Pietro di Bernardone (*c*.1181–1226 AD), who became St. Francis of Assisi; the most renowned of Christian patrons for animals and nature (Haluza-DeLay, 2008). Further, in '*Laudato Si':* on care for our common home', Pope Francis (2015) delivered a moving encyclical, supporting greater human care towards Earth as a theologically considered response to global social and ecological problems. Calling for an 'ecological conversion', the pontiff made the following bold proclamation:

> . . . the ecological crisis is also a summons to profound interior conversion. It must be said that some committed and prayerful Christians, with the excuse of realism and pragmatism, tend to ridicule expressions of concern for the environment. Others are passive; they choose not to change their habits and thus become inconsistent. So what they all need is an 'ecological conversion', whereby the effects of their encounter with Jesus Christ become evident in their relationship with the world around them. Living our

vocation to be protectors of God's handiwork is essential to a life of virtue; it is not an optional or a secondary aspect of our Christian experience.

(Pope Francis, 2015: 158–159)

In response to multilateral talks to address global social and environmental concerns raised at COP23, the Bonn Climate Change Conference (November 2017), Pope Francis expressed his view that US president Donald Trump and his administration's isolationist climate change denialism are on par with 'flat Earth truthers', voicing a pontiff's decree imploring the world's 1.2 billion Catholics to embrace responsible ecotheological interpretations of the Bible's teachings by looking beyond unnecessary consumption, destructive human development initiatives and the alarming threats facing humanity and the environment due to human-induced biodiversity loss and global warming (Pope Francis, 2015; also see Li et al., 2016; Kuruvilla, 2017; Schuldt et al., 2017). It is telling that Pope Francis has drawn his greatest inspirations from Saint Francis of Assisi.

Both stewardship and ecotheological traditions continue to play important roles in shaping Christian canon. Together, they contribute to our understanding of our place within myriad living systems upon which we depend (even if through a hegemonised 'Great Chain of Being' from God to man/woman, to animals, to plants and so forth). We see that the gendered fundamentalism of Christian dogma can conjure conservative interpretations of the Bible that have amplified the hegemonisation of human societies as God's 'gardeners' on Earth that not only position men above women but also distances humanity from other-than-human nature. However, we also note that stewardship and, even more so, ecotheology provide greener paths forward offering considerable encouragement for Christians the world over to honour, celebrate and take great care of God's Earthen gifts, while also caring for each other and ourselves. Granted, the dogmatic side of Christian masculinities has emphasised anthropocentric (indeed androcentric) control over nature, society, marginalised humans and the self in alignment with malestream norms. But, as we have demonstrated here, these constraints are juxtaposed against more politically progressive views of stewardship and ecotheology. Given these elements of Christian world views prioritise (w)holiness and interdependency where life beyond humanity has agency, it is possible that stewardship and ecotheology might find some synergies with the biocentricity of ecological masculinities that we advocate, meaning Christian masculinities cannot be entirely positioned as oppositional to the theories and practices we purport throughout this book.

Last to be considered in this chapter is men's rights masculinities. Located on the far-right of masculinities politics, we proceed to examine this positionality next.

Men's rights groups (toxic/extreme masculinities unleashed)

Men's rights activists (or MRAs) emerged through tense links between 'angry white men', family law, political extremism, domestic terrorism and backslashes against the gains in women's and LGBTIQA+ rights (Messner, 1997; Kimmel, 2013). These groups argue that men are the big losers in contemporary society at the hands of 'reverse sexism' and the eroding of traditional family values in a dichotomising world (Clatterbaugh, 1997: 11–12). The masculinities of these groups commonly share vocal opposition to 'politically correctness' (Keskinen, 2013; Friedersdorf, 2017). Those who subscribe to this view consider that society is placating to feminism and women are taking advantage of men both personally and politically. They argue that this problem is most evident in the alleged mistreatment of some fathers who – they claim – have been deprived of their paternal rights and subjected to systematic discrimination in family law courts, with the explicit intention of marginalising men when spousal separations occur (Boyd and Sheehy, 2016). Men's rights groups are currently experiencing an international resurgence largely in alignment with alt-right movements, involuntarily celibates (or 'incels'), Men Going Their Own Way (MGTOW) groups, culture warriors like Jordon Peterson, white supremacy advocates and neo-fascist groups throughout the Global North (Messner, 2016; Köttig et al. eds., 2017; Williams, 2018). The most extreme of these groups are to be found in the US, where men's rights masculinities formed initially to facilitate family law court reforms in opposition to legislation that – they argue – favour women unfairly and have, in some cases, adopted domestic terrorism tactics as hallmarks of their responses (Ashe, 2007: 57). The foreboding view of these groups is a perception that legal, cultural and economic reforms that aim to even the playing field between women and men are in fact resulting in reverse oppression, placing men as victims that some MRA proponents find enragingly reprehensible.

Men's rights groups are not organised into a cohesive movement per se. Rather, they represent nodes of reactive politics that tend to attract men who have felt hard done by at work or home and are wanting to fight back in the company of other men in order to restore their sense of primacy. These groups have a long history (Dragiewicz and Mann, 2016). Charles V. Metz's (1968) pamphlet, *Divorce and Custody for Men*, frontally attacked feminism and emphasised the 'traditional social roles' of women and men in the context of the need to return to gendered traditions at home and in society. Richard Doyle's (1976) *Rape of the Male* was also influential, building on Metz's traditionalist views, arguing that men are victimised by and subject to misandry and anti-male discrimination. Doyle argued that fear and false accusations pervade men's alleged penchant for sexual misconduct – shifting focus away from sexual assault data and towards the supposed invitations of the victim, resulting in his forming the Men's Defense Association. By the mid 1980s, the National Coalition of Free Men, Divorce Reform Busters, the Men's Rights Association, the Lone Fathers Association, Coalition of American Divorce Reform Elements and Men's Equality Now (which grew into the Coalition of Free Men and Men's Rights Incorporated), emerged as a cadre of outspoken defenders of men's rights. These organisations shared a common agenda that focused on the validation of biological determinism and with it the proclaimed 'natural order' of male domination. They also challenged the political legitimacy of feminism, suggesting that men were – and far from its primary beneficiaries – deeply wounded by contemporary Western society (Farrell, 1974). Building on his previous MRA efforts, Doyle went on to publish a recent book titled *Doyle's War: Save the Males* (2016) where he argued that feminism is a hoax, men's chivalry is misplaced, and restoring equal rights for men is the only salvation for traditional family values, manly virtues and indeed the very survival of civilisation. With the support of such views, these groups continue to champion male domination emboldened by the current resurgence of right wing politics throughout the West. With recent repeals of policies and practices to support gender equity in the US under the Trump administration, we are witnessing the reassertion of control over women's reproductive rights with renewed vigour, particularly by men aligned with this positionality, rendering men's rights activism a wholesale assault on social justice.

Men's rights groups capitalise on a belief that men no longer matter and have been tossed aside, forgotten, ignored and blamed (Dragiewicz and Mann, 2016; Jordan, 2016). The positionality prioritises the plight of working men, who they commonly frame as law-abiding, tax-paying and actively engaged in machinations of society, as targeted, shunned, shamed, persecuted and forgotten (Root, 2016). Their common narrative is the product of valorised gendered traditionalism, characterised by defensiveness and resistance towards responsibility, accountability, and/or attempts to bring about gender equity. We find these sentiments of defensiveness and victimisation to be highly destructive – accentuating the culture wars and driving women, non-binary/genderqueers and men further apart by prioritising differences ahead of cooperation towards gender equity while giving little to no mention of the real costs of male domination on the glocal commons. These various sources of internalised victimisation have propelled members of men's rights groups to bring to bear all the mechanisms of oppression at their disposal to allegedly 'turn the tide' back in working (white) men's favour – to allow the wind to be at men's backs once again (Kimmel, 2008). The claim that men have lost privilege at all is of course nothing more than convenient cherry-picking. Cries of reverse sexism, reverse racism and men's emasculation are, in fact, reactions to limited nominal gains in gender, race and sexual equality; they have no basis in accurate factual analyses, relying instead on contortions of pockets of unsubstantiated data to proffer inflections of lost power and control by a system allegedly pitted against men. Despite this, the proponents of these groups have conveyed – at times – violent backlashes driven by heavy doses of 'aggrieved entitlement' (Kimmel, 2013: 75). They have gained popularity through garnering sympathy and support for men who have struggled (often quietly and for some time) with deep-seated isolation. We suggest that it is more likely the case that recent MRA backed resurgences of male domination are little more than blatant refusal by some men who have traditionally been the prime beneficiaries of masculine hegemonisation to 'be dragged kicking and screaming into the inevitable future' of heterogeneity

(Kimmel, 2013: xii). Instead, MRAs have called for a return to the 'golden age' of industrial/breadwinner hegemonisation (Ashe, 2007: 61). Their proponents claim that the privileges of men and traditional notions of masculinity should not be contested. They justify such claims by citing 'historical legacy, religious fiat, biological destiny and moral legitimacy' of men throughout Western history in forging the power base of male domination that many (white working- and middle-class) men are extremely reluctant to relinquish (Kimmel, 2001: 27). For the purposes of developing our arguments in support of ecological masculinities, we consider men's rights groups to be broadly anti-feminist and overtly misogynistic. In order to articulate an effective ecologised masculinities theory, it is vital that we gain clarity about the drivers of these expressed sentiments of victimisation. With that knowledge, we can then more effectively position ecological masculinities as a support to growing global efforts to achieve gender equity, and greater Earthcare as viable alternatives to these extreme forms of masculinities. This exposes the paradox that many men who align themselves with men's right arguments are in fact projecting their discontents on those subordinated by a sexist, racist, homophobic industrialised hegemony rather than recognising that their lives are in fact being damaged by the very same systemic mechanisms that they are using to reassert their primacy. In this sense, a critical analysis of this movement is particularly useful in helping us interrogate the collapsing of men's victimisation with toxic/extreme beliefs and actions that have the capacity to cause considerable global, regional, local interpersonal and personal harm. We also recognise that men and masculinities associated with this positionality are likely to be some of the most difficult masculinities to engage in exit politics through a process of ecologisation as we formulate it here, since many of the politicised platforms that characterise this positionality are antithetical to the broader, deeper and wider care that we advocate.

Bringing Earth into masculinities politics

Throughout this chapter, we have examined a cross section of research traditions and categories within masculinities politics. We have noted a range of views that expose the ways that male domination consolidates privilege, wealth, power and control over the means of production, women, non-binary/gender-queer people, as well as otherised men. Each analysis we offered considered the characteristics of that positionality relative to an emergent ecologised masculinities theory and its associated practices. It is noteworthy however that none offers a clearly defined approach to masculine ecologisation; references to nature and Earthcare are at best incidental and secondary to other agendas that each positionality holds dear. We note that under the auspices of unchallenged male domination, men will continue to occupy roles that penetrate other-than-human places as frontiersmen, inquisitors, investigators and masters over nature. We also note that when folded into masculinities analyses, nature tends to serve as a place to escape from the straitjacketing of masculine hegemonisation; after all, going 'bush' is often used as a salve for a persistent sense of insufficiency that can accompany contemporary masculinies and materialistic lives (Campbell and Mayerfield Bell, 2000).

We have demonstrated here that the various views that characterise masculinities politics reveal the benefits (for men) and costs (to them and others) of masculine hegemonisation. This is particularly evident when stood against measures of gender, race, politics, religion and legal standing to which we can also add issues of class, sexuality, violence, crime, education, family, popular media and militarism (Kimmel and Aronson, 2004; Connell and Pearse, 2014). As cracks in the substrate of hegemonised masculinities grow throughout civil society and in alignment with our burgeoning social and ecological crises, turning our attention to nature purely for respite, as done largely via the mythopoetic movement, will not suffice since when left unchallenged, men and masculinities take with them to the frontiers of nature the same mechanism of domination that can assault the lives of those who are otherised. As Kimmel and Kaufman (1994: 261) so eloquently put it, in the so-called 'untamed' wilds of other-than-human nature, men and masculinities could 'stake a new claim for manhood' in natural places but in doing so tend to engage similar mechanisms of conquest dressed up in green garb. Conquests (both within the civilised world and beyond) bring with them some (at least temporary) good feelings for the victor, since, in the wilds of nature, men and masculinities get to revel in the thrill of the chase as a rehearsal of societal domination through the ecstatic experience of the successful kill. At the frontier, just as in social arrangements awash with male domination, men and masculinities get to score, bag, cop, earn, prowl, stalk, know, long for, desire, plunder, plough and even rape, just as they do in number in society towards human others. Left unchecked, these patterns readily emerge regardless of the particular positionality a discussion on men and masculinities might examine (Flannigan-Saint-Aubin 1994: 241). To address this adequately, an ecologised masculinities theory must be formulated that is both personal and political and is able to expand and redefine men's lives and the masculinities that shape them.

The different approaches discussed above offer great insight into the complexities of our understandings of men and masculinities. Each positionality captures expressions of masculinities that are unique to their particular politics and practices. Here, we have exposed the need for the following: the importance of supporting feminism (as pointed out by profeminist scholars); the failed possibility of social equity argued by anti-capitalists the rainbow of identities that characterise LGBTIQA+ masculinities; the racist oppression that pervades constructions of masculinity exposed by decolonisation scholars. We have also identified the colonial crossover between black, brown and indigenous masculinities, flagging the need to hear more about the lived experiences of the colonised as marginalised men and their thoughts on manhood, masculinities and Earth. We then considered the deep connection to the self and other men in nature that is characteristic of the mythopoets; the care for communities and Earth that has found voice through Christian stewardship and ecotheology and the reactive and defensive care for men's lives – egregiously misguided by sentiments of victimisation – that MRAs commonly prosecute. Clearly, care is evident in all of the traditions discussed throughout this chapter, but is a human attribute that is unfortunately constrained and misdirected in many men's lives; traditional socialisations have failed to reawaken men's broader, deeper and wider capacities to care for the glocal commons that we believe is possible for all men to imbue.

Having surveyed masculinities politics and noted the absence of ecological masculinities, we turn our attention to those who have addressed the human–nature relationship frontally for some time, exploring discourses in deep ecology, ecological feminism and feminist care theory in order to further assist us as we make the case for ecological masculinities.

Notes

1 For Roslyn Frank (2008: 1), situatedness referred to 'the ways in which individual minds and cognitive processes are shaped by their interaction with socio-cultural structures and practices' when the subject of any given position (but not the position itself) becomes the focus of our attention.
2 The term 'positionalities' refers to taking various positions in relation to other positions within discourses of socio-cultural significance. Consequently, 'positionalities' is used in reference to cultural accounts of social phenomena that create conditions for discrete situatedness.
3 For further clarification of the points of intersection and distinction between 'gender equity' and 'gender equality', also see UNFPA (2005).
4 Of course, sexism not only existed on both sides of the Iron Curtain pre-Perestroika, but also perseveres in post-Soviet and formerly communist states in Eastern Europe and beyond to this day.
5 This is particularly relevant in the US as government support for women's reproductive rights have been alarmingly threatened under the Trump administration, despite generations of hard-fought gains in those rights.
6 We discuss this in greater detail in Chapter 6.

References

Aboim, S. 2016. *Plural Masculinities: The Remaking of the Self in Private Life*. Oxon: Routledge.
ANROWS [Australian National Research Organisation for Women's Safety]. 2016. *Horizons Research Report – October 2015 – Violence against Women: Additional Analysis of the Australian Bureau of Statistics' Personal Safety Survey, 2012 (Issue 01.01/2016)*. Sydney: ANROWS.
Anshelm, J. 2010. 'Among demons and wizards: the nuclear energy discourse in Sweden and the re-enchantment of the World'. *Bulletin of Science, Technology & Society*, 30(1): 43–53.
Ashe, F. 2007. *The New Politics of Masculinity: Men, Power and Resistance*. New York: Routledge.
Berlant, L., and M. Warner. 1995. 'What does queer theory teach us about x?'. *PMLA* 110(3): 343–349.

Berry, R., ed. 2006. *Environmental Stewardship: Critical Perspectives – Past and Present.* London: T&T Clark.

Bird Rose, D. 2016. 'Tag archives: Aboriginal walk-off (country for Yarralin)'. Accessed 1 July 2017. http://deborahbirdrose.com/tag/aboriginal-walk-off

Bliss, S. 1987. 'Revisioning masculinity: a report on the growing men's movement'. *Context: A Quarterly of Humane Sustainable Culture* 16 (spring): 21.

Bliss, S. 1989. 'The wildman, the earth father and my uncle Dale'. *Wingspan – Journal of the Male Spirit* (summer): 10–11.

Bliss, S. 1992. 'What happens at a mythopoetic men's weekend?'. In C. Harding, ed., *Wingspan: Inside the Men's Movement.* New York: St. Martin's Press, 95–99.

Bliss, S. 1995. 'Mythopoetic men's movement'. In M. Kimmel, ed., *The Politics of Manhood: Profeminist Men Respond to the Mythopoetic Men's Movement (and the Mythopoetic Leaders Answer).* Philadelphia: Temple University Press, 292–307.

Bly, R. 1990. *Iron John: A Book About Men.* Boston: Addison-Wesley.

Bowers, C. 1993. *Education, Cultural Myths, and the Ecological Crisis: Toward Deep Changes.* Albany: State University of New York Press.

Boyd, S., and E. Sheehy. 2016. 'Men's groups: challenging feminism'. *Canadian Journal of Women and the Law* 28(1): 5–17

Brod, H. 2002. 'Studying masculinities as subordinate studies'. In J. Gardiner, ed., *Masculinity Studies and Feminist Theory: New Directions.* New York: Columbia University Press, 161–175.

Buckingham, S., and R. Kulcur. 2009. 'Gendered geographies of environmental injustice'. *Antipodes* 41(4): 659–683.

Buckingham, S., and V. Le Masson. eds. 2017. *Understanding Climate Change Through Gender Relations: Routledge Studies in Hazards, Disasters and Climate Change.* Oxon: Routledge.

Bullough, V. 1994. 'On being male in the Middle Ages'. In C. Lees, ed., *Medieval Masculinities: Regarding Men in the Middle Ages.* Minneapolis: University of Minnesota, 31–45.

Butler, C. 2017. 'A fruitless endeavour: confronting the heteronormativity of environmentalism'. In S. MacGregor, ed., *Routledge Handbook of Gender and Environment.* Oxon: Routledge, 270–286.

Callahan, D. 1981. 'What obligations do we have to future generations?'. In E. Partridge, ed., *Responsibilities to Future Generations: Environmental Ethics.* Buffalo: Prometheus Books, 73–85.

Campbell, H., and M. Mayerfeld Bell. 2000. 'The question of rural masculinities'. *Rural Sociology* 65(4): 532–546.

Cappel, J., Clough, D., Deane-Drummond, C., Gottfried, R., Valentine, K., Jones, P., and A. Thompson. 2016. *Ecotheology and Nonhuman Ethics in Society: A Community of Compassion.* New York: Lexington Books.

Cariou, W., Tengan, T., Hokowhitu, B., Justice, D., Scofield, G., Sinclair, N., and R. Van Camp. 2015. *Indigenous Men and Masculinities: Legacies, Identities, Regeneration.* Winnipeg: University of Manitoba Press.

Carrigan, T., Connell, R., and J. Lee. 1987. 'Hard and heavy: toward a new sociology of masculinity'. In M. Kaufman, ed., *Beyond Patriarchy: Essays by Men on Pleasure, Power, and Change.* New York: Oxford University Press, 139–192.

Cherp, A., and R. Mnatsakanian. 2008. 'Environmental degradation in Eastern Europe, Caucasus and Central Asia: past roots, present transition and future hopes'. In D. Heaney, ed., *Eastern Europe, Russia and Central Asia.* London: Routledge, 38–42.

Christensen, A., and S. Jensen. 2014. 'Combining hegemonic masculinity and intersectionality'. *NORMA: International Journal for Masculinity Studies* 9(1): 60–75.

Claeys, P., and D. Delgado Pugley. 2017. 'Peasant and indigenous transnational social movements engaging with climate justice'. *Canadian Journal of Development Studies/ Revue canadienne d'études du développement* 38(3): 325–340.

Clatterbaugh, K. 1997. *Contemporary Perspectives on Masculinities.* Boulder: West-view Press.

Connell, R. 1995. *Masculinities.* Berkeley: University of California Press.

Connell, R. 2000. *The Men and the Boys.* St. Leonards: Allen & Unwin.

Connell, R. 2001. 'The social organization of masculinity'. In S. Whitehead and F. Barrett, eds., *The Masculinities Reader.* Oxford: Blackwell, 30–55.

Connell, R. 2002. *Gender.* Cambridge: Polity.

Connell, R. 2016. 'Masculinities in global perspective: hegemony, contestation, and changing structures of power'. *Theory and Society* 45(4): 303–318.

Connell, R., and R. Pearse. 2014. *Gender: In World Perspective.* Cambridge: Polity.

Conroy, J. 2017. '"Angry white men": the sociologist who studies Trump's base before Trump'. *The Guardian Online.* Accessed 2 November 2017. http://www.theguardian. com/world/2017/feb/27/michael-kimmel-masculinity-far-right-angry-white-men

Devries, K., Mak, J., Garcia-Moreno, C., Petzold, M., Child, J., Falder, G., and C. Pallitto. 2013. 'The global prevalence of intimate partner violence against women'. *Science* 340(6140): 1527–1528.

Di Chiro, G. 2008. 'Living environmentalisms: coalition politics, social reproduction, and environmental justice'. *Environmental Politics* 17(2): 276–298.

Digg. 2017. 'They got their hands on guns anyway: the perpetrators of America's worst mass shootings have one glaring thing in common'. Accessed 19 November 2017. http://digg.com/2017/mass-shooters-domestic-violence

DiPiero, T. 2002. *White Men Aren't.* Durham: Duke University Press.

Dobratz, B., and S. Shanks-Meile. 2000. *White Power, White Pride: The White Separatist Movement in the United States.* Baltimore: Twayne Publishers/Johns Hopkins University Press.

Doyle, R. 1976. *Rape of the Male.* St. Paul: Poor Richard's Press.

Doyle, R. 2016. *Doyle's War: Save the Males.* Minnesota: Forest Lake.

Dragiewicz, M. and R. Mann. 2016. 'Special Edition: fighting feminism–organised opposition to women's rights; Guest editors' introduction'. *International Journal for Crime, Justice and Social Democracy* 5(2): 1–5.

Du Bois, W. 2007[1903]. *The Souls of Black Folk.* Sioux Falls: NuVisions.

Eisenstein, H. 1983. *Contemporary Feminist Thought.* Boston: G. K. Hall.

Elliott, K. 2016. 'Caring masculinities: theorizing an emerging concept'. *Men and Masculinities* 19(3): 240–259.

Everytown for Gun Safety Support Fund. 2015. 'The real story of mass shootings in America: between January 2009 and July 2015, there were at least 133 mass shoot-ings in the U.S. Not all of them make headlines – and the story the data tells is different from the one that mass media would have you expect'. Accessed 1 July 2017. http://everytownresearch.org/mass-shootings

Everytown for Gun Safety Support Fund. 2017. 'Using FBI data and media reports, Everytown for Gun Safety developed an analysis of mass shootings that took place between January 2009 and December 2016'. Accessed 1 July 2017. https://every townresearch.org/reports/mass-shootings-analysis

Fanon, F. 2002[1967]. 'The fact of blackness'. In R. Adams, and D. Savran, eds., *The Masculinity Studies Reader*. Oxford: Blackwell, 232–244.

Farrell, W. 1974. *The Liberated Man*. New York: Random House.

Fasteau, M. 1975. *The Male Machine*. New York: Delta.

Flannigan-Saint-Aubin, A. 1994. 'The male body and literary metaphors for masculinity'. In H. Brod and M. Kaufman, eds., *Theorizing Masculinities*. Thousand Oaks: SAGE Publishing, 239–258.

Flood, M. 2005. 'Men's collective struggle for gender justice: the case of antiviolence activism'. In M. Kimmel, J. Hearn and R. Connell, eds., *Handbook of Studies on Men and Masculinities*. Thousand Oaks: SAGE Publishing, 458–466.

Flood, M., and R. Howson. eds. 2015. *Engaging Men in Building Gender Equality*. Newcastle upon Tyne: Cambridge Scholars.

Frank, R. 2008. 'Introduction: sociocultural situatedness'. In R. Frank, R. Dirven, T. Ziemke and E. Bernárdez, *Body, Language and Mind: Sociocultural Situatedness* (Volume 2). Berlin: Mouton de Gruyter, 1–18.

Franklin, C. 1987. 'Surviving the institutional decimation of black males: causes, consequences, and interventions'. In H. Brod, ed., *The Making of Masculinities: The New Men's Studies*. London: Allen & Unwin, 160–176.

Friedersdorf, C. 2017. 'The politically correct presidency of Donald Trump'. Accessed 17 April 2017. http://www.theatlantic.com/politics/archive/2017/02/the-alt-political-correctness-of-donald-j-trump/515856

Gaard, G. 1997. 'Toward a queer ecofeminism'. *Hypatia* 12(1): 114–137.

Gaard, G. 2011. 'Ecofeminism revisited: rejecting essentialism and re-placing species in a material feminist environmentalism'. *Feminist Formations* 23(2): 26–53.

Gaard, G. 2017. *Critical Ecofeminism (Ecocritical Theory and Practice)*. Lanham: Lexington.

Gambill, E. 2005. *Uneasy Males: The American Men's Movement (1970–2000)*. Lincoln, NE: iUniverse.

Gleeson, H. 2017. 'Toxic masculinity: Will the "war on men" only backfire?'. *ABC News Online*. Accessed24 June 2017. http://www.abc.net.au/news/2017-01-28/toxic-masculinity-war-could-backfire/8207704

Golding, M. 1981. 'Obligation to future generations'. In E. Partridge, ed., *Responsibilities to Future Generations: Environmental Ethics*. Buffalo: Prometheus Books, 61–72.

Goldman, M. 1972. *The Spoils of Progress: Environmental Pollution in the Soviet Union*. Cambridge: MIT Press.

Gray, E. 1982. *Patriarchy as a Conceptual Trap*. Wellesley: Roundtable Press.

Griffin, S. 1978. *Woman and Nature: The Roaring Inside Her*. New York: Harper & Row.

Halberstam, J. 1998. *Female Masculinity*. Durham: Duke University Press.

Halberstam, J. 2005. *In a Queer Time and Place: Transgender Bodies, Subcultural Lives*. New York: New York University Press.

Haluza-DeLay, R. 2008. 'Churches engaging the environment: an autoethnography of obstacles and opportunities'. *Human Ecology Review* 15(1): 71–81.

Hanmer, J. 1990. 'Men, power, and the exploitation of women'. In J. Hearn and D. Morgan, eds., *Men, Masculinities and Social Theory*. London: Unwin Hyman, 21–42.

Haraway, D. 1988. 'Situated knowledges: the science question in feminism and the privilege of partial perspective'. *Feminist Studies* 14 (3): 575–599.

Hatty, S. 2000. *Masculinities, Violence and Culture*. Thousand Oaks: SAGE Publishing.

Hearn, J. 1987. *The Gender of Oppression: Men, Masculinity, and the Critique of Marxism*. New York: St. Martin's Press.

Hearn, J. 1992. *Men in the Public Eye*. London: Routledge

Hearn, J., Nordberg, M., Andersson, K., Balkmar, D., Gottzén, L., Klinth, R., Pringle, K., and L. Sandberg. 2012. 'Hegemonic masculinity and beyond: 40 years of research in Sweden'. *Men and Masculinities* 15(1): 31–55.

Heasley, R. 2005. 'Queer masculinities of straight men: a typology'. *Men and Masculinities* 7(3): 310–320.

Herskovits, M. 1937. 'African gods and Catholic saints in new world negro belief'. *American Anthropologist* 39(4): 635–643.

Hill, H. 2007. 'Befria mannen: idéer om förtryck, frigörelse och förändring hos en svensk mansrörelse under 1970-och tidigt 1980-tal'. PhD diss., Lund University.

Hitzhusen, G. 2007. 'Judeo-Christian theology and the environment: moving beyond scepticism to new sources for environmental education in the United States'. *Environmental Education Research* 13(1): 55–74.

Hoff, B. 1994. 'Warriors and the planet: an interview with Jed Diamond'. *M.E.N. Magazine: A Publication of Seattle Men's Evolvement Network* 5(6): 1, 15–20.

Hoff, B., and Bliss, S. 1995. 'Interview with Shepherd Bliss'. Accessed 11 February 2011. http://www.menweb.org/blissiv.htm

hooks, b. 2004. *The Will to Change: Men, Masculinity, and Love*. New York: Washington Square Press.

Hopkins, P., and G. Noble. 2009. 'Masculinities in place: situated identities, relations and intersectionality'. *Social & Cultural Geography* 10(8): 811–819.

Hughes, R. 2003[1986]. *The Fatal Shore*. London: Vintage.

Jordan, A. 2016. 'Conceptualizing backlash: (UK) men's rights groups, anti-feminism, and postfeminism'. *Canadian Journal of Women and the Law* 28(1): 18–44.

Josephson, P., Dronin, N., Mnatsakanian, R., Cherp, A., Efremenko, D., and V. Larin. 2013. *An Environmental History of Russia*. Cambridge: Cambridge University Press.

Kaijser, A., and A. Kronsell. 2014. 'Climate change through the lens of intersectionality'. *Environmental politics* 23(3): 417–433.

Kaufman, M. 1994. 'Men, feminism, and men's contradictory experiences of power'. In H. Brod and M. Kaufman, eds., *Theorizing Masculinities*. Thousand Oaks: SAGE Publishing, 42–164.

Keen, M. 1984. *Chivalry*. New Haven: Yale University Press.

Kelly, A. 2017. 'The alt-right: reactionary rehabilitation for white masculinity'. *Soundings* 66: 68–78.

Kennedy, K. 2013. 'Death rated from guns, traffic accidents converging'. Accessed 19 November 2017. http://www.usatoday.com/story/news/nation/2013/01/09/guns-traffic-deaths-rates/1784595

Keskinen, S. 2013. 'Antifeminism and white identity politics'. *Nordic Journal of Migration Research* 3(4): 225–232.

Kimmel, M. 1987. 'Men's responses to feminism at the turn of the century'. *Gender & Society* 1(3): 261–283.

Kimmel, M. 1993. 'Clarence, William, Iron Mike, Tailhook, Senator Packwood, Spur Posse, Magic . . . and us'. In E. Buchwald, P. Fletcher, and M. Roth, eds., *Transforming a Rape Culture*. Minneapolis: Milkweed Editions, 119–138.

Kimmel, M. 1995. 'Preface'. In M. Kimmel, ed., *The Politics of Manhood: Profeminist Men Respond to the Mythopoetic Men's Movement (And the Mythopoetic Leaders Answer)*. Philadelphia: Temple University Press, xi–xiii.

Kimmel, M. 1996. *Manhood in America: A Cultural History*. New York: Free Press.
Kimmel, M. 1998. 'Who's afraid of men doing feminism?'. In T. Digby, ed., *Men Doing Feminism*. New York: Routledge, 57–68.
Kimmel, M. 2001. 'Global masculinities: restoration and resistance'. In B. Pease and K. Pringle, eds., *A Man's World: Changing Men's Practices in a Globalized World*. London: Zed Books, 21–37.
Kimmel, M. 2008. *Guyland: The Perilous World Where Boys Become Men*. New York: HarperCollins.
Kimmel, M. 2013. *Angry White Men: American Masculinity at the End of an Era*. New York: Nation Books.
Kimmel, M., and A. Aronson. 2004. *Men and Masculinities: A Social, Cultural, and Historical Encyclopedia*. Santa Barbara: ABC-CLIO.
Kimmel, M., and A. Ferber. 2000. '"White men are this nation": right-wing militias and the restoration of rural American masculinity'. *Rural Sociology* 65(4): 582–604.
Kimmel, M., and M. Kaufman. 1994. 'Weekend warriors: the new men's movement'. In H. Brod and M. Kaufman, eds., *Theorizing Masculinities*. Thousand Oaks: SAGE Publishing, 259–288.
Kimmel, M., and M. Messner. 1989. *Men's Lives*. New York: Macmillan.
Kirsch, M. 2000. *Queer Theory and Social Change*. London: Routledge.
Komarov, B. 1978. *The Destruction of Nature in the Soviet Union*. London: Pluto.
Köttig, M., Bitzan, R., and A. Petö. eds. 2017. *Gender and Far Right Politics in Europe*. Cham: Springer.
Kuruvilla, C. 2017. 'Pope Francis blasts "perverse attitudes" of climate change deniers'. Accessed 19 November 2017. http://www.huffingtonpost.com.au/entry/pop e-francis-climate-change_us_5a0f5525e4b0e97dffed3e0d
Lawlor, R. 1991. *Voices of the First Day: Awakening in the Aboriginal Dreamtime*. Rochester, VT: Inner Traditions International.
Lee, J. 1991. *At My Father's Wedding: Reclaiming Our True Masculinity*. New York: Bantam.
Leopold, A. 1966[1949]. *A Sand County Almanac: With Essays on Conservation from Round River*. New York: Ballantine.
Li, N., Hilgard, J., Scheufele, D., Winneg, K., and K. Jamieson. 2016. 'Cross-pressuring conservative Catholics? Effects of Pope Francis' encyclical on the US public opinion on climate change'. *Climatic Change* 139(3–4): 367–380.
Lovelock, J. 1979. *Gaia: A New Look at Life on Earth*. Oxford: Oxford University Press.
Mac an Ghaill, M. 1994. 'The making of black English masculinities'. In H. Brod and M. Kaufman, eds., *Theorizing Masculinities*. Thousand Oaks: SAGE Publishing, 183–199.
Malm, A. 2015. *Fossil Capital: The Rise of Steam Power and the Roots of Global Warming*. London: Verso.
Marriott, D. 1996. 'Reading black masculinities'. In M. Mac an Ghaill, ed., *Understanding Masculinities: Social Relations and Cultural Arenas*. Buckingham: Open University Press, 185–201.
May, L.Strikwerda, R., and P. Hopkins. 1992. 'Male friendship and intimacy'. In L. May and R. A. Strikwerda, eds., *Rethinking Masculinity: Philosophical Explorations in Light of Feminism*. Lanham: Rowman & Littlefield, 79–94.
McCammack, B. 2007. 'Hot damned America: evangelicalism and the climate change policy debate'. *American Quarterly* 59(3): 645–668.
Mellström, U. 2014. 'Multidimensional masculinities'. *NORMA: International Journal for Masculinity Studies* 9(2): 81–83.

Merchant, C. 1980. *The Death of Nature: Women, Ecology and the Scientific Revolution.* New York: HarperCollins.

Merchant, C. 1996. *Earthcare: Women and the Environment.* New York: Routledge.

Messerschmidt, J. 2012. 'Engendering gendered knowledge: assessing the academic appropriation of hegemonic masculinity'. *Men and Masculinities* 15(1): 56–76.

Messner, M. 1997. *Politics of Masculinities: Men in Movements.* Lanham: AltaMira Press.

Messner, M. 2016. 'Forks in the road of men's gender politics: men's rights vs feminist allies'. *International Journal for Crime, Justice and Social Democracy* 5(2): 6–20.

Metz, C. 1968. *Divorce and Custody for Men.* New York: Doubleday.

Moncrief, L. 1970. 'The cultural basis for our environmental crisis'. *Science* 170 (3957): 508–512.

Moore, R., and D. Gillette. 1990. *King, Warrior, Magician, Lover: Rediscovering the Archetypes of the Mature Masculine.* New York: HarperCollins.

Moosa, C., and N. Tuana. 2014. 'Mapping a research agenda concerning gender and climate change: a review of the literature'. *Hypatia* 29(3): 677–694.

Mortimer-Sandilands, C. 2005. 'Unnatural passions? Notes toward a queer ecology'. In L. Uddin and P. Hobbs, eds., *Invisible Culture: An Electronic Journal for Visual Studies (Issue 9: Nature Loving).* Accessed 1 June 2017. http://www.rochester.edu/in_visible_culture/Issue_9/issue9_sandilands.pdf

Nicholson, H. 2001. *The Knights Hospitaller.* Suffolk: Boydell.

O'Brien, K. 2004. 'An ethics of natureculture and creation: Donna Haraway's cyborg ethics as a resource for ecotheology'. *Ecotheology: Journal of Religion, Nature & the Environment* 9(3): 315–337.

Ortner, S. 1974. 'Is female to male as nature is to culture?'. In M. Rosaldo and L. Lamphere, eds., *Women, Culture, and Society.* Stanford: Stanford University Press, 68–87.

Össbo, Å., and P. Lantto. 2011. 'Colonial tutelage and industrial colonialism: reindeer husbandry and early 20th-century hydroelectric development in Sweden'. *Scandinavian Journal of History* 36(3): 324–348.

Pearse, R. 2017. 'Gender and climate change'. *Wiley Interdisciplinary Reviews: Climate Change* 8(2): 451.

Pease, B. 1998. 'Dividing lines: the politics of the men's movement'. *Community Quarterly: A Journal Focusing on Community Issues* 47: 77–88.

Pease, B. 1999. 'Deconstructing masculinity–reconstructing men'. In B. Pease and J. Fook, eds., *Transforming Social Work Practice: Postmodern Critical Perspectives.* St. Leonards: Allen & Unwin, 97–112.

Pease, B. 2000. *Recreating Men: Postmodern Masculinity Politics.* London: SAGE Publishing.

Pease, B. 2002. *Men and Gender Relations.* Croydon: Tertiary Press.

Pease, B. 2016. 'Masculinism, climate change and "man-made" disasters: towards an environmental profeminist response'. In E. Enarson and B. Pease, eds., *Men, Masculinities and Disaster.* Oxon: Routledge, 21–33.

People's Institute for Survival and Beyond. 2017. 'Undoing racism'. Accessed 17 November 2017. http://www.pisab.org

Pope Francis. 2015. 'Laudato Si': on care for our common home'. Encyclical. Accessed 19 November 2017. http://w2.vatican.va/content/francesco/en/encyclicals/documents/papa-francesco_20150524_enciclica-laudato-si.html

Pulé, P., and M. Hultman. Forthcoming. 'Men and nature: a critical analysis of the mythopoetic men's movement'. In R. Cenamor and S. Brandt, eds., *Ecomasculinities* in *Real and Fictional North America: The Flourishing of New Men*. Lanham: Lexington Books [Rowman & Littlefield].

Quealy, K., and M. Sanger-Katz. 2016. 'Comparing gun deaths by country: the U.S. is in a different world'. *New York Times Online*. Accessed 19 November 2017. http://www.nytimes.com/2016/06/14/upshot/compare-these-gun-death-rates-the-us-is-in-a-different-world.html

Rickards, L., Wiseman, J., and Y. Kashima. 2014. 'Barriers to effective climate change mitigation: the case of senior government and business decision makers'. *Wiley Interdisciplinary Reviews: Climate Change* 5(6): 753–773.

Rivera, J., and D. Miller. 2007. 'Continually neglected: situating natural disasters in the African American experience'. *Journal of Black Studies* 37(4): 502–522.

Roach, C. 2003. *Mother Nature: Popular Culture and Environmental Ethics*. Bloomington: Indiana University Press.

Rogers, R. 2008. 'Beasts, burgers, and hummers: meat and the crisis of masculinity in contemporary television advertisements'. *Environmental Communication* 2(3): 281–301.

Root, W. 2016. *Angry White Male: How the Donald Trump Phenomenon Is Changing America – and What We Can All Do to Save the Middle Class*. New York: Skyhorse.

Ross, A. 1992. 'Wet, dark and low, eco-man evolves from eco-woman'. *Feminism and Postmodernism* 19(2): 205–232.

Ross, L., ed. 2014. *Continuing the War Against Domestic Violence*. Boca Raton: CRC Press.

Schuldt, J., Pearson, A., Romero-Canyas, R., and D. Larson-Konar. 2017. 'Brief exposure to Pope Francis heightens moral beliefs about climate change'. *Climatic Change* 141(2): 167–177.

Schumacher, E. 1973. *Small Is Beautiful: Economics as If People Mattered*. New York: HarperTorch.

Sehlin MacNeil, K. 2017. 'Extractive violence on indigenous country: Sami and Aboriginal views on conflicts and power relations with extractive industries'. PhD diss., Umeå University.

Seidler, V. 1991. *Recreating Sexual Politics: Men, Feminism, and Politics*. London: Routledge.

Seidler, V. 2014. 'Moving ahead: alternative masculinities for a changing world'. In A. Carabí and J. Armengol, eds., *Alternative Masculinities for a Changing World*. New York: Palgrave Macmillan, 219–234.

Sexton, J. 2016. 'Donald Trump's toxic masculinity'. *New York Times Online*. Accessed 12 November 2017. http://www.nytimes.com/2016/10/13/opinion/donald-trumps-toxic-masculinity.html

Seymour, N. 2013. *Strange Natures: Futurity, Empathy, and the Queer Ecological Imagination*. Urbana: University of Illinois Press.

Solnit, R. 2017a. *The Mother of All Questions*. Chicago: Haymarket Books.

Solnit, R. 2017b. 'Rebecca Solnit: let this flood of women's stories never cease'. Accessed 15 November 2017. http://lithub.com/rebecca-solnit-let-this-flood-of-womens-stories-never-cease

Solnit, R. 2017c. 'The fall of Harvey Weinstein should be a moment to challenge extreme masculinity'. *The Guardian*. Accessed15 November 2017. http://www.theguardian.com/commentisfree/2017/oct/12/challenge-extreme-masculinity-harvey-weinstein-degrading-women

Soloway, J. 2016. 'Jill Soloway on Donald Trump, locker rooms and toxic masculinity'. Accessed 17 November 2017. http://time.com/4527277/jill-soloway-donald-trump-locker-rooms-toxic-masculinity

Stanovsky, D. 2007. 'Postcolonial masculinities'. In M. Flood, J. Gardiner, B. Pease and K. Pringle, eds., *International Encyclopaedia of Men and Masculinities*. London: Routledge, 34–47.

Stearns, P. 2001. *Consumerism in World History: The Global Transformation of Desire*. London: Routledge.

Synnott, A. 2009. *Re-thinking Men: Heroes, Villains and Victims*. Surrey: Ashgate.

Tacey, D. 1997. *Remaking Men: Jung, Spirituality and Social Change*. London: Routledge.

Tengan, T. 2002. '(En)gendering colonialism: masculinities in Hawai'i and Aotearoa'. *Cultural Values* 6(3): 239–256.

UNFPA. 2005. 'Frequently asked questions about gender equality'. United Nations Population Fund. Accessed 17 November 2017. http://www.unfpa.org/resources/fre quently-asked-questions-about-gender-equality

UNHCR. 2017. 'Climate change and disaster'. Accessed 14 April 2017. http://www. unhcr.org/en-au/climate-change-and-disasters.html

Waldinger, R. 2016. 'How do we move forward after the election? Lean in!'. Accessed 1 July 2017. http://robertwaldinger.com/move-forward-election-lean

Wardekker, J., Petersen, A., and J. van Der Sluijs. 2009. 'Ethics and public perception of climate change: exploring the Christian voices in the US public debate'. *Global Environmental Change*, 19(4): 512–521.

White Jr., L. 1967. 'The historical roots of our ecologic crisis'. *Science* 155(3767): 1203–1207.

Whyte, K. 2014. 'Indigenous women, climate change impacts, and collective action'. *Hypatia* 29(3): 599–616.

Wicks, S. 1996. *Warriors and Wildmen: Men, Masculinity, and Gender*. Westport: Bergin & Garvey.

Williams, Z. 2018. '"Raw Hatred": why the "incel" movement targets and terrorises women'. *The Guardian* [online]. Accessed 26 April 2018. http://www.theguardian. com/world/2018/apr/25/raw-hatred-why-incel-movement-targets-terrorises-women.

Zawisza, M., Luyt, R., and A. Zawadzka. 2015. 'Societies in transition: are they more sexist? A comparison between Polish, South African and British samples'. *Journal of Gender Studies* 24(1): 38–55.

Zinn, H. 2003[1980]. *A People's History of the United States: 1492–Present* (3rd Edition). Oxon: Routledge.

4 Connecting inner and outer nature

A deeper ecology for the Global North

> . . . the world participates in that which I feel, and the other way about. The world and I are not that far apart, perhaps not even by so much as a millimetre. I have no very clear idea what are the limits of the self; perhaps it flows out and expands, or contracts within. It is never the same. It seems more like a *flow* than anything solid. Is the diversity of feelings that I register only within myself, as if in a kind of box? Is consciousness like some sort of container with pictures of *external* things? That seems nonsensical to me, like an alienation of the world out there and a degradation of the great flow of consciousness [in here].
>
> (Næss and Haukeland, 2002: 23)

A deeper 'total view'

Since the 1960s, the links between the Global North's ecocidal attitudes towards nature (along with the rise of social inequalities) the world over have become increasingly visible. The term ecocide was first used in a larger public event by politicians at the United Nations Conference on the Human Environment in Stockholm (1972) when the Swedish Prime Minister, Olof Palme, accused the US of waging such a war in Vietnam. (Andersson, 2006; Handl, 2012; Crook and Short, 2014). Two main schools of thought emerged in response to the knowledge of ecocide: a light green or 'shallow', more or less business-as-usual approach that at best posited marginal changes to stave off ecological and social decay and became the forerunner for ecological modernisation. This was juxtaposed against what became known as a deep green future, that aimed to adopt a 'deeper total view' of life (Næss, 2005a: 24–25). As we attested in Chapter 2, ecological modernisation has proved ineffective at creating a sustainable world, demonstrating that something more than reform is needed. This telling reality compels us to ensure that our formulation of masculine ecologisation resonates with this deeper total view. One tradition that formalised this into its own distinct discourse is known as the deep, long-range (or simply the deep) ecology movement, which grew out of the musings of its founder, the Norwegian environmental philosopher Arne Næss (27 January 1912 – 12 January 2009) (Næss, 1973; Drengson, 1992).

Næss introduced the term 'deep ecology' at the Third World Future Research Conference in Bucharest in 1972 through his landmark paper, 'The Shallow and the Deep, Long-Range Ecology Movement: A Summary', which promoted the use of 'philosophy and philosophical thinking to help humans overcome the ecological crisis and, ultimately, to restore the Earth to a state of rich and flourishing biological and cultural diversity' (Næss, 2005a: xlv). Deep ecology grew into an international movement beyond Næss's formulation of that work, being championed by a swathe of poets, scholars and activists who took up his teachings, expanding and refining them as the movement evolved (Snyder, 1974; Devall and Sessions, 1985; Zimmerman, 1987; Cheney, 1987; Drengson, 1988; LaChapelle, 1988; Seed et al., 1988; Macy, 1989; Fox, 1990; Rothenberg, 1993; Glasser, 1995; Hallen, 1999; Harding, 2011). One notable aberration among the movement's critics was the considerable debate that ensued in regard to deep ecology's lack of frontal gender considerations – critiques about this limitation being particularly vocalised by ecofeminists (Salleh, 1984; Biehl, 1988; Salleh, 1992; Plumwood, 1993; Mathews, 1994; Slicer, 1995; Naess, 1999a; Warren, 1999; Twine, 2001; Plumwood, 2002). Further critiques of deep ecology in reference to its potential misanthropy were also raised by social ecologists (Bookchin, 1987; Bookchin, 1995; Salleh, 1996). Towards the end of this chapter, we give these critiques our fuller consideration, however, we do not attend explicitly to the critiques levelled at deep ecology by social ecologists here, positioning that discourse as a tacit influence on our thinking. Our particular interest in a critical view of deep ecology is gendered and for this reason we keep our focus on ecofeminist inspired views on the movement. A cadre of scholars and activists have helped us shape ecological masculinities by providing us with important clues about the strengths and the weaknesses of deep ecological thinking in the context of a gendered analysis. But before launching into gendered critiques of the movement, we consider it vital to celebrate and examine the ways that Næss formulated and promoted deep ecology.

Næss defined deep ecology as a new form of environmentalism. He considered it a necessary way to interact with nature and identify our place within it. By deeper, Næss aimed to go right down to those assumptions about the world and our particular relationship with it so that we come to know, feel, trust and identify with that relationship in ways that we can each wholeheartedly and uniquely support (Naess and Haukeland, 2002: 7). Næss did not intend for his deeper total view to be fixed to a particular position as an absolute truth about life. Rather, he referred to a conceptual framework that stressed the importance of an individual's unique sense of reality. In doing so, Næss noted that there is a danger in singular visioning since it can leave an issue under-examined and under-articulated, especially if positions of privilege accompany that view. Deep ecology as he formulated it aimed to counter the mounting evidence of the damage wrought upon Earth, communities and individuals in the post-Second World War industrialised West. His approach was intentionally pluralised. US integral theorist, Michael Zimmerman (1993: 198), noted the following about deep ecology's pluralised and deeper total view:

> Deep ecologists maintain that . . . humanity must move to a new understanding of what humanity and nature *are*, an understanding that is ecocentric, nonanthropocentric, and non-dualistic. Emphasising the need for an ontological shift differentiates deep ecologists from ethicists who seek to extend "moral considerability" to nonhuman beings. Deep ecologists argue that a change in ontology must precede a change in ethical attitudes. A non-dualistic, ecocentric understanding of what things are would lead us to treat nonhuman beings with compassion and care.

Like Næss, Zimmerman supported a deeper understanding of the human–nature relationship. He noted that deep ecology argued for soulful understandings of our unique ontologies (ways of being), suggesting that personal insights about our relationships with nature were necessary precursors to our respective epistemologies (ways of knowing) (Zimmerman, 1987: 21). Speaking fondly of Næss the man and deep ecology in the context of its origins in Norwegian life and culture, close friend, Norwegian compatriot and Qigong master Pamela Hiley (pers. comm., 08/05/17) noted Næss's impatience with the paradoxes of abundance. She cited the tense relationship that many Norwegians experience between celebrating the magnificent wilds of that Nordic land, juxtaposed against the nation's dependence upon the oil industry. She shared that in the last ten years of his life, Næss became increasingly concerned about the great struggle confronting many Norwegians to find balance between their own unique and simple ways (of being one with nature) despite (perhaps in spite of) the ample lives that their oil-rich country has long provided them as a people. This was a view echoed by Kari Marie Norgaard's (2011) year-long study of the citizens of a Norwegian town where she exposed the complexities of localised life, since they on the one hand live well from oil revenue, which, when burned creates toxic emissions, and on the other hand widely claim that Norway is an environmentally friendly country. This double standard echoed the iron grip of monoculturing that masculine hegemonies commonly place upon our lives. After all, it is easy to sidestep celebrating the textured nature of difference when we are operating inside of our own privilege that can be held up as fundamental truths or simply the way that things are – effectively dismissing the inescapable heterogeneity (indeed the paradoxical complexities) of life. To further stress the point, consider the aforementioned example of how extensively Western industrial modern masculinities are infused with sexism, where men can easily avoid examining their own internalised superiority since gender privilege typically blinds them to the costs of male domination on all others and themselves. Similarly, in a world infused with anthropocentrism, we humans are quick to place our own needs, wants and desires above the right to life for other-than-humans. We appear to be very willing to live in full view of our contradictions, deferring to our comforts as our ultimate goal that either distracts or desensitises us.

Næss strove to usurp these paradoxes He suggested that deep ecology's total view adheres to a pluralised context and stresses the need to examine our internal, coherent and mutually supporting beliefs, ideas, values, concepts and categories (Næss, 1989: 37; Riggio, 2015: 77–80). Theoretically speaking, the movement was built on spiritual, literary and social/scientific and philosophical foundations. Næss took stock of Native American traditions, Buddhist and Taoist philosophies, Christian principles, the Yogic and Vedantic philosophies of the *Bhagavad-Gita*, as well as pre-Socratic spiritualities of European paganism. He embraced Henry David Thoreau, John Muir, Aldo Leopold, Rachel Carson, along with Mohandas Gandhi, Benedict Spinoza and James Lovelock. As a praxis, deep ecology formed the basis for embodied processes that were developed and grew to demonstrate considerable successes at enabling individuals to regain energy, creativity and empowerment that would reconnect us to each other, wider nature and cosmic life, giving us the necessary resolve to act on behalf of Earth in being part of it expressing itself in human form through each of us, reflective of our respective uniqueness. Although not a focus of the movement, we note that the praxis of 'nature-oneness' that deep ecology advocated has particular relevance for masculinities, since deep ecology advocated a more humble world view by challenging the internalised superiority of humanity's domination of nature, begging us to similarly challenge the internalised superiority of male domination over all others. Næss argued that no human being has the right to reduce richness and diversity of other-than-human life. However, he suggested that we do have the right to draw from Earth's resources in order to satisfy vital needs – those that maintain life *and* give it deeper meaning. Clearly, by advocating a total view, deep ecology drew from a very wide range of conceptual and practical influences. Næss was a master of zooming out as well as zooming in.

Following in Næss's footsteps, the deeper total view we are subscribing to here draws on many guiding principles, belief systems, philosophies, etc., which comprise the unique foundations of an individual's non-dogmatic and inner wisdoms. When we tune into them, these inner wisdoms can be instrumental in converting the core tenets of deep ecology into customised praxes that manifest in many different (and socially and ecologically beneficial) ways (Quick, 2006: 59–60). We have taken this principle to heart, adapting the notion of complex theories and concurrent pluralised praxes into our formulation of ecological masculinities. From here, we proceed to take a closer look at the core tenets of deep ecology in order to illuminate the important role that the movement plays in our conceptualisation of ecological masculinities. In order to enrich our understanding of the human–nature relationship as it relates to modern Western men and masculinities, we consider Næss the man and the ways his persona shaped the movement, as this gives us some insight into the brilliances and shortcomings of deep ecology for our purposes.

Næss the man

Born in 1912, Arne Dekke Eide Næss was the fourth and unplanned child of a wealthy Bergen family living in Slemdal, in the outskirts of Oslo. He lost his father to cancer before his first birthday and was turned over to the care of the family governess, Mina, who pandered to his every whim while his mother, Christine, grieved. By the time Næss was 4 years old, Mina was dismissed for indulging him too much, setting in place a rift between little Arne and his mother that grew into a deep-seated sense of loss, alienation and mistrust of emotions that had a great bearing on his personal and philosophical development – a level of self-destructive masochism that would later plague his most intimate relationships as much as drive his ecophilosophical brilliance to the fore. He leaned on his older siblings for familial comfort, each gifting him with a penchant for 'simple means' with 'rich ends' that reflected his desire for security that the wealth of his family's heritage accorded. In response to these early challenges the young Arne was most sated by times alone in nature, inventing experiments, developing hypotheses, learning to suspend judgement and falling in love with other-than-human things. Næss was a collector of rocks, stamps, a fearless tree-climber and by the age of 8 had adopted *Hallingskarvet* as his father mountain, giving him a lifelong passion for expansive vistas from which he could survey the world below; climbing Norway's 106 tallest peaks by the age of 17. In these early years he became an accomplished mountaineer, pianist, was introduced to the works of Spinoza and honed his skills as an exhaustive reader in a wide array of disciplines. His quest for knowledge about the cosmos was intuitively philosophical, as well as precise, empirical and scientific, placing a premium on experiential as well as epistemological engagement. Such an approach fascinated him so much that he remarkably completed his PhD at the age of 24 on science as behaviour using an empirical methodology. With a world erupting into global conflict in 1939, Næss, 27 years old and fresh back from a postdoctorate at the University of California (Berkeley), was appointed Chair of Philosophy at the University of Oslo. A year later his homeland was occupied by Nazi Germany. Through those tense years, Næss applied himself to his teaching and research and by 1943 played a crucial role in preventing student deportations for 're-education' in Nazi concentration camps that resulted in his university campus being shut down. From these experiences, Næss gained great affection for Gandhi's notions of greeting your potential or actual adversary with calm and truthful communication; a morality that compelled him by war's end to play a crucial role in reconciliation between Nazi collaborators and the victims of their tyranny. His post-war scholarship pursued the philosophy of science, empirical semantics and the zetetic scepticism of Pyrrho and ended with early retirement in 1969, whereupon he dedicated himself to social and environmental justice activism and deep ecology was born (Næss, 2005a: xxxi–xxxix).

It is important to note that Næss was no misanthrope. A product of his own psychoanalytical journey and stimulated a deep empathy for the suffering of humanity, he volunteered to assist with the treatment of psychiatric patients while in intensive psychoanalysis himself as a younger man. True also to his love for nature, Næss held out a vision for global sustainability that would preserve a quality of life for all humans as a species along with other-than-human others. Indeed, his desire to create the best conditions for humanity to develop a deeper total view of the cosmos necessarily preceded ecological sustainability. He aimed his focus on the social and environmental consequences of the average standard of living for contemporary wealthy societies – not at people as individuals (Næss, 1999c: 467). He argued that there was enough resource on Earth to assure a good quality of life for all species, without detracting from human vital needs:

> It *is* possible to extend care, reinforce it, and cultivate it. Care is not constant or immutable. It is for that reason that I have proposed the motto 'Extended care for nonhuman beings, deepened care for human beings'. The latter is a reminder that there are people living in completely unacceptable destitution, not only ordinary poverty. Everywhere there is deprivation that *must* be eradicated . . . Such deprivation is simply unacceptable.
>
> (Næss and Haukeland, 2002: 107)

Næssian deep ecology marked the need for humanity to take a stand for all life, our own included, since 'the human potential for caring is not static or limited – it can be both extended and deepened', in effect prioritising our need to take great care of each other and ourselves through cooperation and collaboration as we move towards peace, equality and sustainability (Næss, 2005a: xiv). It is interesting to note that deep ecology as Næss posited it relied heavily on the power of reason – that very masculinised human trait. This was a vestige of the younger Næss, who considered that the emotional whims of the feeling body ultimately offer us distractions from the inevitable pain of thinking that cannot be avoided when we fully engage with our world (Rothenberg, 1993). Næss possessed an austere *Panzercharakter.*[1] He embodied the strong Scandinavian premium placed on containment, where one's vulnerability was acknowledged as ripe ground for sharing, but through private machinations that he considered to be quite distinct from the enormous capacities of human logic (Hiley, pers. comm., 08/05/17).[2] As an established professor, Næss duly considered the 'difficulties of suppressing the significance of the development of feelings in human affairs while at the same time worshipping reason. Both are constantly needed' (Næss and Haukeland, 2002: xi). His deep love of nature and an enduring sense of play were minimalist, phlegmatic, aloof and independent; he possessed an enormous capacity to be 'charming, somber and joyful, accountable and carefree' (citing Harold Glasser's 'Introduction', in Næss and Haukeland, 2002: ix–x, xxiv). Næss was a paradox – he lived by the maxim: 'Be still as a mountain | Move like a great river' (Hiley, pers. comm., 08/05/17). He has been described by his friends and family as predictable and evasive, wise and youthful, serious and jovial, grounded in Earth and at the same time ethereally nymph-like; a true 'philosopher of life' who was 'the equivalent of a hunter-gatherer using his wits and intuition to seek out food (for thought) in a fecund landscape' (Næss, 2005a: xix). Some of his closest compatriots referred to him as a seeker, seer, minor prophet, a radical pluralist, aloof and charming, accountable and carefree, arrogant and modest, slippery and precise (Næss, 2005a: xxvi). His approach reflected a love for nature that resulted in positive feelings or his preferred *active emotions* that awaken our greatest capacity to care for others as an integral part of ourselves (Næss and Haukeland, 2002: 2, 9; Næss, 2008: 84). In all these ways, Næss had a keen sense of the power of connectivity. For some fortunate enough to experience his personal life, he was a man of 'higher vibrations' (Hiley, pers. comm., 08/05/17). He dwelled in timelessness, consciousness, lust and simplicity. He is remembered by those who knew him as a human being that reached beyond the binaries of identity and did not languish in the complexities and dramas of daily life.

On one level, it is understandable that Næss was distracted from paying particular attention to the gendered aspects of social and environmental justice. His thinking was focused on the much broader and deeper horizon of the human–nature relationship. Following Næssian deep ecology to its logical conclusions, it was less necessary to dwell on the minutiae of social inequities when all people are potential friends because we are ultimately all connected, even if at times engaged as adversaries, or finding ourselves in starkly different socio-political positions. Næss considered this sensitivity to our immutable connection with each other to be not only unavoidable, but desirable. Turning again to the increasing global polarisation of views about society and environment we are now experiencing, we would benefit from paying particular attention to Næss's generosity, wisdom and embodiment of this point in particular. He sought deeper ecological wisdom by nurturing the positive aspects of emotional intelligence, encouraging the rise of the higher self through 'a broader, richer form of reason that incorporates love, compassion, and identification with all life', aspects of the felt self that he suggested could create mutually reinforcing symbiotic relationships as essential for the healthiest of human lives that rendered his wok the stuff of gestalt ontologies (Næss, 2005a). Such was Næss's 'Self-realization!' (Næss, 2005a: xxiii).

It is important to note that Næss's perspectives on human emotions were not intended to demonise corporeality. On the contrary and in defiance of the Cartesian division that split human individuals off from the world, he considered the human experience as both emotional and rational to the extent that it was not possible to stand outside of the self, since our thoughts, feelings and relationships, were, in his view, inescapably part of our moment-to-moment experiences of living; the emotional aspect of the human experience providing each of us an opportunity to 'pull ourselves together' in order to liberate ourselves from the grip of negative feelings and the impacts they have on the world (Næss and Haukeland, 2002: 15). Næss argued that we must acknowledge and contend with the suffering of the paradoxes that dwell within each of us, in order to cultivate an unnerved calm or 'serenity within oneself', which – he believed – nature could best help each of us find within, especially during the impressionable years between ages 5 and 15 (Næss and Haukeland, 2002: 13, 21, 85). Ideally, we would achieve this on our own, but Næss acknowledged that for most, outside help (such as therapy or contact with nature) was of incalculable worth in moving us along the road to such a goal (Næss and Haukeland, 2002: 38).

Deep ecology examined

Næss's philosophical training shaped him into a deep questioner and thinker first and foremost. He used these talents to create a global movement that championed Earthcare as equal to human care and self-care (Næss, 2008: 20, 27). Deep ecology was intentionally juxtaposed against the reformist tendencies of 'shallow' environmentalism (that we have attested previously, formed the foundations of ecological modernisation), which he considered to, at best, fine-tune human engagements with nature, while not addressing the truer philosophical, economic, social, political and spiritual dilemmas of our times (Fox, 1990: 37–39; Næss and Haukeland, 2002: xxv–xxvi; Næss, 2008: 27). As an avid supporter of this movement, Alan Drengson (1997: 2) noted that deep ecology reopened:

> . . . the conversation with nature and between communities of beings that has been largely interrupted by certain developments in modern industrial society. As a way to an ecologically sound life it involves three elements: experience, practice and theory.

We read these three elements as inner, outer and ideological – respectively. Rather than prioritising human needs and wants over the vital needs of other-than-human others, deep ecology subscribed to a belief in the intrinsic value of all life with the intention of placing human beings on an equal footing with the rest of life on Earth. Deep ecology uncovered a thoughtful environmentalism that aimed to accommodate the right to existence for all living beings (Rothenberg, 1993: 129, 145). This deeper environmentalism guides us to acquire 'a feeling for nature that sees the environmental crisis as a symptom of a psychological or spiritual ailment that afflicts modern humanity in technological societies' (Seed, 2006: 96). The movement explores the ways we think about and interact with all life, with the intent of creating harmony among all species (Devall, 1988: 11). For two prominent spokespeople for biocentrism, Australian activist and philosopher John Seed and US Buddhist ecologist Joanna Macy, deep ecology's transformational potential was an essential aspect of activism as personal praxes. Following Næss's lead, Seed and Macy viewed the conceptualisation of deep ecology as a powerful tool for tangible behavioural change (Seed, 2006: 99; Næss, 2008: 140–141). The deeper truths of deep ecology championed language and embodiment that facilitated authentic sharing and change. The movement enabled individuals and communities to discover silence, deep connectedness to Næss's capital s-'Self' and in doing so, uncover our respective and very personalised encounters with Earth. Deep ecologists were implored to not remain theoreticians but to become practitioners as well, being guided to cross the fjord dividing theory and practice in order to awaken a more truthful dialogue about how it is to be a human in and of Earth. Seed and Macy were instrumental in creating deep ecology practices as means for us to feel the feelings associated with and thereby heal and recover our fullest selves to act decisively in the wake of generations of separation and loss of connection with other-than-human nature (Seed et al., 1988: 14). Deep ecology as embodiment prioritised feeling these feelings through what Seed and Macy referred to as 'The Work that Reconnects' – shaped by the following three processes:

1 'Despair and Empowerment' – or working with the full spectrum of human feelings about the pressing planetary crises
2 'Deep Time, Evolutionary Remembering, The Cosmic Walk' – where we remember our place in the cosmos
3 'The Council of All Beings' – in which we embody and empathise with myriad creatures with whom we share Earth (Seed et al., 1988; Seed, 2006: 100).

The corporeal aspect of deep ecology was designed to awaken the Self identified *with* others, which requires continuous practice to realise and then prevent our nature-connected relationships from fading over time (Bragg, 1996: 96). Building on Macy's 'Despair and Empowerment' work and closely collaborating with Seed, Australian therapist and environmentalist Ruth Rosenhek is credited as another pivotal activist dedicated to the translation of deep ecological processes into practices. She has specifically designed activities to reconnect us with the universal oneness of life and reawaken a passionate sense of care for all living things so that we might – once again – 'think like a mountain' (Seed et al., 1988: 8–9).

In his attempts to bridge this gap between theory and praxes, Næss scribed an 'Apron Diagram' to illustrate the internalisation of deep ecology's conceptual pathway as practitioners of his theories emerged (Næss, 2005a: 75–77). The four 'folds' of the diagram were designed to represent points of intersection between distinct levels of incorporation of deep ecology into our lives. These four levels of incorporation take us from initial ultimate beliefs, challenged by the eight-point platform of deep ecology,[3] that then shape our *a priori* discernment about what we conclude as facts, to become *a posteriori* decisions and actions. These then stimulate deep questioning and in doing so transform our ultimate beliefs about the world and our selves (Clark, 1996: 196; Drengson, 1997: 3; Drengson 2001: 5; Næss, 2003: 270; Næss 2005a: 75–83; Næss 2005b: 63–64; Notario, 2006: 108; Devall, 2010: 5; Drengson and Devall, 2010: 61). Næss was intentionally vague about the precise form of deep questioning he advocated, deferring instead to customised manifestations of deep ecology ('ecosophies' or personal ecological wisdoms) to emerge within the individual (Næss, 2005a: 61; Harding, 2011). In this way, his Apron Diagram was designed to permit the individual to move in both directions from our personal and ultimate premises to the ways we apply them in our particular lives as actions, effectively awakening the deeper Self that is tightly coupled with wider nature (Næss, 2008: 107–111, 168–170). Deep ecology was then an 'articulation of the basic norms within the ecological movement and an application of [Næss's] analytical training to talk in a bureaucratic way. Not to inspire, show style, or be poetic' (Rothenberg, 1993: 133).

Indeed, the Næssian forecast for the twenty-first century indicated that we must necessarily turn towards sustainability (Glasser, 1999: 379). However, Næss was convinced that this was only likely to happen after we suffered enormous ecological and therefore social unrest at the hands of human-imposed abuses (Anker, 1999: 439–440). He was convinced that the only chance we had of securing a sustainable future, one that is both socially and ecologically savvy, was by problematising the selfish aspects of industrialised nations and directly challenging them through non-violent direct actions that facilitated ethical, economic, political and ecological transformations. This view was formative for green political advocacy, which has emerged as a source for radical change as a crucial bulwark against the economic and military hawkishness of governments primarily dominated by men (Næss, 1999b: 445). Such proclamations are chillingly applicable to our times. Take for example the US rhetoric declaring an end to the alleged 'war on coal' along with oil and natural gas, designed to achieve 'energy independence' for that nation and signed as an executive order by US president Donald Trump (29 March, 2017). Trump cited jobs and wealth generation as its predictable priority ahead of the environment (while also lacerating many of that nation's renewable energy along with medical and social welfare programmes), signing the order surrounded by a cluster of delighted white, middle-aged and older men from the US hydrocarbon industries, having ignored the economic, social, political and ecological capital of the clean energy investment supported by the preceding Obama administration (ABC News, 2017). Such ideological struggles have arrested Næss's call for a biocentric future. While there was little mention of male domination or gender politics in Næss's deep ecology, which he formulated long before the hegemonised right wing/social conservative stumping we are experiencing, his unsettling predictions about a twenty-first-century descent into further global social and ecological tumult are now coming home to roost. We need deep ecology more than ever – but it must be translated into terms that are relatable to those men and masculinities that are subsumed within the malestream paradigm of hegemonisation in order to be revived and updated to become more effective at facilitating needed social and environmental change. For Næss, pluralism was essential to achieve this goal.

Ecosophy T

Næss refused to follow a singular path of inquiry. He was most interested to 'see how bad things are and still be able to smile at them . . . [as] the most solid kind of joy' (Rothenberg, 1993: 84). He went to great lengths to ground deep ecology 'in a recognition of the metaphysical fact of interconnectedness' that was something unavoidable when we truly tune into nature and ourselves, precisely because deep ecology's total view is innately present in us all and is simply waiting to be awakened (Mathews, 1991: 148). With this affection for pluralism, he paved a way forward for each of us to harmonise our many and varied beliefs about and experiences with Earth. To assist us with this personal journey, Næss developed the concept of a personalised ecosophy to develop customised norms that serve each of us as moral guides in our respective lives. An ecosopher is someone who recognises the non-accidental necessity to rise above any norm by reaching a perceptible unity with the non-separable whole of life – in other words to see ourselves as one (and an integral) aspect of nature (Anker, 1998; Seed et al., 1988). Elaborating on Næss's ecosophy, Peder Anker (1998: n.p.) suggested that the ecosophised human was on the path to reaching 'an adequate understanding of his or her being-in-nature, an understanding that may be seen . . . as an epistemological re-entry into creative nature'. Developing an ecosophy enables each of us to pay attention to positive feelings about nature that emerge when we commune with a familiar locale. In this sense, the ecosophised Self interpenetrates with the localised aspects of the collective whole, acquiring a respectful and caring degree of thinking and actions consistent with the feelings that come from personalised nature immersion experiences. This deeper approach to the human–nature relationship arises when extended towards a particular natural place that we come to experience as a living and friendly entity unto itself, with which we develop an immediate and intimate relationship. Næss's ecosophisation gave rise to the 'ecological self', which represented an internal state of being, achieved by the individual through various deep identifications with specific surroundings (Næss, 1986a: 3; Naess, 1986b). The ecological self was constructed on the belief that we have been in, of and for nature, from our very beginning as a species and this '*naturally* and beautifully follows norms of strict environmental ethics', resulting in community therapies that heal our relations with all living beings (Seed et al., 1988: 29; Næss, 1995: 14).

The term ecosophy comes from the Greek terms *oikos* (household) and *sophia* (wisdom), which Næss defined as the individualised 'wise discipline of our own actions by living in harmony with nature so as not to damage the integrity of the Earth' (Drengson, 1995: 147). He argued that adopting an individualised ecosophy would capture the truer diversity of deeper total views and that in acknowledging them as unique, we would increase the possibility of greater insights about humanity and the other-than-human world. Næss argued that our respective ecosophies facilitate a healthy process of constant re-evaluating of ideas (Quick, 2006: 63). His particular ecosophy, that being Ecosophy T, was born from his own unique engagement with his cabin retreat, named *Tvergastein* or 'crossed stones'/'stone crosses' that refers to the rock features of his beloved and adopted mountain, *Halingskarvet*, which contain distinctive crystalline patterns used as markers for finding one's way in whiteout conditions that are common to that Norwegian mountain range. It was from his mountain retreat that Næss wrote most extensively about deep ecology (Drengson, 1992: 3–4). Ecosophy T invites us to discover an ecosophical (re)awakening for ourselves by 'always digging down to get to the roots of questions and issues' and in this way, manifests ecocentric practice reflective of a plurality of personal experiences and insights or 'ultimate values' (Drengson, 1992: 3). In this sense Ecosophy T was not only an intensely personal manifestation of deep ecology but was held out by Næss as an example of how we each might manifest our personal relationships with nature as well (Riggio, 2015: 84). He encouraged each of us to develop a unique love for Earth, which is why he did not prescribe an ecosophy for all, but did put forward his own as a model to help guide us. Through Ecosophy T, Næss believed it was vital that we each find our individual ecological wisdoms as integral to achieving his notion of Self-realization! (Drengson, 1992; Drengson, 1999). Alan Drengson and Bill Devall (2010: 58) explained this nuance accordingly:

> Næss was doing something more subtle than many thought. He was not putting forth a single worldview and philosophy of life that everyone should adhere to in support of the international ecology movement. Instead, he is making an empirical claim based on overwhelming evidence that global social movements, from the grass roots up, consist of people with very diverse religious, philosophical, cultural, and personal orientations. Nonetheless, they can agree on certain courses of action and certain broad principles, especially at the international level. As supporters of a given movement, they treat one another with mutual respect.

Consequently, Næss implied that the individual add his or her unique suffix to their personal ecosophy as a distinguishing identity and not emulate his suffix – 'T', even though subsequent deep ecologists like Warwick Fox (1990) argued for our wholesale buy-in to Ecosophy T in honour of Naess's unique capacity for transcendence. For example, those most drawn to explore men and masculinities like Martin and myself (Paul speaking here), where issues such as gender or for that matter class, race and sexual orientation are stood on equal footing with Earthcare, a unique manifestation of ecosophy emerges – for argument's sake an Ecosophy M (for masculinities) – as distinct from a Næssian Ecosophy T. With this in mind, there are some identifiable limitations to deep ecology that are worthy of mention, reflective of our particular interest in men and masculinities.

Ecosophy M

An important lesson to be drawn from deep ecology is its commitment to non-duality. The discourse was intentionally designed to honour the individual *and* the biological/universal, the subject *and* the object, the ego *and* the metaphysical, reason *and* emotion. Despite this, deep ecology's core tenets have – arguably – struggled to challenge the very substance of male domination. That deep ecology did not confront masculine hegemonisation front-on occurred precisely because Næss's Ecosophy T was reflective of Næss the man. Ecosophy T was mapped out as a non-gender-specific and solitary journey that suited his personality and passions best. Næss was, after all, a product of his socio-cultural environment as much as his aristocratic and mountain homes. Privilege can be blinding. Næss avoided one of the core problems afflicting men – that being the conscious or sub-conscious rehearsal of 'going it alone' in order to awaken a deeper Earth wisdom within. He did so precisely because of his heritage; he approached ecosophisation as an isolated, Western, wealthy, white, revered male, effectively muting the presence of a socio-political analysis at the heart of deep ecology since issues of hegemonisation did not impact him negatively – quite the opposite was true. Interestingly, Næss embodied many of the very same criteria that are driving forth ferocious assaults against Earth and human others today. If we think about this in the context of socialisations of traditional masculinities, solo adventures in nature are typical of 'masculine' ways to commune. It is true that developing an ecosophy in alignment with Næss's intent may work well for those of us who enjoy our own company when immersed in our surroundings. However, solitary pursuit does not confront the ways that men are widely conditioned to cut off from others and the world – that particular nuance of deep ecology runs the risk of actually reinforcing men's isolation and it has been our experience in working with men that isolation is one of the root causes of masculine hegemonisation – men dominate more easily when they are not connected to the otherised other that they dominate. In other words, to follow in Næss's footsteps and isolate on a mountain top (or some other place in nature where we feel reverence), to contemplate life and divest ourselves from our communities of intimate human relations in doing so, is to ask us to operate, at least to some degree, within the parameters of the malestream norms. Indeed, our reading of his bio-graphies suggest that Næss was, like most men, subject to his own variations of emotional containment in alignment with the same masculinist narratives that afflict most modern Western men – in this sense Næss was just another guy (Fox, 1990; Rothenberg, 1993; Glasser, 1999; Næss and Haukeland, 2002; Drengson and Devall, 2010).

We are not problematising contemplative time in nature per se. Rather, to build the deep ecology discourse around this practice of personal awa-kening was, in our analysis, too limited to be of great transformative power for many men precisely because this particular nuance was more of the same. This may in fact be a reason that deep ecology has declined in significance as the global economy of the twenty-first century has churned on at the expense of Earth and our communities – it struggled to offer men (in particular) a fresh pathway to deeper Earth connection and failed to recruit and enrol many men, particularly hegemonised men, as agents to end male domination; men who could accentuate gender equity and greater ecological care systemically and personally. We therefore suggest that Næssian deep ecology was too soft on men's internalised super-iorisation by not directly confronting male domination; a critique that shares some semblance of the shortcomings that we have illuminated in reference to the mythopoetic men's movement. Note that we are arguing that deep ecology did not challenge the patterns of internalised super-iorisation in men, which characterise and at the same time afflict tradi-tional Western renditions of masculinities and in doing so, missed a crucial element of subverting one of the root causes of the patterns of oppression that Næss worked tirelessly to eradicate. We also note that to be guided towards an internalised ecosophy in the Næssian sense ran the risk of preaching to the converted and the converted are not the ones who need the message of Næssian ecosophisation as much as it is those who would otherwise go about their business obliviously destroying Earth and dom-inating the marginalised for personal gain. Finally, deep ecology was too isolated to tuck in behind men and masculinities in order to provide custo-mised support – in communion with nature – to help men relinquish the intoxicating privileges of dominating others that have been held as the masculine due for millennia.

We consequently suggest that Næssian deep ecology could have served Earth, human communities and our individual lives better had it included a specific and intentional framework that made the dismantling of malestream norms integral to the ecologisation of men and masculinities (especially those benefiting most from hegemonisation). Such an oversight has cost the global biosphere and our communities dearly as debates about climate change rage; biodiversity loss churns on; the social and political consequences of the (m)Anthropocene become political hot potatoes; gender inequities exacerbate; global citizenship fractures; international conflict descends into the abyss of righteousness, populism, isolationism, protectionism and military and paramilitary heavy-handedness pitted against international and domestic terrorism; all of which have become commonplace. Taken together, these challenges have seemingly reignited traditional and sexist notions of men as protectors and providers, further confusing what it means to be a man in today's world. Ironically, most of these challenges are the products of male domination as they impact structural global, national, regional and local institutionalised mechanisms. They highlight the terrible personal price that Earth, women, non-binary/genderqueer people and marginalised men pay for industrial/breadwinner or ecomodern manifestations of male domination. While this nuance did not feature in Næss's analyses, ecological masculinities follows some of the core tenets of deep ecology, looking further afield and honing the edge of a specific focus on men and masculinities as our unique contribution to reconciling our social and environmental problems.

This is not at all to blame deep ecology for our current and future problems. It is not our intention to dismiss Næss who was indeed a prolific, influential and well-loved philosopher. We do find his offerings extremely valuable and worthy of our reverence. We acknowledge that Næss clearly and deeply loved nature *and* humanity. Nevertheless, it is important to realise that Næss's deep ecology was the work of a philosopher blissfully addicted to the joy and the quiet of wild places, which he paradoxically shared with many companions in dotted bursts of gregarious delight. His journey to the true nature of the human heart was largely a journey through the human mind. If we are to achieve a broad sweeping shift towards a deep green future, we must find a way to bring as many human beings along with us as is possible and in felt ways, along with the power of reason. We must then remain vigilant, accentuating our scepticism of isolation in all its forms; to pursue alternatives to these artefacts of malestream norms; to encourage and support men and masculinities in particular in ways that centralise the felt self – and for many men this means stretching beyond that one permissive masculine emotion – anger (esp. expressed as violence). We must also raise awareness of the value and majesty of Earth and myriad living things. In doing so, we must imbed these awarenesses into our psyches that Næssian ecosophisation demonstrated to us, embracing wilful celebration of life in all its forms as a desirable attribute of modern Western masculinities. In these ways we extend the importance of deep ecology to the level of full humanness, where men and masculinities are reconfigured to champion being of service to the glocal commons. If we heed elements of the erudite lessons from those who have come before us, such as the useful elements of deep ecology, value the emergent blind spots we detect, sharpen our analyses of men and masculinities across the full political spectrum of views and take active steps to subvert the messages of masculine hegemonisation, then we may indeed find ourselves living the truly sustainable lives that Næss and other deep ecologists have so convincingly advocated.

Deep ecology and malestream norms

It is interesting to consider that Næss avoided the full force of his critics. He remained throughout his life 'quite sensitive to questions of identity and difference, and constantly caution[ed] against forms of holism which deny difference' and as a consequence was not personally subject to the intense ire that deep ecology would generate from some of its opponents (Diehm, 2003: 30). Næss (1989: 195) was not averse to embracing our individuality as we strive to reach 'Self-realization!', suggesting that we do not easily 'dissolve like individual drops in the ocean' since '[o]ur care continues to concern the individuals, not any collectivity' but went on to also note that 'the individual is not, and will not be isolatable' even though his practice of deep ecology and many men's lived experiences have suggested otherwise. This was an oversight precisely because individuals were, in Næss's view, separate *and* connected to relational networks of life, at least conceptually. This shaped his relational Self (Deihm, 2003: 31–32). Such views of the Self ←→ other nexus bound self-interest with interest in the general well-being of all life which, on this particular point, brought Næss into direct alignment with Australian radical ecofeminist scholar Val Plumwood. This unintended compatriotism was not indicative of all ecofeminist interpretations of deep ecology, nor for that matter would Plumwood have sat quietly were such an assessment taken to reflect her broader views on deep ecology – which were at times scathing (Plumwood, pers. comm., 19/05/05). From this we are better able to understand why the two discourses collided so hotly, particularly since the 1990s. In *Nature Ethics: An Ecofeminist Perspective*, Marti Kheel (2008) argued that the pervading gender myopia of male environmental leaders marked the need for ecological feminism to be positioned as a feminist-inspired environmental revolution, that deep ecology, beyond Næssian intent, struggled to embrace.

Our task in this book is to persistently problematised 'men' as a binary category (adding Western and white socialisations to further refine our focus). In doing so, we also recognise that men and masculinities are subject to the negative effects of masculine hegemonisation as well. We also note that their ensuing chronic distresses are core drivers for their persistent perpetration of sexist and ecocidal behaviours. The quiescence of deep ecology since its heyday in the 1990s appears to be at least in part a consequence of the movement not having adequately anticipated the impact that sidelining gendered analyses would have on its international appeal and longevity (Salleh, 1998). Looking beyond its Earth wisdom, we have argued throughout this chapter that many men are manipulated by the socialisations of masculine hegemonisation into rigid roles that are *contrary* to what we consider to be their fulllest human natures. They are subject to violence largely at the hands of other men, as are women and Earth. They are pressured into military service and prepared from a very young age to resolve differences of opinion and conflicts with aggression and violence. They continue to be the majority of workers exploited by corporate capitalist means of production. They perform heavy and risky labour in larger number than do women, suffering by far the most industrial injuries. As boys and men, they are isolated socially and from real human contact more so than are girls and women. Boys and men are distanced from their humanity by ridicule mostly from other boys and men. They are likely to die on average seven years younger than women (worldwide) as a consequence of a cross-section of health challenges that they poorly seek preventative or early assistance for. They are trained to exact oppression upon others in exchange for and in order to preserve the privileges of being male (Balser, 1985: 49; Shmerling, 2016). These are just some of the tragic impacts of the internalised superiorisation and ecocidal norms of masculine hegemonisation. Further, the enduring growth edict of capitalism has failed to deliver improved prosperity to working- and middle-class people, flatlining many families' incomes at 1990s levels, which has fed growing resentment among men from these groups in particular (Long and Gillespie, 2016). Population demographics are shifting rapidly on cultural, racial, religious and generational scales. Immigration (legal, illegal and as a consequence of crises) is increasing while straining border security and this is having an impact on men by seemingly threatening their sense of identity, viability, potency and purpose. While white male unemployment is lower than that of men of colour, there has been steady declines in secure positions of employment for white men, which, at least in part, provides an explanation for populist, racist and xenophobic sentiments running rabid throughout the West. The gap between rich and poor within and between global societies continues to grow. There has been a marked decline in levels of trust in the capacity for big government to move beyond internal conflict in order to get things done that will improve men's lives and the lives of those they care about the most – this is being readily taken by some men as indicative of systems failing them and their loved ones. Men can and do readily acquire constructed feelings of declines in power as a consequence of important gains in gender equity and environmental protectionism. This has been further compounded by the challenges of economic decline associated with the exporting of manufacturing jobs to offshore and cheaper labour markets. It has also become commonplace for many women and men to feel less safe in a world where domestic and international terrorism are increasing threats to global and local security. Military options remain a central bargaining chip on the international negotiating table and with this is an exacerbated doubt in governments' capacities to change these situations for the better (OECD, 2015; Barford, 2016; Long and Gillespie, 2016). It is fair to say that in light of these dire circumstances, deep ecology, as it was applied to glocal needs in the 1990s, needs to become more relevant for twenty-first-century circumstances; deep ecology is in need of gendered and structural reactualising.

This chapter has been written largely from the perspective that we owe Næssian deep ecology a debt of much gratitude. We acknowledge that the movement has played a crucial – and indeed favourable – role in bringing to life a deep environmentalism that has profoundly shifted Global Northern ways of being with nature. However, Næss gave birth to a movement that reflected his own preference for a contemplative world view; an active and engaged 'gestalt shift' or 'ontological realism' that insisted we experience the world spontaneously and in doing so embrace our individual communions with nature (Næss, 2005a: xxii). In alignment with Karen Warren's (1999) critique of the absence of gender sensitivities in deep ecology, we have demonstrated that Næssian deep ecology did not reach adequately beyond business-as-usual for men and masculinities. Næss's writings and the practices he advocated did not intend for men and masculinities in particular to eco-sophise as much as humanity writ large. In accentuating empathy, care and acknowledging the intrinsic value for all life, Næssian deep ecology effectively leapt over the gender question by leaving it for those compelled to incorpo-rate it into their particular Ecosophy to address.

Consequently, the contributions of masculine hegemonisation that lay at the heart of our growing social and environmental problems continue to erode the fecundity of the glocal commons. For men already struggling with isola-tion and a disconnect from their emotional literacy, deep ecology did not provide a specific path beyond the structural constrictions of hegemonisation. This raises two questions for us: was deep ecology dismissive of gendered contributions to social and ecological inequalities? And, if so, then did it let hegemonised masculinities off the hook? These questions are not to be underestimated, since modern Western masculinities harbour all the potential of a deeper total view, which we consider to be innately human, beyond gen-dered identities. However, we have argued that deep ecology inadvertently reinforced some of the core elements of male domination that have been instrumental in propelling us towards social and ecological crises by perso-nalising the complexities that accompany gendered identities rather than bringing these insights to the very heart of its analyses – which ecological feminism has aimed to address from its inception. In writing this book, wc approach Earthcare through a gendered lens.

We note that working-, middle- and owning-class white men in particular have little incentive to advocate social and/or ecological equity or to abdicate their primacy and when asked to do so can present powerful, vocal and fore-boding levels of resistance. We see this most fervently in those who have joined the ranks of alt-right shock-politics movements in particular, finding justification in their resistance to broader, deeper and wider care in the wake of feeling left behind. The planet is, consequently, in the throes of a pre-carious time in history that is having far-reaching impacts on repealing poli-cies and practices that progressive movements have fought for in aiming to address generations of social and environmental concerns. The woes of white Western men are worthy of our consideration as well, along with all others, but these concerns must be taken into consideration proportionally; a point of due diligence that backlash movements largely ignore. In order to address this contemporary concern we develop pathways towards masculine ecologisation that Næss and other deep ecologists missed. For these reasons, we build on and look beyond deep ecology, turning our attention to the complex and diverse terrain of gender politics in relationship with Earthcare as an important forerunner to ecological masculinities that deep ecology could not provide. With these shortcomings of deep ecology stood alongside its great wisdoms, we look further afield now to ecological feminism and its associated ecofeminist practices.

Notes

1 *Panzercharakter* is borrowed from the Freudian term defined as the impenetrable shell that a man uses to protect himself from the vagaries of life, and, in doing so, keeps others at arm's length. Næss adopted the self-describing term as a product of extensive Freudian psychoanalysis (Næss, 2005a: xxxi).

2 Used as compulsory tenets of Norwegian philosophical training, Næss scribed six recommendations for communication and argument that centred around the notion of containment: avoid tendentious irrelevance (personal attacks, claims of opponents' motivation, explaining reasons for an argument); avoid tendentious quoting (quotes should not be edited regarding the subject of the debate); avoid tendentious ambiguity (ambiguity can be exploited to support criticism); avoid tendentious use of straw men (assigning views to the opponent that he or she does not hold); avoid tendentious statements of fact (information put forward should never be untrue or incomplete and one should not withhold relevant information); avoid tendentious tones of presentation (irony, sarcasm, pejoratives, exaggeration, subtle or open threats.

3 Being instrumental in shaping our ecologised masculinities theory, deep ecology's eight-point platform, developed by Næss and US deep ecologist George Sessions, is summarised thus: (1) The flourishing of human and other-than-human life on Earth has intrinsic value. The value or worth of an other-than-human is independent of their usefulness for human purposes; (2) Richness and diversity of life forms justifies their intrinsic value and are values themselves (3) Humans have no right to reduce this abundance and diversity except to satisfy vital needs; (4) The flourishing of human life and cultures is compatible with a considerable reduction in human population and the flourishing of other-than-humans requires that to ensure there are fewer resources being consumed by humans and more left to be consumed by other-than-human others (authors' note: of course the economic differentials between people from the Global North and South call this point into question since it is easy to suggest that there ought to be fewer people on the planet when birth rates are inversely correlated with wealth, education and the material 'good life' accorded people of the Global North, whose per capita consumption rates far exceed those in the Global South); (5) Our current interference with other-than-human life is not only excessive, but is also unsustainable and the situation is rapidly worsening; (6) Policy change must bring about transformations of political, social, economic, technological and ideological structures. Were these changes accomplished, the resulting state of affairs would differ from the 'bigness' of the present considerably and would make a more joyful experience of the 'greatness' and in that the connectedness of all things possible; (7) This ideological change prioritises life quality instead of an increasingly higher standard of living. (8) Those who advocate this platform have an obligation to ensure that these changes happen (Devall and Sessions, 1985: 70; Næss, 1986a: 509–510; Drengson, 1992: 4–5; Drengson, 1997: 3–4; Næss and Haukeland, 2002: 108; Naess, 2008: 11–12, 28–31).

References

ABC News. 2017. 'Donald Trump's executive order on energy raises questions about future of Paris climate deal'. Accessed 21 April 2017. http://www.abc.net.au/news/2017-03-29/did-donald-trump-just-kill-the-paris-climate-change-deal/8396158

Andersson, J. 2006. 'Choosing futures: Alva Myrdal and the construction of Swedish futures studies, 1967–1972'. *International Review of Social History*, 51(2): 277–295.

Anker, P. 1998. 'On the ultimate norms in Ecosophy T'. *Trumpeter: Journal of Ecosophy* 15(1). Accessed 15 August 2017. http://trumpeter.athabascau.ca/index.php/trumpet/article/view/152/1323

Anker, P. 1999. 'Remarks on the history of deep ecology'. In N. Witoszek and A. Brennan, eds., *Philosophical Dialogues: Arne Næss and the Progress of Ecophilosophy*. Lanham: Rowman & Littlefield, 431–443.

Balser, D. 1985. Women: Summary Report of the International Women's Conference of Re-evaluation Counseling Communities held in the Netherlands, October 12–17, 1984. Seattle: Rational Island.

Barford, V. 2016. 'Why are Americans so angry?' *BBC News*. Accessed 19 November 2016. http://www.bbc.com/news/magazine-35406324

Biehl, J. 1988. 'What is social ecofeminism?'. *Green Perspectives: A Left Green Publication* 11: 1–8.

Bookchin, M. 1987. 'Social ecology versus "deep ecology": a challenge for the ecology movement'. *Green Perspectives: Newsletter of the Green Program Project* 4–5: 1–23.

Bookchin, M. 1995. *Re-enchanting Humanity: A Defense of the Human Spirit against Anti-Humanism, Misanthropy, Mysticism and Primitivism*. London: Cassell.

Bragg, E. 1996. 'The ecological self: deep ecology meets constructivist self theory'. *Journal of Environmental Psychology* 16(2): 93–108.

Cheney, J. 1987. 'Eco-feminism and deep ecology'. *Environmental Ethics* 9(2): 115–145.

Clark, J. 1996. 'How wide is deep ecology?'. *Inquiry* 39(2): 189–201.

Crook, M., and D. Short. 2014. 'Marx, Lemkin and the genocide–ecocide nexus'. *International Journal of Human Rights* 18(3): 298–319.

Devall, B. 1988. *Simple in Means, Rich in Ends: Practicing Deep Ecology*. Salt Lake City: Peregrine Smith.

Devall, B. 2010. 'Relationship with Arne Næss'. *Trumpeter: Journal of Ecosophy* 26(2): 3–5.

Devall, B., and G. Sessions. 1985. *Deep Ecology: Living as if Nature Mattered*. Layton: Gibbs Smith.

Diehm, C. 2003. 'The self of stars and stone: ecofeminism, deep ecology, and the ecological self'. *Trumpeter: Journal of Ecosophy* 19(3): 31–45.

Drengson, A. 1988. 'Deep ecology: living as if nature mattered by Bill Devall and George Sessions' [book review]. *Environmental Ethics* 10(1): 83–89.

Drengson, A. 1992. 'The long-range deep ecology movement and Arne Næss'. *Trumpeter: Journal of Ecosophy* 9(2). Accessed 1 July 2017. http://trumpeter.athabascau.ca/index.php/trumpet/article/view/425/694

Drengson, A. 1995. *The Practice of Technology: Exploring Technology, Ecophilosophy, and Spiritual Disciplines for Vital Links*. Albany: SUNY Press.

Drengson, A. 1997. 'A model for community economic systems based on ecoforestry'. In A. Drengson and D. Taylor, eds., *Ecoforestry: The Art and Science of Sustainable Forest Use*. Gabriola Island: New Society Publishers, 239–242.

Drengson, A. 2001. 'Education for local and global ecological responsibility: Arne Næss's cross-cultural, ecophilosophy approach'. *Canadian Journal of Environmental Education* 5 (spring): 63–75.

Drengson, A., and B. Devall. 2010. 'The deep ecology movement: origins, development and future prospects'. *Trumpeter: Journal of Ecosophy* 26(2): 48–69.

Fox, W. 1990. *Towards a Transpersonal Ecology: Developing New Foundations for Environmentalism*. London: Shambhala Publications.

Glasser, H. 1995. 'Deep ecology clarified: a few fallacies and misconceptions'. *Trumpeter: Journal of Ecosophy* 12(3): 138–142.

Glasser, H. 1999. 'Næss's deep ecology approach and environmental policy'. In N. Witoszek and A. Brennan, eds., *Philosophical Dialogues: Arne Næss and the Progress of Ecophilosophy*. Lanham: Rowman & Littlefield, 360–390.

Hallen, P. 1999. 'The ecofeminism–deep ecology dialogue: a short commentary on the exchange between Karen Warren and Arne Næss'. In N. Witoszek and A. Brennan, eds., *Philosophical Dialogues: Arne Næss and the Progress of Ecophilosophy*. Lanham, MD: Rowman & Littlefield, 274–280.

Handl, G. 2012. 'Declaration of the United Nations Conference on the Human Environment (Stockholm Declaration), 1972 and the Rio Declaration on Environment and Development, 1992 (United Nations Audiovisual Library of International Law)'. Accessed 6 November 2017. http://legal.un.org/avl/ha/dunche/dunche.html

Harding, S. 2011. 'What is deep ecology?' Schumacher College. Accessed 6 August 2011. http://www.schumachercollege.org.uk/learning-resources/what-is-deep-ecology

Kheel, M. 2008. *Nature Ethics: An Ecofeminist Perspective*. Lanham: Rowman & Littlefield.

LaChapelle, D. 1988. *Sacred Land, Sacred Sex: Rapture of the Deep: Concerning Deep Ecology and Celebrating Life*. Asheville: Kivakí Press.

Long, H., and P. Gillespie. 2016. 'Why Americans are so angry in 2016'. *CNN Money*. Accessed 19 November 2016. http://money.cnn.com/2016/03/09/news/economy/donald-trump-bernie-sanders-angry-america/index.html

Macy, J. 1989. 'Awakening the ecological self'. In J. Plant, ed., *Healing the Wounds: The Promise of Ecofeminism*. Santa Cruz: New Society, 201–211.

Mathews, F. 1991. *The Ecological Self*. Savage: Barnes & Noble.

Mathews, F. 1994. 'Relating to nature: deep ecology or ecofeminism?'. *Trumpeter: Journal of Ecosophy* 11(4): 159–166.

Næss, A. 1973. 'The shallow and the deep, long-range ecology movement: a summary'. *Inquiry* 16: 95–100.

Næss, A. 1986a. 'Intrinsic value: will the defenders of nature please rise?'. In M. Soulé, ed., *Conservation Biology: The Science of Scarcity and Diversity*. Sunderland: Sinauer Associates, 504–515.

Næss, A. 1986b. 'Self-realization: an ecological approach to being in the world'. Paper presented at the Keith Roby Memorial Lecture in Community Science, Murdoch University, March 12.

Næss, A. 1989. *Ecology, Community and Lifestyle*, trans. D. Rothenberg. Cambridge: Cambridge University Press.

Næss, A. 1995. 'The systematization of the logically ultimate norms and hypotheses of Ecosophy T'. In A. Drengson and Y. Inoue, eds., *The Deep Ecology Movement: An Introductory Anthology*. Berkeley: North Atlantic Books, 8–30.

Næss, A. 1999a. 'The ecofeminism versus deep ecology debate'. In N. Witoszek and A. Brennan, eds., *Philosophical Dialogues: Arne Næss and the Progress of Ecophilosophy.* Lanham: Rowman & Littlefield, 270–279.

Næss, A. 1999b. 'Response to Peder Anker'. In N. Witoszek and A. Brennan, eds., *Philosophical Dialogues: Arne Næss and the Progress of Ecophilosophy.* Lanham: Rowman & Littlefield, 444–465.

Næss, A. 1999c. 'Is deep ecology vision a green vision or is it multicolored like the rainbow: an answer to Nona Witoszek'. In N. Witoszek and A. Brennan, eds., *Philosophical Dialogues: Arne Næss and the Progress of Ecophilosophy.* Lanham: Rowman & Littlefield, 466–472.

Næss, A. 2003. 'The deep ecological movement: some philosophical aspects'. In A. Light and H. Rolston III, eds., *Environmental Ethics: An Anthology.* Malden: Blackwell, 262–274.

Næss, A. 2005a. *The Selected Works of Arne Næss: Interpretation and Preciseness (A Contribution to the Theory of Communication).* Dordrecht: Springer.

Næss, A. 2005b. 'The basics of deep ecology'. *Trumpeter: Journal of Ecosophy* 21(1): 61–71.

Næss, A. 2008. *The Ecology of Wisdom: Writings by Arne Næss.* Berkeley: Counterpoint.

Næss, A., and P. Haukeland. 2002. *Life's Philosophy: Reason and Feeling in a Deeper World.* Athens: University of Georgia Press.

Norgaard, K. 2011. *Living in Denial: Climate Change, Emotions, and Everyday Life.* Cambridge: MIT Press.

Notario, M. 2006. 'Meeting with a giant: an informal conversation with Arne Næss'. *Trumpeter: Journal of Ecosophy* 22(1): 101–112.

OECD. 2015. *In It Together: Why Less Inequality Benefits All.* Paris: OECD.

Plumwood, V. 1993. *Feminism and the Mastery of Nature.* London: Routledge.

Quick, T. 2006. 'In praise of Næss's pluralism'. *Trumpeter: Journal of Ecosophy* 22(1): 52–68.

Riggio, A. 2015. *Ecology, Ethics, and the Future of Humanity.* New York: Palgrave Macmillan.

Rothenberg, D. 1993. *Is It Painful to Think? Conversations with Arne Næss.* Minneapolis: University of Minnesota Press.

Salleh, A. 1984. 'Deeper than deep ecology: the eco-feminist connection'. *Environmental Ethics* 6 (winter): 339–345.

Salleh, A. 1992. 'The ecofeminism/deep ecology debate: a reply to patriarchal reason'. *Environmental Ethics* 14 (Fall): 195–216.

Salleh, A. 1996. 'Social ecology and "the man question"'. *Environmental Politics* 5(2): 258–273.

Salleh, A. 1998. 'Deeper than deep ecology: the ecofeminist connection'. In M. Zimmerman, J. Callicott, G. Sessions, K. Warren, and J. Clark, eds., *Environmental Philosophy: From Animal Rights to Radical Ecology.* Upper Saddle Valley: Prentice Hall, 339–345.

Seed, J. 2006. 'Ecopsychology'. Accessed 9 April 2010. http://www.schumachercollege. org.uk/learning-resources/ecopsychology

Seed, J., Macy, J., Fleming, P., and A. Næss. 1988. *Thinking Like a Mountain: Towards a Council of All Beings.* Philadelphia: New Society Publishers.

Shmerling, R. 2016. 'Why men often die earlier than women'. Harvard Health Publications, Harvard Medical School. Accessed 29 April 2017. http://www.health.harvard. edu/blog/why-men-often-die-earlier-than-women-201602199137

Slicer, D. 1995. 'Is there an ecofeminism–deep ecology "debate"?'. *Environmental Ethics* 17 (summer): 151–169.

Snyder, G. 1974. *Turtle Island with 'Four Changes'*. New York: New Directions.

Twine, R. 2001. 'Ma(r)king essence-ecofeminism and embodiment'. *Ethics and the Environment* 6(2): 31–58.

Warren, K. 1999. 'Ecofeminist philosophy and deep ecology.' In N. Witoszek and A. Brennan, eds., *Philosophical Dialogues: Arne Næss and the Progress of Ecophilosophy*. Lanham: Rowman & Littlefield, 255–269.

Zimmerman, M. 1987. 'Feminism, deep ecology, and environmental ethics.' *Environmental Ethics* 9(1): 21–45.

Zimmerman, M. 1993. 'Rethinking the Heidegger–deep ecology relationship'. *Environmental Ethics* 15(3): 195–224.

5   Lessons from ecological feminism

> To reduce human or modern subjectivity to a violent and violating dominating tendency, or to an essential, inevitably harmful collective force, is to misrepresent a minority of all of humanity, and to identify ideologies of domination and disregard for nature as paradigmatic and definitive of all of humanity . . . While there are gendered patterns in relationships with nature . . . sex and gender are interwoven with particulars of class, race, culture and other factors, and so they are also diverse.
>
> (Cuomo, 2017: 288–289)

Gender and environments

Everyone is not treated equally. Similarly, as individuals, we are not having equal impacts on the planet. Some are more complicit in the ills of the world and some are more severely affected than are others. This is a notion that radical and structural feminisms have been championing for some time. While a history of feminist philosophy exists that aimed to extract women and feminine socialisations from associations with nature, there is also a long herstory to the contrary, where 'more nuanced investigations of the complex material, symbolic and ethical relationships between women, animals, and the land have long been prominent in feminist literatures' (Cuomo, 2017: 290). The efforts of feminist scholars who championed both perspectives facilitated the rise of the eminent discourse known as ecological feminism. Chris Cuomo (1998: 6) distinguished 'ecological feminism' from 'ecofeminism' and 'ecofeminists' by noting that the former term is a subset of feminist thinking, while the latter terms link women's empowerment with concerns for Earth through a variety of embodied and politicised perspectives and praxes. To clarify our application of each term in this chapter, we use 'ecological feminism' when discussing the discursive implications of ecological thinking that arose within feminism as a unique and rich body of conceptual work on gender and environments that has formed a distinct and important discourse. We use the terms 'ecofeminism' and 'ecofeminist' here when discussing individuals and their respective interpretations of ecological feminism, accompanied by a plurality of applications (or recommendations for action) that have resulted in a mosaic of manifestations in the real world. In this chapter, we align our work on masculine ecologisation with some elements of ecological feminism, while distancing ourselves from others.

As a subset of the feminist metanarrative, ecological feminism is a third stream that informs ecological masculinities. Further to our cursory introduction to some ecological feminist ideas presented in Chapter 1, we examine the ways that ecological feminism has held men and masculinities accountable for our social and environmental challenges. We recognise that conceptualisations and manifestations of our understandings of men and (especially industrial/breadwinner) masculinities can and must change. Second, we acknowledge that essentialist perspectives on either end of a female–male binary are polarised (and problematic) expressions of a spectrum of views about the ways that gender affects the human–nature relationship. We also note that essentialism is not representative of all ecological feminist theoreticians nor all the ecofeminist practitioners that have presented opinions and actions throughout the gender–nature nexus. Third, we celebrate ecological feminism as the most comprehensive conversation about gender and enivonment of our four chosen streams. We share a material–semiotic view, inspired by – as Donna Haraway puts it – the objective knowledge acquired through biological bodies at historical points in time (Haraway, 1991). We do so to acknowledge subjectivities and to also avoid generalising about women or men's resistance or compliance with social and environmental injustices, noting that the conversation is far more diverse than any gendered essentialism might encourage. Instead, we look to a combined political/personal approach, examining systemic critiques along with personal accountability and responsibility as the most useful strategies for change, keeping our focus on those that are specific to men and masculinities and what ecological feminism might help us learn about and prepare us for as an ecologised masculinities discourse emerges. Of course, we recognise deconstructive analyses in relation to the ways that women, feminine socialisations and Earth are affected by our social and ecological crises as well – albeit in unique ways. Two notable and very recent publications and recommended resources that help us gain further insights into this field are Sherilyn MacGregor's (2017) anthology titled the *Routledge Handbook of Gender and Environment*; and an anthology edited by Susan Buckingham and Virginie Le Masson (2017) titled *Understanding Climate Change through Gender Relations*. An important starting point for our refined examination of ecological feminism is to honour research on the forefront of gender and environments scholarship such as these, as they offer innovative approaches to creating a place at the table for discussion on men, masculinities and Earth to emerge in the wake of compelling (eco)feminist scholarship.

As we have previously acknowledged, men and masculinities are located at the source our social and environmental ills. However, there has been a notable absence of conversations about redefining male socialisations so that masculinities might be reconfigured to support men standing as allies with eco feminists and others in righting these wrongs. These recent developments are worthy of some attention before we continue. MacGregor's (2017: 5, 7, 15) anthology offers us cogent insights into the limitations of original trends in ecofeminist typologising (specifically: cultural, socialist, social and third world ecofeminisms), arguing that we have moved on to perspectives that encompass the broader gender and environments field, of which discussions about men, masculinities and Earth (along with queer ecologies) are a part. In her introductory statements, MacGregor (2017: 7) suggested that historical classifications of ecological feminist scholarship are now mute (and in fact have been contestable all along); shifting her focus to finding threads of thinking and praxes reflecting the pluralism that has long been characteristic of ecofeminist multiplicities. For Buckingham and Le Masson eds. (2017: 2), consideration for gendered complexities and subtitles has been alarmingly absent from debates about global carbon pollution and how nations might respond. This absence threatens mitigating efforts with failure unless and until we accept that gendered inequalities are integral to the alarming predictions of climate science (Buckingham and Le Masson eds., 2017: 2). The social and environmental implications for sidestepping textured gendered debates appear to be dire. We will not offer an in-depth analysis of these matters, but defer to MacGregor, Buckingham and Le Masson (along with others who have greater abilities in these fields of inquiry than either of us) for more informed insights into these discussions. Similarly, our principal purpose in writing this chapter is not to rehash the thoroughly tilled terrain of ecofeminisms. Rather, we examine the trajectory of ecofeminisms that rallied (at times in some tension with each other) around a central concern for the mutual oppression of women and nature by a male-dominated world, presenting five notable threads that we recognise, those being: feminist political ecologies (FPE); feminist science studies, material feminisms and posthumanities; binary ecofeminisms; gender-equitable ecofeminisms; non-binary/genderqueer ecofeminisms. These five threads influence the building blocks for our conceptualisation of masculine ecologisation and its plurality of emergent practical expressions. We examine each of them to aid us in predicting the likely textured trajectory of an emergent discourse on men, masculinities and Earth. We offer a response to this variety of discussions on women, feminine socialisations and Earth as a mirrored analysis to aid us as we unpack the concepts and practices associated with considerations of men, masculinities and Earth. In doing so, we acknowledge that the diversity of views presented by these five threads are products of more than forty years (or arguably of more than a century) of lively feminist debates that have resulted in the rich tapestry that has become ecological feminism.

Herstory of feminist ecologisation

It is difficult to compile a comprehensive herstory of feminist contributions to the intersecting terrain of women, feminine socialisations and Earth. After all, a wide variety of simultaneously evolving views have punctuated these topics for some time. It would also be a misrepresentation of gendered engagements with social and environmental issues to simply offer a timeline of evolving views, since impacts on these emergent discussions have been iterative. Many prominent early feminists recognised the socially and environmentally destructive implications of traditional industrial and modern notions of manhood and masculinities (Laula, 1904; Gilman, 1979[1915]; Wägner, 1941; Carson, 1962). Human rights activist Elsa Laula (1904) provided an early Swedish indigenous view on social and environmental justice, confronting colonisation's impacts on her Saami heritage, as (primarily) white, wealthy men in the Swedish national administration and industries plundered minerals and water resources of her homeland, positioning her as an icon of brave indigenous women's resistance the world over that remains relevant to this day. Charlotte Perkins Gilman's (1979[1915]) *Herland* speaks of a fictitious women's utopia that had no need of men, creating idealised systems freed from those characteristic masculine features of violence and domination. Her novel exposed the ways that women are either revered or desired by men, positing new ways to exalt motherhood while redefining gendered roles; serving as a feminist treatise that was ahead of its time. Elin Wägner (1941) wrote about Sweden's trajectory towards destructive industrial modernisation from the 1930s into the war years. Feminist scholars consider her *Väckarklockan* to be a posthumanities forerunner of ecological feminist thinking (Leppänen, 2008; Leppänen and Svensson, 2016). Further, consider the monumental influence of Rachel Carson (1962), whose ground-breaking exposure of bioaccumulation of toxic synthetic chemicals was one of the most visible contributions to gender and environments concerns before an ecological feminist discourse formally emerged. As Joni Seager (2017: 28) demonstrated, Carson was more of an ecofeminist than was widely acknowledged, since she challenged 'the ascendant view that human progress depended on ever more powerful control over "nature"'. Toxic substances, such as dichloro-diphenyl-trichloroethane (DDT), were not only extensively used on an industrial scale, but had been effectively marketed to domestic markets, with men pictured, spray apparatus in hand, freely distributing what we now widely accept to be one of the most lethal and ecologically damaging substances that humanity has manufactured throughout communities for lawn care, insect-free homes, polio prevention in children, along with accelerating agri-industrial food production in the post-war years.

In the late 1960s women's environmental leadership became increasingly influential. This resulted in, for example, the Green Belt Movement (GBM) originating in Nairobi, Kenya, which championed holistic approaches to localised development strategies. The GBM stressed that environmental care is intimately related to community development, capacity building and empowerment, climate resilience, deliberative democracy and sustainable development strategies, particularly for girls and women throughout the Global South (Maathai, 2004; Green Belt Movement, 2017). Women's activism was central in anti-nuclear movements in the Global North as well (Caldicott, 2006; Kall and

Hultman, forthcoming). Women's leadership courageously reached beyond the constrictions of malestream norms to build the conceptual foundations of ecological feminisms through grass-roots (ecofeminist) actions. These contributions emerged spontaneously across the globe in response to colonialism and industrial modernisation. In this sense, ecofeminist activism (arguably) pre-dated ecological feminist theory (Salleh, pers. comm., 02/01/13).

With these foundational complexities illuminated, we look now to the beginning of ecological feminism as an emerging theoretical field. French feminist scholar Françoise d'Eaubonne coined the term ecofeminism in her pivotal book: *Le féminisme ou la mort* in 1974 (which created a conceptual umbrella for similar active and precursory ideas mentioned above). There, d'Eaubonne argued the need for women to take a lead role in an ecological revolution to usurp male domination in response to its terrible and specific impacts on women and Earth (d'Eaubonne, 1974: 213–252; d'Eaubonne, 1980: 64; Warren, 2000: 21). D'Eaubonne was both a feminist scholar and gender-equity activist. She posited the term ecofeminism to help bring an end to the epic violence of phallocratic civilisations addicted to male domination; her work gave rise to social and environmental movements that were to become powerful expressions of women's intellectual and tangible leadership, which grew to the now internationally renowned discourse, ecological feminism (d'Eaubonne, 1980: 64). Notably, d'Eaubonne did not clarify what her vision for a gendered alternative leadership would look like. Instead, she stressed that men are directly responsible for 'today's deplorable demographic situation, and not only male power; man at every level . . . on the grounds that all society's evils . . . have masculine origins' (d'Eaubonne, 1980: 64). She argued, that men's culpability was evident throughout modern Western socio-political constructs that prop up and are propped up by Western malestreams. Notably, a multiplicity of insights within ecological feminism have since emerged – contributors veering from d'Eaubonne's foundational and misandric opinions (Salleh, 1984; Warren, 1987; Archambault, 1993; Roth-Johnson, 2013). On the other side of the Atlantic, d'Eaubonne's preliminary contributions to the emerging ecological feminist discourse stimulated the publication of Rosemary Radford Ruether's (1975) *New Woman, New Earth*, along with Ynestra King's (1976) courses on ecofeminism that emerged at the Institute for Social Ecology (Vermont, US) (King, 1983; Merchant 2006: 514), Mary Daly's (1978) *Gyn/Ecology: The Metaethics of Radical Ecology* and Susan Griffin's (1978) *Woman and Nature*. To build a truly just and sustainable world, the task ahead was clear:

> Women must see that there can be no liberation for them and no solution to the ecological crisis within a society whose fundamental model of relationships continues to be one of domination. They must unite the demands of the women's movement with those of the ecological movement to envision a radical reshaping of the basic socioeconomic relations and the underlying values of this [male-dominated] society.
>
> (Ruether, 1975: 204)

Ecological feminist statements such as this focused on solving the problems of society and environment through acute analyses of the impacts of gendered socialisations on women and Earth by men (Griffin, 1978: xv; Spretnak, 1990: 9). Ruether (1992: 266), later argued that 'women's liberation' ought to not only be the incorporation of women's wisdom into the supplanting of male domination conceptually speaking. She suggested that ecological feminism could also tangibly steer us away from patterns of isolation towards our world, otherised humans and ourselves (in ways that deep ecology did not). She noted:

> . . . it is impossible to fully add women to this alienated life of males, since the male alienated life-style is only possible by the exploitation of women who remain tied to 'nature'. Rather, what is necessary is a double transformation of both women and men in their relation to each other and to 'nature' . . . The ways of being a person for others and of being a person for oneself need to come together as reciprocal, rather than being split between female and male styles of life . . . Only when men are fully integrated into the culture of daily sustenance of life can men and women together begin to reshape the larger systems of economic, social, and political life.
>
> (Ruether, 1992: 215–216)

This integration of the feminine and masculine principles within us all that Ruether advocated was a 'biophilic mutuality' with great potential to manifest authentic inner and outer security through acceptance, vulnerability, setting limits and acknowledging interdependency, rather than through domination, power and control (Owusu, 2006: 178–179). For Ruether, this was a necessary human process that both women and men must adopt with intention and purpose. Building on these views, Griffin challenged women's alleged frailty, lust and embodiment juxtaposed against the presumed robustness of a hyper-masculinised 'ultimate reality' writ large; an unapologetic proclamation that 'the face of earth is a record of man's sins'. (Griffin 1978: 8–9, 28). The tone of such foundational ecofeminist statements is admittedly binary, if not essentialist. This acknowledged, we recognise in these days of toxic/extreme masculinities revivals and neo-fascist backlashes coupled with a resurgence in industrial extractivism and a dismissive approach to contemporary climate concerns by the US Trump administration, that a new discursive examination of men, masculinities and Earth gives Ruether's forewarnings renewed relevance.

These pioneering perspectives on ecological feminism launched a global process of feminist ecologisation. The discourse was in fact constructed across a broad front of materialist, posthumanist and intersectional analyses of capitalism, reductive science, imperial and colonial history, race, heteronormativity, decolonisation and (andro)anthropocentrism studies (Plumwood, 1993; MacGregor ed., 2017: 1). Ecological feminism continues to contribute provocative and compelling arguments under the auspices of more neutralised studies on gender and the environment. Its proponents seek conceptualisations and actions to help resolve the inherent tensions that have long existed between our understandings of gender and our use/ misuse of nature (MacGregor ed., 2017: 2). Consistent throughout the herstory of ecological feminism is a unifying principle that (like deep ecology) multiplicities offer a sound path forward for protecting and preserving all life. This is an important detail for us to consider since we position ecological masculinities as a discursive compatriot to ecological feminism noting, as we have attested previously, that its unfolding trajectory is likely to be subject to similar complexities.

Ecofeminist pluralities

Ecological feminism has worked across a wide front to explore conditions for women and Earth on the theoretical, policy, practical and psycho-spiritual levels (Alaimo, 1994: 133; Warren, 2002: 39). For some of its early supporters, the discourse celebrated women's apparent inseparable relationship with nature (especially through menses and child birth) that no man could share, while others highlighted the masculine proclivity to commoditise women's bodies in similar ways to industrial/breadwinner and ecomodern commoditisation of Earth's resources, asking men to join the ecofeminist project or better yet 'queer-ise' gendered binaries in order to get beyond those limitations (Gaard, 1997). Such suggestions were not intended to churn out 'girly men' in the Schwarzeneggerian sense that we raised in Chapter 2. Instead, these invitations showed that men could, through an ecologised feminisation process, reconnect with their caring capacities beyond the limitations that essentialised language would otherwise have us believe is the exclusive stuff of women. Ecological feminism grew into a diverse conceptual framework that encouraged practices to manifest feminist ideals of empowerment for women and respect for nature.

We are most interested in pitching our analyses above a granular view of specific ecofeminisms. The discourse evoked the human psychic potential for intellect, feeling, activity and receptivity, advocating richer and more holistic relational experiences between Earth and humanity and among us all as a species as well. This emergent pluralism represented distinct gender and environmental ethics that characterise the discourse to this day. Various emergent ecofeminisms illuminated a number of related paths to meet the challenges of counter-hegemonic thinking, bonded in the common cause of restoring equity for all life through 'carefully considered relational exchanges' specifically between Earth and women, among women and between women and men (Plumwood 2002a: 167). They shared their joint critiques of the hegemonisation that accompanies industrial/breadwinner and ecomodern proclivities for logical and dualistic approaches to reality that are the hallmarks of male domination. A common commitment bonds these various threads of insight to end the mutual mistreatment of women and Earth from a variety of perspectives, that being the need for men and masculinities to be more caring for global, regional and local issues – simultaneously. For Karen Warren (2000: 97), this created ripe conditions for theoretical and ethical nodes (rather than loosely organised claims) to emerge, bound by 'care-sensitive ethics' that emulate a patchwork quilt:

> The 'necessary conditions' of a theory (say, ecofeminist philosophical theory [a.k.a. ecological feminism]) are like borders of a quilt: They delimit the boundary conditions of the theory without dictating beforehand what the interior (the design; the actual patterns) of the quilt does or must look like. The actual design of the quilt will emerge from the diversity of perspectives of quilters who contribute, over time, to the making of the quilt. Theory is not something static, preordained, or carved in stone; it is always *theory-in-process*.

Inspired by the Names Project Quilt that stitched together the names of lives lost to AIDS during the early years of that epidemic without defining how any individual patch symbolises the person deceased, this analogy stressed that quilts are – like theory – self-critical and changing. Their purpose is to capture moments in time that necessarily change with the shifting conditions that they stand for. They can be repaired, replaced or removed if no longer useful to the broader quilt, or, as was Warren's intended analogy, represent those moments within theoretical evolution that no longer align with the theory within which they originated. Quilts are also contextual since they reflect historical, societal, economic and political influences; they may generalise within themselves but play an even more important part in a bigger picture (Warren, 2000: 68). In other words, quilts, like theories, tell stories.

The ecofeminisms examined by Warren (1997: 13–14; Warren, 2000: 98–101) conform to eight necessary boundary conditions that she refered to as 'features' of their collective empirical and linguistic implications. They are:

1   The generalisations within ecofeminisms harbour a set of common beliefs, values, attitudes and assumptions about the ways that environmental destruction disproportionately affects women and children.
2   All ecofeminisms take stands against sexism, racism, classism, naturism, in fact any 'ism of social domination' to ensure that theoretical and practical attempts to make the needs of women and Earth invisible or unimportant (both consciously or unconsciously) are challenged.
3   Each ecofeminism is unavoidably contextual, affected by histories and identities as they are impacted by human–human and human–other-than-human relational exchanges, expressing narratives about the psychology, needs and insights that they each offer, meaning self and story are inextricably linked to contradict the invisibility of women.
4   Differing ethics captured by each ecofeminism give voice to the variety of needs portrayed by women and other-than-human others, prioritising the respectful acknowledgement of difference, effectively challenging

mainstream assumptions about masculinised rationality and feminised Earth.

5   They each accentuate the narratives of the downtrodden and oppressed (specifically women and Earth) to ensure that their respective generalisations are accurately representative, random, right-sized and replicable in order to minimise biases – particularly those that privilege men – by prioritising women-led community efforts and protests that contest male domination.

6   Unnoticed, underplayed and misrepresented messages about women and Earth are valued and prioritised within each ecofeminism, stressing their collective ethical and empirical importance despite individualised differences.

7   All ecofeminisms as nodes within ecological feminism necessarily redefine what it means to be human, placing gender-free or gender-neutral presumptions under the microscope to ensure that politics, policies and philosophies shift away from sexist and ecocidal presumptions.

8   Mainstream communication is considered suspect by the ecological feminist discourse, especially in the ways that it can ascribe assumptions about women, feminine socialisations and Earth while privileging men and masculinities.

Warren considered the ethical distinctions of these ecofeminist nodes within ecological feminism to be distinct narratives of beings-in-relationships, creating a diversity of valuable vehicles for human encounters with other-than-humans, which steer us away from arrogance and encourage loving ('caring') perceptions of difference. She argued that this would result in the three features of her 'care-sensitive ethics' where ecofeminisms:

1   harbour the moral imperative of caring for others and self;
2   are 'situated' rather than ahistorical, transcendent or absolute; and
3   centralise considerations of care resulting in a condition of 'care practices'.

These ethical principles celebrate utility, self-interest, duty and rights as potentially overriding, if not unavoidably conspicuous (Warren, 2000: 104–105, 107–108). Following on from her patchwork quilt analogy, Warren compared these ethics to a 'fruit bowl', where different fruit suit different purposes, desires or intended outcomes of a shared ethical principle of caring for all others and the self – simultaneously and as an antidote to masculine hegemonisation (Warren, 2000: 108–109). Like Greta Gaard (2016: 168) we consider Warren's boundary conditions and care-sensitive ethics to be crucial as we step towards ecological feminist inspired ecological masculinities. Given the significance of ecological feminism to our work, the discourse might be viewed not only as a discursive 'quilt' made of up of a variety of ethical 'fruit' but could also be considered an 'ecosystem' – where respective ecofeminisms interact like organisms linked in intricate relational webs – ensuring that each engages with the other in pulsing exchanges of tension and support that varies according to the inter-relatable conditions throughout the discourse at any particular moment in time. Further, their values, interests and expressions can manifest in any one individual ecofeminist relative to others.

In previous typologies of ecofeminisms, a grouping of three distinct branches (revolutionary – social, reformist/scientific – spiritual/essentialist) frequently appeared in scholarly literature (Spretnak, 1990: 5–6; Hallen, 1988: 18; Lahar, 1991: 34–43; Carlassare, 1992: 53–58; Merchant, 1992: 183–210; Adams, 1993: 1–9; Mies and Shiva, 1993: 13–21, Plumwood, 1993: 8–9, 35–36; Davion, 1994: 17–28; Warren, 1994: 119–123; Sturgeon, 1997: 3–5, 23–58; Warren, 1997: 4; Warren, 2000: 21–41; Buckingham, 2004: 146–154; Norgaard and York, 2005: 506–522; Kheel, 2008: 207–274; Pulé, 2013). As mentioned previously, such categorisations of ecofeminism into three branches has now been superseded by 'more expansive and kaleidoscopic' web (keeping with the ecosystem analogy here) of discursive relationships made up of various threads on gender and environment studies, which also include masculinities studies alongside decolonisation, intersectionality, material feminism and queer ecologies (MacGregor ed., 2017: 5, 15). This dichotomy of ecofeminisms generated politicised tensions across the ecological feminist discourse. Examining these tensions became central to the inquiries that feminist political ecology (FPE) centralised.

Feminist political ecology

FPE is a framework that finds its origins in political ecology, seeking connections between social and ecological injustices, with special attention to development processes in the Global South as they relate to women's politics, economics and experiences (Rocheleau et al., 1996; Nightingale, 2006; Arora-Jonsson, 2013). FPE emerged as a reaction against masculine hegemonisation through an acute focus on women, the environment and development (WED) on global, regional and local scales. Neo-Marxian investigations of women and Earth strongly influenced these ecofeminists, exposing colonial and bourgeois social constructs, arguing that men are complicit in enslaving women and Earth to advance industrial growth and economic development for their own advantage and to the detriment of all. Such discussions were intended to not only expose male oppression patterns, but to also construct 'egalitarian, decentralised, bioregional communities' that captured Western European counter-cultural idealisations of a communitarian *politick* (Biehl, 1988: 62–63, 67–69; Gruen, 1997: 356–374; Salleh, 1998: 323). Drawing on ecosocialist principles and the trajectory of global well-being and human history over time, neo-Marxist ecofeminists noted the impact of these pressures on men's lives, along with otherised others (Mellor, 1992b: 255). They took vocal stands to move away from a world that disadvantages women and Earth through socio-politically redesigning systemic machinations and radically pointing their associated policy changes towards greater collectivisation and care (Mellor, 1992b: 249; Mellor, 1997: 63; Salleh, 1997: 1; Salleh, 2006: 32–37).

Mary Mellor suggested that a 'we' world must supersede masculinist hege-monies, where caring for others and self are tasks shared equally among women and men (Mellor, 1992a: 255, 261). These notions highlighted the need to cauterise corporatisation and end the inequalities associated with industrial extractivism for the mutual benefit of women and Earth, arguing that doing so would be good for men as well (von Werlhof, 2007: 13). FPE is characterised by the view that while the lives of all human beings are rooted in nature, men are rooted in lead roles of creating and managing infrastructural and systemic practices and have become less attuned to the ways that mechanistic decisions impact human (and other-than-human) embodiments (Mellor, 1997: 60; Mellor, 2017: 93).

This focus on issues that are most relevant to WED offers us an alter-native path towards a more just world. WED illuminated social and envir-onmental injustices, especially in the ways that they collide with the industrialisation of the Global North along with those who own the means of production throughout the Global South. This group of ecofeminists also gave attention to dismantling existing Western social constructs through revisions of labour relations. This translated into direct active political engagement through social systems aligned with counter-capitalism (specifi-cally: socialism, Marxism and anarchism), which can better systemically support decentralisation, localisation, collectivisation, self-organising, inten-tional living, technological innovations, local exchange trading systems (LETS), antinuclear and peace activism, coupled with women's liberation movements, alternative economics (and more). They have broadly supported women's active engagements in the preservation of their sovereignty, liveli-hoods and those of their families, to release the grasp of global capitalist commoditisation over women's lives and Earth resources upon which they depend. The link between these insights and a distinct anti-colonial and post-imperialist vision for the world are obvious. Such strategies framed this cadre of ecofeminisms as synonymous with a 'new internationalism', which became particularly relevant as socialist states and ideologies in the latter stages of the last century collapsed. They noted that 'an invisible global politics in which women worldwide are enmeshed in their everyday life; and a convergence of thinking arising from . . . the efforts of women to keep alive the processes that sustain [them]' is necessary if we are to improve girls' and women's lives and health of the entire planet (Mies and Shiva, 1993: 1–2). Further broadening the reach of this thread of ecofeminism, the privileges shared between ruling elites (both men and women) in the Global North and wealthy individuals in the industrialising South was recognisable and highlighted the global reach of Western capitalist hegemonies across the entire planet. An intention to transform modern societies emerged that deferred to the cosmologies and anthropologies of structurally oppressed peoples, of which women offer a visible alternative view. The target of this alternative to masculinist hegemonies was to expose men's internalised superiorisation, translate structural divisions between Earth, women and men and in doing so seek post-industrial, post-colonial, post-imperial and post-structural societies that harmonised with their immediate along with global environments (both natural and constructed) (Ortner, 1974: 68). The central intention of WED has been to bring about radical societal change from the grass roots up, where the health and fecundity of women and Earth could strategically oppose male domination across the planet, noting that women in Global Northern nations must be held similarly accountable for the impacts of transnational consumption on their sisters in the Global South along with their ecological consequences (Bari, 1992: 84).

Building on WED legacies, but questioning the – at-times – essentialist metaphors and assumptions used, some FPE scholars took issue with the way that women–gender–environment connections were examined throughout the literature. For example, Rebecca Elmhirst (2011), protested the absence of FPE in scientific articles before 2011, not because of the avoidance of those views since many studies did hold the same insights and analyses as FPE. Rather, FPE was not adequately credited for these ideas. In the early twenty-first century, feminism and gender studies has of course evolved, Elmhirst suggesting that FPE had to be revitalised. She continued to show that intersectionality theory, where social identities in relation to power, oppression and discrimination meet, can also contribute important perspectives, especially if we broaden the analyses of gender (Elmhirst, 2011). For others, bringing the knowledge of FPE to the heart of Global North analyses means we are better able to take arguments back to the belly of the malestream beast (Arora-Jonsson 2013). Recently, renewed interest in the intersections between masculinities politics and FPE has emerged, questioning the role that men and masculinities might play in a deep green future. As an example, consider the studies by Noémi Gonda (2017), who exposed the ways that masculinities are constructed in Nicaragua and their impacts on climate change mitigation policies.

Consequently, FPE is an important source of inspiration for us. This is especially true when we consider the ways that unequal power relations shape the social and ecological consequences of industrial extractivism (relative to industrial/breadwinner masculinities in particular). Beyond these considerations, some scholars are also investigating the politics of science, materialism and posthumanities studies through feminist lens (Sehlin MacNeil, 2017; Persson et al., 2017).

Feminist science studies, material feminisms and posthumanities

Renewed interests in bodies, species, biodiversity, waste, climate change and so forth, have encouraged fresh feminist inquiries into environmental concerns. Richard Twine (2010) noted that feminist sciences, material feminisms and posthumanities have historically avoided ecological feminism. Twine claimed that new materialist scholarship did not sufficiently acknowledge the important, indeed foundational ecofeminist contributions to our understandings of the human–nature relationship even though elements of material feminism convey many similar ideas (Twine, 2010). We agree with Twine, noting that under the banner of feminist science studies/material feminisms/posthumanities, we find some of the most important sources of inspiration for the future of twenty-first-century ecological feminism.

Feminist science and technology, material feminists and posthumanities scholars draw from five different knowledge traditions that deserve mention here. They are: decolonisation, quantum physics, microbiology, anti-humanism and science and technology studies (Alaimo and Hekman ed., 2008; Bennett, 2010; Coole and Frost eds., 2010; Braidotti, 2013; Chen et al. eds., 2013). Decolonisation studies aims to liberate indigenous people from the influences of colonisation, thereby shifting 'the geography of reasoning' from a Bacon–Newton–Descartes enactment of nature as dead/mechanistic/separated from culture, towards entangled entities of living matter (Tiostanova and Mignolo, 2012: 10, 174). Contemporary decolonisation studies have been shaped by some feminist theorists who analysed resistance towards mining and other extractivist practices (Plumwood, 2002b; Valladares and Boelens, 2017; Öhman, 2016; Schulz, 2017; Yazzie and Baldy eds., 2017). As a second tradition that inspires these deepened views of global problems, quantum physics posits the notion of vibrating strings as the smallest and unpredictable parts of universe. Feminist scholars such as Karen Barad suggested that elements, technologies and particles that are central to quantum research are only understandable in the context of relationship analyses (Barad, 2003). In her influential article on how 'matter comes to matter', Barad (2003) emphasised that light is both particle and wave at the same time, depending on its intra-action with other elements in different arrangements. Notably, neither discursive practices nor material phenomena can be explained in terms of the other, but only when explained together. Third, feminist materialists such as Stacy Alaimo and Susan Heckman eds. (2008) insisted that our microbiological understandings of languages that affirm the materiality of the body as active can be reluctant as much as forces to be reckoned with (Alaimo and Hekman ed., 2008). Interestingly, some ecofeminists have shared this view, thereby making it possible to reconceptualise nature within the human body as anything but mechanistic and dead (Merchant, 1980; Bennett, 2010). A forth source of knowledge that inspires this thread of scholarly work is anti-humanism. Anti-humanism emerged with the 'death of man', as man was understood from the Renaissance onwards. This was a concept proffered by Michel Foucault. It is important that we not confuse 'the death of man' with cynical and nihilistic misanthropy in the form of climate change denialism or neo-fascism. Further, anti-humanism should not pull our attention in the wrong direction since we must look 'more affirmatively towards new alternatives' and 'create alternative ways of conceptualizing the human subject' (Braidotti, 2013: 37). Giving up on humanism (or the rationalist primacy of human importance) does not mean giving up on ourselves. After all, 'where subjectivity begins and ends is too often bound up with fantasies of a human uniqueness in the eyes of God, of escape from materiality, or of mastery of nature' (Bennett, 2010: ix). Understanding the interconnectedness of life is in fact a broadening of care for ourselves. Lastly, we consider arguments from the in-depth case studies associated with science and technology studies. That discourse emphasises materiality as always and already a part of values, ideas, politics and so forth, making the modern claim about separation between culture and nature obsolete (Haraway, 1988; Latour, 2004). By this thesis, unpredictability is neither completely unpredictable, nor completely predictable, but rests on a combination of stability and contingency as vibrant matter (Bennett, 2010).

From these various influential discussions, we recognise that a core ontological idea of feminist science studies/material feminisms/posthumanities is twofold. First, that objects and subjects are heterogeneous. Second, they become what they are in relation to others; let us provincially call them quasi-objects. Quasi-objects (as for example bodies that can be called male) cannot pre-exist as such, but neither can their existence be purely ideological or socially constructed (Serres, 2007). This position moves toward a conception of knowledge-making as a negotiation among human and other-than-human assemblages. We must in fact understand reality as a contingent and antagonistic field filled by heterogeneous material quasi-objects (or in the context of this book: men) which are structured by hegemonic processes (again, in the context of this book: malestream norms). The identity of each element is constitutively split and when an element such as man is part of a chain of equivalence, other possibilities are cancelled: man stood with business suit, money, greed, stock exchange, global through to local exploitation, etc. This suggests that the meaning of man in such a sequence is established in a network of relations beyond single referential materiality (Latour, 1993; Latour, 2004). These lines of inquiry do have similarities with ecology as a science and Earth wisdom as a social movement, drawing from: Baron von Humboldt's 'chain of connection' in natural history; Nicholas of Cusa's 'pantheism'; Pierre Teilhard de Chardin's 'cosmology of evolution'; Ludwig von Bertalanffy's 'organismic conception'; the works of general systems theorists like Ilya Prigogine's insights about cybernetic self-regulation, self-organisation, feedback loops, evolution at the edge of chaos, emergent creativity, system dynamics; Brian Goodwin's 'theoretical biology'; James Lovelock and Lynn Margulis's 'Gaia Theory'. Early on, Charlene Spretnak (1999: 12, 15) raised the alarm about our wholesale collapse into the enervated self at the behest of mechanistic ideologies and their associated mind–body splits. She called for us to assist the mind–body to self-heal through holistic techniques like meditation, prayer and efforts to centre the self in communion and connectivity with Earth. It is understandable that Bruno Latour (2017) in his book *Facing Gaia: Eight Lectures on the New Climatic*

Regime has turned to these types of knowledge systems as well when trying to find meaning in the Anthropocene.

An important insight from this litany of probing scholarships is that we must treat gender as if it were 'matter'. This is not an essentialist, predetermined view. Rather, we seek continuous and heterogeneous ways of justifying the plural complexities of existence for all life as a crucial post-patriarchal approach to ecological masculinities. The assumption about pre-determined characteristics between the sexes have made women synonymous with Earth through Mother Nature rhetoric. This way of thinking has led to objectification of women and has distanced their access to culture; that space largely occupied by men (Alaimo, 2009; Alaimo, 2010). From this, we begin to gain a sense of textured matter that pervades gender identities. Unfortunately, and in agreement with Gaard, we see that feminist science and technology, material feminism and posthumanities scholarship tend to focus more on concepts and theoretical proliferations than political self-reflections and environmental justice actions, since:

> Making connections among posthumanisms, critical animal studies, interdisciplinary gender studies, new feminist materialisms, and the larger eco-cultural critique of a postcolonial vegan ecofeminism will require extending theory from the realm of the purely intellectual to that of the political. In many cases, such connections expose our own role in oppressive structures – as consumers of suffering, as contributors to climate change, as sponsors of global food scarcity – and such exposure is not flattering.
>
> (Gaard, 2017: 126)

Ecological feminism has centralised various interpretations of this collection of ideas from its very beginnings. However, the discourse was credited by some as the source of a 'linguistic turn' within broader feminist scholarship, with Gaard (2017: 118–119) noting that for more than twenty years, the spectre of essentialism haunted ecofeminism, pushing many theorists and activists away out of fear that their work would be tarred with that brush. This is now swinging back the other way as discussions on climate change and the Anthropocene in particular gather momentum, calling our attention – with even greater urgency – to social and environmental concerns in mainstream political debates, supported by fresh research funding.

Returning to some early ecofeminist contributions to inquiries into the human–nature relationship, we note specific mention of embodiment, care and sense-of-place as recurrent fixtures of the ecological feminist discourse. For example, seeking pathways to nourish the vital needs on all life from her adopted home in Western Australia, Canadian environmental philosopher Patsy Hallen (1988: 15–16; also see Hallen, 1989; Hallen, 1994: 18–19; Hallen, 2001; Hallen, 2003) developed theories and practices to awaken 'Living Earth Ethics'. Hallen's efforts to teach and implement her version of ecofeminism was a visceral response to a deep-seated concern that 'as late moderns, we inhabit a deprived world, a world of artifice and simulation, engineered pleasures and electronically produced vistas, where we are distracted, numbed, and lured into being passive spectators' (2001: 224). She chastised the 'frontier ethics' of industrial/breadwinner masculinities, noting that we have been:

> . . . hoodwinked into believing that there are boundless frontiers. We can feel Earth shuddering under the pressure of human malpractices, but we still trust that biotechnology or space science, some theory or invention, will provide the answers to any environmental crisis. We may have been forced to abandon the 'myth of superabundance' but this has been replaced by the 'myth of scientific supremacy'. This swaggering stance is the exemplar of ecological denial . . . Nature is not only more complex than we know. It is more complex than we *can* know. We need an ethically responsive, humble science which is self-reflective, non-reductionist and respectful of the intentionality, agency and awesome powers of the 'more-than-human' world.
>
> (Hallen, 2003: 60)

Responding to the etymology of ecology – a study that she argued is especially accessible to and, indeed, needs women – Hallen (1988: 10) sought a generative, reunifying and whole sense of reality. She summarised her vision for living earth ethics thus:

> If we wish to uncover what is, rather than imposing what is not, if we wish to recognise and allow to flourish the complexity of interacting systems (including ourselves), if we wish to ex-ist rather than in-sist, if we wish to 'let things be' . . . the way in which they are, if we wish to unite our head, hand and heart, we need to care.
>
> (Hallen 1989: 7)

Hallen's wisdom exposed the damaging effects of our loss of care for the glocal commons (Hallen, 2001: 225). She forged forth with her counter-cultural eroticism as central to praxes, which exposed the benefits of post-gendered perceptions of ourselves in society and environment as crucial to our liberation from all systems of oppression. She also steered us in the direction of honouring the simple things in life as vital (intensely embodied and psycho-sensual) contributions to contending with our urgent need to recover an 'ecologically literate citizenry' through daily Earth-connected practices, which harbour great potency to reconstruct an ecologically relational self-identity and enlarge our social-scientific understanding of Earth (Warren, 1987: 18; Hallen, 1988: 10; Hallen, 2001: 218, 226–22).

Hallen was, like other early ecofeminists aligned with this thread of ecological feminism, strongly influenced by deep ecology. She lauded the notion of 'biocentric egalitarianism', valourising those who sought answers to pressing global problems through shared interests in protectiveness, identi-fication with wider nature and intentional shifts away from 'ethics of duty' that are peculiar to hegemonised masculinities. Such thinking deferred instead to 'ethics of care' that draw on the moral sentiment of justice, where we take from Earth only what will meet our 'vital needs' and no more; doing so enables us to (re)ground through the tangible realities of our cosmological rehabilitation (Gilligan, 1982; Mathews, 1991: 47, 147, 150).

The recognition of the internal and logical implications of the connectivity of all living things is peculiar to this branch of ecofeminists (Mathews, 2005: 69). For another Australian environmental philosopher, Freya Mathews, this was an earnest attempt to reunify 'mentality with materiality' that honoured the psychic dimensions of our physical being, helping us arrive at a psycho-physical unity with the cosmos – an ecofeminist metaphysics. Rigorous in her pursuit of such a metaphysics, Mathews argued that epistemological, ontological and spiritual human endeavours become inseparable from the agency that per-vades a 'taken for granted' Earth beneath our feet (Mathews, 2005: 4–5). But this notion of broader synergies with the world around us does not deny the presence of human impacts on Earth and vice versa since with enough time:

> . . . everything is touched by the processes of life, and eventually taken over by them to be fed into the cycle of decay and rebirth. Left to itself, the living world reclaims its own. Things that initially seemed discordant and out of place gradually fall into step with the rest of Creation. Old cars take their place beside old dogs and old trees; antiquity naturalizes even the most jarring of trash.
>
> (Mathews, 1999: 124)

The broader panpsychic care (for humanity *and* Earth) that Mathews formulated called forth the need for us to rededicate ourselves to securing the world and our selves concurrently (Mathews, 2005: 79). This is indicative of the scientific, material and posthuman elements of some ecofeminists that pursued a 'return to nature' as yielding; a wholesale willingness to 'let the world go its own way' so that we might *re*-inhabit place, note that we belong to it and with it and in doing so, fuse our very identities with it as home, securely attaching to it in the same ways that we fall in love (Mathews, 1999: 124; 2005: 19). This was a modern Western interpretation of indigenous wisdoms, inspired by the large quantities of trash that Mathews saw strewn about a remote native community she visited in the Australian outback – reminding us that our discarded items are part of Earth and, in eventually returning to Earth, ought to still be visible so that we sustain our awareness of the cause and effects of waste.

Arresting links between men's oppression of women and indigenous oppression pervaded the various ecofeminist perspectives as well. Australian ecofeminist philosopher Val Plumwood (2002a: 104) noted that man is 'set up as culturally universal', relegating woman as an 'exception, negation or lack of the virtue of the One', being otherised so completely as to be a 'deviation', a 'difference', a 'deficiency' to be 'controlled', 'contained' and 'governed' by mechanisms of hierarchical exclusion; unsurprisingly managed by men. Citing Edward Said's (1978) seminal commentary on 'orientalism' and Benita Parry's (1995) insights on 'resistance theory', Plumwood drew comparable conclusions for colonised people when stood against colonisers (particularly male colonisers). She noted that the colonised becomes a 'dependent', 'illegitimate and refractory foil', a 'lack', a 'negativity', 'disorderly', 'deficient', 'inferior', 'devalued', an 'absence of the coloniser's chief qualities', an offence to 'reason, beauty and order' (Plumwood, 2002a: 105).

Clearly, scientific, material and posthuman feminists have provided us with a plethora of alternatives to masculine hegemonisation. We consider it high time that humanity (Western, white men in particular) hear these calls to not simply welcome more women into the fold of masculine hegemonisation, but to actively usurp the tired, old socially bankrupt and ecologically lacerating elements of malestream norms. In doing so, we aim to replace them with alternatives greatly encouraged by our deep-thinking compatriots that approach worldly engagement from a completely different perspective; we prioritise broader, deeper and wider care that scientific, material and posthuman (eco)feminists have been championing for some time. Taking us far beyond the confines of gendered essentialism, it behoves us to seek their guidance, which provides us with some of the most vital ingredients as we formulate an effective ecologised masculinities theory.

Binary ecofeminisms

As noted in Chapter 1 and revisited in the early stages of this chapter, some ecofeminists have emphasised analyses wedded to biological functions and polarised ideas of sex. We refer to this thread as 'binary ecofeminisms'. The essentialisms that characterise binary ecofeminisms capture the attitudes of those who have focused their attention on women's bodies and stereotypical feminine traits; considered distinct from and oppositional to those of men and masculinities. This thread stands in some tension with the four previous threads, reinforcing a belief that women are inherently closer to nature than are men, assigning fundamental ways of being, thinking and doing to gender roles and bodies. We consider this thread to be an ecofeminist counterpoint to the essentialist understandings of men and masculinities championed by the mythopoetic men's movement that we discussed in Chapter 3. We elaborate on our typology of binary ecofeminisms here to consider the characteristics presented by these ecofeminists in finer detail. We do so to prepare the ground ahead of us, since similar interpretations of men, masculinities and Earth are already present in masculinities politics and will likely find currency as ecological masculinities gathers momentum – more on this in Chapter 8. Through the following examination, we expose the limitations of binary gendered essentialism, paving the way for more fruitful notions of ecofeminism that support gender-equitable and non-binary/genderqueer approaches to masculine ecologisation.

Binary ecofeminisms are characterised by pagan traditions that celebrate goddess worship. They find links with Wiccan witchcraft, Earth rites and rituals and claim that care and love are biological feminine qualities that are not only oppositional but would best replace the habitual hierarchicalising and ecocidal characteristics of hegemonic masculinities. This thread offers women an opportunity to reclaim special pride of place in our societies by valorising them as child-bearers, primary food gatherers and celebrating their crucial roles in social functioning (Godfrey, 2008). There is a widely held belief that women (as distinct from men) have a strong bond with nature since their menstrual cycles (euphemistically referred to as a 'moon cycle'), like the tidal impacts on water movements, are determined by the phases of the moon. These notions point to lunar regulation of women's menses, triggering ovulation, affecting their moods and emotions, while also governing behaviours and attitudes through impacts on their blood, hormones and their souls (Macleod, 2015). Popular culture does not commonly assign similar claims to men's neurobiology, ethology or physiology.

Links between women and Earth have been accentuated by women's capacities to give birth. This has provided binary ecofeminists with embodied connections to broader cycles of life and death, allegedly qualifying them to attune with and therefore speak for nature in ways that men cannot (Daly, 1978; Spretnak, 1986). For essentialist ecofeminists who emerged in the 1960s and 1970s, nature was a spiritual and personal quantity that problematised domineering, scientific and technological approaches of masculinist conventions (Merchant, 1992: 187). Arguing in favour of women's elevation and liberation through the revival of ancient rites and rituals, these ecofeminists dramatised pre-herstoric notions of nature as pregnant, ripe and full, which correlated with celebrations of women as harbingers of life (Musawa, 2010). Monica Sjöö and Barbara Mor (1987: 34) cited Neolithic evidence to support intonations that early Western civilisation was in fact championed by women (circa 10,000 BC), who had woven intricate relationships between human societies and their surroundings, based on communitarian living. Further, it was argued that women (and not men) gained access to love for other women by savouring the sumptuous fullness of Earth goddesses; feminism offering a reawakening of universal oneness and infinite selfhood that many men still deny themselves and deny in women through sexism. In these ways, binary ecofeminists assert that men dethroned and subordinated women and Earth beneath male gods, degrading the organismic and nurturing qualities of both with male-controlled technological and mechanistic ontologies and epistemologies that served as their gap fillers. Ethics of care, reification of the intuitive self, ecologically inspired relational exchanges and a treatise of humans as biologically sexed and socially gendered characterise this stream of ecofeminisms (Merchant, 1992: 191).

However, the distinguishing features of binary ecofeminists came under intense scrutiny. The Mother Earth–Earth Mother nexus that rejoices in a synchronous relationship between menses and lunar cycles (particularly correlated with the new moon) remains debatable, having been substantiated by some investigative data analyses, laboratory experiments and clinical observations, while contested by others (Law, 1986; Rose, 1991; Münster et al., 1992; Chakraborty, 2013). Controversy about the binary nature of some ecofeminisms has continued well into the twenty-first century, building on early and critical interrogations raised by Sherry Ortner (1974) and Carolyn Merchant (1980) who cross-examined their essentialist colleagues (MacGregor, 2006; MacGregor ed., 2017). They suggested, in a similar critique we raised towards the mythopoetic men movement, that essentialist convictions, ironically, enable the mutual devaluing and subordination of women and Earth, since women's labour, like Earth's resources and their similar roles in giving life, ascribes to them terms such as 'virgin', 'fertile' and 'barren' capturing the twinned admonishment of all that patriarchal society has long considered inferior to men (Milner-Barry, 2015). Susan Prentice (1988: 9) chided the idealism of essentialist ecofeminisms. She noted that in examining the sources of our social and environmental problems, we can uncover the foundations of masculine thinking. However, there is a risk that we also directly or indirectly make men innately bad and wrong, effectively advocating for women's biological links with Earth in ways that trivialise the possibilities of nature atonement in boys and men. Janet Biehl (1988) shared similar views in criticising the biological determinism of essentialism for not usurping the injustices of the state. She argued that nature, women *and* men have been negatviely impacted through race, class and gendered oppression. Biehl demonstrated that by elevating women's liberation above men's, we effectively sidestep the historical and logical struggle to free the glocal commons from the whims of capitalism, statehood and wholesale ethnic subjugation prosecuted by men and masculinities for millennia (Biehl, 1991: 50; Merchant, 1992: 194; Otto, 2012: 18). We seek alternative analytics to those offered by binary ecofeminists; looking to socio-politically informed perspectives focused on supporting truer liberation for all. We add that there is further danger in women/Earth essentialist perspectives giving men little reason to prioritise Living Earth Ethics that could otherwise contribute to the disassembling of male domination (Seager, 1993; Sturgeon, 1997; Merchant, 2006).

Our caution about binary ecofeminisms is further informed by Catherine Roach's (2003: 8) *Mother Nature: Popular Culture and Environmental Ethics*. There, Roach offered her considered thoughts about a collapsed Mother Earth–Earth Mother metaphor. She wrote from the perspective of the *good*, the *bad* and the *hurt* ways that humans can invoke ambiguous and uneasy relationships with nature, challenging the presumption that women and Earth are comingled in ways that binary ecofeminisms presume that men are not. Roach's (2003: 45) critiques of essentialism were pragmatic and grounded in ways that transcend gendered polarisations, since:

> On the biological level, although men do not menstruate, bear children, or breast-feed, they do share all other human biological processes (eating, sleeping, eliminating wastes, getting sick, dying); and in their ejaculation

of semen, men have their own direct experience of a tangible stuff of the reproduction of life. Furthermore, there are many women who do not bear children and even more who do not breast feed.

Giving consideration to the 'Love Your Mother' environmental slogan, Roach (1991: 47; 2003: 39–41) criticised the gendered presumption that women as child-bearers and as the main child raisers are 'hard-wired' to commune with Mother Nature in ways that men cannot and will not. The malestream imperative, as she illuminated it, does indeed appear to be a compulsion to in fact 'control your mother' (Roach, 2002: 84). Roach noted that a presumption concocting ecological feminism as better able to connect women with nature and accentuate them as more caring and peaceable, which also portrays men as more aggressive and destructive, was fundamentally flawed. She supported the following kind of inquiry instead:

> If every time someone waves a 'Love Your Mother' banner, this triggers and reinforces assumptions, held at least to some degree in the cultural imagination, that women care more, or more easily, about nature, then what effect do these assumptions have on women's (and men's) lives? And are they true? . . . the problem actually lies in a false hierarchical opposition between the categories of nature and culture themselves.
>
> (Roach, 2002: 40)

Roach suggested that we must look to the nature–culture binary beyond analyses of women and men as discrete genders to transcend the limitations of essentialism. Consistent with these mounting concerns about binary ecofeminisms, we agree that essentialism offers an oversimplified approach to the gendered aspect of the human–nature relationship (Roach, 2003: 45). Essentialist perspectives picture women as 'cleaners and men as mess-makers' in ways that affirmed stereotypes that place 'women back in the traditional housekeeping role of tidying up after men who cannot be expected to do it themselves' and 'lets men off the hook and hooks women as housekeeper, care giver, and nurse' (Roach, 2003: 44). From Roach (2003: 4), we conclude that, 'environmental destruction is self-destruction' regardless of the gendered origins from which malestream norms might originate . The essentialist cultural imagery of the Mother Earth metaphor is not likely to save us, nor Earth, precisely because such messages feed on separation and difference rather than communalism and sameness between women and men, effectively widening the gap between men and Earth, while artificially accentuating women's grounded natures (compounded by the fact that many marginalised men are impacted in similarly negative ways by masculine hegemonisation as are women and non-binary/genderqueer people). Binary ecofeminisms are characterised by potent imageries of men in the world who slay, dig, eviscerate and mutilate Mother Nature's body. They assume that for as long as Earth is 'conceptualised as alive and sensitive, it could be considered a breach of human ethical behavior to carry out destructive acts against it' (Merchant, 1980: 43). This is a noble cause, but one that has not manifested in practice. This tendency to 'sex-type' Earth, women and men excludes men and masculinities from an ecologised discourse in ways that other threads exploring, women, feminine socialisations and Earth do not (Hallen, 1994: 21).

Of course, notions of motherhood are one of the most overt fronts of sexist oppression imposed upon women through persistent denigration, socio-political disadvantaging and associated attempts to control women's reproductive rights (Gaard, 1993: 302; Wolf, 2003). Further complicating the role of women as mothers, Roach interrogated perceptions of the 'Dangerous Mother'; the cruel and torturous man-eater who can strip men back to basics in an instant and at will. She also considered the 'Hurt Mother' who cries out desperately for help, hoping someone will save her from destruction; the environmental movement was built – at least in part – on this presumption that we can and must restore Mother Earth to health after having exhausted her through our wanton exploitation of her riches; ravaging her body in the same ways that women's (and others') bodies are raped (Roach, 2003: 72, 76, 119, 125). These multilayered essentialist approaches by some women set them up to be 'gender soluble' rather than 'separate' selves, reaffirming the insight that not all people bear equal responsibility or accountability for halting human destruction of the environment. We cannot presume all people will behave in caring ways towards Earth or each other . Similarly, we cannot place such holds on women. While it may be true that some men – modern Western men in particular – are more alienated from nature than many women are, it is misguided to presume that men cannot and will not also be caring towards all others and themselves as well (Roach, 2003: 59). Likewise, while environmental degradation persists, we acknowledge that men's reticence to make necessary changes in support of a deep green future is selfish and unthinking, if not malicious. Such nuances are the products of gendered ambivalence. On reflection on the truer nature of human nature, Roach (2003: 6, 8) convincingly argued that:

> Humans are not solely loving, but neither are we inevitably brutish. We are not solely rational beings whose good intentions determine our actions, but neither are we blindly controlled by hidden and selfish agendas that we can never hope to access or change. Probing the deep roots of our ambivalent response to nature can help mitigate feelings of hate toward it.

For Roach, it is precisely this ambivalence and its impacts on contemporary social and environmental justice that was of paramount concern.[1]

Other feminist scholars have joined the voiced concerns about binary ecofeminist attitudes. Turning to social scientific insights on mothering, anthropologist, primatologist and evolutionary theorist Sarah Blaffer Hrdy's (1999) *Mother Nature: Natural Selection and the Female of the Species*, further problematised social conditioning for women to be modest, compliant, non-competitive and sexually reserved – indeed embracing their lot in life to 'conceive, gestate, and suckle babies, period' – in the wake of male biases within science (especially biology). In doing so, she raised an additional cautionary tale about the pitfalls of gendered essentialism (Hrdy, 1999: xiv, 16, 27, 308, 495–496). In *Beyond Mothering Earth: Ecological Citizenship and the Politics of Care*, Sherilyn MacGregor (2006: 5) offered a terse assertion that eco-feminists ought to bring their private experiences into their political activism as a rich contribution to expressive citizenship. Effectively, MacGregor provided us with politicised instructions for activism as praxes. Also consider the indigenous Saami in Sweden who routinely pit themselves against mining exploitations, with women on the frontline struggles firmly merging indigenous heritage with strategic technological and visual choices of powerful 'artivism' reaching beyond the confines of essentialism (and leveraging off the slogan 'we are nature protecting ourselves') (Sjöstedt Landén, 2017).

Through a detailed analysis of French feminist Luce Irigaray's views on essentialism in *Ethics of Eros: Irigaray's Re-writing of the Philosophers*, Tina Chanter (2016) made a compelling point. She noted that some philosophers have tripped over concerns about essentialism to such an extent that it is common for the impact of unfounded misrepresentations and universalisms on post-structural feminist analyses to be glossed over. Attending to this, she suggested that we ought to:

> . . . talk about and find ways of combating sexism, racism, heterosexism, and all the other 'isms' [including ecocide] for which the accusation of essentialism has been allowed to stand. To the extent that essentialism mystifies these urgent and pressing problems it covers over not only the importance of thinking through the question of sexual difference, but also the damaging and dehumanizing dynamics and multiple faces of the imperialism of the same. These dynamics need to be confronted on their own terms – directly, specifically, forcefully, and accurately – not through the vague discourse of essentialism.
>
> (Chanter, 2016: 254)

Essentialist support for a woman–nature nexus is problematic, since supporting women and feminine socialisations as fundamentally 'caring' restricts the ability for men and masculinities to bring such qualities to the fore in their exchanges with Earth, in addition to placing unfair and unrealistic expectations on women and overly generalising about their caring capacities, along with men's supposed lack there-of.

The Mother Earth–Earth Mother association captures restrictions for both women and men. Consequently, binary ecofeminisms stand in considerable tension with the other threads of ecological feminisms we explore. Ultimately, the problems we face at the global level impact us all and together must be problems that we collectively resolve. Accentuating gender difference does little to help move us in this direction. For these reasons, we view gendered essentialism to be exclusionary and problematic for Earth, women *and* men. We need to connect with our own inner natures as well as nature beyond our bodily boundaries. Clearly, stereotyping on either end of the gendered spectrum is troublesome precisely because we then deny many women and men their sovereignty to deviate from socialised norms and in doing so it is human and other-than-human marginalised others who continue to suffer the most.

Gender-equitable ecofeminisms

Other more socio-politically focused environmental feminisms sought ideological and structural changes in the mechanisms of domination that pervade extractive industries. The more visible research of this kind focused on public policy, qualitative/quantitative research, green technologies and the implementation of equal representation in various regulatory organisations. These, what we refer to as gender-equitable, ecofeminists suggest that we need more thoughtful and tempered approaches to developmental policies and practices, where sexism and environmental insensitivity can be corrected by regulations supporting equity for all humans along with considerate use of Earth's resources. These ecofeminists prioritised gender equity as the crucial missing link in creating a socially and ecologically just and sustainable world.

Not as outspoken as binary ecofeminists discussed above, this thread's proponents encourage critical examination of discrete categories within gender–nature discourses to expose the different influences that impact both women and men actively engaged in environmental politics. Studies that support this thread have examined, for example, different patterns of consumption by women and men; highlighting that in general, men have a far heavier ecological footprint than do women (Hanson, 2010; Räty and Carlsson-Kanyama, 2010). When faced with the question of material consumption, ecofeminists such as Ines Weller (2017: 336) noted that '[a]s a rule, more women than men express a willingness to make sustainable consumption choices'. In that study, Weller showed that women on average consume in more environmentally friendly ways than do men. Others exposed that men in general do not care as much for the environment than women (McCright and Sundström, 2013), suggesting that a measure of gendered differences about environmental concerns explains why men on average are less enrolled than the average woman in environmental movements (Grasswick, 2014). These trends expose a general reticence by men to dismantle the structures that create and support their primacy, a trend that appears to not generate resistance in women as deeply. On the other hand, women, especially in the Global North, play significant roles as consumers as well; the social and environmental impacts of that consumption should not be ignored nor let them off the hook either, as we examine the complexities of these issues.

Similarly, environmental organisations remain awash with the presence and impacts of male domination. Men tend to become the leaders of environmental organisations, bringing with them a suite of conscious and unconscious malestream socialisations, with varying levels of willingness to have their dominator patterns challenged (Buckingham and Kulcur, 2009; Stoddart and Tindall, 2011). The same has proved true throughout green politics, where male leadership is also common and with it the presence of sexism – even if unintentional (Jackson, 2017). As an added example, consider the countering efforts of 'gender mainstreaming' at the levels of global governance, which the United Nations Economic and Social Council (ECOSOC) defined as:

> . . . the process of assessing the implications for women and men of any planned action, including legislation, policies or programmes, in all areas and at all levels. It is a strategy for making women's as well as men's concerns and experiences an integral dimension of the design, implementation, monitoring and evaluation of policies and programmes in all political, economic and societal spheres so that women and men benefit equally and inequality is not perpetuated. The ultimate goal is to achieve gender equity.
> (United Nations, 2002: v)

Recommendations such as this aim to level the playing field with the best of intentions to ensure that both women's and men's interests are woven into policies and practices at the very highest levels of governance in equal measure. But such definitions do not include a reconfiguring of the field itself. Women continue to be underrepresented in policy development debates; those present conditioned throughout their entire careers to adhere to masculinist views that dovetail with the pressures and payoffs of malestream norms (Buckingham, 2017). Despite some movement towards gender equity, women are still expected to shoehorn into a man's world.

This inconsistency is not new. We can trace the disparity between the rhetoric and the realities of gender equity at the highest levels of transnational environmental negotiations back to the Rio Earth Summit (1992). At the time of this landmark event, there was a narrow window of great opportunity to institutionalise gender equity along with adequate controls of greenhouse gases. But this opportunity was sadly missed; women representatives in associated business and government agencies assumed roles alongside men in ways that emulated ecomodern masculinities – as watered down 'ecomodern feminists' perhaps. We have not seen a re-gearing of masculinised structures towards the kinds of material, ethical or behavioural innovations that ecological feminism advocates. It appears that the successes of women's empowerment, especially since Rio, have become synonymous with women's ecomodernisation, having them join the ranks of 'green economy boomers' who are and have long been masculinist – a trend that remains with us to this day despite growing support for solving global social and environmental issues and empowering women (Foster, 2017: 220). Theses green economic policies, which have traditionally favoured men's common interests to seek engineering mitigations from an ecomodern perspective, have systematically sidelined relational, sociological and systemic approaches, stopping short of paradigmatic transformations towards a deep green future (Littig, 2017: 324).

Further, consider the ways that gender and mobility interact. Studies of these measures show that the range of mobility for women is notably less than is the case for men (Hanson, 2010). Women also tend to have lower carbon emission correlated with constraints on their spatial mobility, use public transport in higher number, travel shorter distances and are more willing to rely on bicycle or foot transportation, all of which have notable environmental benefits (Hanson, 2010). Through the lens of a development paradigm this is even more visible in the Global South, where cultural and socio-economic factors significantly affect women's mobility, such as restrictions to leave their homes, lack of their own income and access to money, while having greater domestic burdens to bear. Susan Hanson's (2010) research also exposed the complexities involved in accurately analysing these differences, since women can choose to engage in work closer to home for reasons of domestic care or they may choose to take the bus because they are more concerned for the environment, etc. In line with Ines Weller (2017: 337), we recognise that arguments for gender equity play an important role in exposing unequal power relations, raising awareness about gendered differences in consumption patterns and clarifying moralities associated with equal socio-political representation and influence. But mobility and representation become more complex (and more urgent) to achieve when there are planetary boundaries to respect. Within the framework of industrial modernity, women's energy and GDP growth – particularly in the Global North and wealthier segments of Global South communities – could be 'added in' to the same assessments as men's, making problems worse for the masses while some women's lives improve. However, when there are restricted resources and linear progressions towards modernisation which we consider gender neutral, we must ask how we can deal with gender equity in an ecofeminist way? The strategies put in place to achieve UN style gender mainstreaming have categorically failed, since they have at best, merely brought more women into a man's world, with the risks of hypermasculinist patterns repeating irrespective of one's gender and despite the increased women's leadership throughout the Global North. It is our contention that a gender-equitable approach to concerns about women, feminine socialisations and Earth is simply not robust enough. At best, it appears to result in a simple 'shuffling of deck chairs on the *Titanic*' through increased women's representation in the absence of systemic change; hardly the ideal political strategy to steer us away from social and environmental catastrophes if we simply have more women (and for that matter non-binary/genderqueer people) designing and maintaining masculinist business-as-usual approaches to glocal management. A wholesale structural revolution is needed; one that is gender-equitable and systemically transformative.

In the previous section, we noted that binary ecofeminisms skip over the importance of humanity's gendered heterogeneity. Here, we have argued that gender-equitable approaches to our understanding of women, feminine socialisations and Earth run great risk of under-analysing structural relations – even if ecomodernised rather than industrial/breadwinner-ised – effectively sidestepping malestream accountability once again (Arora-Jonsson, 2011). With these inadequacies considered, we look to post-gendered ecofeminisms to seek further guidance.

Non-binary/genderqueer ecofeminisms

Lastly, we consider non-binary/genderqueer examinations of women, feminine socialisations and Earth. There is a growing but still marginal discussion emerging that is now looking at and beyond a focus on gendered and environmental concerns as they relate to women's interests. Joan Roughgarden's (2004) *Evolution's Rainbow*, explored queer pride and diversity since the late 1970s. As an evolutionary biologist, Roughgarden presented evidence of a wide range of different forms of sexual activity and gender roles that exist outside of traditional and binary understandings of gender among humans and in other-than-humans as well. Paying close attention to those other-than-human species that – like humanity – have more than two biological sexes, along with those species who change their sexes and genders under specific ecological conditions, Roughgarden explored the notion of multiple-gendered groups that she organised into families. Her book demonstrated that a wide variety of gendered interactions can be normalised giving us just cause to celebrate diversity and heterogeneity in human identities and beyond (Roughgarden, 2004). Some are now critically exploring the 'cis male/cis female' binary (where 'cis' is Latin for 'on this side of' and refers to gendered identities that match a sexual preference for the opposite gender; considered the diametric alternative to the term 'trans'). These terms are integral to gender research that also included studies on queer ecologies, trans-ecologies as well as contra-malestream ecomasculinities that are introducing fresh lines of inquiry while stretching the bounds of established ecological feminist (and other ecophilosophical) traditions (MacGregor ed., 2017: 15). Reaching further afield than gender-equitable ecofeminisms discussed above, we also note an important development of queering ecofeminisms posited by Greta Gaard (1997) that is now gathering momentum, which we consider at length in Chapter 7 (also see Gaard, 2017). Nicole Seymour (2013) is another valuable contributor to non-binary/genderqueer ecologisation (also see Seymour, 2017). Her insights provide us with important lessons about the knowledge we can gain from queer/trans-marginalisation as we pursue greater care for the glocal commons. Seymour (2017: 255) challenged prejudices that frame trans people as '"unnatural" – not just generally against "Mother Nature's" plan, as lesbian, gay, and bisexual people are often considered, but also literally, physically constructed through medicine, technology, or even toxicity'. She recognised the positive influence of material feminism, but struggled with what she considered to be the troublesome tendency in that discourse to call us back to the 'real' body of women and men that can overlook the lived realities of trans people. Instead she turned towards 'organic transgenderism' as a possibility which 'emerges from an expanded ecological consciousness and environmental ethics' (Seymour, 2017: 257). We agree that if humanity is to strike an inclusive justice-oriented transitions 'from a ciscentric and anthropocentric viewpoint (*most humans are cisgender and therefore cisgenderism must be natural across all life*) to an inclusive, ecocentric viewpoint (*many animals are transgender, transsexual, or intersex; how might that change how we think of ourselves as human animals?*)' (Seymour, 2017: 260). We follow the leadership of scholars such as Roughgarden, MacGregor, Gaard and Seymour, summarising what we consider to be very welcome transformative ideas on gender and environments that are now emerging. The ideological significance of such views for a study on men, masculinities and Earth is expansive.

Cameron Butler (2017) discussed the need to confront the heteronormativity that corrupts environmentalism. Looking beyond the history of national parks (especially in the US), he was not merely critical of preserving nature intrinsically, but intentionally targeted the tendency to use natural areas 'to ensure that straight white men had a space to go to reclaim their masculinity' (Butler 2017: 274; Di Battista et al., 2015; for a historical study in the Swedish context, also see Hjulman, 2017). Butler (2017: 281) insisted that we must pursue 'a deep sense of care for the environment while simultaneously interrogating how "the environment" is conceptualized'. We acknowledge that these views pursue liberatory ideas and engagements with gendered identities and their points of intersection with other-than-human others. These additional and recent contributions, illuminate the capacities of social and environmental justice movements to build solidarities across broad and diverse fronts. Such are the rich counter-malestream and pro-queer responses that are simultaneously emerging across various marginalised and/or so called 'front-line' communities, including scholars and activists exposed to extractivism and the growing implications of climate change (Di Chiro, 2008; Gaard, 2015; Quinn-Thibodeau and Wu, 2016). As twenty-first-century populism blended with toxic/extreme masculinities reverberates around the globe whipped up by alt-right/neo-fascist shock politics, the discontents of nations' dominant (white) populations are becoming more visible, and, alarmingly, the parallels between twentieth-century fascist and 1930s Nazi authoritarianism are clear (Sexton, 2016; McQuade, 2017). This trend calls forth progressive and socially engaged communities to form alliances in proactive response to malestream dogmatisation with alacrity and haste. Non-binary/genderqueer ecologies present us with a convergent front in those margins, compelling us to seek and find the power in heterogeneity, where sex types and identities (or the lack thereof) across all species create dynamic springboards for post-heteronormative masculine ecologisation that we support here.

Threads of a creative quilt

This book would not be possible without the insights of ecological feminism and the efforts of ecofeminists. In this chapter, we have stressed that there is indespensible knowledge, which we have discussed through our consideration of the five ecofeminist threads. We gain ground from each of them in unique ways as they have respectively grappled with our social and environmental plight, bringing to bear a collective response to the world's struggles as (primarily but not exclusively) masculinities problems. Through in-depth case studies and theoretical advancements, feminist political ecologists continue to expose the ways that groups of men acquire societal leadership through extractive processes that have colonial roots and imperial visions for a gendered and hegemonic future. Feminist science/material/posthumanities have been instrumental in reaffirming the need for Global Northern accountability, exposing the culpability of the world's wealthy men in the rise of the (m)Anthropocene. Binary ecofeminisms have overly-relied on gendered stereotypes to expose the ways that men and masculinities are entangled with industrial modern structures and a breadwinner protector/provider ethos, even while rightly noting the ways they are eroding the living conditions for all life (wantonly or not). Gender-equitable ecofeminisms examine the ways that power relations and social inequities are intertwined with environmental politics, seeking fairness through gender-sensitive strategies that simply do not challenge the malestream status quo adequately – demanding an equal place at the table of masculine hegemonisation but struggling to tip that very table on its head and replace it with something new that is more deliberatively democratic. Non-binary/genderqueer ecofeminisms have brought us to a great watershed moment, where the things that define us as individuals and as a species are necessarily composite, reminding us, as does ecology, that resilience is most assured when our environments are woven with webs of complexity. We express our deep gratitude for the diversity of views of the ecological feminist discourse; they have collectively provided important sources of inspiration for an emerging discourse on masculine ecologisation.

In concluding our analyse of ecological feminism, we note that while this stream of thought raises very important questions about masculinities and the ways that men enact those socialisations, its alternative vision that contravenes the structural pressures, personal values and the embodiments of masculine hegemonisation have not successfully taken hold. Ecofeminists were astute at exposing the contributions of men and masculinities to the fog of masculine hegemonisation, offering a variety of interpretations, aspects of which help us create something new, but they have not – on principle – taken men and masculinities there directly. Indeed, this is not the job of individuals speaking on behalf of otherised others. For any conversation on masculine ecologisation to expect that from ecofeminists would in fact be more of the same – men and masculinities relying on women and feminism to make them feel better, act better and/or produce better results for the planet. The ecologised masculinities we envision pays critical homage to the mosaic of personal, political and environmental insights of ecological feminism, taking many of its tenets on board while also seeking unique conceptualisations and praxes, generated by and for men and masculinities as we heed the collective wisdom of this discourse.

We acknowledge that ecological feminist strategies for our common future correctly stopped short of 'cleaning up shop' for men and masculinities and intentionally so, however, an unfortunate consequence of this has been the inadvertent additional distancing of men and masculinities from roles as ecofeminist allies and compatriots in support of a deep green future.

Ecofeminists have understandably lent critical attention to the exploits and destructiveness of hegemonic masculinities and its supporting structures. Meanwhile, these structures continue to resist broader, deeper and wider care. However, as the ecological feminist discourse has grown and diversified, ecofeminist personal politics have refined analyses, pressing the edges of gendered identities as some of the necessary ingredients in Earthcare, helping us see that all cisgender men are not in fact to blame for our social and environmental challenges as individuals, helping us focus the fullest force of this book on structural change. This is a tricky line to walk between exposés of and accountability for oppressions balanced against allegiance building beyond the gender wars. Of course, men (like all others) must be held to account when acting from within the oppressive frameworks of masculine hegemonisation (or any oppression for that matter). This highlights the need to centralise kindness and compassion towards all who join a communal effort in support of the glocal commons. But what of those that are not of this persuasion? How do we lead individuals out of the delusions of their own primacy in support of all life? From our ecofeminist colleagues, we can see that a significant aspect in answering this question must be to direct our attention towards ways we can better support men and masculinities to become more involved in solutions to the social and environmental problems that we face.

If ecological feminism has provided us with pathways that point us in the direction of a deep green future, we note that it is now time for men to follow their lead. We need ecological masculinities that are proactive, productive and reach across the widest possible gendered and political spectrum, just as has emerged throughout ecological feminism over time. To achieve this, we must be willing to look for other options for men and masculinities than the industrial/breadwinner and/or ecomodern offerings of hegemonisation that have accompanied male domination. In presenting such a nuanced approach to this work that tends to the machinations of men and masculinities but focuses on the structural socialisation of internalised superiority that afflict them, we diverge from those (particularly essentialised) ecofeminist who did not attend to an analytical separation between systemic critiques of socialisations and the personal blame of biological determinism. It is our belief that some ecofeminists have understandably expressed great anger, frustration and indeed hurt for the wounds that men and masculinities have inflicted on Earth and human others (women in particular), but have conflated structural and personal accountability and in doing so have constructed some interpretations of ecological feminism as a discourse that many men find difficult to relate to and embrace.

Surely, men can not only cause great harm but can also generate great care towards Earth, human others and themselves? Going forward, the task as we see it is to move beyond gendered binaries and emphasise the possibilities of care that transcend their associated stereotypes. This book is a step in that direction, exploring the possibility of post-gendered critical analyses of the human–nature relationship, while also tending to the importance of gender politics for men and masculinities. From here, we continue to examine the notion of care more closely through our consideration of feminist care theory.

Note

1 This is a point I (Paul speaking here) explored through a literature review and field study of male chimpanzees (*Pan troglodytes*) and bonobos (*Pan paniscus*) that I conducted for my master's research (Pulé, 2003).

References

Adams, C. 1993. 'Introduction'. In C. Adams, ed., *Ecofeminism and the Sacred*. New York: Continuum, 1–12.

Alaimo, S. 1994. 'Cyborg ecofeminist interventions: challenges for an environmental feminism'. *Feminist Studies* 20(1): 133–152.

Alaimo, S. 2009. 'Insurgent vulnerability and the carbon footprint of gender'. *Kvinder, Køn & Forskning* 3–4: 22–35.

Alaimo, S. 2010. 'The naked world: the trans-corporeal ethics of the protesting body'. *Women and Performance: A Journal of Feminist Theory* 20(1): 15–36.

Alaimo, S., and S. Hekman, eds. 2008. *Material Feminisms*. Bloomington: Indiana University Press.

Archambault, A. 1993. 'A critique of ecofeminism'. *Canadian Woman Studies* 13(3): 19–22.

Arora-Jonsson, S. 2011. 'Virtue and vulnerability: discourses on women, gender and climate change'. *Global Environmental Change* 21(2): 744–751.

Arora-Jonsson, S. 2013. *Gender, Development and Environmental Governance: Theorizing Connections*. Oxon: Routledge.

Barad, K. 2003. 'Posthumanist performativity: toward an understanding of how matter comes to matter'. *Signs: Journal of Women in Culture and Society* 28(3): 801 831.

Bari, J. 1992. 'The feminization of earth first!' *Ms.* May/June: 84.

Bennett, J. 2010. *Vibrant Matter: A Political Ecology of Things*. Durham: Duke University Press.

Biehl, J. 1988. 'What is social ecofeminism?' *Green Perspectives: A Left Green Publication* 11: 1–8.

Biehl, J. 1991. *Rethinking Ecofeminist Politics*. Boston: South End Press.

Braidotti, R. 2013. *The Posthuman*. Cambridge: Polity.

Buckingham, S. 2004. 'Ecofeminism in the twenty-first century'. *Geographical Journal* 170 (2 June): 146–154.

Buckingham, S. 2017. 'Gender and climate change politics'. In S. MacGregor, ed., *Routledge Handbook of Gender and Environment*. Oxon: Routledge, 384–397.

Buckingham, S., and R. Kulcur. 2009. 'Gendered geographies of environmental injustice'. *Antipodes* 41(4): 659–683.

Buckingham, S., and V. Le Masson. eds. 2017. *Understanding Climate Change through Gender Relations: Routledge Studies in Hazards, Disasters and Climate Change*. Oxon: Routledge.

Butler, C. 2017. 'A fruitless endeavour: confronting the heteronormativity of environmentalism'. In S. MacGregor, ed., *Routledge Handbook of Gender and Environment*. Oxon: Routledge, 270–286.

Carlassare, E. 1992. 'An exploration of ecofeminism'. Master's diss., University of California, Berkeley.

Caldicott, H. 2006. *Nuclear Power Is Not the Answer*. New York: The New Press.

Carson, R. 1962. *Silent Spring*. Boston: Houghton Mifflin.

Chakraborty, U. 2013. 'Effect of different phases of the lunar month on humans'. *Biological Rhythm Research* 45(3): 383–396.

Chanter, T. 2016. *Ethics of Eros: Irigaray's Re-writing of the Philosophers*. Oxon: Routledge.

Chen, C., MacLeod, J., and A. Neimanis, eds. 2013. *Thinking with Water*. Ontario: McGill-Queen's University Press.

Coole, D., and S. Frost. 2010. eds. *The New Materialisms: Ontology, Agency, and Politics*. Durham: Duke University Press

Cuomo, C. 1998. *Feminism and Ecological Communities: An Ethic of Flourishing*. London: Routledge.

Cuomo, C. 2017. 'Sexual politics in environmental ethics: impacts, causes, alternatives'. InS. Gardiner andA. Thompson, eds.,*The Oxford Handbook of Environmental Ethics*. New York: Oxford University Press, 288–300.

d'Eaubonne, F. 1974. *Le féminisme ou la mort*. Paris: Pierre Horay.

d'Eaubonne, F. 1980. 'Feminism or death'. In E. Marks and I. de Courtivron, eds., *New French Feminisms: An Anthology*. Amherst: University of Massachusetts Press, 64–67.

Daly, M. 1978. *Gyn/Ecology: The Metaethics of Radical Feminism*. London: Women's Press.

Davion, V. 1994. 'Is ecofeminism feminist?'. In K. Warren, ed., *Ecological Feminism*. New York: Routledge, 8–28.

Di Battista, A., Haas, O., and D. Patrick. 2015. 'Conversations in queer ecologies: an editorial'. *UnderCurrents: Journal of Critical Environmental Studies* 19: 3–5.

Di Chiro, G. 2008. 'Living environmentalisms: coalition politics, social reproduction, and environmental justice'. *Environmental Politics* 17(2): 276–298.

Elmhirst, R. 2011. 'Introducing new feminist political ecologies'. *Geoforum* 42(2): 129–132

Foster, E. 2017. 'Gender, environmental governmentality and the discourse of sustainable development'. In S. MacGregor, ed., *Routledge Handbook of Gender and Environment*. Oxon: Routledge, 216–228.

Gaard, G. 1993. 'Ecofeminism and Native American cultures: pushing the limits of cultural imperialism?'. In G. Gaard, ed., *Ecofeminism: Women, Animals, Nature*. Philadelphia: Temple University Press, 295–314.

Gaard, G. 1997. 'Toward a queer ecofeminism'. *Hypatia* 12(1): 114–137.

Gaard, G. 2015. 'Ecofeminism and climate change'. *Women's Studies International Forum* 49: 20–33.

Gaard, G. 2016. 'From "cli-fi" to critical ecofeminism: narratives of climate change and climate justice'. In M. Phillips and N. Rumens, eds., *Contemporary Perspectives on Ecofeminism*. Oxon: Routledge, 169–192.

Gaard, G. 2017. 'Posthumanism, ecofeminism, and inter-species relations'. In S. MacGregor, ed., *Routledge Handbook of Gender and Environment*. Oxon: Routledge, 115–130.

Gilligan, C. 1982. *In a Different Voice: Psychological Theory and Women's Development*. Cambridge: Harvard University Press.

Gilman, C. 1979[1915]. *Herland*. New York: Pantheon.

Godfrey, P. 2008. 'Ecofeminist cosmology in practice: genesis farm and the embodiment of sustainable solutions'. *Capitalism Nature Socialism* 19(2): 96–114.

Gonda, N. 2017. 'Revealing the patriarchal sides of climate change adaptation through intersectionality: a case study from Nicaragua'. In S. Buckingham and V. le Masson, eds., *Understanding Climate Change through Gender Relations*. Oxon: Routledge, 173–189.

Grasswick, H. 2014. 'Climate change science and responsible trust: a situated approach'. *Hypatia* 29(3): 541–557.

Green Belt Movement. 2017. 'The Green Belt movement'. Accessed 8 November 2017. http://www.greenbeltmovement.org

Griffin, S. 1978. *Woman and Nature: The Roaring Inside Her*. New York: Harper & Row.

Gruen, L. 1997. 'Revaluing nature'. In K. Warren, ed., *Ecofeminism: Women, Culture, Nature*. Bloomington: Indiana University Press, 356–374.

Hallen, P. 1988. 'Making peace with the environment: why ecology needs feminism'. *Canadian Women's Studies (Les cahiers de la femme)* 9(1): 9–19.

Hallen, P. 1989. 'Careful of science: a feminist critique of science'. *Trumpeter Journal of Ecosophy* 6(1): 3–8.

Hallen, P. 1994. 'Reawakening the erotic'. *Habitat Australia*February: 18–21.

Hallen, P. 2001. 'Recovering the wildness in ecofeminism'. *Women's Studies Quarterly* 29(1/2): 216–233.

Hallen, P. 2003. 'The art of impurity'. *Ethics and the Environment* 8(1): 57–60.

Hanson, S. 2010. 'Gender and mobility: new approaches for informing sustainability'. *Gender, Place & Culture* 17(1): 5–23.

Haraway, D. 1988. 'Situated knowledges: the science question in feminism and the privilege of partial perspective'. *Feminist Studies* 14(3): 575–599.

Haraway, D. 1991. *Simians, Cyborgs, and Women: The Reinvention of Nature*. London: Routledge.

Hjulman, T. 2017. 'Ett med naturen: En studie av hur naturen omförhandlades i mellankrigstidens konflikter mellan naturskydd och samiska rättigheter'. PhD diss., Luleå tekniska universitet.

Hrdy, S. 1999. *Mother Nature: Natural Selection and the Female of the Species*. London: Chatto & Windus.

Jackson, S. 2017. 'Gender politics in Green parties'. In S. MacGregor, ed., *Routledge Handbook of Gender and Environment*. Oxon: Routledge, 304–317.

Kall A-S and M. Hultman. Forthcoming. 'Women for peace and small scale renewables. Anti-nuclear mobilization in 1970s Sweden'. In *La Camera Blu*. Federico II Open Access University Press: Napoli.

Kheel, M. 2008. *Nature Ethics: An Ecofeminist Perspective*. Plymouth: Rowman & Littlefield.

King, Y. 1983. 'The ecofeminist imperative'. In L. Caldecott and S. Leland, eds., *Reclaim the Earth: Women Speak out for Life on Earth*. London: Women's Press, 9–14.

Lahar, S. 1991. 'Ecofeminist theory and grassroots politics'. *Hypatia: A Journal of Feminist Philosophy* 6(1): 28–45.

Latour, B. 1993. *We Have Never Been Modern*. Cambridge: Harvard University Press.

Latour, B. 2004. *Politics of Nature: How to Bring the Sciences into Democracy*. Cambridge: Harvard University Press.

Latour, B. 2017. *Facing Gaia: Eight Lectures on the New Climatic Regime*. Cambridge: Polity.

Laula, E. 1904. *Inför lif eller död?: sanningsord i de lappska förhållandena*. Gaaltije.

Law, S. 1986. 'The regulation of menstrual cycle and its relationship to the moon'. *Acta Obstet Gynecol Scand*. 65(1): 45–48.

Leppänen, K. 2008. *Elin Wägner's Alarm Clock: Ecofeminist Theory in the Interwar Era*. Lanham: Lexington.

Leppänen, K., and T. Svensson. 2016. 'Om naturupplevelser hos Elin Wägner och Hagar Olsson. Lästa i eko-och vithetskritisk belysning'. *Tidskrift för genusvetenskap*, 37(1): 11–31.

Littig, B. 2017. 'Good green jobs for whom? A feminist critique of the green economy'. In S. MacGregor, ed., *Routledge Handbook of Gender and Environment*. Oxon: Routledge, 318–330.

Maathai, W. 2004. *The Green Belt Movement: Sharing the Approach and the Experience*. New York: Lantern Books.

MacGregor, S. 2006. *Beyond Mothering Earth: Ecological Citizenship and the Politics of Care*. Vancouver: University of British Columbia Press.

MacGregor, S., ed. 2017. *Routledge Handbook of Gender and Environment*. Oxon: Routledge.

Macleod, N. 2015. 'Moon cycles and women'. Accessed 2 May 2017. http://www.menstruation.com.au/periodpages/mooncycles.html

Mathews, F. 1991. *The Ecological Self*. Savage: Barnes & Noble.

Mathews, F. 1999. 'Letting the world grow old: an ethos of countermodernity'. *Worldviews: Environment, Culture, Religion* 3(2): 243–271.

Mathews, F. 2005. *Reinhabiting Reality: Towards a Recovery of Culture*. Sydney: University of New South Wales Press.

McCright, A., and A. Sundström. 2013. 'Examining gender differences in environmental concern in the Swedish general public, 1990–2011'. *International Journal of Sociology* 43(4): 63–86.

McQuade, J. 2017. 'Can we compare Trump's USA to Nazi Germany?'. Accessed 12 November 2017. http://www.gatescambridge.org/multimedia/blog/can-we-compare-trump%E2%80%99s-usa-nazi-germany

Mellor, M. 1992a. *Breaking the Boundaries: Towards a Feminist Green Socialism*. London: Virago.

Mellor, M. 1992b. 'Green politics: ecofeminine or ecomasculine?'. *Environmental Politics* 1(2): 229–251.

Mellor, M. 1997. *Feminism and Ecology*. New York: New York University Press.

Mellor, M. 2017. 'Ecofeminist political economy: a green and feminist agenda'. In S. MacGregor, ed., *Routledge Handbook of Gender and Environment*. Oxon: Routledge, 86–100.

Merchant, C. 1980. *The Death of Nature: Women, Ecology and the Scientific Revolution*. New York: HarperCollins.

Merchant, C. 1992. *Radical Ecology: The Search for a Liveable World*. New York: Routledge.

Merchant, C. 2006. 'The scientific revolution and the death of nature'. *Isis* 97(3): 513–533.

Mies, M. and V. Shiva. 1993. 'Introduction: why we wrote this book together'. In M. Mies and V. Shiva, eds., *Ecofeminism*. Halifax: Zed Books, 1–21.

Milner-Barry, S. 2015. 'The term "mother nature" reinforces the idea that both women and nature should be subjugated'. Accessed 2 May 2017. https://qz.com/562833/the-term-mother-nature-reinforces-the-idea-that-both-women-and-nature-should-be-subjugated

Münster, K., Schmidt, L., and P. Helm. 1992. 'Length and variation of menstrual cycle – a cross-sectional study from a Danish county'. *British Journal of Obstetrics and Gynaecology* 99(5): 422–429.

Musawa. 2010. *In the Spirit of We'moon: Celebrating 30 Years: An Anthology of Art and Writing.* Wolf Creek: Mother Tongue Ink.

Nightingale, A. 2006. 'The nature of gender: work, gender, and environment'. *Environment and Planning D: Society and space* 24(2): 165–185.

Norgaard, K., and R. York. 2005. 'Gender equity and state environmentalism'. *Gender and Society* 19(4): 506–522.

Öhman, M. 2016. 'TechnoVisions of a Sámi cyborg: reclaiming Sámi body-, land-, and waterscapes after a century of colonial exploitations in Sábme'. In A. Hussenlus, K. Scantlebury, K. Anderssone, and A. Gulberg, eds., *Interstitial Spaces: A Model for Transgressive Processes.* New York: Springer, 63–98.

Ortner, S. 1974. 'Is female to male as nature is to culture?'. In M. Rosaldo and L. Lamphere eds., *Women, Culture, and Society.* Stanford: Stanford University Press, 68–87.

Otto, E. 2012. 'Ecofeminist theories of liberation in the science fiction of Sally Miller Gearhart, Ursula K. Le Guin, and Joan Slonczewski'. In D. Vakoch, ed., *Feminist Ecocriticism: Environment, Women, and Literature.* Lanham: Lexington, 13–38.

Owusu, R. 2006. *Kwame Nkrumah's Liberation Thought: A Paradigm for Religious Advocacy in Contemporary Ghana.* Asmara: Africa World Press.

Parry, B. 1995. 'Problems in current theories of colonial discourse'. In B. Ashcroft, G. Griffiths, and H. Tiffin, eds., *The Post-Colonial Studies Reader.* London: Routledge, 36–44.

Persson, S., Harnesk, D., and M. Islar. 2017. 'What local people? Examining the Gállok mining conflict and the rights of the Sámi population in terms of justice and power'. *Geoforum* 86: 20–29.

Plumwood, V. 1993. *Feminism and the Mastery of Nature.* London: Routledge.

Plumwood, V. 2002a. *Environmental Culture: The Ecological Crisis of Reason.* London: Routledge.

Plumwood, V. 2002b. 'Decolonisation relationships with nature'. *PAN: Philosophy Activism Nature* 2: 7–30.

Prentice, S. 1988. 'Taking sides: what's wrong with eco-feminism?'. *Women and Environments* 10 (spring): 9–10.

Pulé, P. 2003. 'Us and them: primate science and the union of the rational self with the intuitive self'. Master's diss., Schumacher College, Plymouth University.

Pulé P. 2013. 'A declaration of caring: towards an ecological masculinism'. PhD diss., Murdoch University.

Quinn-Thibodeau, T. and B. Wu. 2016. 'NGOs and the climate justice movement in the age of Trumpism'. *Development* 59(3–4): 251–256.

Räty, R., and A. Carlsson-Kanyama. 2010. 'Energy consumption by gender in some European countries'. *Energy Policy* 38(1): 646–649.

Roach, C. 1991. 'Loving your mother: on the woman–nature relation'. *Hypatia* 6(1): 46–59.

Roach, C. 2002. 'Getting back at mother nature'. *Sierra* 87(3): 84.

Roach, C. 2003. *Mother Nature: Popular Culture and Environmental Ethics.* Bloomington: Indiana University Press.

Rocheleau, D., Thomas-Slayter, B., and E. Wangari. 1996. *Feminist Political Ecology: Global Issues and Local Experience.* London: Routledge

Rose, E. 1991. 'The good mother: from Gaia to Gilead'. *Frontiers: A Journal of Women Studies* 12(1): 77–97.

Roth-Johnson, D. 2013. 'Back to the future: Françoise d'Eaubonne, ecofeminism and ecological crisis'. *International Journal of Literary Humanities* 10(3): 51–61.

Roughgarden, J. 2004. *Evolution's Rainbow: Diversity, Gender, and Sexuality in Nature and People.* Berkeley: University of California Press.

Ruether, R. 1975. *New Women New Earth: Sexist Ideologies and Human Liberation.* Minneapolis: Winston Press.

Ruether, R. 1992. *Gaia and God: An Ecofeminist Theology of Earth Healing.* New York: HarperCollins.

Said, E. 1978. *Orientalism.* New York: Pantheon.

Salleh, A. 1984. 'Deeper than deep ecology: the eco-feminist connection'. *Environmental Ethics* 6 (winter): 339–345.

Salleh, A. 1997. *Ecofeminism as Politics: Nature, Marx and the Postmodern.* London: Zed Books.

Salleh, A. 1998. 'Deeper than deep ecology: the ecofeminist connection'. In M. Zimmerman, J. Callicott, G. Sessions, K. Warren, and J. Clark, eds., *Environmental Philosophy: From Animal Rights to Radical Ecology.* Upper Saddle Valley, NJ: Prentice Hall, 339–345.

Salleh, A. 2006. 'Towards an inclusive solidarity on the left: editor's introduction'. *Capitalism Nature Socialism* 17(4): 32–37.

Schulz, K. 2017. 'Decolonizing political ecology: ontology, technology and "critical" enchantment'. *Journal of Political Ecology* 24: 126.

Seager, J. 1993. *Earth Follies: Coming to Feminist Terms with the Global Environmental Crisis.* New York: Routledge.

Seager, J. 2017. 'Rachel Carson was right – then, and now'. In S. MacGregor, ed., *Routledge Handbook of Gender and Environment.* Oxon: Routledge, 27–42.

Sehlin MacNeil, K. 2017. 'Extractive violence on indigenous country: Sami and Aboriginal views on conflicts and power relations with extractive industries'. PhD diss., Umeå University.

Serres, M. 2007. *The Parasite.* Minneapolis: University of Minnesota Press.

Sexton, J. 2016. 'Donald Trump's toxic masculinity'. *New York Times Online.* Accessed 12 November 2017. http://www.nytimes.com/2016/10/13/opinion/donald-trumps-toxic-masculinity.html

Seymour, N. 2013. *Strange Natures: Futurity, Empathy, and the Queer Ecological Imagination.* Urbana: University of Illinois Press.

Seymour, N. 2017. 'Transgender environments'. In S. MacGregor, ed., *Routledge Handbook of Gender and Environment.* Oxon: Routledge, 253–269.

Sjöö, M., and B. Mor. 1987. *The Great Cosmic Mother: Rediscovering the Religion of the Earth.* San Francisco: HarperSanFrancisco.

Sjöstedt Landén, A. 2017. 'En berättelse om motstånd mot gruvexploatering-en berättelse om Norrland'. *Brännpunkt Norrland*, redigerad av A. Öhman, and B. Nilsson. Umeå: H: Ströms.

Spretnak, C. 1986. *The Spiritual Dimension of Green Politics.* Rochester: Inner Traditions/Bear.

Spretnak, C. 1990. 'Ecofeminism: our roots and flowering'. In I. Diamond and G. Orenstein, eds., *Reweaving the World: The Emergence of Ecofeminism.* San Francisco: Sierra Club Books, 3–14.

Spretnak, C. 1999. *The Resurgence of the Real: Body, Nature and Place in a Hypermodern World.* New York: Routledge.

Stoddart, M., and D. Tindall. 2011. 'Ecofeminism, hegemonic masculinity, and environmental movement participation in British Columbia, Canada, 1998–2007: "women always clean up the mess"'. *Sociological Spectrum* 31(3): 342–368.

Sturgeon, N. 1997. *Ecofeminist Natures: Race, Gender, Feminist Theory, and Political Action.* New York: Routledge.

Tiostanova, M., and W. Mignolo. 2012. *Learning to Unlearn: Decolonial Reflections from Eurasia and the Americas.* Columbus: Ohio State University Press.

Twine, R. 2010. 'Intersectional disgust? Animals and (eco)feminism'. *Feminism & Psychology* 20(3): 397–406.

United Nations. 2002. *Gendering Mainstreaming: An Overview.* New York: Office of the Special Adviser on Gender Issues, Department of Economic and Social Affairs.

Valladares, C., and R. Boelens. 2017. 'Extractivism and the rights of nature: governmentality, "convenient communities" and epistemic pacts in Ecuador'. *Environmental Politics* 26(6): 1015–1034.

von Werlhof, C. 2007. 'No critique of capitalism without a critique of patriarchy! Why the left is no alternative'. *Capitalism Nature Socialism,* 18(1): 13–27.

Wägner, E. 1941. *Väckarklocka,* Stockholm: Bonniers.

Warren, K. 1987. 'Feminism and ecology: making connections'. *Environmental Ethics* 9 (Spring): 3–20.

Warren, K. 1994. 'Towards an ecofeminist peace politics'. In K. Warren, ed., *Ecological Feminism.* New York: Routledge, 179–199.

Warren, K. 1997. 'Taking empirical data seriously: an ecofeminist philosophical perspective'. In K. Warren, ed., *Ecofeminism: Women, Culture, Nature.* Bloomington: Indiana University Press, 3–20.

Warren, K. 2000. *Ecofeminist Philosophy: A Western Perspective on What It Is and Why It Matters.* Lanham: Rowman & Littlefield .

Warren, K. 2002. 'Response to my critics (defending *Ecofeminist Philosophy*)'. *Ethics and the Environment* 7(2): 39–59.

Weller, I. 2017. 'Gender dimensions of consumption'. In S. MacGregor, ed., *Routledge Handbook of Gender and Environment.* Oxon: Routledge, 331–344.

Wolf, N. 2003. *Misconceptions: Truth, Lies, and the Unexpected on the Journey to Motherhood.* New York: Anchor.

Yazzie, M., and C. Baldy, eds. 2017. 'Decolonization: indigeneity, education & society'. *Home Page Online.* Accessed 15 July 2017. http://decolonization.org/index.php/des/index

6   Caring for the 'glocal' commons

Everyone cares . . . human survival depends on care. Infants are entirely help-
less and would perish without some degree of care. As a result, we can say that
all of us . . . have been involved in a caring relationship.

(DeFalco, 2016: 6)

The possibilities of care

Care is a contested concept (Clement, 2007: 301). The term is derived from
the Old English *caru* that reflected suffering, sorrow, lamentation or mourning
and has come to be associated with notions of concern, heed, attention,
regard, caution and the burden of inescapable responsibility. While notions of
care are traditionally associated with women and feminine socialisations, primatologist Sandra Blaffer Hrdy (1999: 207) argued that '"[i]nstincts" to care
slumber in the hearts of primate males, including men', meaning that care has
been integral to masculinities since the dawn of our species as well.

Widely used as both a noun and a verb, care is a complex term. Considered a
human virtue entangled and juxtaposed against discussions on justice, care harbours social values of both private and public significance that are contingent on
who determines care, how that care is mediated, what quality of care is offered and
how the care being offered is received (Curtin, 1991; Tronto, 1993a; Benner et al.,
1996). Care can have great consequences, providing material, emotional or psychic
sustenance to some while emaciating those who are otherised. Care emerges
through both giving and receiving. Care can provide a sense of accomplishment as
well as the fulfilment of obligations or it can leave us feeling used (Bubeck, 1995:
150). Care is a common fixture of our daily lives, traversing the boundary between
others and ourselves, instigating a variety of caring actions. Indeed '[c]are is prob-
ably the most deeply fundamental value' for human beings to assume (Held, 2006:
17). Consequently, care has many meanings and applications for our daily lives. In
the context of masculine hegemonisation, capacities to care for others and ourselves continue to be conflated with justice. For example, care has recently been
enmeshed with mechanisms of justice, along with calls for better education and
healthcare for all (Hart, 2013; Patrick et al., 2016; Fernandes-Jesus et al., 2017).
But this dissonance need not erode the potency of conversations about care.

Throughout this book, we have returned to the notion that men's lives are in fact richer, more meaningful, more diverse and longer lived when they are connected with others. This is particularly true if those relational exchanges are awash with care from both ends (towards men and from men towards others) with men living much better lives as a result. Consider the study on adult development which tracked 268 Harvard graduates from classes 1939 to 1944 compared to 456 men who grew up in inner-city Boston of a similar age. This study is deemed to be the longest research project focused on uncovering the secret to real happiness (Harvard Second Generation Study, 2017). Examining ageing, relational and neuroscientific indicators, Harvard psychiatry professor Robert Waldinger demonstrated that close relationships, relationships of high quality and those that are the most stable resulted in the best of emotional and physiological outcomes for men (Lewis, 2015). Consider this statement from Waldinger et al. (2015: 23) speaking to 'lessons on the good life' that makes a strong case for the value of copious care for men in particular:

> The feeling that one can rely on an intimate partner in times of need is likely to foster a greater sense of wellbeing in the face of life's daily stresses and uncertainties and this feeling is likely to inform the evaluation of how satisfied partners are in their relationships. Conversely, lack of comfort with caregiving or caretaking and the sense that a partner cannot be relied on for support, might well contribute to more frequent conflicts in the marriage, particularly as needs for support increase with age.

Granted, the positive outcomes for overall well-being are evident when being cared for. However, the form of care studied above might go well for those who receive that care but says little about the ripple effects of that care on others or the negative impacts of conveying care myopically when care is disseminated unevenly. Hegemonic masculinities promote caring in precisely these predetermined ways. As we have argued, men's myopic care has deleterious social and environmental consequences. Take for example men serving in military and paramilitary services (socially devastating and ecocidal practices), the unbridled passions of men supporting national football teams (their sport dependent on fossil fuels) or the bureaucratic implementations of care by a public servant who holds an influential position in government (bogging people and processes down in red tape that can occur to them as profoundly uncaring). Examining these permutations on care further still, consider that men do have emotional intelligence, providing them with capacities to empathise with others, passing their assessment of situations through ethical filters that assist them to care. Such qualities are considered to be reflective of someone who is comfortable with themselves, the world around them and the social networks that they are immersed in (Goleman, 1995: 45). These are some of the key qualities of an emotionally literate person.

Men can develop 'ecological intelligence' as well. They can do so naturally and alongside calls for increased emotional intelligence:

> Today's threats demand that we hone a new sensibility, the capacity to recognize the hidden web of connections between human activity and nature's systems and the subtle complexities of their intersections. This awakening to new possibilities must result in a collective eye opening, a shift in our most basic assumptions and perceptions, one that will drive changes in commerce and industry as well as in our individual actions and behaviours.
>
> (Goleman, 2009: 43)

It is important to stress that the term 'ecological' Goleman used here referred to an intimate understanding of the living Earth and our role within it, while 'intelligence' spoke to our capacity to learn and adapt to environmental stimuli so that we can deal effectively with the challenges that are confronting us (Goleman, 2009: 43). Fresh waves of academic and activist advocacy for Earth jurisprudence are responding to human-induced ecocides. They represent the psychological benefits we gain from Earthcare to avert *solastalgia* – the psychic and existential distress caused by environmental harm that affects us precisely because we are connected to Earth as home (Albrecht, 2005). Rights-of-nature movements are now setting frameworks in place to mandate legal obligations to care for the glocal commons (and this means tending to the local social and ecological needs in our immediate lives and surrounds that then radiate out towards global concerns). These responses are inescapably entwined with our own self-care (Stone, 2010[1972]; Higgins et al., 2013). This is a revolutionary development, with legal proceedings now shifting and shaping the human–nature relationship through, for example, a recent landmark determination that the New Zealand North Island Whanganui River has been awarded ancestral and legal 'personhood', representing a major international victory for global indigenous Earth wisdom. This has paved the way for the Uttarakhand court in India to follow suit on behalf of the mighty Ganges River, even if some sections of both rivers are deemed ecologically 'dead' at this time (Roy, 2017; Safi, 2017). As these innovations unfold, what might more ecologised expressions of masculine care look like? Returning to Waldinger's reference to caring attachment as central to 'the good life' and Goleman's 'new sensibility' in order to achieve heightened environmental intelligence, men and masculinities are being called to proactively combine the internal and external glocalisations of care – away from industrial/breadwinner and ecomodern masculinities and towards ecological masculinities. But this life of broader caring attachment, this new sensibility, remains the allusive exception rather than the rule, especially for Western men. To be male and to care continues to be not only myopic, but a fraught expression of masculinities as well.

Utilitarian care

Masculine hegemonisation supports expressions of care for select others and ourselves, but in ways that protect and preserve male domination. Care has, unfortunately, been steeped in a utilitarian tradition for so long as to have a normalising effect on the ways we conceptualise and extend care to others. This manifestation of other-care offers at best a near-sighted perspective of how that care might benefit the one caring as they extend their care to the one being cared for. This reveals the heart of the matter. Men and masculinities are subject to a 'care myopia', which can contradict traditional notions of manhood and must be transformed. Let us consider industrial/breadwinner approaches to care as we seek new horizons of care for men and masculinities.

Traditionally, care has been embedded within debates about the morality of right and wrong and good and bad. Shelley Taylor (2002: 123) argued that men's isolation tends to bind them to duty, honour and the justification of their own existence to make a difference in the world from an egocentric rather than egoless place, meaning that men are widely socialised to be less relational than women – in other words men possess ethics of care, but how that care manifests is defnined by gender identity, relationships and individual lived experiences. Men's myopic care is the product of a long history of conditioning.

Henry Sidgwick (1901) suggested that our hedonistic tendencies compel us to seek out and maintain beauty in order to tantalise the human mind. He followed in the footsteps of utilitarian philosophers like Jeremy Bentham and John Stuart Mill, echoing Bentham's 'greatest happiness for the greatest number' by noting that:

> . . . when we are computing how much happiness a given state of the world involves, we should give equal weight to any two equally happy people. And it's pretty obvious why it is generally conducive to the general happiness that each individual should distribute his beneficence in the channels marked out by commonly recognised ties and claims.
>
> (Sidgwick, 1901: 210)

Such proximal care has throughout history been applied unequally – directing care to some beyond ourselves. This unequal distribution of care remains commonplace in Western traditions; our virtuosity towards others has long been an equation – a functional imperative that has at best served self, with special dues of kindness being extended to those who stand in close relation to ourselves (Sidgwick, 1901: 242; Schneewind, 1977). More contemporary studies on ecosystem services demonstrate a similar view of utilitarian care (Kosoy and Corbera, 2010; Jackson and Palmer, 2015; Puig de la Bellacasa, 2015). If we problematise this rationale, we note traditional justifications for this conditional extension of care to something or someone outside of ourselves neatly aligns with the self-serving imperatives of capitalism, which is of course created, managed and maintained by hegemonic masculinities. In alignment with the utilitarian tradition that has shaped the West, we typically extend care only in order to get something for ourselves in return. Effectively, human care has been positioned as a balance sheet, where extending care to others is dependent on and respondent to our own inner agency gaining benefit from doing so. We behave admirably when we care, hoping quietly that caring might compensate our vagaries with acts that ultimately self-serve. This subjective rationale for our caring continues to settle on feeling good about ourselves through our pursuit of the good for others and is optional, being enacted only if we are so inclined (Slote, 1997: 228; Darwall, 2002: 36–37, 49). Such views on care are not merely conditional. They are also located in the context of the reductive constructs that pervade masculine hegemonisation in the context of care, which separate the human mind from embodied exchanges between others and ourselves, giving little if any consideration to notions of the intrinsic value and the equal rights of all life that we have discussed above. In relegating care to abstraction, the logical exercise of caring beyond ourselves operates independently from the happiness, perfection or excellence that we might gain when we offer our care to others as an honouring of their intrinsic value. This conditionality is not the kind of care we are interested in.

In this chapter, we reach beyond utilitarian approaches to care, prioritising the right of existence for all life in alignment with profeminist masculinities politics as well as our deep ecological and ecological feminist forebears. Concurring with Tammy Shel (2009: 122), we note that '[t]here must be conditions for the full development of human beings and satisfaction of their basic needs as individuals, . . . through caring for an explorative, creative, and critical education' beyond 'performance ideology of one-dimensional society', rendering concurrent care for all others and ourselves a vital step in a sustainable future. Consequently, we look to non-utilitarian insights in order to assist us to locate care at the heart of masculine ecologisation. To this end, we discovered that feminist care theory offers great guidance to traditional notions of care. We proceed to support the (re)awakening of broader masculine capacities to care.

Feminist theories on care

Virginia Held elaborated on our understanding of the distinction, first posited by Nel Noddings, between 'caring about' (a state of nurturing caring ideas and intentions) versus 'caring for' (the hands-on application of caring for) something or someone. Held (1995: 102–105) noted that:

If caring involves a commitment, then caring must have an object. Thus, caring is necessarily relational. We say that we care for or about something or someone. We can distinguish 'caring about' from 'caring for' based on the objects of caring. Caring about refers to less concrete objects; it is characterized by a more general form of commitment. Caring for implies a specific, particular object that is the focus of caring. The boundaries between caring about and caring for are not so neat as these statements imply. Nonetheless, this distinction is useful in revealing something about the way we think of caring in our society.

These distinctions are significant. They have also been thoroughly interrogated by Held and other scholars (Chodorow, 1978; Ruddick, 1980; Gilligan, 1986; Friedman, 1993; Plumwood, 1993; Tronto, 1993a; Tronto, 1993b; Noddings, 1995; Ruddick, 1995; Held, 2006; Shel, 2007). We do not claim to give a total overview of this field of study here. For expediency and to keep our focus on masculine ecologisation, we collapse these distinctions, using the terms 'care' and 'caring' throughout this chapter to refer to both nuanced applications in the broader context. We do so in order to include both the conceptual notions of caring 'ethically' speaking and tangible and applied notions of caring in the 'societal' sense in honour of the extensive contributions offered by feminist care theorists whose work has preceded ours (Held, 1993: 9–10; Noddings, 2002: 2).

The moral pragmatism associated with care effectively narrows the bandwidth of permissible caring behaviours in alignment with the constrictions of masculine hegemonies. Care has been relegated not only as self-serving but is also divested from emotional investment in the broader well-being of others – an all too convenient alignment with malestream socialisations of men and masculinities. This is understandable if we view the world through the lens of masculine hegemonisation. After all, there is little incentive to extend broader care to non-proximal others when we are steeped in traditional notions of hegemonic masculinities. Contrary to this care myopia, some men do find themselves serving in caring roles at work or home that test the bounds of traditional expressions of masculine care. For example, Peter Singer (1993: 90–91) noted that many fathers care deeply for their children but are still constrained by expressions of that care through protector/provider roles rather than valorising emotional literacy. It is far from unusal for men to serve as nurses, teachers, land carers, social/ environmental activists and so forth; all being roles that call on them to engage not just in their utilitarian capacities to care, but their active, embodied and emotionally guided connectivity with others as well; their empathy moving them to act caringly in very tangible ways. As a consequence, we acknowledge that the permissible expressions of care as they impact men and masculinities stretch beyond the bounds of utilitarian notions of care, even though the ways that women and men demonstrate care might differ.

Consider early works on feminised care. We acknowledge Mary Wollstonecraft (1792), Catharine Beecher and Harriet Stowe (1869) and Charlotte Perkins Gilman (1979[1915]) who offered instrumental elucidations that challenged stereotypical assumptions about women and care. Forty years ago through her influential book: *The Reproduction of Mothering*, Nancy Chodorow (1978) placed the mother–daughter relationship under the microscope, critically analysing the ways that women are socialised to assume roles as mothers and primary childcarers. Using notable links between human psyche and culture as well as psychoanalysis and sociology, Chodorow explored the social mechanisms that determine how women consider themselves heterosexual, why they have urges to mother, what personality traits are woman specific and how male domination can be interrogated and transformed to embrace greater care in order to help share the caring load. She noted that women's ego boundaries are less firm than men's and that this accounted for the psychological predisposition imposed upon women to become mothers and primary childcarers to the detriment of their economic and social freedoms – those freedoms being occupied in far greater number by men. However, our primary attention in this chapter is levelled at more recent contributions to our understandings of care (building momentum since the 1980s).

These scholarly interrogations are foundational to what has come to be referred to as feminist care theory. We principally credit the formal emergence of this discourse to Carol Gilligan and Nel Noddings, whose investigations of care instigated considerable further thoughts and applications of care from which we have drawn great sustenance for the theories and praxes we advocate throughout this book. While deemed controversial on account of an apparent essentialism, Gilligan's (1982) *In a Different Voice: Psychological Theory and Women's Development* provided an important feminist contribution to our understandings of care. There, Gilligan ascribed differing feminine and masculine engagements with care not to the biology of our bodies. Rather, she considered distinct articulations of care to be matters of theme; her research demonstrated that both women and men harboured care, with women tending to adopt relational complexities in order to articulate care and men rationalising care as an equation governed by righteousness. From these investigations, Gilligan concluded that societal care would atrophy without women's care. She demonstrated that women's care was an alternative perspective that required recognition as an equally legitimate form of moral reasoning. This, she argued, was commonly obscured by liberal justice traditions manufactured and controlled primarily by men, which overshadowed women's care with mechanisms of autonomous and independent assessments of who to care for, when to care about them and how that care would be expressed and applied. Central to Gilligan's argument was her observation that this gendered care differential between women and men found its roots in the ways girls and boys are differently cared for as infants and small children, resulting in different experiences for children of both genders. This in turn set girls and boys on distinct courses to express care in notably different ways as adults. In making such claims, Gilligan became one of the first vocal proponents of a view that might loosely be defined as 'difference theory'.

Building on Gilligan's work, feminist educator and philosopher, Nel Noddings (1984), wrote another important feminist contribution about care in the context of moral education titled *Caring: A Feminine Approach to Ethics and Moral Education.* She noted that women enter into moral action (and therefore the praxes of care) through 'different doors' than do men. Recognising that women and feminised approaches to care are characterised by deliberative, direct and textured approaches to care, Noddings linked women's care to states of mental suffering or 'engrossment' predetermined by our burdens, our sources of anxiety and the constraints of our fears. From these origins, she argued, we are motivated to act caringly towards something or someone beyond ourselves in nuanced ways, where the one caring sets the terms upon which they extend their care to the one being cared for (Noddings, 1984: 9). In this way, Noddings considered care contextual, being a receptive concept that was subject to shared control and mutual exchanges between the one caring and the one being cared for. She argued that initiating care could occur by being available to offer care either as sentiment or by being in need or want of receiving caring acts. In fact, Noddings (1984: 148) dedicated a chapter in her book to caring for plants, animals, things and ideas, arguing that broader care was an implicit aspect of human care as well.

It is true that we can feel similar levels of care towards other-than-humans as we can towards our own species. This broader care includes our care for animals and plants as other-than-human 'persons' (Singer, 1979: 93, 97; also see Singer, 1975; Singer, 1993; Regan, 1995; Webster, 2005; Spira and Singer, 2006). However, Noddings ascribed receptivity, relatedness and responsiveness as intractable moral consequences of care, suggesting that the obligation of the one caring dissipates only when the one being cared for (either human or other-than-human) did not or could not receive that care. In this sense, Noddings contested Singer's call to end speciesism, suggesting instead that care for animals only extends to those who are sufficiently proximal to the one caring as to complete or reciprocate their care. She argued that our recognition of and longing for primal relatedness to life writ large generates fulfilment and joy, which, in turn, sustains the one caring (Freedberg, 1993: 536). Rita Manning (1992a, also see Manning, 1992b; Manning, 1996) extended Noddings's arguments, suggesting that our obligations to care for other-than-humans such as pets, livestock and wild animals was predetermined by the customised relational exchanges we have with those creatures that we share our respective lives. Carol Adams (1990) analyses of the sexual politics of meat preempted this argument, prioritising broad applications of love and empathy for other-than-humans over the rationalism and pragmatism of rights-based arguments. Daniel Engster (2006) wrestled with the entanglement between care and dependency, considering this delineation as definitive by arguing that those animals that are not dependent on humans are not in need of our care, even though industrial livestock practices often fall far short of this mark. Ecological feminist Marti Kheel (2008) interrogated animal care through the lens of moral obligation, asserting that all animals are unique as species and as individuals; that industrial/breadwinner masculinities have constructed the rationalisation, mechanisation and abstraction of animal husbandry and should be contested as a consequence.

It is notable, that Noddings, unlike Gilligan, gave some consideration to other-than-human care. She then proceeded to revisit and expand on her earlier claims about human and other-than-human care through a more recent book titled *Starting at Home* (Noddings, 2002). In that revised examination of care, she responded to judgements about care as a 'fine domestic theory', designating ethics of care as learnt at home (particularly between parent and child), which then held with it great power to radiate out to 'large-scale macro-issues' at the societal and global levels. Noddings posited that in order to effectively address some of our most pressing pla-netary problems, we must look to the domestic arena for guidance – our ethics of global justice being born out of our domicile ethics of care. She called forth the 'relational self' to supersede the 'autonomous self', ampli-fying consideration for *all* of those included in a network of care. Noddings (2002: 3) affirmed the concept of 'caring about' as an important motiva-tional stage for inspiring local and global justice. She contended that while it is impossible to care about all, especially distant others, we must strive for interdependence and from there recognise that it is impossible for us to shirk responsibility for injuries inflicted upon others and ourselves, effec-tively providing potent motivation for policies and practices that meet the needs of all. Unfortunately, Noddings stopped short of holding to account the challenges confronting this broader care. A tertiary examination of care was left to other feminist scholars who expanded the topic's body of knowl-edge beyond the discourse's foundations, giving considerable additional sub-stance to the applications of feminist care theory.

Applied care

Applied care can be self-serving or benevolent. In a defiant gesture of resisting men's consolidation of power, Joan Tronto (1995: 102) explained that care is often accompanied by a concurrent sense of acceptance of our-selves as well as responsibility for the well-being of others, whether wilfully/ dutifully imposed or innate. She argued that care was not restricted solely to human interactions, but could be applied to the relational exchanges between humans and our world (Tronto, 1993a: 102–103). Tronto demonstrated that care reflects the efforts we express in order to sustain the best of outcomes for others and is, notably, widely devalued, underpaid and consolidated in the powerless sectors of society, consequently and not surprisingly veneered in feminisation (Tronto, 1995: 113). She suggested that when we care, we are willing to work for others, make sacrifices, acquire and expend material resources, express emotional connection and invest energy in the one being cared for. For Tronto (1993a: 105– 108), care provides a suite of activities that maintain, contain and repair the human world in order to help make it more liveable by integrating environmentally, embodied and self-caring acts. She argued that care has both conceptual and practical faces expressed through four phases reflective of a broad cross section of ethics of care:

- Caring about: awareness of and attention to the need for care to be extended to humans and other-than-humans
- Taking care of: assuming responsibility for the needs of humans and other-than-humans that represents a preliminary form of caring
- Care-giving: meeting some or all of the other's needs for care as the more substantial and directive form of caring
- Care-receiving: the receiver responds to the care being offered, their response potentially requiring more care

(Tronto, 1998: 16–17)

Feminist philosopher Peta Bowden located care along a broad spectrum of interpretations, relationships and circumstances reflective of mothering, friendship, nursing and citizenship; each quality harbouring distinct embodied characteristics within the carer. Bowden (1997: 1–2) considered the nature of caring to be dichotomous reflections of pluralised aims and outcomes. She emphasised the epistemological insights about care as practice, which extend beyond care theory. Bowden investigated moral theories of justice that encompass care. She compared broader-scale care reflective of the masculine tendency to focus one's attention on dispassionate institutions with the supposed mundane routines of caring for someone or something on a daily basis, arguing that personal care is complex, relational and located at the very heart of our interactions with all humans and other-than-humans. Bowden's care was intensely subjective and intricately connected to conflicting ethical considerations of responsiveness, self-understanding, reciprocity, trust, respect, openness and vulnerability (Bowden, 1997: 16–17).

William S. Hamrick (2002: 75–76) located his thoughts on care along a continuum between caring about another and caring for them (synonymous with Noddings's use of these distinctions). This differentiated approach to care was originally defined by Max Scheler (1954) as 'fellow-feeling', which operated across the following four-part scale:

1   An immediate community of feeling: sympathy and care for the joys and sorrows of the other that is non-sensory given we can never actually feel another's feelings for them
2   Genuine 'fellow-feeling': care towards humans and other-than-humans through reduction of their suffering or celebration of their joys,

distinguished by feeling vicariously with them or actively participating in their feelings through commiseration

3   Mere emotional infection: caring about the experience of the other through contagion of their sorrow or joy, but doing so devoid of intentional directedness of feeling or participation in the feelings of the other

4   Authentic 'emotional identification': where involuntary and unconscious care results in one's ability to identify with the experience of the other, which requires both caring about and caring for them – simultaneously

For Virginia Held (2006: 18), care was the most basic of moral values, traditionally relegated to patronising machinations within private dom-iciles, which have long been ascribed as women's realm. As both labour and as an ideal, she argued that care is constrained by patriarchy. She shed light on masculine care, which has been largely confined to impera-tives of corporate, military, legal or governmental care, as well as being located as 'higher pursuits' than, for example, child raising, education, responding to the needs of others, achieving peace and treasuring the environment. For Held, caring relations were instrumental in forging global and interdependent civil societies based on peace, respect, improved conditions for children and environmental sustainability; that contrary to self-interest, care is instrumental in promoting healthy social relations and creating strong community bonds. Marilyn Friedman argued that caring on the global scale has typically manifested through foreign aid, welfare assistance, disaster relief and social services all designed to ease the suf-fering of others through systemic means – largely managed by men (1993: 266–267). Notably, her analyses of global applications of care did not extend to Earthcare.

For Tammy Shel (2007), caring for others reflected the meaning we attach to our relationships with them. Shel categorised caring in action according to the following criteria:

•   Inclusive caring: idealised caring that stems from love for all others (care for humanity, nature – the entire Earth and life within it), resulting from the humanisation of all people, all genders and includes a will to share Earth with other-than-human nature as well
•   Selective caring: care extended to those we are closest to, our discernment guided by biases, prejudices and the restrictions of malestream norms, with varying degrees of inclusivity and exclusivity
•   Adaptive and resistant caring: care that is compliant with malestream norms, or works intentionally against them to ensure otherised others are empowered
•   Cultural caring: care that is encouraged within a specific cultural context that may vary considerably between one society and the next

- Authentic and aesthetic caring: care and nurturing between teachers and students based on testing and academic accomplishment, which is gauged by the performances of the students in reflection of the effective care given to them by their teacher, such that they gain more opportunities and thereby advance their future prospects (Shel, 2007: 12–14)

Cognisant of these various permutations on care, we note further sub-elements that have emerged throughout the discourse. Stan van Hooft (1995: 29–30) agreed with Noddings that care could imply burden, a motivational disposition, a worry; where being attentive to behaviours, acting caringly towards others, taking care of them, or being fond of them – all required effort. Like Bowden, Uma Narayan (1997) viewed colonisation and subjugation of the colonised as motivated by care, albeit laced with selfish gains. In *Love's Labor*, Eva Kittay (1999) examined the instructive nature of care for the seriously disabled. There, Kittay held out the principle that theories of justice, in alignment with those advocated by John Rawls, are dependent upon the principles and practices of care. Seeking a path beyond essentialism, Kittay suggested that conceptual and institutional reform were necessary elements in achieving equality for care workers. Stephen Darwall's (2002: 37–38) 'rational care theory' suggested that when we care for others, we promote their welfare; we seek 'the good' for them. To do so effectively, we must see ourselves as care-worthy as well. Like Held, Kittay considered care to be a practice more so than a virtue. Els Maeckelberghe (2004: 3) explored feminist ethics of care in the context of human vulnerability and interdependence, arguing that Western cultures are steeped in a tradition of trapping women (and not men) into the tasks of tending to the needs of others at the expense of themselves. These complexities apply to the human–human relationship and other-than-human care as well, rendering the possible applications of care to be self-serving as much as broadly benevolent.

Caring for other-than-humans and other-than-human-care

With the failure of utilitarian care to adequately address global climate change, more strategies are now taking shape to varying degrees of success. For example, take the Reducing Emissions from Deforestation and forest Degradation (REDD) issue along with REDD+, which focused attention on the Global South, was originally raised as a concern at the 1992 Rio de Janeiro Earth Summit, but did so by preserving colonial structures. Consider also the carbon markets of the EU that failed to adequately tend to global climate concerns (Hultman and Yaras, 2012; Higgins et al., 2013). These ecomodern strategies are fraught, taking us down political, social and ecological dead ends, subject to the short-term whims of governments, which the US withdrawal from the 2015 COP21 Paris climate accord exemplifies. A plethora of industrial/breadwinner examples abound and are dire. Driven by greed, workers directed by their corporate employers fell the 500-year-old, 90-metre Tasmanian mountain ash (*Eucalyptus regnans*), which is second in height only to the ancient

Californian redwoods (*Sequoia sempervirens*); the majesty of such a tree is translated into linear metres of lumber generating gross profit for the company who then pays the feller handsomely to do their bidding. The industrialisation of meat production and processing is intentionally designed to deaden both worker and consumer care for the plight of the individual cow whose flesh is packaged for consumption by obscuring its sentience (Hamrick, 2002: 102). Through these terse examples, we are reminded that humans have been managing care by selectively and simultaneously amplifying and then silencing our capacities to take note of and be accountable for our impacts on human and other-than-humans. As a species, we have commonly compartmentalised our care. By doing so, it becomes more possible to turn a blind eye to the potentially horrendous consequences of our actions. It is our view that such traditions are products of masculine hegemonisation that can and must change.

Maria Puig de la Bellacasa (2012) discussed the need for thinking with (and sometimes against) care as a term when practising environmental research. She suggested that 'care for' ought to be understood as carrying an embodied possibility of making a difference. In a later paper she agreed with David Harvey that the habitual time–space compression that characterises capitalism made caring for soil and other-than-humans difficult, but was a much-needed act if we are to expose and better manage the root causes of our environmental problems (Puig de la Bellacasa, 2015). A closer examination of care not only as a practice but also as a concept, reveals that its various applications are widely contested, some scholars attempting to arrest its ambiguities as a 'slave morality' that is empirically flawed, theoretically divergent, parochial and in its simplest forms, essentialist (Sander-Staudt, 2017). Conversely, care can tend to the needs of all other-than-humans as well as ourselves. The term and its varied interpretations share in common an emphasis on relational proximity between other-than-humans and ourselves. The ways we understand and speak about care and the ways we act caringly are subject to the status of the relationship between others and ourselves and is not in fact confined to gendered socialisations that shape our identities. This post-gendered perspective on care illuminates the presence (or absence) of ethics of care within an individual or other-than-humans. Put simply and in alignment with these various propositions about care, *all* human beings care and that care can extend beyond the bounds of our own species to include infinite capacities to care for other-than-human life as well.

However, a powerful differential between other-than-humans and ourselves has persisted into the present. As we discussed in Chapter 3 in reference to Christian masculinities, humans commonly operate as stewards over other-than-human nature. This has facilitated the accumulation of material possessions, along with the shaping of our values, creativity, laws, the systems we manufacture and subsidise, along with the definitions and ways that we apply our intellect. In doing so, our species uses masculinist logics of domination to subordinate other living things, effectively exposing the (m)Anthropocene, which has prosecuted the mandate that we ought to be in possession of and control other-than-human life, while making the best of things for ourselves. Little wonder that human development and ecocide commonly go hand-in-hand.

Feminist care theory offers us further questions to consider about caring as it applies to the human–nature relationship. Is it not possible for humans to be cared for by other-than-humans? For example, why does the dog attack its master's would-be attacker? Is the dog only concerned about its next meal? We know, that care exists among other-than-humans within and between species as well (Masson and McCarthy, 1995: 1–4; Nealon, 2015; Vieira et al. eds., 2015; Lewis-Jones, 2016; Ryan, 2016). Could it not be possible that other-than-humans can care for each other and can also extend that care towards humans as well – would this not seem to any pet owner to be self-evident? A well-researched example of this suggest that some species of trees demonstrate sentient care for each other, even after one of the trees is no longer 'alive' (of course also then raising questions about what we actually mean by referring to a tree as sentient) (Wohlleben, 2016). Is it not possible that sentience can be met with mutual relational exchanges between other species and our own? Beyond human agency, is it not true that life cares for life? Noddings alluded to these transcendental questions about care beyond the human realm by stressing that while our conscious care for others is commonly restricted, we are able to perceive the vital nature of our caring exchanges with all others, beyond our own human experience – we feel empathy and in doing so awaken our broader care for life beyond our own immediate realm. This appears to be true for other species as well (Noddings, 1984: 149).

When we partition our care, we run great risk of bringing forward sinister aspects of ourselves that contain and control the ways we offer our greatest good to others – we become conditional. This applies not simply in the ways we interact with each other, but also in the ways that we are caring or careless towards other-than-human life as well. Our care can be suppressed by the mechanisms of oppression that separate the other from ourselves. When we oppress in the name of self-care, we are, in effect, stripping away our full humanness to give permission to the oppressor within to arise. Hamrick (2002: 124) poignantly argued that when we create walls and separate ourselves off from the eternal interconnections between others and ourselves, we erode our humanity. This denial of attachment to the other can result not only in a separation from other-than-human nature, but can also create sufficient moral desolation and cognitive numbing as to enable repeated acts of cruelty towards both human and other-than-humans to emerge from within us – cruelty that can only be enacted when we deny our care (Puig de la Bellacasa, 2017). Our socialisations (not our human natures) are at the root of the ways we suppress our care for the glocal commons, with men and masculinities being the heaviest recipients of such conditioning, resulting in the highest levels of care myopia that embolden the sentiments of male domination.

Indeed, human history offers innumerable examples of the less-than-caring aspects of masculinities, much of which has resulted in great harm to many humans and the planet. Suppression of social or environmental accountability becomes more evident when men's livelihoods are dependent on ignoring destruction that has been brought about by one's own actions. As the social and environmental consequences of this care myopia bites ever deeper into the fabric of life on Earth, the need to forge a deep green future is increasingly urgent – perhaps precisely because our care is an inseparable aspect of our humanness. Ground is being gained. Consider the following examples: Western municipalities routinely recycle domestic waste; triple bottom lining is a more common aspect of contemporary corporate modelling; concerns about climate change have transitioned into transnational policies that are proving to stand the test of time (and political whims), renewables are significantly superseding fossil fuels; rivers are being restored; poisons are being banned; endangered species are being revived; local community initiatives are being reprioritised. We argue that all of these examples (limited though they are) are the result of our being willing and able to identify with other-than-human aspects of Earth as precious and fragile. In doing so, we are simply heeding the call to treat our Earth fellows along with ourselves with the utmost care (Hamrick, 2002: 123, 152–168). For each of these examples and the plethora of others that accompany them, men and masculinities are welcomed, present and vital contributors to such a changing tide.

So, all of us are affected – overtly or covertly – by the oscillating journey of mind, body and spirit between carelessness and great care (de Waal, 1996; Goodall and Berman, 1999). When we acknowledge our attachment to the glocal commons, extending care to all life on Earth becomes an inseparable element of being human. In doing so, we harness our goodness, expressing love, concern and gratitude to others and ourselves. In alignment with feminist care theorists (and contrary to utilitarians), when we are in this fullest human capacity, we are compelled to care beyond selfish bounds – we minimise the suffering of all others without effort or fear of loss of self – regardless of our gendered identities. This is a journey that is deeply embedded within the human psyche. All humans care (DeFalco, 2016: 6). Men are humans too; our care is inescapable – it may be socially supressed or confined behind the veneer of malestream norms, but it lingers in the hearts of all men, awaiting acknowledgement and connection to the glocal commons.

Men, Masculinities and care

Throughout this book we have argued that expressions of masculine care beyond malestream norms are still not widely socially sanctioned. Instead, male domination places expectations on men to fight with each other and the world in a struggle for social primacy. Men who have adopted industrial/breadwinner and ecomodern masculinities have internalised the belief, values and actions that male domination accords over and above care. There is however no 'free lunch' for men that blindly embrace masculine hegemonisation. To operate within the internalised superiorisation that accompanies male domination requires a substantial suppression of emotional literacy. Effectively, men have hoarded leadership, been socially, economically and politically rewarded in the private and public spheres and bolstered by an expectation that these benefits are theirs for the taking. These accoutrements of male domination lay at the heart of men's internalised superiorisation and has been emboldened by socially sanctioned forms of myopic care. However, when men pause enough to look at their lives from a place of broader, deeper and wider care, many are able to see that they have traded their relational selves for their socio-political and economic primacy and the ways that they are able to show care is in fact psychospiritually emaciated (Holmgren and Hearn, 2009). This is not a new insight. Roger Horrocks (1994: 1) noted that in exchange for dominance, traditional masculine identities are accompanied by emptiness, impotence and rage along with feeling abused, unacknowledged and victimised, typically resulting in what he summarised to as 'emotional autism, emptiness and despair'. The balance sheet for men and masculinities is grim; social primacy traded against connection with others and self, resulting in what Harvey Jackins (1999) referred to as men's chronic 'feeling badly' feelings which, we suggest, are the natural consequences of hegemonic masculine impacts on Earth, our communities, each other and ourselves.

This is not to say that masculinities have not, or cannot authentically care. On the contrary, we note that masculine care has traditionally been present but has been positioned as less central to core notions of masculinities (Morrell et al., 2016). So, men do care, but when they do, their masculinity is commonly called into question (take for example judgments of men serving as kindergarten teachers or male nurses stood against those serving as engineers, politicians and policy makers). We note that the stigmas attached to caring can be raised in status by assigning increased power and remuneration to certain roles in society in order to 'sanctify' that kind of care, especially when those roles are commonly occupied by men (e.g. the cook becomes a chef, the nurse becomes the nurse practitioner and the activist becomes the politician) (Björk and Härenstam, 2016). These linguistic and positional qualifications protect and preserve men's privileges in connection with industrial/breadwinner sentiments, effectively reinforcing male domination by further emboldening masculine primacy through societally sanctified expressions of care. Sadly in the cultural context of the modern West, our care is shaped by the ways that we are gender socialised. Accordingly, there is a need to expand conversations about care beyond feminist ideals (Tronto, 1993a: 101). We must also be willing and able to enrich and expand our definitions of care as they relate to men's lives and masculine identities as well. In other words, we need to stop pinning care in its broadest sense on women and things feminised and begin to see care as integral to men and masculinities as well. We can achieve this by firstly noting that men, like women, naturally care – that caring is a post-gendered pursuit – a human quality that we all possess. From there, we must then create the right conditions for men and masculinities to demonstrate care across a broader spectrum of ethical and behavioural possibilities than is currently the case. We make this distinction precisely because the broader care we call for has not been a presiding feature of masculine hegemonisation throughout our history – especially among wealthy, Western, white males who typically monopolise privileged positions. This proposition challenges men and masculinities to turn away from capacities to confine and/or outsource care that have freed men (particularly those in industrial/breadwinner roles) to focus on alleged 'higher' pursuits of care at the meta-level (Tronto, 2006).

Care for the glocal commons needs to become broadly acceptable for constructions of masculinities if we are to live in equitable societies and within planetary boundaries. Indeed, the broader care we call for here must include care for Earth, communities, families, each other and ourselves – simultaneously and over time (Pulé, 2013; Puig de la Bellacasa, 2015). We must continue to challenge the prescriptive notions that women have long been expected to caringly tend to the hearth in domestic subservience and to take second place in civil society just as we must be willing to interrogate men's care myopia that has long been restricted to reaching rational goals such as protecting and providing for one's family domestically or tending to noble public pursuits for the sake of structural flourishing (Gilmore, 1990: 42; Tronto, 1993a: 118–119). So, while we acknowledge that men can be and indeed are caring, we criticise malestream norms that have been built into the kinds of permissible care associated with masculinities throughout the West to date. We expose this constrained approach to men's care for its role in letting male domination off the hook, since sanctioned masculine care has been located as 'not' feminised care. Adding economic, social and political upheaval to this equation we begin to see that correlated with the recent rise of populism throughout the West are tense views that men in particular have been short-changed by neo-liberalism; their traditional avenues of expressing care (especially through diminished roles of protecting and providing) have been faltering as global socio-economic machinations and their ecological consequences reach advanced stages of distress. In other words, the sanctified pathways of expressing masculine care have been failing. For many, the solution has been a hard right wing swing where the war drum, chest beating, sexualising of women and wealth accumulation have been reignited as the sacrosanct mechanisms that will ensure a patriarchal revival and breathe new life into masculine hegemonisation, in the promise of giving men in particular an opportunity to feel good about themselves once again (encoded in, for example, the 'Make America Great Again' slogan). These forms of right wing industrial/breadwinner masculinities will continue to bring with them enacted and restrictive policies and practices. Uunder the auspices of malestream sanction, and nationalistic notions of a kind of paternalism that produces seemingly wonderful outcomes for some are clearly devastating the lives of many others with dire consequences for life on Earth.

Softer, kinder and warmer

Ecologisation is one way to achieve a mature and caring demeanour that is reflective of our fullest humanity. Indeed, for the caring person (regardless of gendered identity), it can be difficult to reconcile the cognitive dissonance that accompanies a life of privilege at others' expense. Similarly, it is difficult for a truly caring person to position themselves above others in subordinating ways, as is charactcristic of masculine hegemonies. To achieve greater care we must allow masculinised civic justice to meet with feminised empathy, not only conceptually, but specifically within and between men, masculinities and Earth.

Men are socialised to be discerning about when and how they access and express their care. Western societies are dominated by utilitarian approaches instructing men to care for their families, communities, their nations and the elements of their lives that they hold dear. Despite our species' nature-immersed origins, many modern Western men find it difficult to assume social or environmental responsibility when their salaries require of them that they – at least to some degree – ignore or justify the social and environmental consequences of their actions. Unfortunately, contra-hegemonic examples of broader, deeper and wider masculine care remain rare. It is a hallmark of malestream norms that our livelihoods (indeed our very senses of self) are tightly interwoven with moncy, prestige, power, control and the valorising of personal gain, which have been prioritised ahead of the social and ecological consequences of our actions as a species. Indeed, the entire global human economy functions on an assumption that men – in particular (but not exclusively) – will serve global mechanisms of productivity and are trained to do so from very early in life, effectively being raised to become 'human doings' rather than 'human beings'. We need men on the broadest of levels to become softer, kinder, warmer, more caring and fuller human beings, who both conceptually and in practical terms, live in the knowledge that they are integral parts of an intricate living planet. To be, think and do otherwise is to accelerate planetary social and ecological demise.

A by-product of these prescriptions of masculinities is a less-engaged life in the Næssean sense discussed in Chapter 4. Like Næss (1986: 16), we suggest that pleasure, happiness and his notion of 'Self-Realization!'

are paramount pursuits and are dependent upon the degree to which we bring awareness to our humanness, which shapes our ability to access authentic gestures of care that we believe are innate. To be such a man is to cut against the grain of malestream norms, to prioritise relational intimacy over being right and in doing so, to care deeply for others and ourselves – concurrently. Men who adopt masculinities that prioritise these alternative, deeper expressions of care capitalise on a unique and remarkable human endowment to live in communion with the glocal commons; a perspective that may well have been easier to access for women but is sorely needed for all life to flourish. Forging a deep green future is, after all, no longer a radical ecotopic dream. It is, rather, a necessity if we are to truly address the human impacts on Earth, our societies and ourselves. We are being called to the defence of the glocal commons like never before and the role of men and masculinities in response to this call is crucial. If we avoid extending care to Earth, others and ourselves we are in effect continuing to corrode our own full humanity along with our integral ecological presence on the planet; as much as we destroy the fecundity of Earth's living systems for present and future generations of life, we also destroy ourselves. In Section Three of this book, we unpack our notion of ecological masculinities, which is designed to subvert this trend.

References

Adams, C. 1990. *The Sexual Politics of Meat.* New York: Continuum.

Albrecht, G. 2005. 'Solastalgia, a new concept in human health and identity'. *Philosophy Activism Nature* 3: 41–44.

Beecher, C., and H. Stowe. 1869. *The American Woman's Home, or, Principles of Domestic Science: Being a Guide to the Formation and Maintenance of Economical, Healthful, Beautiful, and Christian Homes.* New York: J. B. Ford.

Benner, P., Tanner, C., and C. Chesla. 1996. *Expertise in Nursing Practice: Caring, Clinical Judgment and Ethics.* New York: Springer.

Björk, L. and Härenstam, A. 2016. 'Differences in organizational preconditions for managers in genderized municipal services'. *Scandinavian Journal of Management* 32(4): 209–219.

Bowden, P. 1997. *Caring: Gender-Sensitive Ethics.* London: Routledge.

Bubeck, D. 1995. *Care, Gender, and Justice.* Oxford: Oxford University Press.

Chodorow, N. 1978. *The Reproduction of Mothering: Psychoanalysis and the Sociology of Gender.* Berkeley, CA: University of California Press.

Clement, G. 2007. 'The ethic of care and the problem of wild animals'. In J. Donovan and C. Adams, eds., *The Feminist Care Tradition in Animal Ethics: A Reader.* New York: Columbia University Press, 301–315.

Curtin, D. 1991. 'Towards an ecological ethic of care'. *Hypatia* 6(1): 62–74.

Darwall, S. 2002. *Welfare and Rational Care.* Princeton: Princeton University Press.

DeFalco, A. 2016. *Imagining Care: Responsibility, Dependency, and Canadian Literature.* Toronto: University of Toronto Press.

de Waal, F. 1996. *Good Natured: The Origins of Right and Wrong in Humans and Other Animals.* Cambridge: Harvard University Press.

Engster, D. 2006. 'Care ethics and animal welfare'. *Journal of Social Philosophy* 37(4): 521–536.

Fernandes-Jesus, M., Carvalho, A., Fernandes, L., and S. Bento. 2017. 'Community engagement in the transition movement: views and practices in Portuguese initiatives'. *Local Environment* 22(12): 1546–1562.

Freedberg, S. 1993. 'The feminine ethic of care and the professionalization of social work'. *Social Work* 38(5): 535–540.

Friedman, M. 1993. 'Beyond caring: the de-moralization of gender'. In M. Larrabee, ed., *An Ethic of Care: Feminist Interdisciplinary Perspectives.* New York: Routledge, 258–273.

Gilligan, C. 1982. *In a Different Voice: Psychological Theory and Women's Development.* Cambridge: Harvard University Press.

Gilligan, C. 1986. 'Reply to critics'. *Journal of Women in Culture and Society* 11(2): 324–333.

Gilman, C. 1979[1915]. *Herland.* New York: Pantheon.

Gilmore, D. 1990. *Manhood in the Making: Cultural Concepts of Masculinity.* New Haven: Yale University Press.

Goleman, D. 1995. *Emotional Intelligence: Why It Can Matter More than IQ.* New York: Bantam.

Goleman, D. 2009. *Ecological Intelligence: How Knowing the Hidden Impacts of What We Buy Can Change Everything.* New York: Broadway Books.

Goodall, J., and P. Berman. 1999. *Reasons for Hope: A Spiritual Journey.* New York: Warner Books.

Hamrick, W. 2002. *Kindness and the Good Society: Connections of the Heart.* Albany: State University of New York Press.

Hart, R. 2013. *Children's Participation: The Theory and Practice of Involving Young Citizens in Community Development and Environmental Care.* Milton Park: Earthscan.

Harvard Second Generation Study. 2017. 'Study of adult development'. Accessed 19 May 2017. http://www.adultdevelopmentstudy.org/grantandglueckstudy

Held, V. 1993. *Feminist Morality: Transforming Culture, Society, and Politics.* Chicago: University of Chicago Press.

Held, V. 1995. 'Introduction'. In V. Held, ed., *Justice and Care: Essential Readings in Feminist Ethics.* Boulder: Westview Press, 1–6.

Held, V. 2006. *The Ethics of Care: Personal, Political, and Global.* Oxford: Oxford University Press.

Higgins, P., Short, D., and N. South. 2013. 'Protecting the planet: a proposal for a law of ecocide'. *Crime, Law and Social Change* 59(3): 251–266.

Holmgren, L., and J. Hearn. 2009. 'Framing "men in feminism": theoretical locations, local contexts and practical passings in men's gender-conscious positionings on gender equality and feminism'. *Journal of Gender Studies* 18(4): 403–418.

Horrocks, R. 1994. *Masculinity in Crisis: Myths, Fantasies, Realities.* London: Macmillan.

Hrdy, S. 1999. *Mother Nature: Natural Selection and the Female of the Species.* London: Chatto & Windus.

Hultman, M., and A. Yaras. 2012. 'The socio-technological history of hydrogen and fuel cells in Sweden 1978–2005: mapping the innovation trajectory'. *International Journal of Hydrogen Energy* 37(17): 12043–12053.

Jackins, H. 1999. *The Human Male: A Men's Liberation Draft Policy*. Seattle: Rational Island Publishers.

Jackson, S., and L. Palmer. 2015. 'Reconceptualizing ecosystem services: possibilities for cultivating and valuing the ethics and practices of care'. *Progress in Human Geography* 39(2): 122–145.

Kheel, M. 2008. *Nature Ethics: An Ecofeminist Perspective*. Plymouth: Rowman & Littlefield.

Kittay, E. 1999. *Love's Labor: Essays on Women, Equality, and Dependency*. New York: Routledge.

Kosoy, N., and E. Corbera. 2010. 'Payments for ecosystem services as commodity fetishism'. *Ecological Economics* 69(6): 1228–1236.

Lewis, T. 2015. 'A Harvard psychiatrist says 3 things are the secret to real happiness'. *Business Insider Online*. Accessed 6 June 2017. http://www.businessinsider.com.au/robert-waldinger-says-3-things-are-the-secret-to-happiness-2015-12?r=US&IR=T

Lewis-Jones, K. 2016. 'People and plants'. *Environment and Society* 7(1): 1–7.

Maeckelberghe, E. 2004. 'Feminist ethic of care: a third alternative approach'. *Health Care Analysis* 12(4): 317–327.

Manning, R. 1992a. 'Just caring'. In E. Cole and S. McQuinn, eds., *Explorations in Feminist Ethics: Theory and Practice*. Bloomington: Indiana University Press, 45–54.

Manning, R. 1992b. *Speaking from the Heart: A Feminist Perspective on Ethics*. Lanham: Rowman & Littlefield.

Manning, R. 1996. 'Caring For Animals'. In J. Donovan and C. Adams, eds., *Beyond Animals Rights: A Feminist Caring Ethics for the Treatment of Animals*. New York: Continuum, 103–125.

Masson, J., and S. McCarthy, S. 1995. *When Elephants Weep: The Emotional Lives of Animals*. New York: Dell Publishing.

Morrell, R., Dunkle, K., Ibragimov, U., and R. Jewkes. 2016. 'Fathers who care and those that don't: men and childcare in South Africa'. *South African Review of Sociology* 47(4): 80–105.

Næss, A. 1986. 'Self-realization: an ecological approach to being in the world'. Paper presented at the Keith Roby Memorial Lecture in Community Science, Murdoch University, 12 March.

Narayan, U. 1997. *Dislocating Cultures: Identities, Traditions and Third World Women*. New York: Routledge.

Nealon, J. 2015. *Plant Theory: Biopower and Vegetable Life*. Stanford: Stanford University Press.

Noddings, N. 1984. *Caring: A Feminine Approach to Ethics and Moral Education*. Berkeley: University of California Press.

Noddings, N. 1995. 'Caring'. In V. Held, ed., *Justice and Care: Essential Readings in Feminist Ethics*. Boulder: Westview Press, 7–30.

Noddings, N. 2002. *Starting at Home: Caring and Social Policy*. Berkeley: University of California Press.

Patrick, R., Dooris, M., and B. Poland. 2016. 'Healthy cities and the transition movement: converging towards ecological well-being?'. *Global health promotion* 23(1): 90–93.

Plumwood, V. 1993. *Feminism and the Mastery of Nature*. London: Routledge.

Puig de la Bellacasa, M. 2012. 'Nothing comes without its world: thinking with care'. *Sociological Review* 60(2): 197–216.

Puig de la Bellacasa, M. 2015. 'Making time for soil: technoscientific futurity and the pace of care'. *Social Studies of Science* 45(5): 691–716.

Puig de la Bellacasa, M. 2017. *Matters of Care: Speculative Ethics in More than Human Worlds*. Minneapolis: University of Minnesota Press.

Pulé, P. 2013. 'A declaration of caring: towards an ecological masculinism'. PhD diss., Murdoch University.

Regan, T. 1995. 'The burden of complicity'. In S. Coe, ed., *Dead Meat: With an Essay by Alexander Cockburn*. New York: Four Walls Eight Windows, 1–4

Roy, E. 2017. 'New Zealand river granted same legal rights as human being: after 140 years of negotiation, Māori tribe wins recognition for Whanganui river, meaning it must be treated as a living entity'. Accessed 17 July 2017. http://www.theguardian.com/world/2017/mar/16/new-zealand-river-granted-same-legal-rights-as- human-being

Ruddick, S. 1980. 'Maternal thinking'. *Feminist Studies* 6(2): 342–367.

Ruddick, S. 1995. 'Injustice in families: assault and domination'. In V. Held, ed., *Justice and Care: Essential Readings in Feminist Ethics*. Boulder: Westview Press, 203–224.

Ryan, J. 2016. 'Planting the eco-humanities? Climate change, poetic narratives, and botanical lives'. *Rupkatha Journal on Interdisciplinary Studies in Humanities* 8(3): 61–70.

Safi, M. 2017. 'Ganges and Yamuna rivers granted the same legal rights as human beings'. Accessed 20 November 2017. http://www.theguardian.com/world/2017/mar/21/ganges-and-yamuna-rivers-granted-same-legal-rights-as-human-beings

Sander-Staudt, M. 2017. 'Care ethics'. Accessed 14 May 2017. http://www.iep.utm.edu/care-eth/#H1

Scheler, M. 1954. *The Nature of Sympathy*, trans. P. Heath. New Haven: Yale University Press.

Schneewind, J. 1977. *Sidgwick's Ethics and Victorian Moral Philosophy*. Oxford: Oxford University Press.

Shel, T. 2007. *The Ethics of Caring: Bridging Pedagogy and Utopia*. Rotterdam: Sense Publishers.

Shel, T. 2009. 'The Dialectic of Tolerance and Intolerance in the Ethics of Caring'. In D. Kellner, T. Lewis, C. Pierce, and D. Cho, eds., *Marcuse's Challenge to Education*. Lanham: Rowman & Littlefield, 117–130.

Sidgwick, H. 1901. *The Methods of Ethics* (6th Edition). Indianapolis: Hackett.

Singer, P. 1975. *Animal Liberation: A New Ethics for Our Treatment of Animals*. London: Jonathan Cape.

Singer, P. 1979. *Practical Ethics*. Cambridge: Cambridge University Press.

Singer, P. 1993. *Practical Ethics* (2nd Edition). Cambridge: Cambridge University Press.

Slote, M. 1997. 'Virtue ethics'. In M. Baron, P. Pettit, and M. Slote, eds., *Three Methods of Ethics: A Debate*. Malden: Blackwell, 173–238.

Spira, H., and P. Singer. 2006. *Ten Points for Activists*. Oxford: Blackwell.

Stone, C. 2010[1972]. *Should Trees Have Standing? Towards Rights for Natural Objects*. Palo Alto: Tioga.

Taylor, S. 2002. *The Tending Instinct: How Nurturing is Essential to Who We Are and How We Live*. New York: Time Books.

Tronto, J. 1992. 'Women and caring: what can feminists learn about morality from caring?'. In A. Jaggar and S. Bordo, eds., *Gender/Body/knowledge: Feminist*

Reconstructions of Being and Knowing. New Brunswick: Rutgers University Press, 172–187.

Tronto, J. 1993a. *Moral Boundaries: A Political Argument for an Ethic of Care*. New York: Routledge.

Tronto, J. 1993b. 'Beyond gender difference to a theory of care'. In M. Larrabee, ed., *An Ethic of Care: Feminist Interdisciplinary Perspectives*. New York: Routledge, 240–257.

Tronto, J. 1995. 'Women and caring: what can feminists learn about morality from caring?'. In V. Held, ed., *Justice and Care: Essential Readings in Feminist Ethics*. Boulder: Westview Press, 101–116.

Tronto, J. 1998. 'An ethic of care'. *Generations: Journal of the American Society on Aging* 22(3): 15–19.

Tronto, J. 2006. 'Vicious circles of privatized caring'. In M. Hamington and D. Miller, eds., *Socializing Care: Feminist Ethics and Public Issues*. Lanham: Rowman and Littlefield, 3–25.

van Hooft, S. 1995. *Caring: An Essay in the Philosophy of Ethics*. Boulder: University of Colorado Press.

Vieira, P., Gagliano, M., and J. Ryan, eds. 2015. *The Green Thread: Dialogues with the Vegetal World*. Lanham: Lexington Books

Waldinger, R., Cohen, S., Schulz, M., and J. Crowell. 2015. 'Security of attachment to spouses in late life: concurrent and prospective links with cognitive and emotional wellbeing'. *Clinical Psychological Science* 3(4): 516–529.

Webster, J. 2005. *Animal Welfare: Limping Towards Eden: A Practical Approach to Redressing the Problem of Our Dominion Over the Animals*. Oxford: Blackwell.

Wohlleben, P. 2016. *The Hidden Life of Trees*. Carlton: Black Inc.

Wollstonecraft, M. 1792. *A Vindication of the Rights of Woman: With Strictures on Political and Moral Subjects*. London: J. Johnson.

Section III

Ecological masculinities: an emerging conversation

7 Headwaters

Previous research on men, masculinities and Earth

> It may be true that cultures preceding the rise of state societies . . . had no ideologies of dominating nature. It may also be true that many women today, for not only biological but also historical and social reasons, retain character-istics of sympathy and care that many men, for social reasons, have lost (although men, as humans, are also biologically equipped for caring). However, reifying these differences into a 'male' and 'female nature' tends to exclude the possibility that men may become caring, and it imposes a moral agenda on women to somehow 'save' society from the damage that some men have historically wrought.
>
> (Biehl, 1988: 63)

A pivotal juncture

Western industrialised civilisation is at a pivotal social and environmental juncture. We have arrived here as a direct consequence of the resource colo-nialism, consumer habits and the perpetrator–victim dynamics of the wealthy Global North (which is being exacerbated by the aspiring middle and owning classes of the Global South). The choices we have made and are still making will have considerable bearing on the health and fecundity of both human and other-than-human life on Earth. Throughout Section Two, we stressed that should we continue along paths of industrial/breadwinner denial and/or ecomodern greenwashing, we are certain to get more of the same – burgeon-ing social inequities and accelerating ecological demise. Recent history demonstrates that unfettered growth, if left to be managed by neo-liberal reforms, will not provide us with a panacea. What we are witnessing instead is resurgent and disgruntled populism, nationalism, xenophobia, hatred, unkind-ness, religious zealotry, misogyny, racism, isolationism, greater wealth for some and greater poverty for the marginalised masses, along with ever-grow-ing ecological degradation for myriad other-than-humans with whom we share the planet.

Resistance to these trends is growing. Some are choosing to transition beyond the old and tired social norms that emphasise human (especially male) domination by celebrating our place within the glocal commons. This alternative offers a broader approach to the ways we care for life, prioritising present and future generations of all others along with ourselves. Our suggested path for men, masculinities and Earth rests on an assumption that ecological indicators such as climatic change are 'canaries in the coalmine', offering us compelling evidence to foster alternatives that will steer us away from this pathological growth ideology that has characterised Western industrial capitalist societies and has resulted in unjust global relational exchanges (Hultman and Anshelm, 2015: 30; Hultman, 2017b). This new possibility we turn to is ecologised, gender-sensitive and broadly caring. We visualise it as an estuary where the four streams of masculinities politics, deep ecology, ecological feminism and feminist care theory that we have discussed above gather, their 'waters' mixing and carrying with them various materials that (as they wash up upon the shore) we can use to build ecological masculinities (as if it were a shelter on the banks of this estuary). The materials from these aforementioned four streams present us with theories and praxes in a punctuated manner drawn from a wide array of contributors. They collectively offer us important insights into the central role that men and masculinities play in the social and environmental problems we face (Pulé, 2013; Hultman, 2016: 28). Spurred on by these various influences, we argue it is vital that we build a new theory and its associated praxes for the benefit of all life. We proceed now to take a closer look at other materials that have come before us. In this chapter, we gather these previous works into seven thematic groups, laying them out on the shore in front of us – so to speak – in order to determine what additional materials we have to work with and what is missing that we will need to freshly generate for ecological masculinities to arise. In offering the analyses that follow, we not only summarise the contributions of others to masculine ecologisation. We also demonstrate that no one to date has formulated a sufficiently rigorous theoretical framework under which all of these contributions can gather – at least until the writing of this book. With this in mind, we begin with the oldest of those contributions; a mythological deity, whose presence in the vernacular of Western culture remains subtle, but profound.

The Euro-pagan Green Man

Environmental history is dotted with an intriguing figure. Though marginalised in the contemporary Global North, Earth-immersed masculinities have a long history of Euro-pagan rites and rituals associated with the Green Man (Basford, 1978). The Green Man has been visible in European folklore with effigies appearing as cathedral carved heads throughout that region since the eleventh century. These representations of the Green Man manifested through a heterogeneous variety of features. He is commonly portrayed as a simple and singular face or sprouting head shrouded or made from leaves and foliage that became a symbol of rebirth (Basford, 1978; Anderson, 1990).

The Green Man has been a subversive and recurring archetypal presence in the modern West. He is thought to have first appeared in the Danube region during the Neolithic period (*c.*8500 BC) and is widely considered the long-held mascot of European embodiments of wild nature. He has donned various forms as Western Europe's original Rumpelstiltskin, Haussibut, Heinnekin, Hämmerlein, Hinkebein, Berit, Robin Hood, Puck, Robin Goodfellow, sitting among the mythical characters of Europe's ancient forests (fairies, dwarves, trolls, gnomes, elves, kobolds, leprechauns) as a mischievous Earthen fertility spirit capable of raucous frivolity or great terror, demanding food and drink from mortals in exchange for patronage and safe passage through the 'wilds' of nature (Russell, 2002: 52–53). He is most prevalent in architecture throughout Western Europe from the Gothic period of the so-called Dark Ages; reaching his socio-cultural height of visibility at the very time that Western European maleness was repressing the feminised emotional, sensual and esoteric aspects of the human experience through the witch hunts. The Green Man has stood quietly as a bulwark against the fortified warrior-hero that has also characterised Western Europe since the Dark Ages (Matthews, 2001: 8, 16, 27). These two renditions of maleness might be viewed as opposite expressions of the same self: *Logos* and *Eros*. The knight, recoiled behind his bravado and protecting his inner vulnerabilities from the onslaught of the corporeal world with lance and shield, is juxtaposed against the fully expressed, sensuous and embodied self of the Green Man (Cheetham, 2005: 115). In the latter we find the imp, the trickster, the boyishness within, who unapologetically exposes what lurks beneath the mighty knight's shining armour. He is the masculine face of Earth and represents an alternative maleness that enables men to 'come to their senses' and sink into their bodies, while bearing witness to the 'greater circles of experience beyond bound linear thinking' (Anderson, 1990: 219). The Green Man is nature's organic matter personified; his flesh has merged with the wilds of untamed lands for centuries. He offers a winding path towards a 'masculine revolution' of rounded, integrated and raw masculinities that, through the mythopoetic men's movement and other enactments across masculinities politics, has experienced some semblance of a contemporary Western revival.

Julia Somerset (Lady Raglan) (1939) reintroduced the Green Man to the vernacular of Western counterculture in 1939 (Livingstone, 2016). His sexual potency has been used in recent history to support those recovering from the trauma of the HIV/AIDS epidemic. He has been adopted by fringe groups as well, positioned as the centrepiece of some rites and rituals in, for example, queer communities. Carolyn Dinshaw (2017) linked the Green Man to the Radical Faeries in Bettina Bildhauer and Christopher Jones' anthology *The Middle Ages in the Modern World*. Dinshaw (2015) had previously noted that the Radical Faeries celebrated and prioritised 'authentic, transhistorical, universal gay subjectivity and belonging' as a point of connection and empathy for those who have felt violently colonised by industrial/breadwinner masculinities, which has applications to both LGBTIQA+ communities along with other-than-human others. The Radical Faeries were founded in 1979 by US gay men who followed in the footsteps of movements towards feminist/ lesbian collectives, many of whom were blending their politics and sexualities with back-to-the-land ideologies (Livingstone, 2016). The Radical Faeries remain active to this day, having revived maypole rituals, adopted effeminate pagan rites that prioritised nature-immersed expressions of masculinities as paths towards sexual and spiritual liberation. The Faeries have sought alternative pathways for recovering from colonial and homophobic trauma (Livingstone, 2016). However, they have not provided an overall popular Green Man revival. Rather, the Faeries have woven his presence into some of the ways they practise their alternative views and in doing so have built a bridge between a 'complex political context' and medieval and mythological renditions of Euro-pagan masculinities, encouraging the appropriation of the Green Man as an overt challenge to 'settler colonial logic' and the oppressive heteronormative machinations that have accompanied hegemonic masculinities, which they seek to dismiss (Hennen, 2008).

Perspectives such as these do press the edges of malestream norms and open up the possibility of a heterogeneity of masculinities and nature. However, they can still remain within the confines of stereotypical masculine behaviours even as they attempt to challenge popular notions of manhood, ascribing traits of the Green Man as trickster to men's bodies. This notion is worthy of further examination, suggesting that there is a need to look more broadly at the possibilities of the Green Man archetype for men, women and non-binary/genderqueer people alike. Additional research of that nature is the task of subsequent publications.

In the following section, we note that the Green Man has found his way into the contemporary rites and rituals of the mythopoetic men's movement as well, but in superficial applications throughout that community at best.

Essentialised Earth-honouring

Through the mythopoetic men's movement, urban, suburban and rural men alike have joined these challenges to traditional notions of masculinities in large number. For example, the ManKind Project (2017) claimed to have initiated more than 60,000 men worldwide. They have prioritised men's communion with each other and self typically in natural settings, aiming to sharpen men's roles in being of service to the world. We give mythopoesis deeper consideration here by revisiting Shepherd Bliss as one of the movement's notable early and academically trained advocates. We do so because the mythopoets represent the most influential praxis-oriented contributors to the intersecting terrain about men, masculinities and Earth and are almost exclusively concentrated in the Global North. In Chapter 3, we introduced Bliss's contributions to ideas of masculinity and environment, arguing that his notion of 'eco-masculinity' offered a preliminary scholarly response to growing ecological feminist concerns about the impacts of masculine hegemonisation on women and Earth. We offer an analysis of Bliss's personal journey relative to the impact of the foundational arguments for his eco-masculinity on the mythopoetic men's movement.

As an army officer from a distinguished US military family, Bliss acquired an acute understanding of the pressure placed on men to adhere to industrial/ breadwinner identities. Coming to prominence as a mythopoetic men's leader in the movements formative years, Bliss took a stand for the re-mythologising of modern Western men and masculinities. He celebrated the Ancient Greek legend of Orpheus, wild Pan, young David of the Old Testament, the Aztec plumed serpent Quetzalcoatl, the Hopi hump-backed trickster and fertility deity Kokopelli (whom he named his Sebastopol, CA berry farm after), Western pagan fairy tales, Jungian archetypal psychology along with the teachings of St. Francis of Assisi, John Muir, Henry David Thoreau, Walt Whitman, Mahatma Gandhi and Frederico Garcia Lorca and the poetry of Mary Oliver (Bliss, 1995). Leveraging off these esoteric, spiritual and literary environmental greats, Bliss argued in favour of a nature-connected 'mature' masculinity that he suggested would emerge when we reconcile the most pressing issues afflicting many men's lives, those being: psychotherapeutically healing father wounds, deepening friendship bonds among men of various ages, investigating and educating men about medical/health issues, developing modes of intimacy between women and men that are tender and warm beyond sexuality, training men to acquire authentic and expansive emotional vocabularies and celebrating masculine physicality, all of which, he argued, ought to be explored in the company of fellow men in natural settings and in doing so would result in the wholesale redefining of traditional Western masculine norms (Bliss, 1987).

Bliss's advocacy for an ecologically inspired masculine ontology was his response to perceived missing or inadequate mature masculinities that must be retrieved, achieved and stands as complementary to femininity (Kimmel, 1993: 4; Bliss, 1995b; Mason, 2006: 17–18). In his pursuit of the mature masculine, Bliss attempted to distance himself from his violent military 'warrior' past. Motivated by his deep concern for the health and well-being of Earth, he confronted technology, soldiering, nuclear weaponry and men's addiction to power that, he argued, continued to collectively pollute Earth as the most pressing universal evils of our time. Noting that a mythopoetic warrior ethos was failing to cauterise these violations of life, he pointed us towards '[d]eveloping eco-masculinity' that he suggested 'can help men to play our part to generate what is being lost' (Hoff and Bliss, 1995; also see Bliss, 1995: 304). There may well have been a post-patriarchal intention to develop personally aware and politically wise men through Bliss's work, but he did not specify what his rendition of 'eco-masculinity' might help men find nor how they might find it.

The rites and rituals that have come to characterise men's mythopoesis continue to draw on animals, plants and nature effigies. They embolden a sense of place in communities of men in bioregional contexts, but have calcified a tradition of sidestepping frontal critiques of male domination and its many personal (internal and domestic) and political (external and structural) guises. Bliss and his mythopoetic compatriots effectively supported the empowerment of men as individuals but struggled to facilitate their 'powering down' in broader structural contexts (Magnuson, 2007). Further, the movement's instrumental use of nature has earned a reputation for enabling men to gain deeper access to themselves, however, nature has remained a foil for this deep inner work throughout men's mythopoetry. Further, Bliss's eco-masculinity stopped short of a critical analysis of gendered essentialism and as a consequence the movement remained tainted by a routine return to hegemonised roles in the lives of many men once their mythopoetic trainings were complete; their connections to life missions in service to the greater good devoid of structural analyses and remaining myopic even if much more deeply caring towards world, others and self (Ferber, 2000; Magnuson, 2007; Gremillion, 2011). Granted, broader systemic understandings of the benefits and costs of masculine primacy have and will continue to make their way into some mythopoetic men's events. But nature-inspired rites and rituals, when blended with pop psychology, has a long legacy of distracting men from bringing an end to broader systemic oppressions (both internalised superiorisation as a point source and its external manifestations through a plethora of perpetrations that men enact) as well as the persistent destruction of nature at men's hands while enthralled by their collective efforts to facilitate personal growth and development. Arguably, Bliss's notions of eco-masculinity were fixated on being personally complementary to men's empowerment. Unfortunately, this meant that critical analyses of structural oppressions slipped into the background.

Other understandings of men, masculinities and Earth have since emerged with much more nuanced and structural levels of insight. Scholars examining nature-inspired literature provide us with another approach to our understandings of masculine ecologisation. We turn our attention to the gendered considerations in ecocriticism next.

Ecocritical masculinities

The field of ecocriticism has offered literary scholars opportunities to disentangle masculinities and the environment. They cross-examine protagonists as exemplars of idealised ecomasculinities that might hold out – albeit fictitious – alternative paths forward for men and masculinities in deeper relationship with Earth (Buell, 2005; Woodward, 2008; Oppermann, 2011). Other scholars have explicitly focused on intersectional studies of extreme sports, film and US literature while also exploring transformative impacts of these activities on shifting men's attitudes towards more ecologically considerate paradigms (Cornelius, 2011; Salovaara, 2015; Brandt, 2017). Foremost of these is Mark Allister's (2004) anthology *Ecoman: New Perspectives on Masculinity and Nature*.

Allister's anthology grew out of a series of essays presented at a plenary session called 'Men and Nature: Perspectives on Masculinity and the More-Than-Human World' at the 2001 conference of the Association for the Study of Literature and the Environment in Flagstaff, Arizona, US. Seeking fresh insights about men, masculinities and Earth, *Ecoman* illuminated an inherent tension between traditional masculine identity and 'wilderness', giving special reference to the North American myth of masculinity by exploring concepts of 'the wild' relative to Eurocentric compulsions to dominate nature. The anthology's contributors shared a common starting point for discussions on the topic, agreeing that the North American male psyche is embedded within nature through frontier-smenship, which was inescapably centred on conquest – of women, indigenous people and the resource riches of wilderness. In the book's preamble, Allister framed an emerging discussion on 'frontier ecocriticism' which he presented as a fresh analysis of social constructions of masculinity. His argument was primarily 'theoretical, city-oriented, and focused on violence, race, and sexual orientation' (Allister, 2004: 6). The anthology also revealed the existence of intersecting considerations of social and environmental justice among men. In line with some of the mythopoetic ideals we have discussed above, Allister compiled arguments that men can and do actively seek out their wild natures, which lies dormant and bound during weekdays to:

> . . . an electrified, wired office, but on weekend or vacations he hits the road on a bike or in a boat, or competes in extreme sports, or hikes with expensive gear through stunning mountain landscapes. In any case, 'nature' is a thing out there to be enjoyed, certainly not lived in. Nature is for self-congratulation: 'I am still a natural man'.
>
> (Allister, 2004: 5)

In this sense, the anthology placed a spotlight on today's ecomodern man; a wilderness user, a consumer of the out of doors validating masculine identity in the wake of the castrating drudgery of modern (working- and middle-class) post-industrial and urban/suburban life. Also, consider the literary reverence for hunting (Hemingway, 1936; Snyder, 1960; Abbey, 1988). This canon has reached acclaimed levels of appeal. In a chapter titled 'Deerslayer with a Degree', John Tallmadge (2004: 22) claimed that 'we need new models of manhood if we are to achieve durable, sustainable and honourable relations between human culture and the rest of life'. However, Tallmadge failed to tell us how to achieve these new models of modern Western manhood other than evoking a forum for boys' initiation into manhood through hunting. Further, the implicit hegemonic relationship between the hunter and the hunted was not deconstructed; the masculinised self as dominator entering nature as a 'taker' who extracts his quarry was for Tallmadge emblematic of a man's victory against the odds through a successful hunt that, he argued, equated to the successes (indeed the excesses) of the masculine self in the 'man-made' world. The hunted's agency and inherent worth did not make mention. Nor did the impact of the loss of that individual animal on its ecosystem. The specifics of hunting as a supposed masculine rite were not illuminated, rendering Tallmadge's contribution to our understandings of the quintessential 'ecoman' as superficial at best.

Allister (2004: 7– 8) positioned *Ecoman* as a companion to ecofeminism. However, to our reading this was not evident throughout the book, since various contributors provided cursory arguments for masculine ecologisation that did not delve into the political machinations nor the sociological and ecological consequences of malestream norms that we consider to be necessary in order to justify it as ecological feminist complement. For example, consider Scott Slovic's chapter 'Taking Care: Toward an Ecomasculinist Literary Criticism?'. This was the only chapter in Allister's anthology that discussed ecofeminism directly and beyond Allister's initial mention. We note that Slovic did not overtly position his rendition of ecomen as allies to ecofeminist causes, alluding instead to that classic sexist retort of, feminist hysteria, since, in his view:

> . . . it is perhaps inevitable that a social movement [such as ecological feminism] should root itself in some form of critique, the way in which this critique is voiced has everything to do with how widely the views of the movement are embraced. It is all too common that visions of social reform are expressed in language so angry and self-righteous that potential supporters are put off, scared away, or otherwise disenfranchised.
>
> (Slovic, 2004: 71)

Slovic criticised ecological feminism as a 'tacit inversion of traditional, European, male-centred hierarchies of value . . . although scholars have been reluctant to admit this', suggesting that some ecofeminists sought women's moral superiority over men as a flipped view to their historical subjugation by sexism (Slovic, 2004: 71). In effect, Slovic claimed 'reverse sexism', placing his perspective at odds with the ecological feminism as a discourse deeply steeped in oppression theory that has thoroughly debunked notions of reverse oppression (Slovic, 2004: 71–72). This perspective is shared by many mythopoets, men's rights activists and Christian masculinities traditionalists, whose concerns for men have continued to be vocalised in various forms of backlash politics espousing protective rebuttals to malestream critiques by feminists, ecofeminists and profeminists (Harding ed., 1992). Slovic effectively positioned himself as a leading ecocritic, baulking at dissecting the social commentary of a structural analysis in favour of 'paying attention' to nature from the creative vantage of ecocriticism (Slovic 1992: 17, 171; Satterfield and Slovic, 2004: 1). Further, he stopped short of demonstrating how men might actively facilitate ecologically responsible human–nature relationships – other than stating that they should. Like other contributors to Allister's anthology, Slovic did not formulate a conceptually sound nor practically applicable ecologised masculinities theory or praxis. For these reasons, *Ecoman* achieved its claim of (at best) being a 'preliminary mention' of the need to bring masculinities–nature relationship into more acute focus. Despite its great promise, it did not provide us with what we consider to be the essential transdisciplinary ingredients and needed theoretical framework that would initiate a new discourse on men, masculinities and Earth. Others in the ecocritical field have since offered fresher perspectives on the topic since *Ecoman* was published, but have also, in our view, suffered from similar shortcoming (Cornelius, 2011).

Recent fresh investigations of the borderlands of men's bodies pitted against nature was conducted by Finnish researcher Harri Salovaara. In a paper titled '"A Fine Line": Crossing and Erecting Borders in Representing Male Athletes' Relationships to Nature', Salovaara (2015a) provided an intersectional analysis of extreme sports, which proved to be foundational for his doctoral research titled *Male Adventure Athletes and Their Relationships to Nature* (2015b). Salovaara has positioned himself as a multidisciplinary scholar. Shaped by ecocriticism, gender studies and masculinities politics, he has been investigating an 'ecomasculine' viewpoint through the lens of masculine/feminine markers and how their borders are blurred (Salovaara, 2015a: 77). Juxtaposing his examination of male extreme athletes in adventure films with their female counterparts, Salovaara discovered notable language differences in actors of extreme athleticism; women athletes being described as 'graceful', 'emotional' and 'nature connected' while their male counterparts were represented by terms such as 'hardened', 'possessing', 'wanting', 'conquering', 'strong', 'masochistic', 'warring', 'working-class', 'roughneck', 'tough guys' who habitually push through their pain. Salovaara offered a poignant framework for investigating the impact of this gendered lexicon on men's bodies when portrayed in films of high adventure (Salovaara, 2015a: 81). The films studies reinforced stereotypical gendered differences – women commonly portrayed as blending in, while men sought the reassurance and exhilaration of forging forth and conquering. But Salovaara was critical of this essentialism, noting that gendered polarisations can become blurred in extreme sports as well, with male femininity arising through necessary knowledge of the body and self while female masculinity could place demands on women to dig deep, be brave, 'have balls' and confront the life-threatening dangers on the climb with gusto (Salovaara, 2015a: 82). His analysis suggested that the gendered lines of extreme sport are in fact vague and therefore contestable. Salovaara is currently proceeding with notions of 'ecological protest masculinities' that can foist male extreme athletes into self-reflexivity and regenerative personal and environmental practices through increased care for others and self. These represent qualities that can (and do) cut against the grain of masculine hegemonisation. We consider Salovaara's views useful. They provide us with a reflexive perspective on ecocriticism in outdoor adventure film and the ways that this medium contributes to gender stereotyping in the various practices that people engage with. We also note a compelling argument in support of transitions from ethics of conquest to ethics of connection through his work.

Another anthology, *Masculinities and Literary Studies: Intersections and New Directions* by Josep Armengol et al., appeared in 2017. Chapter 12 by Stefan Brandt is titled 'The "Wild, Wild World": Masculinity and the Environment in the American Literary Imagination', while Chapter 13 by Requena-Pelegrí is titled 'Green Intersections: Caring Masculinities and the Environmental Crisis'. Both are worthy of our specific consideration here for their respective references to ecomasculinities. In Brandt's chapter, we are taken on a journey of man-making with Rough Rider and quintessential US outdoorsman Teddy Roosevelt. Brandt argued that cool nerves, horsemanship, hardihood, endurance, keen eyesight and hunting prowess were the hallmarks of premium manhood, epitomised in the ways that Roosevelt instilled (indeed imposed) these characteristics upon his son and imprinted this and associated heroic symbolisms upon the US masculine psyche that has shaped generations of US men (and beyond) (Brandt, 2017: 133). Brandt acknowledged that postmodern literature has challenged these masculinities stereotypes, laying the foundations for an 'eco-masculinity' that he defined as 'an increased sense of awareness of the problematic dimensions of manliness' to emerge (Brandt, 2017: 139). Brandt has been particularly interested in considering this locus through an ecocritical lens. He suggested that by maintaining its characteristic 'earth-centred approach to literary studies', ecocriticism maintains its Rooseveltian foundations that runs the risk – as ecofeminists have demonstrated – of androcentric dualising. Brandt offered us a compelling analysis and an important source for studying modern Western masculine hegemonisation in US ecocriticism, one that might help us better understand why many Western men portray a care myopia and why the rites and rituals of the mythopoets resisted structural analysis. After all, a Rooseveltian persona has comprehensively woven its way into the very fabric of US culture (and beyond), placing limits on what is acceptable for modern Western manliness. We note however that in his chapter, Brandt did not provide us with a clear vision of the socio-political and ecological consequences of this legacy. Rather he left that to inference. Similarly, he did not offer men and masculinities clear alternatives beyond his critiques of an archetypal Rooseveltian frontiersmenship.

Turning to Requena-Pelegrí's important chapter in the same anthology, where she discussed caring masculinities and the environmental crisis, we are presented with an intersectional and literary analysis of masculinities politics and care theory. There, Requena-Pelegrí argued that masculinities are unavoidably entangled with care for others (both human and other-than-human), positing that although 'care has featured prominently in the studies on men and masculinities of the preceding decades' and has been essentialised and '[t]raditionally encoded as feminine and thus relegated to the undervalued realm of emotions', it is important to also recognise that 'care

has historically been antagonised from normative definitions of masculinity'
(Requena-Pelegrí, 2017: 143–144). Building on Connell's 'patriarchal dividend',
Requena-Pelegrí agreed that:

> . . . if the demands of normative masculinity have required men to stand
> up to the requirements of a performance of gender based on, among other
> aspects, domination, violence, aggression, emotional restraint, or competi-
> tiveness, these aspects have also been transferred to actual environmental
> interventions as well as literary constructions of the natural world.
>
> (Requena-Pelegrí, 2017: 145)

In the absence of critically problematising masculinities, well-meaning, environmentally caring men run the risk of repeating the same patterns as their
industrial/breadwinner fellows, even within the intended alternative masculinities of environmentalism. The institutionalisation of male domination does
not conveniently disappear simply because we examine masculinities through
the lens of care. Effective social and environmental interventions as praxes
require intentional interrogations of masculine hegemonisation as vital and
structurally focused starting points.

Looking further still at the ecocritical discourse, we also note the work of
Uche Peter Umezurike (forthcoming) titled 'The Eco(logical) Border
Man: Masculinities in Jim Lynch's Border Songs'. Following a similar vein to
Brandt and Requena-Pelegrí, Umezurike's paper explored the paradoxes of
the story's protagonist – Brandon Vanderkool – who, as a gentle-spirited
border patrolman, lived in constant tension with the subversive violence of
the US borderlands with Canada; Brandon's 'ball-busting' job in the wilds
between two nations placing him at odds with his demure persona. We consider Umezurike's analysis intriguing.

Our respective experiences in our exchanges with individuals and groups of
men (Martin and Paul speaking here as activists more than scholars) have forged
a telling rule – the thicker a man's armour, the greater his vulnerability within.
Ecocriticism, when collapsed with ecomasculinities, appears to readily accentuate this notion, but typically does not delve into the gender politics that
created it. If we are to shift the tide away from masculine hegemonisation, a
path towards effective ecologisation must include both the reconciliation of
personal paradoxes along with structural analyses. These ecocritical 'ecomen'
must be sufficiently internally resourced to stand peacefully at the borders of
their own psyches. Umezurike shared this view, envisioning:

> An ecoman, a man comfortable in his dyslexia, his failures, gracelessness,
> emotionality, and relationality with things posited as the other – the nat-
> ural, the feminine, the alien . . . a point of reference, inspiring us to forge
> and foster a community grounded on caring for and caring about nature
> and all that coexists with humanity on planet earth.
>
> (Umezurike, forthcoming)

The ecologised protagonists that our literary compatriots have been eloquently examining are not simple fictions written to entertain us. Rather, they have real world relevance. They can also be considered more than real, since the narratives they enrich represent longings or idealisations that impact masculine socialisations and their implications for the ways boys are raised, men act and women and non-binary/genderqueer people manifest their internal masculinities. These complexities accentuate the dissonance of identity politics that are embroiled in fresh battles at the frontline of the culture wars; they hold out the possibility of attaining something new and different to toxic/extreme masculinities and in doing so tip us towards the appeal of ecologisation in the broader relational (if not also biocentric) sense. Some of these protagonists (such as Umezurike's analysis of Brandon) are portrayed as being in great conflict with male-stream imaginary, while others (such as Brandt's analysis of Roosevelt) examine ways that the male psyche is seemingly addictively embedded within nature through conquest. We recognise that these tensions are products of a long tradition. After all, ecocritics and nature writers have been drawn to the intersections of masculinities and active encounters with nature for some time.

Given the impact of works such as these on our perceptions of men, masculinities and Earth, hunting masculinities and the eco-warriors that resist them and other forms of Earth utilitarianism are worthy of our consideration as well. We turn our attention to notions of natural resource use by environmental historians next.

Stalking nature

Environmental historians have provided us with deconstructive contributions to discussions on men, masculinities and Earth in reference to hunting (Bouchier and Cruikshank, 1997; Loo, 2001; Smalley, 2005; Sramek, 2006). Will Abberley provided an interesting analysis of the interspecies encounters captured in Darwin's and Wallace's respective travel memoirs. Abberley showed that a distanced restraint of emotions when encountering other-than-human nature was juxtaposed against the thrill of the hunt as two characteristic and divergent expressions of Victorian masculinities (Abberley, 2017). Other historical research prior to Abberley's has focused on the ways that environmental movements have provided us with useful insights into the values and practices of Earthcare as they are impacted by gender identities. One revealing example is provided by Willeen Keough's examination of the masculinities associated with the Newfoundland pack-ice seal hunt that became an icon of environmental activism through intense media coverage that started in the latter part of the twentieth century. In a paper titled '(Re-) telling Newfoundland Sealing Masculinity: Narrative and Counter-narrative', Keough (2010) assessed thirty-two interviews with career sealers and seal hunt protestors, examining definitions and embodiments of 'man the hunter' – the warrior pitted against apparent protest masculinities adopted by the gentle, greener and ethically motivated ecomasculinities of environmental activists. Positioning the former as protagonists and the latter as antagonists, Keough described the seal hunters as self-professed family men and community members, with many considering themselves good Christians, intractably engaged in their rough-and-tumble roles as breadwinners. She demonstrated that the activists possessed the moral high ground of the pack-ice conflict, but suggested that this was little more than 'scuttlebutt', highlighting that in doing so, activists borrowed similar imagery to represent themselves as did the sealers they opposed by dressing in camouflage gear, racing to the 'front line' to do battle against their foes, all the while their conceptualisations of their masculinities aligned with combative traditions that are replete throughout Western malestreams (Keough, 2010: 2). In this sense, Keough's criticisms were levelled at the subtext of gendered identities more than at the warring sides of the seal hunt itself.

A similar case study, published by Erik Loomis (2017), explored the intersection between masculinities and forestry. Loomis observed the ways that logger unions constructed a certain strand of industrial/breadwinner subculture, which was contrasted against that of factory working men. Even though both groups were beholden to large corporations, the loggers were portrayed (by their unions in particular) as a liberated proletariat, strong, clean and mentally alert, defining themselves through brute force and personal bravery that distinguished them from men of the factory floor who were enmeshed with risky and unhealthy mills as expendable simpletons and industrial slaves (Loomis, 2017: 37, 40). Loomis (2017: 42) proposed that ending forms of resource extraction could also end demeaning forms of masculinities and considered this to be a vital consideration in any proactive future for both men and sustainable economies. This is an important insight in connection with the urgent need to transition to renewables from hydrocarbon industries in light of the alarming ecocidal evidence of global climate change associated with fossil-fuel production and consumption.

These studies exposed a telling paradox that echoed our previous analyses of the mythopoetic men's movement. Sealers, loggers and factory workers alike are embodied examples of a long tradition of hardening up, especially in the difficult initial period of establishing one's self professionally (take, for example, the first 20 to 50 seal pup kills), which, when combined with a life of hardship at both work and home demands that any normal man must simply get the job done and come home in one piece, putting his emotional self aside in order to survive both physically and psychologically (since, as one sealer stated, 'dead is dead') (Keough, 2010: 141). This leaves little room for the self-confronting process of structural analyses since for many men it is simply enough to put food on the table and endure another day, or better yet, feel content with the accomplishment of having met the social expectations placed upon them to put self aside in order to protect and provide for one's family. These perspectives demonstrate that men's conditioning around care for community and family supersedes self-care, and certainly Earthcare, providing a telling characteristic of industrial/breadwinner masculinities, which has far-reaching applications (and implications) in defining the socio-cultural mores of resource extraction (Miller, 2004; Milnes and Haney, 2017). Regardless of one's role within or in opposition to extractive industries, we can infer from studies such as these that in the absence of deconstructive analyses of masculinities, malestream norms readily pervade men's spaces. The penchant to adopt patterns of male domination drive both ends of social and environmental justice debates in ways that miss the deeper issue at hand.

Clearly an effective ecologised masculinities theory must adopt a socio-political analysis that ecocriticism does not. We must facilitate the movement of masculine hegemonisation beyond immediate embodiments, reaching for examinations of men's bodies and psyches to articulate strategies that circumvent hegemonisation from repeating again and again. After all, if working men are the inescapable champions of 'dead being dead' and eco-warriors are contemporary 'saviours' (code for righteous knights in shining armour), we need to go further still to truly ecologise masculinities in light of the shortfalls of both extremes.

Given their closer proximity to the land enmeshed with localised through to globalised politics and economics, an examination of men in the environmental movement might shed structural light on intersections between regional issues and human encounters with Earth.

Men in the environmental movement

We return now to more closely consider a paper by Raewyn Connell (1990) titled 'A Whole New World: Remaking Masculinity in the Context of the Environmental Movement'. Connell provided us with one of the earliest scholarly analyses of environmentally considerate men in the Australian context. In the 1980s, feminism (and ecological feminism in particular) began to play a more influential role in shaping the Australian environmental agenda. This brought to bear the need for men in that nation's environmental movement to rethink their exchanges with women and Earth. Some men embraced this nuance, which had the effect of producing emergent reconstructions of masculinities for those individuals, the communities they engaged with and the environmental causes they espoused. Surveying the life histories of six men (aged 22–50) who were actively engaged in 'green politics', Connell's study concluded that:

> . . . the men found a distinctive mixture of personal relationships and cultural ideals. This politics engaged their lives at more than one level and met a variety of needs – for solidarity with others, for moral clarity, for a sense of personal worth. This engagement was important in producing a gender politics. The movement had leverage, so to speak, on its participants' emotional life.

(Connell, 1990: 462)

Connell's research demonstrated that caring for Earth can raise men's consciousness in ways that also broaden their political and personal encounters, with great potential to prepare them for challenging masculine hegemonisation internally and externally.

The men in Connell's study provided us with a unique perspective. They were not 'day-trippers playing at being the Sensitive New Man' as many men have habitually done so through mythopoetry (Connell, 1955: 136). Rather, the men interviewed by Connell (1990: 471) were committed to 'real and far-reaching politics of personality' in both principle and practice, even as they collided with the structural oppressions that confronted their communities. Connell found that despite strong resistance from the malestream, these men demonstrated some level of success at challenging traditional notions of masculine hegemonisation by engaging in an ecological discourse that had gained initial prominence in the late 1960s and began to make noticeable inroads into the fabric of Western social and environmental policies and practices by the 1980s (Hultman, 2015b). Connell (1990: 463–464) suggested that under the influence of feminism, these men tilled 'fertile ground for a politics of masculinity' that could reconfigure their lives and in doing so would facilitate profound changes in their relational exchanges with human and other-than-human others alike. Citing the links between environmental activism and the need to engage emotionally with the world, Connell (1995: 120) proposed that these 'environmentally sensitive' men launched direct challenges to hegemonic masculinity through: ideologies of equity; an emphasis on collectivism and solidarity; active engagement in personal growth and celebrating the organic wholeness of all life. However, the men that Connell researched articulated the cognitive dissonance associated with the 'gender vertigo' that accompanied their efforts, noting that making their politics visible brought their respective senses of manhood into question, resulting in perceived and real marginalisation from malestream norms (Connell, 1995: 127–128, 141–142). Responding to Connell's exploration of their lives, these men revealed that adopting overt anti-hegemonic politics posed a very real threat that cut deep into their psyches, conveying in no uncertain terms that they were being perceived as gender traitors by some in adopting radical social and environmental ethics. Their defiance of malestream manliness resulted in a clear message that gender 'betrayal' is a big 'no-no' if one is wanting to remain a recipient of the social primacy promised men by a sexist and nature-destroying society.

In a similar vein to Connell and while on a fellowship in New Zealand, I (Martin speaking here) examined the personal and professional machinations of Māori architect Rau Hoskins (Hultman, 2014). In that study, I considered Hoskins' views on the built environment, noting that here was a man who had studied indigenous and hybrid construction techniques, developing a unique brand of architecture shaped by more than 1,300 years of kinship links and Earth wisdoms. Hoskins and his colleagues drew information from their clients by unpacking their specific interests and desires; the end product being customised dwelling designs that took these personal particulars on board alongside considerations for the natural environment on site, in order to craft structures that would enrich cultural exchanges and facilitate greater connectivity between the indoors and out of doors (designTRIBE, 2017). The rhetoric of this sounds enlivening. But even here, market forces have great sway in determining building ordinances, placing economic pressures ahead of sustainable technologies. Effectively, they wed the services of inspiring individuals like Rau Hoskins to select clients who either can pay handsomely out of pocket or have access to funding support. This then restricts the benefits of such efforts, that harbour great potential to transform national policies on building codes and sustainability ratings, to the wealthy. Naturally, as an architect, Hoskins's practice was dependent on the resources of his clientele and in this sense the nature of his architecture remains constrained by the capitalist economic system within which it is performed.

As with this Hultman study, Connell confirmed that attempts to subvert male domination and ecological destruction through avant-garde strategies is persistently constrained by both social and market forces if not outright 'gender reprimand', representing severe barriers against the shifts towards ecological masculinities that we advocate throughout this book. From both studies, we learn that the malestream bastion standing in the way of masculine ecologisation is monumental for many men. To get beyond it, Connell suggested that men must shift to a new ideological terrain 'where the social/structural sources of emotional contradiction can be addressed directly. As radical feminism purported, this requires a shift to the level of collective practice that is far from the norm for most men who have been socialised for millennia to go it alone (Connell, 1990: 473). We can equate this recommendation to a remaking of the masculine self through consciousness-raising as concurrent ontological shifts at home and in broader social contexts, which could then manifest a 'gendered counter-sexist politics for men who reject hegemonic masculinity' and are thereby better equipped to widen the scope of their countercultural efforts in the face of foreboding oppositional pressures (Connell, 1990: 476).

The broader links between men, masculinities and the localised implications of pressing social and environmental issues provides us with some additional considerations. Take for example, a paper titled 'Masculinism, Climate Change and "Man-made" Disasters: Toward an Environmentalist Profeminist Response', by Australian sociologist Bob Pease (2016). Pease offered an important contribution to our understandings of ecomasculinities in the context of disaster response and management; a context within which masculine interactions with other-than-human nature can be particularly acute. He was suspicious of attempts to encourage men's deeper communion with nature in a mythopoetic way, since the history of those efforts has at best encouraged men to 'seek to find redeeming features in traditional masculinity in response to eco-feminist critiques' (Pease, 2014: 65). He noted that:

> Given the wide acknowledgement among feminist scholars that hege-
> monic masculinity is associated with a dominator relationship to nature
> (Twine, 1997), it is curious that there has been so little critical masculi-
> nities scholarship on men's relationship with nature. Much of the early
> engagement with nature from mythopoetic writers (Bly, 1990; Moore and
> Gillette, 1990) had an essentialist premise that men had an essential core
> that was connected with nature that they needed to reclaim. Notwith-
> standing the essentialist writings of the mythopoetic writers on 'the wild
> man' and other mythical beings, most masculinity theorists have neglected
> a critical interrogation of men and the natural world.
>
> (Pease, 2014: 65)

We agree with Pease's critique here, noting the importance of looking beyond
gender binaries as we articulate our theoretical framing of masculine ecologisation, but we intentionally dwell on ecological masculinities as a necessary
step to help us get there. After-all, shifting to a new ideological terrain in
order to reconfigure masculinities personally and politically is of course no
simple matter. Take for example analyses of climate change (Anshelm and
Hultman, 2014), as well as environmental activist responses to it, particularly
since the 1960s and 1970s (Melosi, 1987; Rome, 2003; Hazlett, 2004). In both
cases, deconstructive analyses are unavoidably gendered.

Ecologising masculinities in order to bring about greater care towards
humans and others requires multifaceted approaches to care for the glocal
commons. It is not sufficient for masculine care to be overly localised (and
therefore myopic) just as it is inadequate to overly rationalise the need for
structurally sensitive masculine care in pursuit of globalised social and environmental justice. We consider the two to be entwined necessities. To further
stress the point, consider some recent research of the environmental movement
by Jody Chan and Joe Curnow (2017). Based on an extensive participatory
study of a student environmental group, these researchers discovered that men
(particularly white men) tend to occupy airtime in conversations and more
readily hold themselves as experts, conveying rational arguments, seeking
practical solutions and drawing up lists of tasks to get there (Chan and
Curnow, 2017: 83). Another study by Susan Buckingham and Rakibe Kulcur
(2009) exposed the presence of men's entitlement even within environmental
movements where political sensitivities are generally on high alert. The same
pattern of malestream disruption of transformative gender relations has been
witnessed in green party politics in the Global North where industrial/bread-
winner norms have been exposed, but inadequately replaced with what we
categorise as ecomodern responses (Jackson, 2017: 310). We draw the conclusion that personal and structural transformation must be a two-way street,
with intersecting paths that deserve to be taken seriously since environmental
awareness does not automatically translate into gender equity, nor vice versa.
While the alternative politics of social and environmental justice activists play
an important role in helping to address glocal concerns, self-reflection on the

personal level must also be present. This way, we ensure that men at the boundaries along with socially sanctioned protocols, dispute resolution pathways and community agreements about the ways that they interact with Earth, others and self, do in fact challenge hegemonic masculinities and proactively facilitate masculine ecologisation. With this in mind, we hold an optimistic view that men and masculinities can, do and will take these steps, positioning ecological masculinities as both a conceptual alternative and a pluralised pathway to get us there. Consistent with this intention, we proceed to examine masculinities beyond urban and suburban spaces.

Farming men and the sociology of rural masculinities

Rural sociology broadly examines the sociological implications of life beyond cities. This field of study originates in investigations of agriculture, food production and the spatial geography of rural and remote regions. Some scholars of the field pay attention to the intersection of gender identities and the environment and their geographically specific practices (Bell, 2000; Campbell and Mayerfeld Bell, 2000; Laoire, 2001; Campbell et al. eds., 2006). Other scholars focus on outdoor activities such as fishing, hunting and industrial labour in the context of natural resource extraction (Saugeres, 2002; Brandth and Haugen, 2005; Keller and Jones, 2008; Venkatesh, 2017), as well as studies on changing identities in the countryside as they are shaped by economic perturbations (Brandth and Haugen, 2000). Rural sociology also discusses countercultural and ecologically friendly practices as sources of deeper understanding of men, masculinities and Earth through examinations of rural communes and back-to-land intentional communities.

We first consider farming and rural masculinities through an examination of the master's thesis in social work completed by James Donaldson (1990a). Donaldson spoke to an emergent 'ecomasculine spirit' reflective of a select group of farming men that he referred to as 'male ecological leaders'. As a social worker, he was interested in discovering the impact of environmentalism on masculine socialisation among a group of male environmental activists living in various small fruit-producing communities in north-central Washington State in the US. Donaldson paid particular attention to the socio-political aspects of his research sample, exploring their beliefs around cross-cultural issues, the exploitation of minorities in rural regions, social oppression, gendered approaches to labour (including parenting), views on manhood and the ways that environmental awareness shaped their feelings and actions in response to social and environmental injustices. The men he studied shared a willingness to 'practice truth, and to find the sacred connections of farming again [actively facilitating] the restoration of agricultural character to the world' through artisan-agricultural ethics (Donaldson, 1990a: 21–22; Donaldson, 1990b: 5). Of course, the farming practices employed by these men were 'alternative', relying on lowered pesticide and fertiliser inputs, biological control methods, soil care, crop rotation and developing local climatic knowledge, reflective of the men's collective commitment to sustainability. They emphasised biodynamic and bioregional approaches to farm stewardship. He positioned 'back-to-the-land' movements such as those studied as vital contributors to raised social and environmental consciousness, arguing that the ecological age, embodied by these men, would occur through an ecocentric post-patriarchal world-view in the following politically, socially and ecologically desirable ways:

- Resist further environmental abuse wherever it occurs in order to reduce the damage we are inflicting on the environment and delay looming crises while we pursue other approaches
- Educate citizens and leaders about the relationship between human welfare and environmental quality as well as the causes of environmental crises and the steps needed to resolve them
- Redefine key concepts including critical and economic and political principles, so that our basic interactions can be oriented towards achieving a sustainable balance between human societies and Earth
- Expand existing institutions and build new ones designed to sustain and nurture human activities that occur in balance with nature
- Combine environmental and human rights protection efforts as indivisible aspects of a unified strategy that forges a sustainable world for all

(Donaldson, 1990a: 19–20)

Donaldson saw the men he studied as environmental leaders pulling embodiments of modern masculinities away from malestream norms by:

> . . . developing a new ecomasculine spirit of fierce courage which will disavow the supermale image of the power-tripping corporate executive. Maybe they will come up with a picture of the emptiness of the position of power and the tragedy of the isolated role of the male who seeks esteem in raw power and privilege from economic gain even at the expense of the mothering earth.
>
> (Donaldson, 1990b: 5)

Underestimating the essentialism of 'motherising' Earth, Donaldson considered these men were best placed among men in general to implement the imperatives of ecologisation. In his view, they represented a vanguard creating the historical process of ecomasculinity in real time. They served as 'social actors' not only 'surveying their own historical process' but were also actively engaged in creating 'new ecological symbols expressing the meaning of their existence' by 'attempting the ordering of a society based on ecological principles and practices' (Donaldson, 1991: 7). They embraced education, critical analyses, along with capacities to actively engage with civil society at personal, familial, local and regional levels. The valuative choices of these farming men directly impacted their lived experiences at home as well; their 'spirits could become enhanced through nurturing and caring' for all others that then facilitated alternative manifestations of masculinities, distancing them from the male domination patterns that pervade mainstream society in the ways they interacted with and tended to their families (Donaldson, 1990a: 23). This was particularly evident in their commitments to conscious fathering. However, Donaldson did not address any need to end male domination. He made no mention of transforming hegemonic behaviours between women and men nor among the men themselves. Notably, in the Global North, farming operations are changing but largely remain a man's world (Stenbacka, 2007: 87–88; Graeub et al. 2016). Relative to farm management as industrial scale agribusinesses in the Global North, the work that women do on farms continues to be under-recognised and undervalued (Hultman, 2015a). The practical applications of rural men's interpersonal interactions were lost in the study's focus on countercultural masculine intent, as if their primary focus was facing outward to challenge the malestream world that seemingly distracted them from also facing inwards to address their own internalised dominator patterns.

Donaldson's study noted that, in choosing a back-to-the-land lifestyle, some rural men were at high risk of being otherised for challenging the benefits of hegemonic masculine compliance; in effect colliding with the 'patriarchal dividend' (Connell, 1995). This represented a big hurdle against comprehensive gender equity in their daily lives and was likely a primary cause for their falling short of addressing their own internalised superiorisation. Also, while the demographics of these men were not fully revealed, Donaldson's research indirectly exposed the limitations of ecotopic approaches to life reflective of the 'white, middle-class ghettos' that characterise environmentally aware populations to this day (Bawden, 2015). He proceeded to argue that with our growing environmental dangers 'there were ecologically aware men who had, at the centre of their lives, their place and their people', which further emboldened the protector/provider ethos that pervades malestream norms (Donaldson, 1990a: 25). While localised successes were noted, the men Donaldson studied had negligible impacts on the broader societal forces that he acknowledged were destroying Earth – they were in effect separatists, reflective of an elite who could afford to hide out from Western malestreams – at least in principle. Sadly, their anti-hegemonic intentions had little or no impact on oppression mechanisms beyond their localised ecotopias. Consequently, the impact of these men's ecomasculine strategies on their societal and interpersonal relations was suspect; far from the serious protest masculinities that they aspired to achieve. These critiques are similar to those raised against various ecovillages as well (Jarvis, 2017). Through the lens of our analyses of an effective masculine ecologisation, we conclude that Donaldson's study highlighted the shortcomings of any rural separatism that shuns masculine hegemonisation where it fails to translate into broad scale systemic as well as nuanced interpersonal social and environmental justice. While it is alluring for some men to ecologise in the quiet and tranquil environs of rural communities, we cannot assume that these localised hide-aways from urban landscapes will automatically translate into broad-scale de-hegemonisation or more preferably outright ecologisation.

The process of ecologisation must be more intentional than that in our view, being structural as well as personal, global as well as local, finding application in urban settings as much as in the remote nooks where wilder nature is at our fingertips, such that men of the soil stand alongside men of urban and suburban communities to facilitate ecologisation on the broadest of fronts. Learning from the short-comings of Donaldson's farming men, we note the importance of building ecological masculinities across a broad political and personal front. We recognise that metropolises are particularly important to target – taking ecologisation to 'the belly of the beast' so to speak. Adopting a deeper view than Donaldson's 'land settlers', we note that urban environs represent the most socially tumultuous, eco-logically devastating, structurally visible, ethnically diverse, economically variable and geopolitically influential locales for post-hegemonised masculinities to arise that pulls our attention back towards masculinities in metropolitan contexts. One successful example of this recommendation was implemented in the Spring of 2018 in Järna, Sweden, under the name of *Under Tallarna*; a systemically critical gather-in that accomplished precisely this needed union of personal and political examinations of human/Earth encounters under the auspices of rural, suburban and urban considerations.

Reconsider the references to those who are moving away from the indus-trial means of agricultural production. Through back-to-the-land movements, we are bearing witness to rural, suburban and urban forms of ecological masculinities. These agricultural populations who are subject to unique challanges are of keen interest to some sociologists (Peter et al., 2000; Lavire, 2002). The structural issues examined by such studies can be of assis-tance to any effective ecologised masculinities discourse, shedding light on those who are engaged with rural regions (such as farmers, many of whom are men) that commonly develop an intimacy with the land in ways that scholars do not. Meanwhile, other scholars offer some important connections between localised concerns and pressing global issues (such as climate change) (Alston, 2015). Hugh Campbell and Michael Mayerfeld Bell (2000) approached the topic from both ends. They considered rural inquiries into masculinities and masculinities inquires into rural studies, positioning their research in alignment with Connell as a contribution to feminist analyses of agri-culture. Their research contested previously held notions that masculinities were monolithic 'sex roles' suffering from great 'crises', recommending that we ought to consider 'rural masculinity' as subject to 'symbolic, discursive, or ideological' constructions instead (Campbell and Mayerfeld Bell, 2000: 532, 534). Such stu-dies brought the gendered complexities of rural communities into acute focus, noting that when we assume farmers are men, we pigeonhole rural men and women. Doing so, we run the risk of presuming that farming men will work hard, compete and isolate as good working men should and that the women in their lives are invisible (Campbell and Mayerfeld Bell, 2000: 540).

In another study on environmental justice and rural concerns, David Pellow claimed that an adequate gendered dimension was missing from rural studies. He argued that we must give:

. . . greater attention to the ways in which gender and sexuality might work in rural environmental (in)justice contexts . . . since . . . rural 'natural' spaces in the U.S. have historically been socially constructed not only through discourses that are racialized, but also in ways that are deeply masculinist, patriarchal, and heteronormative. Ecofeminism and feminist theory offer strong tools for making these connections.

(Pellow, 2016: 5)

From views such as this, we are reminded that rural studies can expose strongholds of masculine hegemonisation, situating masculine identities beyond suburban and urban environs as legitimate and worthy of our attention as well (Campbell and Mayerfeld Bell, 2000: 540). We note that these considerations will serve the process of greater global sustainability best if we are able to tend to the needs of men and masculinities on the broadest front. For these reasons, we believe that studies on agriculture, farming men and rural sociology offer us important additional areas for further research on ecological masculinities.

Feminist-inspired ecomasculinities

As we attested in Chapter 5, ecofeminists have taken the lead in exposing the ways that malestream myopia has been impacting otherised humans and other-than-humans. Some have been heeding their calls. Shortly after Connell's pivotal paper discussed above, ecofeminist-inspired scholar Richard Twine (1995) emerged as an additional and important contributor to the links between men, masculinities and nature. In a provoking post on the Essex Ecofem Listserv, he raised the question: where are all the ecomasculinists? Twine stated the following:

While there are some men writing in ecofeminism . . . there does not seem to be any literature on how the environmental and feminist movements together form a strong critique Of[sic] the dominant Western masculine tradition. Does anyone know of any critical examinations (specifically ecofeminist critiques) of this position, particularly one that addresses masculinity rather than patriarchy. While non-essentialist ecofeminists have pointed out the problems of a simple celebration of the 'feminine' there seems to be a theoretical gap on the reformulation of masculinity in the light of feminism. Do we still wish to keep some degree of polarity or are we looking at the creation of an androgynous gender? Any responses would be hugely appreciated!

(Twine, 1995: n.p)

But for a brief exchange between Twine and Amanda Swarr (née Lock), Niamh Moore, Sandra Russon and Karen Barnhardt, followed later by a more considered response from Lee Hall (2005), this listserv exchange did not lead to a deeper study of the validity (or not) of an emergent 'ecomasculinity' as a grounded theory and/or practice. Twine (1997) proceeded to post 'Masculinity, Nature, Ecofeminism' on the same listserv, offering more of his thinking in response to his own adroit question from 1995. That posting also drew from Connell's (1995) critical insights about hegemonic masculinity while lambasting the then peaking mythopoetic men's movement, Twine noting that:

> . . . we can do much better than Robert Bly's essentialised narrative of the 'Wild Man' as a way of representing nature and masculinity. I feel that there is an absence of writing on the relationship between masculinity and nature even though it has been recognised for a long time that hegemonic masculinity is partly configured by a dominating and alienated relation to nature. Moreover, in discussions of men and emotions, or men and violence, or men and embodiment the category of 'nature' is always lurking there in the background yet is not given sufficient direct attention.
>
> (Twine,1997: 1)

Twine argued in favour of the de-hegemonisation of men and masculinities. He linked this to the ways that men engage with nature, steering away from the feminisation, romanticisation and dominator patterns that conveniently avoid explorations of men, masculinities and Earth. As an alternative, he celebrated the notion that 'ecological politics provides an important way in which (profeminist) men can subvert, albeit indirectly, hegemonic masculinity and then potentially create new, mutually enriching and non-oppressive conversations between men and nature' (Twine, 1997: 6). He maintained that it was ecofeminist politics that best exposed 'male physical and emotional vulnerability' in ways that might ease 'the stress and illness that goes with its denial' (Twine, 1997: 5). For Twine, such politics were a voice in the wilderness of ecologised masculinities, since it was not the task of ecofeminists to advance discourses towards ecomasculinities, given the distance between masculinity and nature was amplified by male domination. That, he contended, was the work of male scholars aligned with ecological feminism; a poignant insight that contributed significantly to the emergence of this book.

Twine suggested that it was essential for men to develop emotional relationships with nature along with ecofeminist-inspired structural analyses. A vital ingredient in this was for them to recognise that men are unmarked and must aspire to 'something counter to hegemonic masculinity' (Twine, 1997: 2). In a later paper titled 'Ma(r)king Essence-Ecofeminism and Embodiment' Twine (2001) reiterated the longstanding ecofeminist conviction that women are not only seen to be closer to nature than men but are also deemed to be more 'embodied'. This was a notion in alignment with Joane Nagel's (2003) exploration of sexuality in the context of ethnicity, racial diversity and nationalism and the ways it shapes our perceptions of difference across communities and cultures, particularly in reference to conflicts between people and place. This perceptible difference, Twine (2001: 32–33) contended, highlighted the possibility for men to gain insights from women's lived experiences in order to resolve the anxiety of their collective master identity by embracing the revealing aspects and social constructions of 'marked' bodies. Thinking here about a football game as an analogy, participants that are 'unmarked' on the field are free to play in whatever way they like while 'marked' players are checked and contained by their competitors who restrict their actions on the field. In socio-cultural landscapes, the same holds true for men as unmarked 'players' compared to women, non-binary/genderqueer people (and also other-than-human others) as marked 'players' who are devalued by the master identity of malestream norms. This distinction is particularly acute for wealthy, white men in the context of class, gender, sexuality, species and race privileges (Twine 2001: 40–48). Twine (2001) proposed that this intentional masculine embodiment could increase men's sensual capacity such that they might stretch beyond functioning minds that robotically control us to become bodies impacted by and impacting upon nature, each other and self. He suggested that men's marked embodiment could enliven their sensual capacities to develop texture in their lives beyond serving as mere automatons beholden to corporate capitalism. Such a perspective may also include increased acceptance of bodily functions – odours, secretions, actions, as well as embracing all of the human body, including the emotions (Twine 2001: 40). He argued that embracing marked embodiment could shift perceptions of the masculine self away from men's disdain and self-loathing and common loathing of human and other-than-human others, effectively softening the boundaries between masculinity and nature so that men might no longer be 'sealed off' from the world around them (Twine 2001: 44). Twine's (2001: 48) ma(r)king of the masculine body with an *essence of flesh* carried with it 'connotations of animality, femininity, sexuality, and nature', subverting the hegemonic norms of the heteronormative malestream, where those that are marked might gain equal consideration to unmarked men. Twine's preambles on the subject were formative, but he too did not provide us with a road map for masculine ecologisation. His deference to ecofeminism was in effect a shortcut that many men could not connect with or relate to; he did not offer a metanarrative on the subject for others to explore and unpack. Instead, his compelling queries about the need for an emergent international discourse on masculine ecologisation diffused for the best part of twenty years.

In a presentation at the Sixteenth Americas Conference on Information Systems, David Kreps (2010) provided us with another nuanced and ecofeminist-inspired contribution to ecological masculinities. In this rather obscure paper on the topic of ecologised masculinities that reflected his expertise in the information and communications technology (ICT) space, Kreps echoed ecofeminist Chris Cuomo's (2002) assertion that 'environmental malfeasance is a product of masculinist, colonial and capitalist assumptions and practices'

(Kreps, 2010: 4–5). He introduced the need for 'eco-masculinities' as the best philosophical and critical pathway to reconciling the inherent tensions of gendered and environmental debates, applying this contention to the ways we use ICTs and the impacts that this use has both socially and environmentally. Kreps was a proponent of models of behaviour change that would bring about more ecologically sensitive and altruistic social and economic actions by rebalancing socio-technical encounters as they differed between women and men. We acknowledge the validity of Kreps' contention that 'eco-masculinities' can be informed by a critical view of our domestic use of information technologies. Their foreboding presence in the home is indeed increasingly coupled with rising rates of per capita energy consumption in Western nations and individual habituated behaviours that create additional distance between us in our social lives, effectively cauterising our skills in social plasticity (Kreps 2010: 2). But Kreps's unpacking of gender-sensitive eco-masculinities as a salve to the deadening impacts of ICT stopped there. We consider Kreps' analysis a long bow to draw given the fact that ICTs additionally divorce the self from visceral engagements with Earth beyond highly processed use of raw materials to manufacture devices. Applying his notions of eco-masculinities to ICT may well have highlighted the impact of such thinking on one of the more gender unequal and highly resource-dependent industries on the planet. But, beyond assertions that technology is gendered and its use must become pro-environmental and profeminist, Kreps did not explicate how his eco-masculinities might attend to our looming social and environmental problems. Indeed, the absence of a call to use ICTs with greater gender and environmental sensitivity suffered from a similar void in theoretical framing for his eco-masculinities as we have demonstrated above.

A final compelling academic contribution to masculine ecologisation that is at the centre of our thinking is an article by ecofeminist scholar, activist and filmmaker, Greta Gaard, titled 'Toward New EcoMasculinities, EcoGenders, and EcoSexualities' published in Carol Adams and Lori Gruen's (2014) anthology *Ecofeminism: Feminist Intersections with Other Animals and Earth*. Gaard (2014: 225–226) made a strong case for our need to create 'radical democratic social movements of eco-activists and scholars' through an intentional deconstruction of the role of the 'dominant Master Self . . . in order to recognise and enact eco-political sustainability and ecological genders . . . to start thinking about eco-masculinity'. Gaard applied Karren Warren's (1990) eight feminist boundary conditions (mentioned previously) to her suggested ecological masculinity in noting the need to become: resistant to patterns of social domination; ethically contextual; cognisant of women's voices; aligned with ethical theories in process and over time; sensitive to the perspectives of otherised others; unapologetically subjective and willing to centralise the views of those who are marginalised; critical of the misrepresentation of traditional ethics and considerate of alternatives; critically redefining of

214 Ecological masculinities

our understandings of the human condition (Gaard, 2014: 231; Gaard, 2017: 168). She challenged the currency of traditional manifestations of masculinity under capitalism, seeking cooperation and true democracy that would substitute masculine hegemonisation with caring masculinities, where men in particular might embrace their capacities to nurture what they create, relinquish control, engage their emotions, champion ecological sustainability, honour other-than-human others and prioritise eco-justice (Gaard, 2014: 237). Gaard insisted that the most productive approach to resolving the conundrums of the gender–nature nexus is 'to envision diverse expressions of eco-genders – not just eco-masculinities but also eco-femme and eco-trans identities – as well' (Gaard, 2014: 238). She has since further parried with the topic of ecological masculinities in *Critical Ecofeminism* (Gaard, 2017: 163–169). Continuing to leverage off Warren's (1990: 141) previous work, Gaard (2017: 168) referenced 'feminist ecomasculinities' as fundamentally relational, objectionable to 'abstract individualism' and posited that 'all human identities and moral conducts are best understood "in terms of networks or webs of historical and concrete relationships"'. Gaard (2014: 230) rightly highlighted that 'neither ecocriticism, nor men's studies, nor queer ecologies, nor (to date) ecofeminism has offered a theoretically sophisticated foray into the potentials for eco-masculinities' in our pursuit of needed planetary solutions. She also noted that while alternatives to 'hegemonic, antiecological masculinism may again be possible', an effective ecologised masculinities theory requires deep consideration of prior works from the fields of ecojustice, philosophy and activism (Gaard, 2017: 166). We have heeded this call.

Gaard also provided helpful critical analyses of our respective and previously published contributions to men, masculinities and Earth. She astutely noted that in my case (Martin speaking here), more was needed to be made of the heterosexism implicit in hegemonic constructions of masculinity. This was a fair critique of my work. At the time of publishing my early contributions to masculinity and the environment, my primary concern was to deconstruct the impacts of hegemonic masculinities on environmental politics, which was in my view problematically dominated by ecomodern masculinities, especially in relation to climate change and energy debates (Hultman, 2013; Anshelm and Hultman, 2014). My research has since broadened to include a wider scope of considerations in developing an effective masculine ecologisation process. I have found much inspiration and support for theorising on men, masculinities and Earth from trans- and queer-ecologies, acknowledging that Gaard (and others) contributed to ecologised masculinities by bringing forth crucial ideas of plural identities as well as intersectionality, which I have aimed to support in subsequent publications (Hultman, 2017a: 248; Hultman 2017b: 95–96).

In Paul's doctoral research (Pulé, 2013), Gaard detected an intention to subvert 'daring' masculinities with greater care for self, society and environment through politicised shifts away from masculine hegemonisation

(Gaard, 2017: 168–169). She correctly noted that in my doctoral research on the topic (Paul speaking here), I had not adequately analysed the precursory contributions of key ecofeminist scholars (specifically: Salleh, 1984; Plumwood, 1993; Warren, 1994; Salleh 1997; Warren, 1997; Warren, 2000), who had previously rationalised gender–nature discourses beyond the need for a feminist-inspired revisionism of men, masculinities and Earth. Furthermore, Gaard identified that my dissertation did not sufficiently interrogate the significance of structural influences such as race, class, sexuality and culture in shaping an effective masculine ecologisation. We both recognise Gaard's comments as some of the most recent scholarly contributions to a rigorous analysis of conversations about masculine ecologisation to date. We also acknowledge that these critiques of our respective earlier works have since shifted our attention towards the value of trans- and queer-ecologies in ways we had both previously missed. Gaard's contributions to our understanding of men, masculinities and Earth are illuminating along with other celebrated influences as we articulate transitions from masculine hegemonisation to ecologisation.

Gathering materials (a summary)

This chapter has provided a broad literature review of works on or related to the topic of masculine ecologisation. Returning to our metaphor of the four streams carrying rich ingredients into an estuary, we have above surveyed each of the key materials available to us to work with.

The cluster of previous research considered in this chapter has exposed a perennial but increasing interest in the intersecting terrain of men, masculinities and Earth. We have been particularly encouraged by our discovery of a growing list of conceptual developments on men, masculinities and Earth we have given consideration here, indicating that our in-depth analyses of this topic is not completely new – even if we have now gathered them together for the first time under the banner of a new conversation that we call ecological masculinities. We have intentionally worked with this transdisciplinarity throughout this literature review chapter, learning from various discursive historical and contemporary contributors as we have explored the values and practises they have each discussed. This is not to say that we can simply caste our thoughts forward by looking backwards. Rather, we have aimed to demonstrate here that directly challenging overt industrial/breadwinner hegemonisation and the inadequacies of ecomodern masculinities has been tepidly underway for some time. We position ourselves as two among this growing community of thinkers and actors who are seeking alternatives to masculine hegemonisation by crafting this book as a masculine ecologisation metanarrative, replete with a framework for pluralised praxes to emerge.

Our task in Chapter 8 is to look beyond this collection of materials that will help us build our ecological masculinities shelter. This is an exercise that recognises the necessity of achieving a deep green future through more considered and confronting approaches to men, masculinities and Earth. The project ahead that we envision is: ontological and epistemological; deconstructive of notions of man, male, manhood and masculinities; cognisant of self-identity, familial relations, community engagement, localised economics; sensitive to the ways that power (beyond domination) is conveyed throughout society and in our exchanges with other-than-human others. Such a project is both personal and political, finding application from the most urban of metropolises to the remotest of farms, wildernesses and cultural landscapes. Our rendition of ecological masculinities attempts to facilitate transitions where self becomes Self in the deep ecological sense, radiating out into the relational exchanges that are not only integral to our individual lives but redefines the very machinations of our interactions among ourselves and human and other-than-human others as well. Such a project is intended to redefine masculine relational exchanges and raise their capacities to care for all life.

In concluding this chapter, we have acknowledged debts of gratitude to those who have come before us, carefully examined the materials they provided and in doing so, identified what is still needed for an effective ecologised masculinities theory and its associated practices to emerge. Now laid out on the shores of our estuary, these materials equip us well to build a shelter where unique expressions of masculine ecologisation can occur. Chapter 8 is dedicated to that process through the conceptual and tangible elements of ecological masculinities.

References

Abberley, W. 2017. '"The love of the chase is an inherent delight in man": hunting and masculine emotions in the Victorian zoologist's travel memoir'. In S. MacGregor and N. Seymour, eds., *Men and Nature: Hegemonic Masculinities and Environmental Change*. Munich: RCC Perspectives, 61–68.

Abbey, E. 1988. *The Fool's Progress: An Honest Novel*. New York: Henry Holt.

Adams, C., and L. Gruen, eds. 2014. *Ecofeminism: Feminist Intersections With Other Animals & The Earth*. New York: Bloomsbury.

Allister, M. 2004. 'Introduction'. In M. Allister, ed. *Ecoman: New Perspectives on Masculinity and Nature*. Charlottesville: University of Virginia Press, 1–16.

Alston, M. 2015. *Women and Climate Change in Bangladesh*. Oxon: Routledge.

Anderson, W. 1990. *Green Man: The Archetype of Our Oneness with Nature*. London: HarperCollins Publishers.

Anshelm, J., and M. Hultman. 2014. 'A green fatwā? Climate change as a threat to the masculinity of industrial modernity'. *NORMA: International Journal for Masculinity Studies* 9(2): 84–96.

Basford, K. 1978. *The Green Man*. New York: Brewer.

Bawden, T. 2015. 'Green movement must escape its "white, middle-class ghetto" says Friend of the Earth chief Craig Bennett'. Accessed 22 October 2017. http://www.

independent.co.uk/environment/green-movement-must-escape-its-white-middle-cla
ss-ghetto-says-friends-of-the-earth-chief-craig-10366564.html

Bell, D. 2000. 'Farm boys and wild men: rurality, masculinity, and homosexuality'. *Rural Sociology* 65(4): 547–561.

Biehl, J. 1988. 'What is social ecofeminism?'. *Green Perspectives: A Left Green Publication* 11: 1–8.

Bildhauer, B., and C. Jones, eds. 2017. *The Middle Ages in the Modern World: Twenty-first century perspectives*. London: OUP/British Academy.

Bliss, S. 1987. 'Revisioning masculinity: a report on the growing men's movement'. *In Context: A Quarterly of Humane Sustainable Culture* 16 (Spring): 21.

Bliss, S. 1995. 'Mythopoetic men's movement'. In M. Kimmel, ed., *The Politics of Manhood: Profeminist Men Respond to the Mythopoetic Men's Movement (and the Mythopoetic Leaders Answer)*. Philadelphia: Temple University Press, 292–307.

Bly, R. 1990. *Iron John: A Book About Men*. Boston: Addison-Wesley.

Bouchier, N., and K. Cruikshank. 1997. '"Sportsmen and pothunters": environment, conservation, and class in the fishery of Hamilton Harbour, 1858–1914'. *Sport History Review* 28(1): 1–18.

Brandt, S. 2017. 'The "wild, wild world": masculinity and the environment in the American literary imagination'. In J. Armengol, M. Bosch-Vilarrubias, À. Carabí and T. Requena-Pelegrí, eds., *Routledge Advances in Feminist Studies and Intersectionality*. New York: Routledge, 133–143.

Brandth, B., and M. Haugen. 2000. 'From lumberjack to business manager: masculinity in the Norwegian forestry press'. *Journal of Rural Studies* 16(3): 343–355.

Brandth, B., and M. Haugen. 2005. 'Doing rural masculinity – from logging to out-field tourism'. *Journal of Gender Studies* 14(1): 13–22.

Buckingham, S. 2010. 'Call in the women'. *Nature* 468(7323): 502.

Buckingham, S., and R. Kulcur. 2009. Gendered geographies of environmental injustice. *Antipode* 41(4): 659–683.

Buell, L. 2005. *The Future of Environmental Criticism: Environmental Crisis and Literary Imagination*. Malden: Blackwell.

Campbell, H., and M. Mayerfeld Bell. 2000. 'The question of rural masculinities'. *Rural Sociology* 65(4): 532–546.

Campbell, H., Mayerfeld Bell, M., and M. Finney. eds. 2006. *Country Boys: Masculinity and Rural Life*. University Park: Penn State Press.

Chan, J., and J. Curnow. 2017. 'Taking up space: men, masculinity, and the student climate movement'. In S. MacGregor and N. Seymour, eds., *Men and Nature: Hegemonic Masculinities and Environmental Change*. Munich: RCC Perspectives, 77–85.

Cheetham, T. 2005. *Green Man, Earth Angel: The Prophetic Tradition and Battle for the Soul of the World*. Albany: State University of New York Press.

Connell, R. 1990. 'A whole new world: remaking masculinity in the context of the environmental movement'. *Gender and Society* 4(4): 452–478.

Connell, R. 1995. *Masculinities*. Berkeley: University of California Press.

Cornelius, M. 2011. 'Beefy guys and brawny dolls: he-man, the masters of the universe, and gay clone culture'. In M. Cornelius, ed., *Of Muscles and Men: Essays on the Sword and Sandal Film*. Jefferson: McFarland and Company, Inc., 154–174.

Cuomo, C. 2002. 'On ecofeminist philosophy'. *Ethics and the Environment* 7(2): 1–11.

designTRIBE. 2017. Rau Hoskins. Accessed 31 October 2017. http://www.designtribe.
co.nz/en/people.html

Dinshaw, C. 2015. 'I've got you under my skin: the green man, trans-species bodies, and queer worldmaking – Carolyn Dinshaw talk'. Talk presented at Helen C. White Hall, University of Wisconsin, Madison, 5 February.

Dinshaw, C. 2017. 'Black skin, green masks: medieval foliate heads, racial trauma, and queer world-making'. In B. Bildhauer and C. Jones, eds., *The Middle Ages in the Modern World*. Oxford: Oxford University Press, 276–304.

Donaldson, J. 1990a. 'The beliefs of male ecological leaders regarding the impact of ecological movements on the socialization of the masculine role'. Master's diss., Heritage College.

Donaldson, J. 1990b. 'Ecomasculinity on the rise'. *Wingspan: Journal of the Male Spirit* summer5: 8.

Donaldson, J. 1991. 'Thunder stick, a sacred symbol for men in Australia and the Americas'. *Journal of Vancouver M.E.N.* 1(2). Accessed 22 October 2017. https://a rchive.org/stream/thunderstick/1.2_djvu.txt

Ferber, A. 2000. 'Racial warriors and weekend warriors: the construction of masculinity in mythopoetic and white supremacist discourse'. *Men and Masculinities* 3(1): 30–56.

Gaard, G. 2014. 'Towards new ecomasculinities, ecogenders, and ecosexualities'. In C. Adams and L. Gruen, eds., *Ecofeminism: Feminist Intersections with Other Animals and the Earth*. New York: Bloomsbury, 225–240.

Gaard, G. 2017. *Critical Ecofeminism (Ecocritical Theory and Practice)*. Lanham MD: Lexington Books.

Graeub, B., Chappell, M., Whitman, H., Ledermann, S., Kerr, R., and B. Gemmill-Herren. 2016. 'The state of family farms in the world'. *World Development* 87: 1–15.

Gremillion, H. 2011. 'Feminism and the mythopoetic men's movement: Some shared concepts of gender'. *Women's Studies Journal* 25(2): 43.

Hall, L. 2005. 'Ecofem listserv: reflections on the masculine hegemon: a reply to Richard Twine'. Accessed 14 December 2005. http://richardtwine.com/ecofem/reflec tions%20on%20the%20masculine%20hegemon%20-%20a%20reply%20to%20richa rd%20twineef.pdf

Harding, C. ed. 1992. *Wingspan: Inside the Men's Movement*. New York: St. Martin's Press.

Hazlett, M. 2004. '"Woman vs. man vs. bugs": gender and popular ecology in early reactions to *Silent Spring*'. *Environmental History* 9(4): 701–729.

Hemingway, E. 1936. 'The short happy life of Francis Macomber'. *Cosmopolitan* September: 30–33.

Hennen, P. 2008. *Faeries, Bears, and Leathermen: Men in Community Queering the Masculine*. Chicago: University of Chicago Press.

Hoff, B., and Bliss, S. 1995. 'Interview with Shepherd Bliss'. Accessed 11 February 2011. http://www.menweb.org/blissiv.htm

Hultman, M. 2013. 'The making of an environmental hero: a history of ecomodern masculinity, fuel cells and Arnold Schwarzenegger'. *Environmental Humanities* 2(1): 79–99.

Hultman, M. 2014. 'How to meet? Research on ecopreneurship with Sámi and Māori'. Paper presented at international workshop Ethics in Indigenous Research – Past Experiences, Future Challenges, Umeå, 3–5 March.

Hultman, M. 2015a. *Att lokalisera ekonomin: Lokalekonomiska analyser, snedställdhet, kvinnors företagande och hållbar landsbygdsutveckling*. Norrköping: Linköpings universitet, Centrum för kommunstrategiska.

Hultman, M. 2015b. *Den inställda omställningen: svensk energi-och miljöpolitik i möjligheternas tid 1980–1991*. Möklinta: Gidlunds.

Hultman, M. 2016. 'Gröna män? Konceptualisering av industrimodern, ekomodern och ekologisk maskulinitet'. In *Kulturella Perspektiv, Environmental Humanities* (vol. 1 – special issue): s.28–39.

Hultman, M. 2017a. 'Exploring industrial, ecomodern, and ecological masculinities'. In S. MacGregor, ed., *Routledge Handbook of Gender and Environment*. Oxon: Routledge, 239–252.

Hultman, M. 2017b. 'Natures of masculinities: conceptualising industrial, ecomodern and ecological masculinities'. In S. Buckingham and V. le Masson, eds., *Understanding Climate Change through Gender Relations*. Oxon: Routledge, 239–252.

Hultman, M., and Anshelm, J. 2015. 'Masculinities of global climate change: exploring ecomodern, industrial and ecological masculinity'. Paper presented at Work in a Warming World (W3) Workshop: Climate Change, Gender and Work in Rich Countries, Simon Fraser University, Vancouver, June.

Jackson, S. 2017. 'Gender politics in green parties'. In S. MacGregor, ed., *Routledge Handbook of Gender and Environment*. Oxon: Routledge, 304–317.

Jarvis, H. 2017. 'Intentional gender-democratic and sustainable communities'. In S. MacGregor, ed., *Routledge Handbook of Gender and Environment*. Oxon: Routledge, 433–446.

Keller, J., and A. Jones. 2008. 'Brokeback mountain: masculinity and manhood'. *Studies in Popular Culture* 30(2): 21–36.

Keough, W. 2010. '(Re-)telling Newfoundland sealing masculinity: narrative and counter-narrative'. *Journal of the Canadian Historical Association/Revue de la Société historique du Canada* 21(1): 131–150.

Kimmel, M. 1993. 'Clarence William, Iron Mike, Tailhook, Senator Packwood, Spur Posse, Magic . . . and us'. In E. Buchwald, P. Fletcher, and M. Roth, eds., *Transforming Rape Culture*. Minneapolis: Milkweed Editions, 119–138.

Kreps, D. 2010. 'Introducing eco-masculinities: how a masculine discursive subject approach to the individual differences theory of gender and IT impacts an environmental informatics project'. *Proceedings of the Sixteenth Americas Conference on Information Systems*. Lima: Association for Information Systems.

Laoire, C. 2001. 'A matter of life and death Men, masculinities, and staying "behind in rural Ireland"'. *Sociologia Ruralis* 41(2): 220–236.

Laoire, C. 2002. 'Young farmers, masculinities and change in rural Ireland'. *Irish Geography* 35(1): 16–27.

Livingstone, J. 2016. 'The remarkable persistence of the Green Man'. Accessed 18 June 2017. http://www.newyorker.com/books/page-turner/the-remarkable-persistence-of-the-green-man

Loo, T. 2001. 'Of moose and men: hunting for masculinities in British Columbia, 1880–1939'. *Western Historical Quarterly* 32(3): 296–319.

Loomis, E. 2017. 'Masculinity, work, and the industrial forest in the US Pacific Northwest'. In S. MacGregor and N. Seymour, eds., *Men and Nature: Hegemonic Masculinities and Environmental Change*. Munich: RCC Perspectives, 37–43.

Magnuson, E. 2007. 'Creating culture in the mythopoetic men's movement: an ethnographic study of micro-level leadership and socialization'. *Journal of Men's Studies* 15(1): 31–56.

ManKind Project. 2017. 'The ManKind Project'. Accessed 12 June 2017. https://mkpa u.org

Mason, C. 2006. *Crossing into Manhood: A Men's Studies Curriculum*. New York: Cambria Press.

Matthews, J. 2001. *The Quest for the Green Man*. Wheaton: Quest Books Theological Publishing House.

Melosi, M. 1987. 'Lyndon Johnson and environmental policy'. In R. Devine, ed., *The Johnson Years (Volume 2)*. Lawrence: Wiley, 113–149.

Miller, G. 2004. 'Frontier masculinity in the oil industry: the experience of women engineers'. *Gender, Work & Organization* 11(1): 47–73.

Milnes, T. and Haney, T. 2017. '"There's always winners and losers": traditional masculinity, resource dependence and post-disaster environmental complacency'. *Environmental Sociology* 3(3): 260–273.

Moore, R., and D. Gillette. 1990. *King, Warrior, Magician, Lover: Rediscovering the Archetypes of the Mature Masculine*. New York: HarperSanFrancisco.

Nagel, J. 2003. *Race, Ethnicity, and Sexuality: Intimate Intersections, Forbidden Frontiers*. Oxford: Oxford University Press.

Oppermann, S. 2011. 'The future of ecocriticism: present currents'. In S. Oppermann, U. Özdag, N. Özkan, and S. Slovic, eds., *The Future of Ecocriticism: New Horizons*. Newcastle upon Tyne: Cambridge Scholars, 14–29.

Pease, B. 2014. 'Reconstructing masculinity or ending manhood? The potential and limitations of transforming masculine subjectivities for gender equality'. In A. Carabí and J. Armengol, eds., *Alternative Masculinities for a Changing World*. New York: Palgrave Macmillan, 17–34.

Pease, B. 2016. 'Masculinism, climate change and "man-made" disasters: toward an environmentalist profeminist response'. In E. Enarson and B. Pease, eds., *Men, Masculinities and Disaster*. Oxon: Routledge, 21–33.

Pellow, D. 2016. 'Environmental justice and rural studies: a critical conversation and invitation to collaboration'. *Journal of Rural Studies* 47(38): 1–6.

Peter, G., Bell, M., Jarnagin, S., and D. Bauer. 2000. 'Coming back across the fence: Masculinity and the transition to sustainable agriculture'. *Rural sociology* 65(2): 215–233.

Plumwood, V. 1993. *Feminism and the Mastery of Nature*. London: Routledge.

Pulé, P. 2013. 'A declaration of caring: towards an ecological masculinism'. PhD diss., Murdoch University.

Requena-Pelegrí, T. 2017. 'Green intersections: caring masculinities and the environmental crisis'. In J. Armengol and M. Vilarrubias, eds., *Masculinities and Literary Studies: Intersections and New Directions*. New York: Routledge, 143–152.

Rome, A. 2003. '"Give Earth a chance": the environmental movement and the sixties'. *Journal of American History* 90(2): 525–554.

Russell, B. 2002. *History of Western Philosophy*. London: Routledge.

Salleh, A. 1984. 'Deeper than deep ecology: the eco-feminist connection'. *Environmental Ethics* 6 (winter): 339–345.

Salleh, A. 1997. *Ecofeminism as Politics: Nature, Marx and the Postmodern*. London: Zed Books.

Salovaara, H. 2015a. '"A fine line": crossing and erecting borders in representing male athlete's relationships to nature'. In D. Rellstab and N. Siponkoski, eds., *Rajojen dynamiikkaa, Gränsernas dynamik, Borders under Negotiation, Grenzen und ihre Dynamik*. VAKKI-symposiumi XXXV 12–13. 2. 2015. VAKKI Publications 4. Vaasa, (77–85).

Salovaara, H. 2015b. 'Male adventure athletes and their relationships to nature'. Accessed 23 May 2017. https://www.researchgate.net/publication/303234498_Male_Adventure_Athletes_and_Their_Relationship_to_Nature

Satterfield, T. and S. Slovic. 2004. 'Introduction: what's nature worth?'. In T. Satterfield and S. Slovic, eds., *What's Nature Worth? Narrative Expressions of Environmental Values*. Salt Lake City: University of Utah Press, 1–17. http://www.menweb.org/blis beyo.htm

Saugeres, L. 2002. 'Of tractors and men: masculinity, technology and power in a French farming community'. *Sociologia Ruralis* 42(2): 143–159.

Slovic, S. 1992. *Seeking Awareness in American Nature Writing: Henry Thoreau, Annie Dillard, Edward Abbey, Wendell Berry, Barry Lopez*. Salt Lake City: University of Utah Press.

Slovic, S. 2004. 'Taking care: toward an ecomasculinist literary criticism?'. In M. Allister, ed., *Ecoman: New Perspectives on Masculinity and Nature*. Charlottesville: University of Virginia Press, 66–82.

Smalley, A. 2005. '"I just like to kill things"': women, men and the gender of sport hunting in the United States, 1940–1973'. *Gender & History* 17(1): 183–209.

Snyder, G. 1960. *Myths and Texts*. New York: New Directions.

Somerset, J. 1939. 'The "Green Man" in church architecture'. *Folklore* 50(1): 45–57.

Sramek, J. 2006. '"Face him like a Briton": tiger hunting, imperialism, and British masculinity in colonial India, 1800–1875'. *Victorian Studies* 48(4): 659–680.

Stenbacka, S. 2007. 'Rural identities in transition: male unemployment and everyday practice in northern Sweden'. In I. Morell and B. Bock, eds., *Gender Regimes, Citizen Participation and Rural Restructuring (Research in Rural Sociology and Development Volume 13)*. Bingley: Emerald, 83–111.

Tallmadge, J. 2004. 'Deerslayer with a degree'. In M. Allister, ed., *Ecoman: New Perspectives on Masculinity and Nature*. Charlottesville: University of Virginia Press, 17–27.

Twine, R. 1995. 'Ecofem Listserv: where are all the ecomasculinists?'. Essex Ecofem Listserv [10–21 November]. Accessed 12 December 2010. http://www.mail-archive.com/ecofem@csf.colorado.edu/msg00852.html

Twine, R. 1997. 'Ecofem Listserv: masculinity, nature, ecofeminism'. Accessed 26 August 2004. http://richardtwine.com/ecofem/masc.pdf

Twine, R. 2001. 'Ma(r)king essence-ecofeminism and embodiment'. *Ethics and the Environment* 6(2): 31–58.

Umezurike, U. Forthcoming. 'The eco(logical) border man: masculinities in Jim Lynch's Border Songs'.

Venkatesh, V. 2017. 'Bodies, spaces, and transitions in Alberto Rodríguez's Grupo 7 (2012) and La isla minima (2014)'. In D. Ochoa and M. DiFrancesco, eds., *Gender in Spanish Urban Spaces: Literary and Visual Narratives of the New Millennium*. Cham: Springer, 31–52.

Warren, K. 1990. 'The power and the promise of ecological feminism'. *Environmental Ethics* 12(2): 125–146.

Warren, K. 1994. 'Towards an ecofeminist peace politics'. In K. Warren, ed., *Ecological Feminism*. London: Routledge, 179–199.

Warren, K. 1997. 'Taking empirical data seriously: an ecofeminist philosophical perspective'. In K. Warren, ed., *Ecofeminism: Women, Culture, Nature*. Bloomington: Indiana University Press, 3–20.

Warren, K. 2000. *Ecofeminist Philosophy: A Western Perspective on What It Is and Why It Matters.* Lanham: Rowman & Littlefield.

Woodward, W. 2008. "'The nature feeling': ecological masculinities in some recent popular texts'. In D. Wylie, ed., *Toxic Belonging? Identity and Ecology in Southern Africa.* Newcastle upon Tyne: Cambridge Scholars, 143–157.

8 Ecological masculinities

Giving ADAM-n

> Patriarchy has shaped most contemporary industrial-capitalist cultures, so ecomasculinities would need to recognize and resist the identity-shaping economic structures of industrial capitalism, its inherent rewards based on hierarchies of race/class/gender/age/ability/species/sex/sexuality, and its implicit demands for ceaseless work, production, competition, and achievement. With ecofeminist values at heart, ecomasculinities would develop beyond merely rejecting the bifurcation of heterogendered traits, values, and behaviors: ecomasculinity/ies would enact a diversity of ecological behaviors that celebrate and sustain biodiversity and ecological justice, interspecies community, ecoeroticisms, ecological economies, playfulness, and direct action resistance to corporate capitalist ecodevastations. Already, developments are underway.
>
> (Gaard, 2017: 168)

Being Earth

The critical analyses we have presented throughout this book have formed the conceptual foundations of ecological masculinities. Our four streams (and other contributions) have provided us with an abundance of resources to work with as we chart a course towards ecological masculinities. In examining them piece by piece, we have been preparing ourselves to construct a new discourse for ecological masculinities. We have given previous scholarship due thought and reflection. In doing so, we have also discovered what we consider to be missing components for any effective theory for ecological masculinities that can also be manifested within each of us as personal embodiments. After all, beyond the realm of ideas, Earth is not simply something out there to be cared for, but is always and already part of us as well.

The evidence to support such a view is mounting. We acknowledge that the resources we have considered are only some of the many possible influences on the men, masculinities and Earth nexus. Along with the social sciences and humanities, the natural sciences are also dedicated to unpacking our entanglements with human and other-than-human others, revealing the complex web of intractable relationships that Earth supports, which we can examine both qualitatively and quantitatively. The solidarity that these disciplines reveal is also finding further footing in renewed examinations of political ecology (MacGregor, 2010; Elmhirst, 2011), vegan ecofeminism (Gaard, 2017), material feminism and decolonisation discourses (Gaski, 2013). We also recognise important agentic explorations of transitional change through: the ecological self (Mathews, 2017), anar-cho-socialism, ecological citizenship (Dobson, 2003), feminist political economics (Gibson-Graham, 2014) and the conceptualisations of Earthlings. Viewing our planet through these calls to action, we see that our own well-being along with that of all life are one and the same. With this, we recognise the acute need to infuse the transformative energies of social and environmental justice movements into ecological masculinities. While there are many ways we can respond, the choices we make and how we act towards Earth, others and self are reaping both positive and negative consequences. Shaped by these many Earth wisdoms, we contest the extractivist sentiments of industrial/breadwinner masculinities and the insufficiencies of ecomodern masculinities. Instead, we acknowledge that as scholar activists we are actors simultaneously enthralled in ideological and embodied de/reconstructions of masculinities and men's lives. Consequently, this chapter gathers together both political and personal elements of the intersecting terrain between men, masculinities and Earth. Working with these knowledges, we embrace what Australian environmental philosopher Freya Mathews (2017: 66–68,) referred to as 'strategic modalities' or an 'attentiveness to the particular that is guided, like one's responses in a martial context, by one's own vital interests' reminding us of the utter concreteness of an 'engaged form of agency' that insists we know our-selves in place and in relationship with all others.[1] Kneading this concept further still, ecofeminist Mary Phillips (2016: 468) reminded us that embodied care 'foregrounds connectivity and entangled materialisations ... [providing] a starting place from which to re-figure the postmaternal through a radical and liberatory focus on embodied relatedness'. If such wisdoms are correct – as we believe they are – then it is self-evident that we must move beyond the harmful aspects of masculine hegemonisation, end male domination and reconfigure modern Western masculinities towards greater care for the glocal commons. In light of the social and ecological failures of industrial/breadwinner and ecomodern masculinities, this chapter formulates a theoretically grounded and practically applicable process that describes what we have referred to throughout this book as ecological masculinities.

We now stand on estuarine shores, so to speak. The masculine ecolo-gisation process we propose is both interactive/political and con-templative/personal – a combination of reflection and action, making a construction project (such as building a shelter) a fitting analogy for this final chapter.

[Stream one] masculinities politics

The developments across masculinities politics provided us with a plurality of views on men and masculinities that are spread across a spectrum of views. We duly considered this pluralism, focusing our attention on the various ways that men and masculinities collide with care towards humans and other-than-humans within and beyond each of us and our personal politics. Through that analysis, we aimed to reach all men while also giving consideration to the masculinities that dwell within them and in women and non-binary/genderqueer people as well.[2] Accordingly, we shed light on the different ways that human others can attend to levels of masculine care – arguing that what popular culture problematically refers to as 'masculine' principles and practices are present in all human beings. That said, we noted a strong alignment of our work with profeminist views, remaining critical of masculine privileging and thereby recognising that men's sense of powerlessness and pain are, paradoxically, caused by their own internalised superiorisation. However, we recognised that for many men, such an overt anti-patriarchal stance can be unsettling, since it raises questions about the traditional configurations of modern Western manhood and masculinities; a necessary dissonance in our view that gives men and masculinities fresh horizons to strive for. In our consideration of masculinities politics, we have argued that men's ecological consciousness-raising (particularly through men's mythopoetry) has inadequately supported the liberation of all humans and other-than-humans in the wake of its focus on individuation (Kimmel 1998: 60). The task of shifting away from masculine hegemonisation has clearly not been taken up by the malestream status quo. We acknowledged that the omission (or at the very least the marginalisation) of frontal challenges to masculine ecologisation have still not been effectively conceptualised nor practised within that tradition (Gremillion, 2011; Magnuson, 2016). We also recognised that profeminist masculinities scholars and activists have been primarily focused on community, domestic and family violence but that there has been a lack of analyses of masculine impacts on Earth not only within profeminist positionalities but throughout masculinities politics.

[Stream two] deep ecology

Giving consideration to the human–nature relationship as it stands today, we have argued that ecomodernism (championed by shallow environmentalists) has failed to find solutions to the challenges we face. Worse, neo-liberalism entered the new millennium on par with extractivist industrial funding of climate change denialists who have strengthened the interests of corporate capitalism at great risk to the survival of many species on Earth. The main protagonists in this trend have been industrial modernists, who have challenged policy reforms, resisted social and environmental transformations and in doing so have emboldened right wing salvos in the culture wars. In the shadow of these growing threats to global sustainability, industrialisation, especially in the form of resource extraction and dependencies on hydrocarbons, have pushed back against techno-responses such as the renewable energy industry. These pressures continue to gain ground, entangling themselves with masculinist social entitlements (particularly for Western white men), resulting in, for example, continued erosion of Earth's biodiversity and widening gaps between the rich and poor. Sadly, our social and environmental challenges have worsened right at the critical point in history where we needed to urgently redress the ways we care for the glocal commons.

At the same time, notions of Earth sentience have struggled to gain purchase at the highest levels of governance – for example, having seen their heyday in the 1990s, ecophilosophers met the new millennium with ideological quiescence on the global stage. This was despite Næss's deep ecology being timed perfectly to address pressing environmental concerns, but the movement failed to gain critical purchase. In revisiting the wisdoms of deep ecology, we have aimed at reconsidering the wounds created by industrial modernisation from a valuative perspective. Our intention has been to note a profound and deep knowing about the intrinsic value of all life that exposes the folly of industrial/breadwinner and eco-modern rationalisations. From deep ecology, we learned of the value of pluralised literal and psychospiritual relationships with other-than-human nature. Deep ecology has compelled us to know, feel, trust and identify with Earth as part of ourselves while recognising ourselves as part of Earth, calling us to shift our perceptions of and responses to the human–nature relationship away from anthropocentrism and towards biocentrism. This imperative that humans do not have the right to reduce the richness and diversity of other-than-human life, but ought to only draw vital needs from Earth's resources, has particular relevance for today's environmental justice movements.

In surveying contemporary conversations about gender and environments, we found that material feminisms and posthumanities have offered transformative views aligning with the calls of environmental movements such as 'be the change you wish to see in the world', 'think globally, act locally', 'water is life' and 'we are Earth protecting itself', which capture progressive sentiments of broader, deeper and wider Earth care. Returning to some of deep ecology's core tenets, we noted that Næss's Ecosophy T offers each of us individualised pathways towards his notion of 'Self-realization!' in connection with all life. We have borrowed that particular feature from deep ecology to help shape our pluralised formulation of ecological masculinities.

We also determined that deep ecology was rightfully criticised for distancing itself from socio-political analyses around race and gender in particular, its Ecosophy T reflective of the repose and wildness experiencing that Næss the man so joyously advocated – but did so in ways that were isolationist artefacts of his privileged, white, Western, modern and industrialised life. This critique provided us with a clear sense of the importance of bringing men's isolation to the centre of our arguments (that deep ecologists have traditionally omitted), considering contradictions to this as vital ingredients in our masculine ecologisation process in order for men and masculinities in particular to reawaken broader, deeper and wider care.

[Stream three] ecological feminism

Our third stream of influence provided us with the most important socio-political analyses for our work. This stream shed light on power relations between women and men that echoes the utilitarian damage to Earth being done by humanity in the name of profit-driven growth and development policies and practices. The levels of analytical sophistication that we have found in our study of ecological feminism are indeed pivotal However, the textured views throughout that discourse vary considerably, motivating us to not only distance ourselves from binary ecofeminists in particular, but to cross-examine our own work for elements of essentialism that we then have attempted to eliminate. That said, we honoured the important notion many ecofeminists have posited that there can be no liberation for men, women, nor non-binary/genderqueer people and no adequate solution to ecological crises in societies whose fundamental models of relationship valorise male domination. We take this to be a core principle within ecological masculinities as well, noting that it aligns with and is principally informed by ecological feminism.

We find important ontological insights from some ecofeminisms that shed great light on the material-semiotics of our world. This holds true for the ways that our work has been shaped and refined by the posthumanities and material feminism. These refinements challenge us to find just cause to support broader care for the glocal commons in which we are all a part. We have suggested that this broader, deeper and wider care is integral to fresh formulations of masculinities. Our reason for persisting with the concept of ecological masculinities, despite the risks of binary gendered interpretations of our work, is quite simple: at the level of popular culture and in the broader sentiments of civic society, men and masculinities have proved to be broadly resistant to feminism in its many guises. We take this as a clear indicator of the need for languaging and application of very similar ecologised imperatives to our feminist compatriots, which will slip between malestream armouring to facilitate change. We see this as effective not only in the fields of scholastic ideology where we would find ourselves willing to dispense with the need for a unique conversation about masculine ecologisation, but also at the coal face with men who would otherwise not give such notions a second thought. From ecological feminism, we have learned about the importance and the great value of positioning ourselves and this work as translations of feminist, profeminist and ecofeminist ideals that men might be able to better heed.

[Stream four] feminist care theory

Our fourth stream delivered a textured understanding of feminist care theory. Inspired by this stream, we were able to zoom in on conceptualisations of care. We recognised that care requires an investment of time and is an embodied practice. We also suggested that care pervades masculinities to the extent that we believe it should, but in practical terms is frequently narrowly applied or hidden. We argued that malestream socialisations of care are consequently myopic. Stepping beyond malestream hegemonic constraints, our call for this kind of masculine care stretches beyond the immediate relational proximities for men and masculinities as a necessary and expansive approach to our formulation of masculine ecologisation. In practical terms this leads us to revisit our central premise for ecological masculinities: *all masculinities have infinite capacities to care, which can be expressed towards Earth, human others and ourselves – simultaneously.* Of course, we do not, nor can we care for all others all of the time. We are, however, suggesting that possibilities for care are expansive and infinite. For example, many men may struggle to conjure up care for themselves from within – yielding to lives rife with 'shoulds' that leave little room for their own care. As a consequence, men are commonly jammed into stereotypical protector/provider credos of malestream norms that undercut their capacities to care. This central premise challenges the presumption that modern Western men and masculinities are the Earth's great anathema. However, if all masculinities are potentially infinitely caring, then broader, deeper and wider masculine care becomes at least possible, if not fundamental to preferred and new levels of masculine socialisation – that we think of as ecologised in the broader, relational sense. We posit this premise to 'kick the door open' (using a gendered expression intentionally here) for all men, regardless of their locale in the morass of masculinities politics; to actively engage in the transformative process from hegemonisation to ecologisation. We argued that in the absence of such a premise, men are boxed in, which sets them up to continue to be considered the big problem, but does not offer them a path towards being part of our needed social and environmental solutions. Our concern here stresses that if we do not create space for this pathway of broader, deeper and wider masculine care as an exit politics to emerge, then we remain complicit in generating great human suffering and accentuated ecological demise in the wake of male domination. As scholar activists dedicated to de/reconstructions of the social and environmental implications of masculinities, we could not rest with such an outcome. This drove us to support and encourage ecologised reformulations of modern Western men and masculinities.

Further material to consider

Our ecological masculinities shelter is no ordinary structure. We visualise this shelter to be a place of respite and reorganisation, a safe container that facilitates transformations from hegemonisation to ecologisation in men and in masculine identities. Keeping with the analogy, we also sought additional materials at the water's edge or just inland from our estuarine shore. These localised materials fill some of the gaps in our resource needs and assist us in ways that the materials from our four streams have not.

They offer us unique and focused perspectives on men and masculinities that our predecessors missed. We considered those materials in Chapter 7 and summarise them again here.

Considerations of the Green Man rekindled the mischievous and playful elements of masculinities. His revival has turned our attention to a masculinised form of Earthen frolicking, giving men cause to consider what it might be like to live an unarmoured life. However, this revival did not offer us a comprehensive response to the pressing issues of our times. We also discovered the post-patriarchal intention among a small number of mythopoets (with special reference to Shepherd Bliss) whose primary motivations were to develop self-aware, community-connected wise men in service to Earth, others and self. In practice, dismantling structural oppressions has not featured in the mythopoetic men's movement, which has instead emphasised rites and rituals for men, in the company of other men, using nature at best as a backdrop to personal growth and development.

Further to Mark Allister's (2004) anthology *Ecoman*, our ecocritical colleagues explored protagonists in sources of fiction that offered us vivid imagery of alternative and ecologised performances of masculinities (Woodward, 2008; Brandt, 2017; Requena-Pelegrí, 2017; Cenamor and Brandt eds., forthcoming; Umezurike, forthcoming). These various explorations of the veritable 'ecoman' represent fictional experiments in masculinities imbued with real-world invitations for masculine ecologisation that bring together traumas and triumphs of lived experiences with needed social and environmental change. While many of these analyses are rich and eloquent, they are seldom structural, rendering them of limited benefit for our purposes since ecological masculinities necessarily prioritises political transformations that align with profeminist care for the glocal commons. However, this does appear to be changing; ecocriticism remains devoid of structurally inspired, historically informed as well as progressive and forward-looking analyses about the implications of men, masculinities and Earth.

Examinations of hunting and other forms of death in nature that dovetail with malestream rites and rituals highlight characteristics of masculinities that are timeless and increasingly problematic. Parallels were drawn with the masculinities of extractivism and the appeal of male adventurers pitted against the severity of nature. We took the view that any analyses of extractivism are best served by addressing their intersections with men's lives and masculinities as edifices of gender identity, since, for example, women and non-binary/gender-queer people hunt as well, and in doing so engage their masculinities within. Regarding men's efforts in the environmental movement, we noted that there is a persistent tendency to set high ideals in counter-cultural settings that readily confront the enormity of masculine hegemonisation, making it extremely difficult for men to successfully embrace ecologisation – their socialisations rendering them resistant to bite the hand that feeds them. We found an ideological willingness on the part of some men to ecologise in alignment with their socio-political ideals only to then collide with deeply entrenched patterns within themselves and/or the socio-cultural mechanisms they are resisting, making an effective leap towards ecological masculinities challenging and raising the sceptre that the gender politics of their lives are awash with contradictions.

Scholars studying farming and rural sociology exposed the politicised embodiments of some farming men in rural, suburban and urban communities who have attempted to critically transcend the constraints of industrial/breadwinner and ecomodern masculinities and in doing so, imbibe their lives with variations of ecological masculinities. We contended that this is a version of white, privileged escapism that does little to transform the mechanism of oppression that accompany male domination writ large. We add that very few people living in the planet's metropolises (where most humans dwell) will find a back-to-the-land ethos relatable or applicable since many agrarian ecotopic sentiments have proved to be infiltrated by malestream norms. This is predictable despite the best of intentions by some back-to-the-landers to adopt alternative (and more equitable) gender politics, noting that such practises often miss (and would benefit from) continuous re-vitalisation by ecofeminst analyses.

Finally, we gave consideration to the pivotal role that feminist-inspired scholars have raised questions and sought answers to the topic of masculine ecologisation. Connell's case studies of men in the environmental movement, Twine's 'marked' ecofeminist analyses, Krep's gendered study of ICT and Gaard's queer and (eco)feminist ecomasculinities have reminded us of the individual and discursive complexities/possibilities that a study on men, masculinities and Earth provokes. While precursory, these contributions to masculine ecologisation have given us much to work with.

Shelter on estuarine shores

Having revisited the contributions of previous scholarship and what we bring with us, we proceed now with building our ecological masculinities shelter on estuarine shores. We apply this analogy from the science of freshwater ecology precisely because estuaries are great mixing places; locales where materials from far and wide gather, producing some of the richest ecosystems on the planet. Humans have chosen to live alongside estuaries throughout history in large number, using waterways as transport pathways for the goods of trade along with cultural exchanges. These blended waters have supported ecosystems from which humans have foraged, farmed, hunted and gathered. Estuaries have been great givers of life to humanity throughout the ages. But they have also been polluted by our wastes as if the by-products of our production systems would disappear when thrown into their waters. Accordingly, estuaries are ideal places to pay attention to complex issues and develop strategies for change. It is here that we build our ecological masculinities shelter. While relying on the materials that have travelled downstream from masculinities politics, deep ecology, ecological feminism and feminist care theory, we have also recognised the necessity of combining them with materials from previous research we 'found on these estuarine shores' and have summarised above.

We visualise shelter building as a timeless act for our species. This construction project is not only a place of respite. It is an organising node as well, a place where others can gather with us or we can sit in quiet contemplation to confront hegemonisation within, around us and from there respond to it with our particular manifestations of masculine ecologisation. In this sense, our shelter is intended to facilitate ecologisation in our respective lives as we each find ways to generate broader care for the glocal commons from within. We envision an Earth-immersive vernacular structure given its materials are drawn from its estuarine surroundings.[3] In pondering the contributions of those who have come before us, we have noted that these offerings have not provided us with a comprehensive, conceptually rigorous or practically applicable ecologised masculinities theory nor have they shown us how masculine ecologisation might be applied in people's daily lives (the lives of men in particular). Discovering the ways we can better support men and masculinities to give ADAM-n all the more for our glocal commons is the principal aim of the remainder of this book.

Giving ADAM-n

We now proceed to introduce a process that provides alternatives to the isolation, emotional repression, competitiveness and aggression that are symptoms of malestream norms. We do so through the ADAM-n model. This process is our tangible contribution to exit politics from masculine hegemonisation to ecologisation.

The ADAM-n model is designed to break down our vision for masculine ecologisation into clear action steps or precepts. This is our suggested pathway to the praxes of ecological masculinities. The term 'ADAM-n' is a play on a 'new kind of Adam' that stands as an alternative to the gendered norms portrayed by Christianity in the Garden of Eden where man (a.k.a. Adam) fell from God's grace to the depths of bestiality and sins of the flesh allegedly brought forth by disobedient woman (a.k.a. Eve, made from Adam's rib) and the satanical serpent.[4] We use 'ADAM-n' as a takeback term at a time when we are facing obscene expressions of toxic/extreme masculinities along with pressing geopolitical challenges on a planetary scale brought forth by human-centred, malestream and market forces that are wantonly devastating Earth's living systems. Our use of the term ADAM-n is intended to help open fresh pathways for the widest possible audience to attend to these pressing concerns. We have designed the ADAM-n model to support the transformation of masculinities (and men's lives in particular) towards ecologisation. Our ADAM-n model is framed around five precepts that we introduce below to help guide us towards greater care for the glocal commons. These precepts define a process but do not predetermine an outcome. We offer them as a practical pathway so that individualised leadership can emerge through a staged process of ecologisation with the intent of

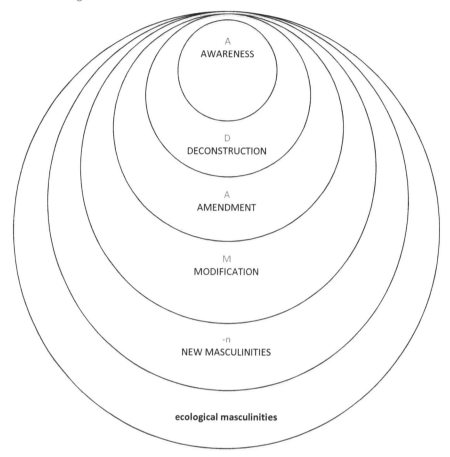

Figure 8.1 The ADAM-n model – five precepts to facilitate masculine ecologisation

leveraging forward personal and political transformations beyond male-stream norms (see Figure 8.1).

In order to clarify the process of masculine ecologisation that we advocate, we expand on these five precepts next. We frame them as personal guides of political significance.

A: Awareness

> *Create strategies to raise self-awareness and awareness about issues that concern you in the world by educating yourself about them.*

By 'awareness' we prioritise a willingness to look at an issue from as many sides as is possible in keeping your capacities for critical analysis engaged. Our intention here is to encourage you to take a position on something based on accurate information as opposed to echo-chambered judgements and unconsidered reactions that might be largely informed by prejudices, values, economic circumstances and expectations around power.[5] The instruction at the heart of this precept is a step that might be considered simple in principle but extremely complex in practice. Giving many different sides of an issue due consideration requires a willingness to reserve one's judgement and – frankly – to listen. A crucial part of developing the capacity for this level of awareness where you can survey a spectrum of views is to acquire emotional literacy and with that a capacity to self-manage your own feelings. One crucial element of developing these skills is to heal your internal hurts so you are less likely to project, presume or perform reactively. There are of course a plethora of modalities to guide you here, which we leave to your choosing.

Our contention is that men oppress because of a lack of self-awareness and a socialised compulsion to locate themselves in power positions justified by male dominated societies, which stems from the impact of early conditioning to isolate. We recognise that this is not the whole story nor is it something unique to men. However, we keep our focus on men here for the sake of a bounded discussion, we highlight men's internalised superiorisation as a meta-symptom of the chronic hurts that result from malestream masculine socialisations as they are laid into boys before they become men. These chronic men's oppressor patterns are pervasive because masculine socialisation persist in alignment with materialist, consumerist, capitalist, fossil-fuel-based societies; they are entangled with a myopic approach to care which hinges on an 'us versus them-ness' that creates distance and difference rather than sameness. This makes it more possible to shut off awareness, divorce ourselves from our impacts on others and rationalise our own positions as right and good while viewing others as wrong and bad; which holds particularly true for men. This dynamic is exemplified by the hegemonic masculinities that pervade climate change denialist communities that are largely populated by and primarily represent the socio-political and economic interests of rich, white, Western men. A compelling additional remedy for a pervasive lack of self-awareness and awareness of our impacts on others that accompanies malestream norms is to intentionally build relational closeness with others and the self.

We note that personal reflexivity, which develops (or deepens) awareness, is a crucial first step in moving from hegemonisation to ecologisation. Australian deep ecologist John Seed exemplified this notion of awareness in stating that 'I am protecting the rain forest' precisely because 'I am part of the rainforest protecting itself. I am that part of the rainforest recently emerged into human thinking' (Macy, 2013: 147). As an outspoken rainforest activist, Seed was compelled to care for the survival and flourishing of the rainforest he was protecting because his other/self-identification rendered his well-being and the needs of the rainforest as indistinguishable (in the deep ecological sense discussed in Chapter 4). Awareness opens us to the wisdoms of our full humanity, which is inescapably in and of Earth. When we enter this level of awareness, it becomes more difficult to cause harm to others since to do so is to harm ourselves and dismiss the inherent worth and sovereignty of human and other-than-human others.

As you ignite or deepen your level of awareness towards others and your relational proximity to them, it becomes easier to consider others as equally valuable as yourself. This broader Self-identification! (and we are intentionally echoing deep ecology here) is taken to be a vital ingredient in an effective transition from hegemonisation to ecologisation; an artefact of our humanity.

D: Deconstruction

Critically analyse the mechanisms of domination that drive extractive industries and pay attention to their broader social and environmental consequences.

Building on the awareness developed above, this second precept is a call to detect the ways that global, regional and local markets shape systems, communities and your own life. Central to a pursuit of economic growth is self-interest, which diminishes care for the glocal commons and challenges your capacities to care for those beyond yourself and your immediate life.

Many of us settle for socially, ecologically or personally destructive jobs simply to make ends meet in a material world. We do so despite our intuitive wisdoms that would have us engage in acts of service, passion and create a legacy of having been of service in this life for the good of all. This is particularly intense for many men, given traditional masculine socialisations not only point many men in the direction of isolation but also demand that they serve as principal breadwinners for their families – often at the expense of their self-care. One way of transcending this is to make the link between the familial strain and personal sacrifices that can accompany employment demands. If you find yourself in a position where, through this deconstructive step, it becomes self-evident that you are being used to concentrate profits into the hands of the wealthy and the compensation you receive for the costs incurred are not balanced or ethically aligned with your core values, then we encourage you to pay attention to this discord. An essential part of this deconstructive precept is to recognise that workers are understandably enmeshed in providing for themselves and their loved ones; many are dependent on mechanistic and pragmatic systems of resource extractivism. However, where the consequences of that work are socially and ecologically harmful, it is important to remain cognisant and critical of the systems that place such pressures upon us. One technique we suggest here is *maieutics* – the Socratic method of 'dialectical midwifery' or seeking knowledge through persistent questioning that results in stimulating discussions between other and self that provoke critical thinking and can, in doing so, reconcile dissonance. Deconstruction, as we visualise it, is intentionally pragmatic, logical and rationally focused. It speaks to that element of malestream masculine socialisations that hooks into the conditioning of men in particular (but not to the exclusion of women and/or non-binary/genderqueer people) to engage in logical reasoning.

Deconstruction celebrates the pragmatism of the masculine self, since a key component of this precept is to take an analytical view of logics of domination, how they impact the world, your communities, those you care for in your immediate proximity and, of course, yourself. With this, we acknowledge Naomi Klein's proposition in her most recent book titled *No Is Not Enough: Resisting Trump's New Shock Politics and Winning the World We Need* (2017), where deconstruction must be accompanied by your active engagement in reconstructing the world you want to inhabit. This is a call to pursue a life of service with gusto, as best you are able. In doing so, we point you in the direction of joining the caring majority to do no harm to others or yourself (Hippocratic Oath resounding in your ears) as we collectively reach towards 'a radically better future' for all (Klein, 2017).

A: Amendment

As your awareness is raised and you identify the impacts of hegemonisation on individuals, communities and nature, take time to consider the costs that others and you yourself incur, your role in perpetuating those costs and how you could make amends for them (either directly or indirectly).

We recognise that our lives are awash with contradictions. Using ourselves as examples here, as Westerners, we both consume substantial amounts of resources in using computers to write this book. We have both also invested money and time in flights to work on manuscripts together, given we live on opposite ends of the globe and have communicated extensively using our smart phones to keep each other up to date with moment-to-moment developments. Like most of you, even the basic elements of our lives, such as shopping for groceries, results in an accumulation of plastics and other wastes and as a consequence, we too are causing deleterious impacts on the planet. Similarly, we both encounter challenges with family, friends and colleagues and have both experienced responding to these situations in ways that are less than ideal for the long-term sustainability of those relationships. We are not puritans nor ecotopians; if we were, we could not have written this book – and this is arguably a symptom of our world.

This precept is an opportunity to embrace course correction. By making amends with yourself first, it is our belief that you are in a better position to desire and enact behavioural change. In doing so, you are less likely to repeat behavioural patterns that are causing you and others harm. We also suggest that it is vital to acknowledge the ways in which you are having detrimental impacts on Earth's living systems and/or on the relationships with those in your life. That acknowledgement might be directed at Earth or a human other, but that is secondary to our principal intent here. We are most interested in your capacity to make amends from your end of an exchange with another and in coming to recognise places where you might have erred, to then be accountable and take responsibility, by owning your shortcomings and finding ways to reconcile those within yourself (this might be a personal journey, or might be one that requires therapeutic help or the support of an elder). From there, should it be appropriate (and safe) to do so, we encourage you to seek amendment with Earth or human other as an external manifestation.

Making amends can have confronting implications. Take violence as a foreboding example, which has acute relevance for men, who are – statistically speaking – by far the most common per capita perpetrators of violence against Earth, human others, each other and self. In Australia, male suicides are approximately three times higher than those for females on account of men's fearlessness, pain insensitivity, greater access to and more willing choice of lethal methods coupled with their socialisations towards thwarted belong-ingness perceived burdensomeness, distress avoidance, poor emotional literacy, stoicism, social isolation, lack of help-seeking strategies, weakness stigmatisa-tion, solitary problem solving tendencies, inertia towards support services and a gendered trend of feeling misunderstood and ignored (APS, 2012). This alarming litany of malestream socialisations additionally contributes to 58 per cent of all violent assaults in Australia being men perpetrating that violence against other men, while women are three times more likely to be subject to domestic violence by someone they know (usually an intimate male partner), than are men (ABS, 2013; Mindframe, 2016). With an eruption of allegations against high-ranking, wealthy and extremely powerful men in recent times, such as through the #MeToo movement, it is clear that men have much to be uniquely answerable to in this regard. Of course, men are not the only perpetrators of physical, sexual or emotional violence, but data on men's violence exposes some of the deep-seated dysfunctions that lie at the very heart of masculine socialisations. This, together with the knowledge that many men in general, and rich wealthy leaders in particular, are the most common perpetrators of violence against the planet, is yet another and alarming outcome of the destructive mechanisms of malestream norms. Making amends for the perpetration of violence and doing the work to prevent it from happening in the first place are vital steps in the masculine journey towards ecologisation.

M: Modification

With social and environmental injustices as well as your own role in them exposed and with you now set on course towards something new and different, strive to modify your thoughts, words and deeds to support greater care for all others and yourself – simultaneously.

This precept represents a reconstructive step, which may sound logical and linear but in somatic terms is more likely the equivalent of two steps forward, one to the side and one back, before it is forward again in the ecologisation process we advocate. We have asked you to examine mechanisms of oppression that impact you or that you participate in at the expense of others and in doing so, to take ownership of those actions as essential ingredients in being responsible for them. In reaching a point of accountability, we then pointed you in the direction of making amends towards others and self. Now is the time to find alternative paths forward in your relational exchanges on both scales. As our previous exploration of masculine ecologisation has attested, attempts to subvert male domination and malestream disruptions to the ecological integrity of Earth are difficult to articulate and enact. We present an opportunity for you to make this transition, by focusing specifically on (re)connecting with your ecological self, actively engaging in recovering your own full humanness and from there choosing paths of action towards others and for yourself that prioritise broader, deeper and wider care.

Modification as we formulate it here illuminates a willingness to embrace new social structures, behaviours and levels of emotional awareness. To be clear, we distinguish our use of the term 'modification' from 'behaviour modification' in the formal psychological sense precisely because the latter relies on managing the human spirit with an array of 'punishments' to change behaviours. We are not talking about this sort of modification, recognising that some of the terrible messages accompanying malestream norms are that masculinities are in crises, that men are entitled to dominate, or they are bad and wrong and in being broken in key places they are in need of repair (Levant, 1997). Such messages cause many men to retreat into defensive mode, often manifesting through offensive behaviours and making critical analyses of concerns about their lives and impacts on others extremely difficult to articulate in ways that engage with the issues afflicting them constructively throughout popular culture. Of course, we agree that there are many aspects of malestream norms that deserve detailed interrogation and have joined our feminist colleagues in this task at length above. For the purposes of reaching the widest audience possible, our intention here is to engage all men and all masculinities in a process of ecologisation, which needs greater societal and personal awareness coupled with strategically and intentionally 'powering men down' from the structural legacies of male domination. For us, ecologisation and men's powering down to reconnect with their fullest human selves go hand in hand.

Our use of modification refers to cultivating and engaging thoughts, beliefs and actions that support social and/or environmental justice. This is the reconstructive aspect of masculine ecologisation, where you are able to use the insights you have acquired about the world and your place within in it to prioritise relational proximity between all others and yourself. Note that we are speaking in general terms intentionally; the ecological masculinities we envision are not prescriptive. We encourage you to take up the challenge of discovering what precise form of modification you could assume. As a guide, consider the following transitions that might arise for you as a conscious career change or shift in life priorities: supporting equal rights for first nations people; standing in solidarity with people of colour, women or non-binary/ genderqueer people by developing values and resource shifts that embrace diversity and respect the sovereignty of others; advocating for the needs of children with special needs; dedicating some of your time to your spiritual community; educating yourself and actively engaging in deliberative democracy where consensus decision making plays a central role (Bessette, 1980; Bohman and Rehg eds., 1997); forfeiting flying in favour of trains when travelling and offsetting your carbon footprint effectively should flying be chosen; being an active and conscious parent, which may mean prioritising your child's needs ahead of your career; developing counselling skills as an enrichment of a hairstylist's career; pursuing professional development in the social services, or small scale renewable technologies; conducting research on the links between coral bleaching and climate change; implementing mining rehabilitation strategies as a consultant or company employee; practicing catch and release when sport fishing; harvesting sustainable forest products while protecting and preserving old growth stands or salvaging logging within ecologically sustainable limits; purchasing organic/free-range animal products, hunting for your meat and only harvesting what is actually needed, or better yet, choosing a meat-reduced or meat-free diet, etc. In ways such as these, we are asking you to prioritise broader, deeper and wider (a.k.a. relational) care.

Accompanying this precept, we encourage you to honour the social, cultural and spiritual wisdom of others and within yourself. Seek modifications in your life that shift your impact on the world from that of a taker to that of a leaver (Quinn, 1992), or if you already have elements of this present in your life, then deepen and accentuate them. Here, we are primarily positing an attitudinal modification that shifts your focus away from self-serving strategies and towards those that orient you to a life of service to the relationships (on planetary, local and intimate scales – reflective of the glocal commons) that you are intricately interwoven with. Recall that we use the term 'ecological' in the broader relational sense and place the onus on you to define the precise form that this will take in your life. Modification encourages you to work towards the ending of socio-cultural divisions within Western societies and to determine what levels of use of Earth's resources are acceptable when you are dedicated to improving the lives of all. Accordingly, modification as we envision it here prioritises ending all oppressions, pointing you in a direction of leadership towards that goal.

-n: Nourish new masculinities

We use '-n' to represent a plurality of new masculinities that can emerge as a result of the masculine ecologisation process we have introduced above. With this, we advocate the denormalising of hegemonic masculinities, seeking new forms of masculinities that celebrate broader, deeper and wider care.

In order to translate the previous four precepts into applications for the widest array of men's lives and masculine identities, we ask you to point yourself in the direction of a life of service. The new kinds of 'Adam' we are advocating here are those connected to the broader majesty of life. Consequently, '-n' as our fifth precept is the galvanising aspect of ecological masculinities. Within this precept there are four elements to consider, which are unique to each person. There are of course many more elements that could be included. The four we offer here are intended to help frame the beginning of a much deeper conversation for you to have with yourself and your communities of support. As you are able to clarify them, they will lead you to a shortlist of actions reflective of your vocation in life, such as those we exemplified above.[6] They are:

1   **Zeal:** these are the activities that you value most and want to spend the bulk of your time doing. They ignite drivers within you. They motivate you to actively engage with others and to deeply connect with yourself. They may be a certain sport, local politics, gardening, doing crafts, painting, making music, visiting museums, photographing landscapes or sharing knowledge through teaching. You may have one activity or several that generate zeal within you. Whatever it is, you will know that you are on the right track if you take stock of what you effortlessly spend time doing with your days that feeds your curiosity and motivates you to act. Choose those activities that could be combined with broader, deeper and wider care for the glocal commons. These activities will engage you with the world around you. They will embolden you rather than deplete you. Notice what activities launch you out of bed in the morning with enthusiasm to greet the day. If you do not experience this, imagine what activities they might be. I (Martin speaking here) am reminded of my sheer enthusiasm about pondering sustainable technologies and designs such as permaculture blended with Māori Earth wisdoms that have proved the test of time, when studying architect and ecopreneur Rau Hoskins during my time in New Zealand (Hultman, 2014).

2   **Superpower:** these are the skills in your life that you are naturally adept at. They may be long-distance running, shooting hoops, balancing budgets, listening earnestly to others as an emotional support, doing mathematics, teaching emotional literacy, writing books, modelling, building homes, etc. These talents are your special gifts in this life. We consider it vital that you get familiar with them if you have not done so already, especially those that can be implemented for the concurrent benefit of the planet and yourself. They may be in some sense genetic or socialised gifts, but either way, they are the special contributions that you make when you are at your best, which flow through you and from you out into the world with little effort. In my case (Paul speaking here), a curiosity about men is the product of years as a youth wondering why it was difficult to be close with men and what I might do to change that. From that early experience, I have found ways to make a living out of studying, mentoring, working alongside, teaching and writing about men. As a further example, think here of the trauma of isolation that afflicted Arne Næss's

younger years that then served him to both deeply connect with human others and then seek solitude to deeply connect and write about the intrinsic value of nature at *Tvergastein,* his mountain retreat.

3   **Hurts:** these are your unique set of wounds that have shaped you into who you are in the world today. They are likely to be difficult experiences, such as sexual abuse, beatings, abandonment, shaming, etc. These will be unique to your story and with some reflection (if you have not done so already) it is likely that you will recognise these incidences to be the places that you have accumulated hurts, either from others or yourself (or both). These hurtful experiences typically result in wounds; they can be powerful guides. When you look back at them they will, like a trail of crumbs, lead you to the things in your life that you are either avoiding because of the pain associated with them, or that have motivated you to tackle out in the world with passion and drive. We recommend that when delving into your hurts, that you do so through a structured journey of personal development that creates some framing for you as you enter this shadowy part of your history or in the safety of a support group of some form and/or with a therapist, elder, mentor, life coach or dear friend.

4   **Wish:** this fourth part of discovering your vocation reflects your wish(es) for the world. Here, you will find a voice within that will be gnawingly saying over and again: 'I wish someone would do something about' such-and-such. Take as an example Rachel Carson who developed her special gift of translating research into easily digested but frightening facts about industrial modern society's killing of birds by chemicals. Or consider Boyan Slat, the 19-year-old Dutch-born Croatian inventor who, in 2013, created the Ocean Cleanup Foundation in response to the high level of plastics he saw in the ocean on a diving trip in Greece. Your wish is that thing, or that suite of things, which you earnestly want someone, somewhere, to change. This wish will reveal some of best places for you to apply your superpower.

Through these four key parts of the self, we encourage you to cultivate and connect with your unique vocation in life that has a positive impact on the glocal commons. Together, they help you find answers to this important question: how can your life be of best service to the betterment of all others and yourself – simultaneously? We have discovered through our respective journeys that pursuing one's vocation is a powerful way to answer such a question. Using some form of a meditative, reflexive or spiritual practice is the final element that draws all four parts of yourself into clarity and is the last step we encourage you to take. We have found that contemporary and socio-culturally respectful rites of passage, yoga, meditative practices, prayer, growing vegetables, foraging for wild mushrooms, long back-country hikes, swimming in oceans, lakes and streams, actively engaging in community projects, rewilding and investing energy into building and maintaining deep, warm and authentic relationships with others, particularly elders and/or mentors, can be just some of the many useful strategies that are available to support you discovering what your unique vocation might be. In all cases, regardless of the infinite number of possibilities that are available, the one common denominator among them all will be care. You will find that whatever it is that you settle on as your vocation, it will unavoidably include some unique way for you to contribute to caring for the glocal commons. Engaging your passions can have profound structural consequences. It is for this reason that we consider the emergence of ecologised masculinities indicated by '-n' to be the galvanising precept of the masculine ecologisation process we have charted, which is both personal and political.

Masculine ecologisation: hope for our common future

Collectively, these five precepts of the ADAM-n model are designed to care for the glocal commons not simply in sentiment but in action as well; we all need to walk the talk of broader, deeper and wider care more so than ever. In solidarity with other forms of care for Earth, community and self that we have honoured throughout this book, we recognise the need for simultaneous transformation on both individual and systemic levels. The overall message we convey to you through the ADAM-n model is to concurrently 'give a damn' about all others and yourself; encouraging you to discover or deepen your connection to a vocation. Take time to explore what such a life might look like for you, or if you already feel focused on a vocation, what can you do to take your leadership presence in the world to the next level in service to the greater good? There are many different ways to create this level of connection to others and yourself. In my particular case (Paul speaking here), staffing rites of passage experiences in the Australia desert where colleagues and I camped for two weeks, living close to Earth and supporting participants to have solo time proved to be particularly important as a reflexive time for me personally and gave me much guidance for my professional development. I have also spent periods intensively practicing yoga, tending to my garden and taking vigorous walks. These are some of the main meditative practices (at the time of writing this book) that have enabled me to (re)gain and maintain clarity about my vocation. For me (Martin speaking here) it is three forms of meeting other people that have encouraged me to become a leader. First was when I met transitional agents in Sweden and New Zealand who in a passionate and clear way put their broader, deeper and wider care for Earth, society and self into action through their support for the glocal commons. Second was my work with the local community in my rural home village of Bestorp where I was met with so much love and happiness when working for the common good of localised people and place. Third, I found great joy in forest and field sojourns. They have become integral to my contemplative time where inner rejuvenation and passionate commitment to my professional pursuits need exploring the other-than-human world. From these reflexive moments, I have been motivated to join or lead transformative organisations such as the Swedish National Transition Board, the SweMineTechNet research network and Environmental Posthumanities Network that hosts an art and humanities collaboration with environmental activists dealing with resource issues.

For both of us as scholar activists, academic pursuits must be accompanied by action. For example, Paul has worked as a men's mentor and outdoor educator, he loves to hike in backcountry places and pursues networks of relationships around the world with gusto. Martin has stopped flying, sold his car, is a dedicated vegetarian as is his family, buys organic food, has voluntarily implemented non-shopping years in solidarity with environmental refugees suffering from the injustices brought upon them by continuing colonial and fossil fuel dependent consumerism. Far from having resolved the contradictions in our respective lives, we are both constantly facing our own challenges and shortcomings. We anticipate that this will be the same for you as well, holding masculine ecologisation as a transitional journey rather than a definitive destination. In both of our cases, the five precepts of our ADAM-n model serve as framing rather than directives.

We encourage you to employ your own rites, rituals or practices and to take the ADAM-n model as a guide to reach and enrich the ways you engage with the world with deepening care. You may find that consciously parenting your children, participating in spiritual rituals and ceremonies or climbing a mountain are more appropriate forums for you than we have mentioned above. Our intention is to encourage precisely this level of pluralism, since preferred contemplative practices will vary greatly from individual to individual. Further, these opportunities for deeper reflection and connection between others and yourself will likely emerge through several practices that nurture you for the betterment of the planet. The onus is then on you to find a healthy balance amongst them. Through the ADAM-n model, we have attempted to create the foundations to support these resultant expressions of your life that prioritise care for the glocal commons. Through that discovery we anticipate that you will create unique ways of being, thinking and doing ecological masculinities. Returning to Figure 8.1, notice that our illustration of the five precepts of the ADAM-n model is 'nested'. This is intentional since the precepts are enmeshed. They describe a process that leads us from hegemonisation to ecologisation; each precept building on the next, collectively creating a pathway that any individual can take towards ecological masculinities.

As we conclude this chapter and bring this book to a close, we note that we have now completed our ecological masculinities shelter on estuarine shores. This shelter is intended to be a place where we can go through a metamorphosis from hegemonisation to ecologisation; a transformation from the limits of industrial/breadwinner masculinities and the illusions and inadequacies of ecomodern masculinities to the infinite possibilities of ecological masculinities not only for the benefit of the world, or those you love or are closely connected with, but for yourself as well. As humans, we are in and of this Earth. Our process of ecologisation starts right in the centre of the self, empowering us to break free from masculine hegemonisation. Our intention has been to facilitate a transformative experience for you as the reader; it certainly has been that for us, as the authors, comparing notes, discussing points of detail and finding ways to say what we both have wanted to say. We invite you to use the theoretical foundations and practical guidance that we have offered here to carry you through your own unique transformation towards ecological masculinities. We welcome you to this process, hoping that this book assists you in manifesting a path that is supportive for all life on Earth as much as it is empowering for you as well. After all, we are, each of us, special and unique forms of Earth defending itself.

Notes

1 We take agency in this sense to be part of larger actor-networks where the possibility for transformation points us towards egalitarian ideals (Jagers et al., 2014).

2 It is precisely for these reasons that this book has a principal focus on men but aims to have a broader scope of relevance for all people, regardless of their biology or identity.

3 This construction aspect of our analogy is inspired by Rau Hoskins, who has dedicated his life to exploring architectural designs that are connected to holistic world views on how to integrate new technologies with old traditions. Hoskins designed structures of sharing and caring through distributed systems in which the resources of the land that can serve as building materials are held in common. He struggled with the way that traditional Eurocentric architecture alienates humans from the environment, which motivated him to create dwellings that encourage people to spend more time outdoors (Hultman, 2017). Taking Hoskins's views to heart, our ecological masculinities shelter is not a single design nor is it a solitary structure. The notion of building a shelter on estuarine shores is a far cry from the isolated refuge of mountain retreats and in this sense, we explore the nuances of our relational selves both inwardly through moment of quiet contemplation and outwardly through active engagement with our surroundings and those who are integral to our respective lives.

4 We were inspired to adopt this nomenclature of ADAM-n as a direct result of email communications with one of Paul's doctoral dissertation examiners, Gender and Culture Studies Professor Catherine Roach (University of Alabama, US) who, on 11 June 2011, suggested that ADAM-n would be a fitting acronym for our model. This same contention was independently corroborated by T. Anne Dabb on 5 May 2017, who graciously offered detailed comments of an identical nature on reading early drafts of this book's manuscript. It is worth noting that the phrase 'give a damn' is also drawn from its use in *Gone with the Wind* (1939). Rhett Butler's (Clarke Gable) famous retort to Scarlett O'Hara (Vivien Leigh), declared that he no longer cared what came of Scarlett as the Confederacy fell apart in the latter stages of the American Civil War. This particular phrase rose to notoriety through its profanity as well as its overt indication of a lack of care from the character of an iconic, daring and wealthy white man towards someone he had previously loved, had exchanged intimacy with and intended at one point to marry. The phrase was, interestingly, voted the 'number one movie line of all time' by the American Film Institute (2005) (Hanna, 2011) capturing the degree to which men's expressed lack of care has remained socially sanctioned into the twenty-first century; popular culture still acknowledging a hyper-masculinised, entitled, affluent, drunken, violent rogue, personified as Rhett Butler, as characteristic of one of the most celebrated of modern Western masculinities – capable of doing whatever he pleased at will and with little

regard for the consequential impact on others, including walking out on them in the face of a collapsing world. The parallels with the toxic/extreme masculinities personified by Donald Trump are arresting.

5 Consider the concept of 'mansplaining' – explaining something in a condescending or patronising manner typically by a man to a woman – as a notable example of the latter. This concept was discussed (though not coined) by Rebecca Solnit (2014 [2008]) and first appeared on a Tomdispatch.com alternative online media post. While contested by some as pejorative, essentialist and dismissive (xoJane [Lesley], 2012; Young, 2013, Young, 2016; MPR News, 2016), the concept exemplifies the point we are making here very well that malestream socialisations condition men to readily override the sovereignty of others as a means of asserting their presumed power – what we refer to as their 'internalised superiorisation'. This is but one – albeit a contested – example from popular culture that illustrates the ways that male domination conditions men to run roughshod over others that are marginalised by masculine hegemonisation.

6 We acknowledge these four parts that in combination support you to discover your vocation as adaptations of a model originally developed by David Fabricius (2011) that he referred to as 'Life Purpose – REVEALED', which is no longer in circulation. We extend a debt of gratitude to Fabricius for this inspiration.

References

ABS [Australian Bureau of Statistics]. 2013. '4125.0 – gender indicators, Australia, Jan 2013 – suicide (key series)'. Accessed 30 October 2017. http://www.abs.gov.au/aussta ts/abs@.nsf/Lookup/by%20Subject/4125.0~Jan%202013~Main%20Fea tures~Suicides~3240

APS [Australian Psychological Society]. 2012. 'Insights into men's suicide'. Accessed 30 October 2017. http://www.psychology.org.au/inpsych/2012/august/beaton

Bessette, J. 1980. 'Deliberative democracy: the majority principle in republican government'. In R. Goldwin and W. Schambra, eds., *How Democratic Is the Constitution?* Washington, DC: American Enterprise Institute, 102–116.

Bohman, J., and W. Rehg. eds. 1997. *Deliberative Democracy: Essays on Reason and Politics*. Cambridge: MIT Press.

Brandt, S. 2017. 'The wild, wild world: masculinity and the environment in the American literary imagination'. In J. Armengol, M. Bosch Vilarrubias, À. Carabí, and T. Requena-Pelegrí, eds., *Routledge Advances in Feminist Studies and Intersectionality*. New York: Routledge, 133–143.

Cenamor, R., and S. Brandt, eds. Forthcoming. *Ecomasculinities in Real and Fictional North America: The Flourishing of New Men*. Lanham: Lexington Book [Rowman & Littlefield].

Dobson, A. 2003. *Citizenship and the Environment*. Oxford: Oxford University Press.

Elmhirst, R. 2011. 'Introducing new feminist political ecologies'. *Geoforum* 42(2): 129–132.

Fabricius, D. 2011. 'The Vital Seven with David Fabricius | The Shift Network'. Accessed 1 November 2017. https://shiftnetworkcourses.com/course/VitalSeven

Gaard, G. 2017. *Critical Ecofeminism (Ecocritical Theory and Practice)*. Lanham: Lexington Books.

Gaski, H. 2013. 'Indigenism and cosmopolitanism: a pan-Sámi view of the indigenous perspective in Sámi culture and research'. *AlterNative* 9(2): 113–124.

Gibson-Graham, J. 2014. 'Being the revolution, or, how to live in a "more-than-capitalist" world threatened with extinction'. *Rethinking Marxism* 26(1): 76–94.

Gremillion, T. 2011. 'Setting the foundation: climate change adaptation at the local level'. *Environmental Law* 41: 1221–1253.

Hanna, L. 2011. '"Frankly my dear, I don't give a damn" voted greatest movie line of all time: As lines go it was, frankly, a good one'. Accessed 19 January 2013. http://www.mirror.co.uk/tv/tv-news/frankly-my-dear-i-dont-give-a-damn-115670

Hultman, M. 2014. 'How to meet? Research on ecopreneurship with Sámi and Māori'. Paper presented at international workshop Ethics in Indigenous Research – Past Experiences, Future Challenges, Umeå, 3–5 March.

Hultman, M. 2017. 'Exploring industrial, ecomodern, and ecological masculinities'. In S. MacGregor, ed., *Routledge Handbook of Gender and Environment*. Oxon: Routledge, 239–252.

Jagers, S., Martinsson, J., and S. Matti. 2014. 'Ecological citizenship: a driver of pro-environmental behaviour?'. *Environmental Politics* 23(3): 434–453.

Kimmel, M. 1998. 'Who's afraid of men doing feminism?'. In T. Digby, ed., *Men Doing Feminism*. New York: Routledge, by 57–68.

Klein, N. 2017. *No Is Not Enough: Resisting Trump's Shock Politics and Winning the World We Need*. Chicago: Haymarket Books.

Levant, R. 1997. 'The masculinity crisis'. *Journal of Men's Studies* 5: 221–231.

MacGregor, S. 2010. '"Gender and climate change": from impacts to discourses'. *Journal of the Indian Ocean Region* 6(2): 223–238.

Macy, J. 2013. 'The Greening of the Self'. In L. Vaughan-Lee, ed., *Spiritual Ecology: The Cry of the Earth*. Point Reyes: The Golden Sufi Center, 145–158.

Magnuson, E. 2016. *Changing Men, Transforming Culture: Inside the Men's Movement*. Oxon: Routledge.

Mathews, F. 2017. 'The dilemma of dualism'. In S. MacGregor, ed., *Routledge Handbook of Gender and Environment*. Oxon: Routledge, 54–70.

McLeod, N. 2015. 'Moon cycles and women'. Accessed 2 May 2017. http://www.menstruation.com.au/periodpages/mooncycles.html

Mindframe. 2016. 'Facts and stats about suicide in Australia'. Accessed 30 October 2017. http://himh.clients.squiz.net/mindframe/for-media/reporting-suicide/facts-and-stats

MPR News. 2016. 'Do we need a different word for "mansplaining"?'. Accessed 29 October 2017. http://www.mprnews.org/story/2016/12/19/mansplaining-as-a-term

Phillips, M. 2016. 'Embodied care and planet earth: ecofeminism, maternalism and postmaternalism'. *Australian Feminist Studies* 31(90): 468–485.

Quinn, D. 1992. *Ishmael*. New York: Bantam Books.

Requena-Pelegrí, T. 2017. 'Green intersections: caring masculinities and the environmental crisis'. In J. Armengol and M. Vilarrubias, eds., *Masculinities and Literary Studies: Intersections and New Directions*. New York: Routledge, 143–152.

Solnit, R. 2014[2008]. *Men Explain Things To Me: And Other Essays*. Chicago: Haymarket Books.

Umezurike U. Forthcoming. 'The Eco(logical) Border Man: Masculinities in Jim Lynch's Border Songs.'

Woodward, W. 2008. '"The nature feeling": ecological masculinities in some recent popular texts'. In D. Wylie, ed., *Toxic Belonging? Identity and Ecology. Southern Africa*. Newcastle upon Tyne: Cambridge Scholars, 143–157.

xoJane.com [Lesley]. 2012. 'Why you'll never hear me use the term "mansplain"'. Accessed 29 October 2017. http://www.xojane.com/issues/why-you-ll-never-hear-me-use-term-mansplain

Young, C. 2013. 'Is the patriarchy dead?'. Accessed 20 October 2017. http://reason. com/archives/2013/09/29/is-the-patriarchy-dead

Young, C. 2016. 'Feminists treat men badly. It's bad for feminism'. *Washington Post*. Accessed 29 October 2017. http://www.washingtonpost.com/posteverything/wp/2016/ 06/30/feminists-treat-men-badly-its-bad-for-feminism/?utm_term=.2636eaa2d079

Index